SLAVERY AND THE POI

Geography played a key role in Britain's long national debate over slavery. Writers on both sides of the question represented the sites of slavery – Africa, the Caribbean, and the British Isles – as fully imagined places and the basis for a pro- or anti-slavery political agenda. With the help of twenty-first-century theories of space and place, Elizabeth A. Bohls examines the writings of planters, slaves, soldiers, sailors, and travelers whose diverse geographical and social locations inflect their representations of slavery. She shows how these writers use discourses of aesthetics, natural history, cultural geography, and gendered domesticity to engage with the slavery debate. Six inter-linked case studies, including Scottish mercenary John Stedman and domestic slave Mary Prince, examine the power of these discourses to represent the places of slavery, setting slaves' narratives in dialogue with pro-slavery texts, and highlighting in the latter previously unnoticed traces of the enslaved.

ELIZABETH A. BOHLS, an associate professor of English at the University of Oregon, is author of *Women Travel Writers and the Language of Aesthetics, 1716–1818* (Cambridge, 1995), *Romantic Literature and Postcolonial Studies* (2013), and co-editor with Ian Duncan of *Travel Writing 1700–1830* (2005).

CAMBRIDGE STUDIES IN ROMANTICISM

This series aims to foster the best new work in one of the most challenging fields within English literary studies. From the early 1780s to the early 1830s a formidable array of talented men and women took to literary composition, not just in poetry, which some of them famously transformed, but in many modes of writing. The expansion of publishing created new opportunities for writers, and the political stakes of what they wrote were raised again by what Wordsworth called those "great national events" that were "almost daily taking place": the French Revolution, the Napoleonic and American wars, urbanization, industrialization, religious revival, an expanded empire abroad and the reform movement at home. This was an enormous ambition, even when it pretended otherwise. The relations among science, philosophy, religion, and literature were reworked in texts such as *Frankenstein* and *Biographia Literaria*; gender relations in *A Vindication of the Rights of Woman* and *Don Juan*; journalism by Cobbett and Hazlitt; poetic form, content, and style by the Lake School and the Cockney School. Outside Shakespeare studies, probably no body of writing has produced such a wealth of comment or done so much to shape the responses of modern criticism. This indeed is the period that saw the emergence of those notions of "literature" and of literary history, especially national literary history, on which modern scholarship in English has been founded.

The categories produced by Romanticism have also been challenged by recent historicist arguments. The task of the series is to engage both with a challenging corpus of Romantic writings and with the changing field of criticism they have helped to shape. As with other literary series published by Cambridge, this one will represent the work of both younger and more established scholars, on either side of the Atlantic and elsewhere.

For a complete list of titles published see end of book.

SLAVERY AND THE POLITICS OF PLACE

Representing the Colonial Caribbean, 1770–1833

ELIZABETH A. BOHLS

CAMBRIDGE
UNIVERSITY PRESS

CAMBRIDGE
UNIVERSITY PRESS

University Printing House, Cambridge CB2 8BS, United Kingdom

One Liberty Plaza, 20th Floor, New York, NY 10006, USA

477 Williamstown Road, Port Melbourne, VIC 3207, Australia

4843/24, 2nd Floor, Ansari Road, Daryaganj, Delhi - 110002, India

79 Anson Road, #06-04/06, Singapore 079906

Cambridge University Press is part of the University of Cambridge.

It furthers the University's mission by disseminating knowledge in the pursuit of
education, learning and research at the highest international levels of excellence.

www.cambridge.org
Information on this title: www.cambridge.org/9781107438163

First published 2014
First paperback edition 2017

A catalogue record for this publication is available from the British Library

ISBN 978-1-107-07934-2 Hardback
ISBN 978-1-107-43816-3 Paperback

Cambridge University Press has no responsibility for the persistence or
accuracy of URLs for external or third-party internet websites referred to in
this publication, and does not guarantee that any content on such websites is,
or will remain, accurate or appropriate.

Contents

v

Illustrations

Acknowledgments

This book has been long in the making and reflects generous support from numerous individuals and institutions. I thank the Oregon Humanities Center and the Center for the Study of Women in Society for research fellowships. The University of Oregon (UO) English Department has supported me through the years in various ways, in particular with a research term at a crucial juncture. Special thanks go to former Department Head Harry Wonham and Associate Head Paul Peppis. I have been fortunate to present my research at a number of venues, including the Modern Language Association, the American Society for Eighteenth-Century Studies conference, the Interdisciplinary Nineteenth-Century Studies, the Society for Early American Studies, the American Historical Association, and the American Anthropological Association. Special thanks go to the McNeil Center for Early American Studies and the organizers of its Interdisciplinary Seminar in Atlantic Studies, in particular to Toni Bowers; to Alan Bewell for organizing the MLA session where I first aired my ideas about Equiano; and to Vin Carretta and George Boulukos for joining a later Equiano session. I thank the graduate students in my 2006 seminar, "British Slavery, Atlantic Ghosts," for lively discussions.

A number of colleagues and friends took the time to read and comment on parts of the book. I thank Leon Chai, Elizabeth Heckendorn Cook, Dianne Dugaw, David Lambert, Janet Sorensen, Dick Stein, and the members of the UO Early Modern reading group, EMODS, including Leah Middlebrook, Dan Rosenberg, Gordon Sayre, and Melissa Walter. Lise Nelson was an indispensable guide during my forays into geography and theories of place. Trevor Burnard and Paul Youngquist kindly answered queries, and Kerry Sinanan generously shared unpublished work. Dan Rosenberg orchestrated UO's purchase of the Eighteenth-Century Collections Online (ECCO) database, an essential research tool. I thank the helpful and professional librarians and staff at the National Library of Jamaica, especially Genevieve Jones-Edman; the James Ford Bell Library at the University of Minnesota, especially Associate Curator Margaret Borg; the British Library; and the UO's Knight Library. Marina Hirsch provided impeccable editing and proofreading. I am especially grateful to the anonymous reader at Cambridge University Press for astonishingly detailed, informed, and valuable guidance on revisions and to Linda Bree for shepherding the project through review.

Support of a different kind came from colleagues and friends in Eugene and elsewhere, including Marilyn Booth, Lara Bovilsky, Leon Chai and Cara Ryan, Ruth Clogston, Chris and Jenny Ellis, Karen Ford, Sangita Gopal, Lisa Redford and Sergei Bogdanov, and Gordon Sayre. Two groups joined me in essential activities: thanks to the Walking Ladies (Louise Bishop, Kathleen Karlyn, and Joanne Kent) and Drinking Ladies (Sara Hodges and Marjorie Taylor) for invaluable advice and encouragement. My family has lived with the project for a number of years. My mom, Mary Bohls, is a quiet, steadfast presence. My dad, Allen Bohls (1928–2011), taught me high standards and pride in one's work. My father-in-law, Andy Doe, and the East Coast Doe clan have been unfailingly supportive. I thank my sons, Casey and Cooper Doe – who have grown up with this book – for cheerful company, climbing tips, and trash TV. Finally, Chris Doe deserves more gratitude than words can express. This book is dedicated to him, again and always, with love.

Earlier versions of parts of Chapters 1, 3, and 6 appeared in the following: *The Country and the City Revisited*, edited by Donna Landry, Gerald MacLean, and Joseph P. Ward (Cambridge University Press, 1999); a special issue of *European Romantic Review* on the Picturesque, edited by Gary Harrison and Jillian Heydt-Stevenson (2002); and *Women on the Verge of Home*, edited by Bilinda Straight (SUNY Press, 2005).

Captive spaces

I have often wondered how English people can go out into the West
Indies and act in such a beastly manner.
                    The History of Mary Prince, a West Indian Slave

I begin with a captive: not a slave but rather the planter William Beckford,
illegitimate scion of the super-rich Beckford clan. He has just made the
transatlantic voyage back from Jamaica, where he owns three sugar plantations. On his way to London, his post-chaise meets a carriage containing
his cousin Richard, a London merchant to whom he owes £25,000, and
two bailiffs, who arrest him for debt.[1] Imagine the bankrupt planter pining
and fuming in London's Fleet Prison from 1786 until the late 1790s, passing
the time by writing his massive two-volume *Descriptive Account of the Island
of Jamaica* (1790). Immobilized in a London jail by the financial and legal
system that had supported him through decades of flamboyant prosperity,
what does Beckford decide to do? He takes readers on a picturesque tour
of a colony on the other side of the Atlantic, detailing its scenic attractions
for those unable to sail to the New World.

His choice is not as whimsical as it may seem. Beckford's work of discursive place-making served the interests of his planter peers at a time
when the source of their fortunes – the institution of slavery – was under
attack from an increasingly powerful abolitionist movement. In *Slavery
and Human Progress*, David Brion Davis discusses a fundamental shift in
metropolitan attitudes toward slavery starting in the 1760s and 1770s: from
acceptance, or at least toleration, to a sense that slavery was fundamentally
wrong and destined – sooner or later – to end. This shift was accompanied
by "a profound change in the basic paradigm of social geography." The
problem of slavery, in other words, became spatialized.[2] This process coincided with the first stirrings of the abolitionist movement, which coalesced
in the 1770s and 1780s, marked by the founding of the Society for Effecting
the Abolition of the Slave Trade (SEAST) in 1787.

Abolitionists constructed Britain's slave colonies as aberrant places in need of metropolitan intervention. Their humanitarian narrative depended on a notion of collective responsibility for distant others: they felt compelled to rescue West Indian slaves from their corrupt Creole owners. This "othering" of the West Indies was central, the geographer David Lambert suggests, not only to the success of the abolitionist movement but also more broadly "to the forging of British metropolitan identity in the late eighteenth and early nineteenth centuries."[3] Anti-slavery activists strove, with considerable success, to paint the colonists as un-British and to define Britishness against colonial corruption. Of course, powerful pro-slavery interests fought back with all of the means at their disposal. Britain's protracted national debate over slavery was a war of representation, fought in numerous venues and modes. A key tactic in this struggle forms my topic as I examine a range of writings by people with varying stakes in the political struggle over slavery. They represent the nodes of the Atlantic system – the sites of slavery, including not only the West Indies but also Africa, the source of their captive labor; and the British Isles, the destination of their produce and profits – as fully imagined places, vividly described in ways that support a particular political vision, whether pro- or anti-slavery.

This is a book about the places that slavery made. Beginning in the fifteenth century, colonization and slavery shaped the ecologies, economies, and societies of the Caribbean islands: took them captive, so to speak, hostage to the political and economic imperatives of the empire. The mid-seventeenth-century "Sugar Revolution" generated large-scale agribusiness, including the proto-industrial management of enslaved bodies and labor in plantations.[4] By the 1770s, Britain's mature sugar colonies had become slave societies with distinctive customs, landscapes, and histories. However, they were also nodes in an Atlantic network connecting the Caribbean with Europe and Africa in circuits of exchange, carrying constant flows of bodies, goods, and ideas. Slavery's captive spaces were the quintessentially modern product of a capitalist economy and a colonial society, assembled on tropical terrain: displaced, deracinated people living in relations of compulsion and surveillance for the benefit of owners an ocean away.

The expanding field of Atlantic Studies has been shifting our conceptual focus from nations and national traditions to the dynamic connections among them.[5] Paul Gilroy's influential *The Black Atlantic* put slavery where it belongs: at the center of these super-regional economies and histories. Gilroy's main concern is with later black intellectuals (i.e., Douglass, DuBois, and Wright) who creatively wrought the legacy of slavery into countercultures of modernity. However, his powerful conceptual framework – the "transcultural, international formation" that was and is the Black Atlantic – directs our attention to mass mobility: the 10 million captive Africans who endured the abjection of the Middle Passage and – those who survived – permanently changed the shape and color of Western modernity.

Movement is essential to this project. All of the writings I discuss belong – in one way or another – to the capacious genre of travel writing: texts that bring faraway places home to readers unable to travel there physically. Because travel writing chronicles movement to and through places, it renders those places for readers, searching out terms to convey travelers' experience to distant minds. The academic study of travel writing has expanded in recent years, another body of work that grounds this study. Its popularity in the eighteenth and nineteenth centuries cannot be understood apart from colonial expansion. It addressed a curiosity about the wider world, driven by Britons' vested interests in the far-flung spaces into which their empire was expanding or might in the future expand.[6]

People traveled varying routes across the captive spaces of the Atlantic, depending on who they were and what they owned – or who owned them. A plantation owner based in the English countryside, like Sir Thomas Bertram in Jane Austen's *Mansfield Park*, might need to travel to Antigua or Jamaica to inspect his property and check up on those administering it. Conversely, planters resident in the islands returned on occasion to the "mother country" to spend their fortunes (or, like Beckford, to try to repair them). They sent their children home to be educated because the colonies lacked good schools. Soldiers and civil servants, from humble to grand, could be posted to one colony or another as customs collectors, defense forces, and colonial governors. The risk of tropical disease meant that many would never return.

Enslaved people traveled as well.[7] The Middle Passage obviously does not fit received ideas of travel, with its "history of European, literary, male, bourgeois, scientific, heroic, recreational, meanings and practices," as James Clifford observes. However, even conditions as harsh as those on the slave ships did not prevent travel from becoming a source of significant experience, knowledge, and cultural production. Slavery created "diasporic and migrant . . . cultures of displacement and transportation" whose creativity shaped our modern world. Olaudah Equiano and Mary Prince, the enslaved travelers whose narratives I study, had survival skills honed by their suffering. Their travels fostered what Clifford calls "discrepant cosmopolitanism": moving beyond local attachments, they became citizens of the Atlantic world.[8] To read their so-called slave narratives as travel writing is to realize that they are in dialogue with travel writing as it is conventionally understood. As I uncover their sophisticated engagement with the same discourses and paradigms invoked by more privileged writers, texts authored by enslaved people offer an invaluable counterpoint.

A wealth of recent scholarship on British slavery and the abolitionist movement informs my study. As postcolonial criticism continues to decenter literary and cultural studies of the long eighteenth century, scholars of colonial slavery have been especially productive, although much remains to be done.[9] The essays in Paul Youngquist and Frances Botkin's recent online collection, *Circulations: Romanticism and the Black Atlantic*, are an outstanding example. As their introduction reminds us, the maritime economy of the Atlantic drove the booming prosperity of the eighteenth-century British Empire, and the Caribbean slave colonies comprised its core. "The West Indies are not the edge of Empire. They are its engine: the economic, material, and cultural condition of British prosperity and dominion during the Romantic era."[10]

The colonization of the Caribbean basin by the European empires – beginning with Spain and including Holland, Britain, France, Portugal, and even Denmark – formed part of what we can call "early globalization." Although most scholarship on "globalization" covers the twentieth and twenty-first centuries, some geographers believe the term can be usefully applied beginning as early as 1500.[11] In the early modern period, expanding European networks of transportation, trade, and colonization established new links between Europe and other parts of the world for the circulation of ships, people, goods, and capital. By the late 1700s, the material culture of the British Empire flowed through well-developed circuits connecting Western Europe with the Americas, Africa, and India. The Caribbean provides an especially compelling example of imperial interconnectedness. Its lucrative agrarian capitalism, grounded in plantation agriculture, depended on the global circulation of plants, people, implements, and supplies. The Caribbean's global connections linked it (through the metropolitan center) to Britain's interests across the world.

One example of this imperial reach is Sir Joseph Banks's 1790s scheme to transplant Tahitian breadfruit to the Caribbean to feed enslaved laborers. Banks, the botanist who accompanied Captain James Cook on his first voyage to the Pacific (1768–72), later became President of the Royal Society, turning his scientific authority and political influence to imperialist ends. Banks pioneered the systematization of scientific knowledge at the imperial center, building complex networks to connect areas of scientific research around the world. The Royal Botanic Gardens at Kew anchored a worldwide botanical network. Plants could be taken from one colony, carefully nursed, and transported to another – putting both exploration and science in the service of the empire. The first attempt to transport breadfruit plants in 1787 was thwarted by the notorious mutiny on the *HMS Bounty*, but Captain Bligh's second attempt in 1791 was successful (except that most West Indians, for various reasons, rejected the breadfruit as food).[12]

Sugar cane was an introduced species, taken from the Canary Islands to Hispaniola, from Sicily via Madeira to Brazil, and then to the Lesser Antilles.[13] The mature sugar colonies were intertwined with Europe as metropolitan populations consumed their product with an appetite that became part of daily life. The anthropologist Sidney Mintz observes, "Tobacco, sugar, and tea were the first objects within capitalism that conveyed with their use the complex idea that one could *become* different by *consuming* differently." The availability of these addictive tropical products modified personal and national identities. "Like tea, sugar came to define English 'character.'"[14] This created need generated immense profits. In addition to squandering their wealth on high living, colonials reinvested it in manufactured goods for their plantations and more shiploads of enslaved Africans to replace those who died of deprivation and overwork.

What type of places were Britain's Caribbean sugar colonies in the half-century or so before emancipation? They were organized for sugar production: that was their "purpose and place in the British Empire."[15] Jamaica was by far the biggest colony and it is the topic of the majority of texts I discuss, so I use it as my example. Jamaica was extraordinarily wealthy – by 1774 the richest colony in British America. Individual Jamaican colonists were the richest people in the British Empire.[16] A substantial proportion of planters were absentees (i.e., about one-sixth in 1774, including the island's wealthiest landowners) who spent their fortunes in the British Isles and hired others to manage their estates. Of those residing on the island, relatively few had their wives and families with them. Jamaica was considered "a place in which to make a fortune, not to make a life." White Jamaica was far from a proper bourgeois society. Rather, it was "a model of disorder, licentious sexuality, illegitimacy, irregularity, with colored mistresses kept openly, and concubinage a completely accepted form." Many eighteenth-century Jamaicans were avaricious and self-absorbed, "addicted to ostentatious display and devoted to luxury," spending their wealth on "lavish feasting, copious drinking, and all manner of sexual and sensuous delights."[17]

The enslaved majority had scant part of these enjoyments, except for interracial sex – much of it non-consensual or quasi-consensual (as the notorious diaries of the slave owner Thomas Thistlewood reveal).[18] By the latter half of the eighteenth century, the enslaved outnumbered white colonists more than 10 to 1. Of these, 75 to 80 percent were African-born. The continuing, massive importation of captive Africans fueled agricultural expansion and replaced the large numbers of laborers who "failed to thrive due to poor diet, debilitating work regimes, and brutal treatment."[19] The enslaved were taken from various regions of West and Central Africa and mingled every which way through sale and dispersal from ships to plantations. They spoke different languages and practiced various religions, including Islam. Despite all of this upheaval, displaced Africans and their island-born cohorts together managed to develop a rich and dynamic cultural life, combining elements of African and European language, music, and religion into new, hybrid cultural forms. Fighting dehumanization, they achieved "some measure of self-expression within an overall structure of fierce repression, social disruption, and constant uncertainty."[20]

White Jamaican culture was hybridized as well: a Creole culture, shaped by the conditions of island life, with the white minority surrounded and intimately served by their human property. "The plantation complex during slavery produced an amalgamated culture from which the master class could not insulate itself."[21] Snobbish metropolitan observers such as Lady Maria Nugent (discussed in Chapter 5) noticed the influence of the enslaved on their owners' speech, diet, and behavior. Nugent wrote, "Many of the ladies who have not been educated in England, speak a sort of broken English, with an indolent drawling out of their words, that is very tiresome if not disgusting. I stood next to a lady one night, near a window, and by way of saying something, remarked that the air was much cooler than usual; to which she answered, 'Yes, ma'am, *him rail-ly too fra-ish.*'[22] The groundbreaking work of Edward (Kamau) Brathwaite famously studied the formation of the Jamaican Creole society through the reciprocal shaping of white and black, master and captive. Rather than debased and degenerate – as it appeared to many metropolitan writers – Brathwaite argues that the Creole society was (and is) dynamic and creative, although white Jamaicans, crippled by racism, refused to recognize this.[23]

What is the relationship between slavery and ideas of race? Its exact nature remains controversial. The Trinidadian historian Eric Williams claimed polemically in 1944: "Slavery was not born of racism: rather, racism was the consequence of slavery."[24] This approach refuses to accept racism as eternal and essential, an unfortunate fact of life. Rather, it has a history:

a history inseparable from the history of the captive spaces of the Atlantic system – the history of enslavement, plantation agriculture, and nascent capitalism. Theories of race or human variety have drawn widespread scholarly interest in recent years; many scholars agree that the decades discussed in this book witnessed significant change in prevalent accounts of human variety. "By the early nineteenth century...what increasingly served to distinguish one people from another was not their religion, their degree of 'civilization,' their customs or their beliefs, but rather their anatomy and external appearance." This shift prepared the way for the more dogmatic racism of the late nineteenth and twentieth centuries.[25]

Race is not my central topic; however, ideas about race, or human variety, are unavoidably woven throughout the process of discursive place-making. Textual representations of the captive spaces of the British Atlantic were driven by the political debate over slavery. The discursive resources engaged in that debate were steeped in assumptions about groups of people and their connection to the places they inhabit. The discourses of aesthetics and natural history, in particular, are intertwined with ideas of race in ways that individual chapters explore. Writers' identities and their stakes in the slavery debate involve skin color as well as nationality, occupation, gender, and free or enslaved status. Skin color or physiognomy, national or regional origin, climate and culture, and the connections among them enter into the texts I discuss in ways that are symptomatic of the evolving character of theories of human variety during the late eighteenth and early nineteenth centuries.

I draw my working definition of "place" from a range of recent work by geographers – in particular, feminist geographers such as Doreen Massey and Linda McDowell. One geographer defines "place" as "space invested with meaning in the context of power." Places "are not given but produced by human activity": the production of place is a project with an inevitable political dimension.[26] If space is undifferentiated, Cartesian – pure potential, as it were – then places are what human societies make of the spaces they occupy. The project of place-making is collective, contentious, and open-ended. At an individual level, the social and the spatial converge to generate each person's sense of place, "constructed out of a particular constellation of social relations, meeting and weaving together at a particular locus." It follows that, as McDowell states, "occupants of the same Cartesian spaces may live in very different 'places.'"[27] Caribbean planters and their human property starkly exemplify this truth, as this book describes. Depending on who is writing, Jamaica or Antigua can be either paradise or purgatory.

Of course, the power to invest these colonial spaces with textual meaning was not evenly distributed between white colonists and their human property. Each group's sense of place nonetheless functioned as a limit or horizon for that of the other. During the decades of the abolition controversy, a few enslaved men and women – with the support of metropolitan allies – were able to intervene in the representational contest over the captive spaces of the British West Indies. Access to print, of course, was highly restricted for the enslaved and formerly enslaved. Reconstructing the traces of enslaved people and other subalterns from the archives remains a methodological challenge for postcolonial critics but one that we cannot avoid.[28] This study attempts to set the voices and traces of the enslaved in dialogue with those (far more plentiful in the printed record) of slave owners.

The politics of slavery, I argue, played out to a significant degree as a politics of place. Edward Said famously identified the struggle over imaginative geography as crucial to the culture of imperialism. The imaginative geography of the Atlantic Triangle and the places that its perverse geometry connected became the object of a high-stakes contest during the final decades of British colonial slavery. I examine the process of place-making in various types of texts by writers with diverse stakes in the region. The politics of place is also a politics of identity: planters, slaves, soldiers, sailors, wives, and other travelers bore varying relationships to slavery's captive spaces. For example, we return to our woeful prisoner in London's Fleet Prison. For this member of the West Indian planter elite – cultured cosmopolitan, patron of the arts, former master of many fertile acres and hundreds of slaves – the place that is Jamaica signifies both high-risk investment and intense aesthetic appeal. Sugar planting is a "high-wire act," vulnerable to damage by pests, hurricanes, slave revolt, and price fluctuation: a drama of extremes carried out by larger-than-life characters. Having taken the risk and suffered the fall, Beckford languishes across the Atlantic from his beloved island, feeling very sorry for himself and describing Jamaica for metropolitan readers using the powerful modern discourse of aesthetics.

Why aesthetics? This may seem a surprising category with which to begin a discussion of the spaces that slavery made. Aesthetics, after all, appears closer to pure philosophy than to politics; it is a category strongly marked as extra-historical or psychological. Such assumptions are precisely what made aesthetics attractive to elite writers for constructing colonial space, and they tended to insulate their work from the scrutiny of postcolonial criticism. However, aesthetics exemplifies the distinctively modern discursive resources used to produce places as colonial – to take them captive, as the chapter title indicates. Colonial modernity demanded "non-localized forms of action and vision" – that is, what John Durham Peters calls "bifocality": a dual vision encompassing both the near and the far, the local and the imperial or global.[29] Planter writers such as Beckford exploit the bifocal capacity of aesthetics to enact imaginative intertwinement between colony and metropole, at the same time obscuring the ugliness of slavery's site-specific practices. The discursive construction of place, in this instance, paradoxically involves undoing the purely local (if there is any such thing). These bifocal discourses are at the center of this book. Six interlinked case studies analyze their use by colonial writers to represent the captive spaces of the British Caribbean and to contest the politics of place.

The definition of politics at work in this study is clearly a broad one, encompassing more than only the doings of Parliament, the West India lobby, and the Abolition Society. Although the political struggle culminated in the landmark legislative actions of 1807 and 1833, which abolished the slave trade and emancipated British slaves, the cultural politics of slavery and colonialism was fought out in many venues. Explicit persuasion played a part, but opinion and hegemony also could be crafted through subtler means – importantly, I contend, through the powerful discourses of place the use of which this book explores.[30] The discourses with which I am most concerned – although they were used to construct the colonial periphery – were central to the eighteenth-century epistemic shift known as the Enlightenment. Their emergence marked the onset of modernity and coincided with the peak of British slavery. The case studies in my chapters offer snapshots from the confrontation between slavery and modernity, a later phase of which concerns Gilroy in *The Black Atlantic*. Historians have claimed that the profits of Britain's colonial plantations fueled investment in industrialization.[31] If slavery was indeed a "midwife" to industrial capitalism, what was its relation to the modern division of knowledge emerging around the same time? A partial answer may reside in these writers' politically inflected deployment of an array of distinctively modern discourses to render, contest, or obscure the captive spaces of the British Atlantic.

I first consider the language of aesthetics. One defining feature of the Enlightenment was the "invention of the aesthetic as an autonomous discursive realm." The German Alexander Baumgarten coined the term around 1750, although a concept recognizable as disinterested aesthetic perception emerged in British aesthetic thought as early as 1710. A wide range of eighteenth-century writings on the Caribbean – colonial histories, natural histories, and travelogues – draws heavily on the language of landscape aesthetics, in which aesthetic disinterestedness takes the form of the viewer's distance from the aesthetic object, the natural prospect, or scene.[32] The islands' tropical beauty might seem to make aesthetic discourse a natural fit for them; however, seventeenth-century accounts of the area focus less on the islands' beauty than on their productive potential to serve European needs and desires. By the period that is the concern of this study, the emphasis had shifted – or at least broadened – to encompass a fascination with the islands' scenic appeal. I previously sought to explain the appeal of aesthetics to the apologists of slavery.[33] Chapter 1 traces the shifting fate of a particular aesthetic paradigm – that is, the picturesque – in books about Jamaica the authors of which stood in varying relations to its colonial economy and society.

The slave colony does not exactly lend itself to the picturesque. That a number of writers nonetheless brought the two together during the decades-long lifespan of the picturesque fad – the same decades that saw the rise and eventual triumph of the abolition movement – bespeaks their motivation to assimilate the West Indies to the English countryside, where planters aspired to spend their retirement and their colonial fortunes. The empire, Simon Pugh observes, "was the countryside writ large: an idyllic retreat, an escape, and the opportunity to make a fortune."[34] Picturesque aesthetics overwrote the tropics with European nature, remaking Jamaica into an English countryside or Italian *campagna* with a difference. However, that difference – the insurmountable distance or gap between colony and metropole – comes inexorably to the fore in the texts of the planter picturesque. The difference is slavery, which happened in the colony but sustained the imperial economy. The planter writers that I discuss – Edward Long, William Beckford, and Matthew Lewis – and the artist James Hakewill put picturesque aesthetics to work to beautify the slave colony and keep its ugly realities at arm's length. Their success was very partial, as my readings reveal. Each version of the planter picturesque is differently eroded by the hazards of colonial life and the unruly presence of Jamaica's enslaved majority.

Natural history, along with aesthetics, dominated published British discourse about the Caribbean from Hans Sloane in 1719 through the eighteenth century and beyond. Scientific and economic interest in Caribbean plants and animals filled the subscription lists of lushly illustrated volumes, including Hughes's *Natural History of Barbados* and Browne's *Civil and Natural History of Jamaica*. For Michel Foucault (1994), as is well known, the ordered tabulation of living beings typifies the eighteenth-century *episteme*, or regime of truth. Natural historians needed specimens and information as their raw material; to procure them, they needed help from the human inhabitants of the areas they studied – whether these "boots on the ground" were those of colonial whites, native peoples, or slaves. These unequal collaborations produced knowledge that was truly bifocal: bringing together local, colonial contributions and metropolitan agendas.[35]

Chapter 2 studies the natural-history practice of one atypical scientist, the Scottish mercenary John Stedman, in the context of his life as a soldier in a Caribbean slave colony. Tensions between natural history and slavery and between Enlightenment science and colonial brutality shape his sprawling, self-contradictory *Narrative of a Five Years Expedition against the Revolted Negroes of Surinam*. Although the place that Stedman's book describes is not a British but rather a Dutch colony, it was written for a British readership and its sensational illustrations of slave torture helped to fuel Britain's anti-slavery movement. As the soldier describes his process of tropical seasoning – his harrowing encounter with an alien terrain that begins to kill soldiers almost as soon as they arrive – he works to assimilate Suriname's unfamiliar organisms to European conventions of description, depiction, and classification. The tension between the distancing discourse of natural history and the soldier's close encounters with tropical terrain yields a fractured sense of place. Stedman praises the colony's productivity but is drawn to the forest-subsistence skills of his elusive adversaries, the Suriname Maroons. Their skillful navigation of the jungle that threatens to devour the Europeans forms a counterpoint to the decontextualizing discourse of natural history.

Geography cannot be called an Enlightenment discipline in the same way as aesthetics and natural history. As a body of knowledge, of course, it dates to antiquity. However, geography underwent a significant transformation during the Enlightenment, as Charles W. J. Withers argues in a seminal article. He connects geography's emergence as a modern discipline (dated by David Stoddart to 1769, the year that Cook entered the Pacific) with "'the globalizing project of natural history,' which, like geography, sought to represent, to classify, and to order the world."[36] Both geography and natural history are centrally concerned with place. European exploration was "figuratively, a process of collecting places hitherto unknown to the European gaze" – places that were literal sites for collecting new organisms: plants and animals (and human beings) indigenous to them. The work of classifying these organisms was a metaphorical placing, putting the world in place: "place [as] a symptom of rationalizing order . . . consistent with other metaphors used in understanding that quintessentially metaphorical project, (the) Enlightenment itself."[37]

British writers about the Caribbean took part in this process in ways that served their political aims. Chapter 3 traces the struggle over the imaginative geography of the Atlantic system through several eventful decades. Colonial history was a genre with an agenda, written primarily by planters and slave owners and geared to defending the system that provided their livelihood. The colonial histories that I discuss present not so much history – in the sense of a narrative of past events – as portraits of a place, justifying in various ways the colonies' value to the imperial state. One way that they do this is through imaginative geography: mapping the nodes of the Atlantic system and the relationships among them. The terms of this justification shifted with the march of events. Edward Long's *History of Jamaica* defends slavery in 1774 with a confidence no longer available to Bryan Edwards when he published his *History of the West Indies* in 1793. In the interval, the abolitionist movement had been organized, achieving an impressive hegemony over the terms of the national debate. Abolitionist writers, including Anthony Benezet and Thomas Clarkson, had developed their own version of Atlantic geography, striving to isolate the West Indies as an un-British pocket of corruption, fundamentally different from the morally upright center of the empire. Edwards's response is measured, conceding much to his opponents in the service of the West India interest's core agenda of preserving slavery and the slave trade.

Meanwhile, another epochal event of the 1790s – overshadowed in historical memory by the upheavals in France but for colonials more immediate and menacing – occurred on an island that for Edwards and his fellow Jamaica planters was too close to home. This was the massive and bloody 1791 insurrection in the French colony of Saint Domingue (i.e., present-day Haiti). Edwards visited Saint Domingue in 1791 with a delegation sent by the governor of Jamaica in response to French planters' pleas for help.[38] His second, very different, colonial history, *An Historical Survey of the French Colony of St. Domingue* (1797), revisits Atlantic geography in inflammatory rhetoric attuned to the reactionary mood of the mid-1790s. Chapter 3 concludes by contrasting Edwards's apocalyptic vision with that of a very different colonial historian. Marcus Rainsford, an Anglo-Irish officer, served in the Caribbean and spent several months on Saint Domingue in 1797–8. *An Historical Account of the Black Empire of Hayti* (1805) reverses the conventional binary asserted by the two earlier colonial historians: that is, white Europeans as possessing a monopoly on civilization, black Africans as essentially savage. Rainsford's book hints at a utopian potential that would remain largely unfulfilled as Haiti struggled to survive in the midst of a hostile hemisphere.

Chapter 4 returns to the early years of the abolitionist movement to consider the well-known and controversial figure of Olaudah Equiano or Gustavus Vassa. Manumitted through his own efforts, "the African" took up his pen in the cause of his captive "countrymen." His autobiography, launched into the lively pamphlet war of the late 1780s, presents his version of the abolitionist geography examined in Chapter 3. However, as Equiano works to redraw the pro-slavery map of the Atlantic system, subtle but significant departures put space between the former captive and his white allies. Much has been said about Equiano's elusive identity and his means of narrating it, especially because we now know that he may not have been African at all.[39] However, no one has read the *Interesting Narrative* as a polemic of place, a contribution to remapping the Atlantic system as a circuit of freedom. Its author, a professional sailor, probably logged as many miles after his manumission as before. His choice to include so much material about his travels as a free man underlines the importance of place and mobility to his self-definition. As he narrates his multiple journeys, the strategic, geographically defined identities of "the African" and the black Briton give way to the discrepant cosmopolitanism of the sailor – a member of a multi-ethnic maritime proletariat – and the anti-slavery activist.[40]

The final discourse of place is the gendered discourse of home. Here, the modern European gender system intersects with colonialism through the dual meanings of "home" as "native land" and "family dwelling." Colonial women – white and black, free and enslaved – shared a special relationship to home as domesticity by virtue of their gender. If home – as separate spheres ideology would have it – was women's domain, then colonial women bore a special responsibility for re-creating home, in both senses, on colonial soil. Enslaved women were enlisted in this project: as concubines, when white women were scarce, or as household workers, like Mary Prince. Her household labor allowed Prince a close-up view of the radical disjunction between the dystopian reality of domesticity in a slave society and the metropolitan ideal of domestic gender relations. My analysis assumes a large body of research on the Enlightenment transformation of knowledge about sex and gender. Based on the assumption of incommensurable difference between the sexes and conditioned by the economic reorganization that preceded and founded the Industrial Revolution, gender ideology mapped sexual difference onto the spaces of everyday life so as to assign home to women and tether them to the home.[41] Although actual practice often may have broken with this prescription, the rhetoric of separate spheres continued to hold considerable power well beyond the period of this study – power sufficient to underwrite white colonial women's unique contribution to the imperial project: that is, reestablishing the domestic sphere at far-flung locations.

Chapter 5 turns to unpublished journals by white women sojourning in the West Indies.[42] Janet Schaw and Maria Nugent, female dependents of civil servants working in Britain's Caribbean colonies, recorded their experience in a form whose informality, immediacy, and temporally unfolding structure lends itself to making a case for women's privileged role as carriers of the "emotional furniture" (so to speak) that could turn a slave colony into a home of sorts. Work by Anne McClintock (1997) and others established the importance of the "cult of domesticity" to the imperial project in later historical periods. In the pre-emancipation West Indies, white women were relatively few; those who landed there had much to overlook. Although these diarists did a good job of not seeing what they were not supposed to see, we eventually realize that both were well aware of the sex and violence integral to the slave society: that is, the institution of concubinage and the routine physical punishment of enslaved men and women. Their focus, however, is elsewhere. Schaw carries the virtues of home from her beloved Scotland to a slave colony populated by enterprising Scots. Nugent works hard to clean up Jamaica, or at least the governor's mansion, clearing away literal and figurative dirt and imposing metropolitan norms on the alien Creole society. For these women, the productive potential of modern femininity both enables and limits the labor of place-making.

Mary Prince, meanwhile, performed labor of a different kind – hard, body-wrecking work – in the colonial households of sadistic masters and mistresses. The humblest of the authors in this study, she spent much of her life working in the homes of slave owners in Bermuda, Antigua, and London. Her domestic labor and involuntary journeys positioned her to critique the concept of home in both of its senses. The enslaved woman's experience of home and family stood in bitter contrast to the prescriptive ideals of metropolitan gender ideology. This becomes clear in her autobiography, *The History of Mary Prince, a West Indian Slave*, which is the subject of Chapter 6. Sponsored by and dictated to the London abolitionists who encouraged her last recorded journey – that is, out of her owner's door to freedom – the book was published near the end of the successful campaign for emancipation. Reading the *History* as a travel narrative and its narrator as a traveler tests the limits of the concepts of home and travel. How is each conditioned by power and privilege or the lack thereof? Can an enslaved person be a traveler? Can she have a home? One woman's answers to these questions form an apt conclusion to a study of the sites of slavery – the places and imaginary geographies that slavery made. The movement of people on a massive scale from Africa to the Americas throughout the centuries of New World slavery was the first of those large-scale, involuntary modern dislocations at the center of postcolonial and postmodern debates about identity, place, and nation.[43] Mary Prince's story is noteworthy for the way she turned the geographical awareness gained from a lifetime of involuntary travel into the power to transgress the boundaries of her owners' racialized map of the world. She walked out of their door into a London street – from a site of slavery to a place of freedom. On this short but momentous journey, her first fully voluntary one, the battered former captive became a bold traveler indeed.

Slavery and the Politics of Place studies the discursive construction of the places of British slavery in a group of key texts. The struggle over geography – that is, the construction of social space using powerful modern forms of knowledge in the service of a cultural politics of place – shaped Britain's long-lasting national debate about colonial slavery. Not only politicians and journalists but also planters, soldiers, British ladies, and a few exceptional black men and women took part in this textual tug-of-war. At stake, alongside hundreds of thousands of pounds in human property and lucrative trade, was a nation's sense of itself as deserving of its vast prosperity and power. Drawing a mental map of the Atlantic Triangle and coloring its spaces with the appropriate moral shadings was a collective endeavor – an ongoing cultural negotiation from which we still have much to learn.

CHAPTER I

The planter picturesque

> There is something particularly picturesque and striking in a gang of
> negroes, when employed in cutting canes upon the swelling projec-
> tions of a hill.
>
> William Beckford, *A Descriptive Account of the Island of Jamaica*

Enslaved workers cutting sugar cane are probably not the first image that
comes to mind at the mention of the picturesque; most of the scholarship
on this late-eighteenth-century phenomenon focuses on the British Isles.
A few scholars analyze the explorer picturesque and the picturesque of the
settler colonist. What was the fate of the picturesque in the Caribbean
exploitation colonies?[1] This chapter traces the planter picturesque through
books on Jamaica from Edward Long's 1774 *History of Jamaica* to James
Hakewill's 1825 *A Picturesque Tour of the Island of Jamaica*. Colonization,
sugar, and slavery made the West Indies. Three traumatic events shaped
these islands: the eradication of their first inhabitants, the arrival of many
thousands of captive Africans, and the degradation of their environment
through sugar monoculture.[2] These planter writers use the language of
landscape aesthetics to reimagine the traces of trauma in the form of
aesthetic appeal. Each of their picturesque re-creations of the slave colony
responds to the political circumstances of a specific moment in the historical
trajectory of British slavery and the abolitionist movement. In these books,
the politics of slavery emerges as a politics of place. Using successive versions
of picturesque aesthetics, planter writers present Jamaica to metropolitan
readers as the place that its proprietors want and need it to be. As they
paint their writers' hopes and dreams onto the tropical landscape, however,
these texts also disclose the tensions running throughout the slave society
and the slave owners' fears, most of which were eventually realized.

As a discourse of place, the picturesque is paradoxically placeless,
grounded in mobility and comparison.[3] Viewing land as landscape was
first made possible through the fifteenth-century invention of pictorial

perspective, which the geographer David Harvey attributes in part to the flow of geographical knowledge from voyages of discovery: "knowledge about a wider world that had somehow to be absorbed and represented."[4] Conceiving of space from an individual standpoint made it possible (among its many consequences) to see land as landscape, staged or framed, as if in a painting. The word "landscape" entered the English language in 1598, designating a type of painting and, in 1632, according to the *Oxford English Dictionary* (OED), as a "view or prospect of natural inland scenery, such as can be taken in at a glance from one point of view." By the eighteenth century, John Barrell argues, an educated person would have found it difficult to describe, see, or even think of land "as a visual phenomenon, except as mediated through particular notions of form."[5]

These formal paradigms move us toward the picturesque. They derived, as it happens, from paintings of Italy – in particular, the enormously influential landscapes of Claude Lorrain and Salvator Rosa. This influence was made possible by early modern circuits of travel – in particular, the Grand Tour of Europe – circuits that were contemporaneous with those connecting England to its New World colonies from the early seventeenth century. Thus, early picturesque tourists paradoxically praised native beauty spots "by invoking idealized foreign models."[6] The ability to compare places with one another, and with ideal models or formal criteria, took for granted a privileged mobility that also fostered an "improving" attitude toward nature.

This chapter examines four versions of the planter picturesque, each specific to its historical moment in the trajectory of British slavery: its apogee, its first real political crisis, its post-abolition reconfiguration, and its protracted endgame. To represent a slave colony to metropolitan readers necessarily intervened in the politics of slavery. The picturesque is central to the politics of place that plays out in each text. Each is shaped by its author's specific and sometimes conflicted relationship to the island of Jamaica[7]; to its inhabitants, enslaved and free; and to his own status as a slave owner. Let us, then, preliminarily locate each of our planter authors in time and space.

Edward Long published his massive and influential *History of Jamaica* in 1774, two years after the Mansfield Decision had signaled the approaching necessity of politically defending the institution of slavery but before the abolitionist movement had coalesced as a political force.[8] Long, the son of a planter, married into another wealthy planter clan. He lived 12 years on the island, serving in its Assembly and as an Admiralty judge, before retiring to England, where he passed his sugar-funded leisure by writing his *History* (for which he had gathered material during his time on the island). William Beckford, illegitimate scion of an even wealthier colonial family, also lived on Jamaica as a planter (and patron of the arts) until his return to England in 1786. Far from enjoying a leisurely life, he was thrown into London's Fleet Prison for debt. While incarcerated, he wrote *A Descriptive Account of the Island of Jamaica,* published in 1790 at the height of the abolition controversy and the Abolition Society's clout.

Our third planter author, Mathew Gregory Lewis, differs significantly from Long and Beckford. Although both sides of his family had ties to Jamaica, Lewis's father left the island as a child and never returned; Lewis himself never lived there. Estranged from his father as a young man in 1802, the son had no expectation of inheriting two sugar plantations, which had helped fund his privileged upbringing, when his father died in 1812. Meanwhile, Matthew Lewis built a London career as a popular author, starting with his notorious Gothic novel, *The Monk* (1796), and followed by successful stage melodramas, stories, poems, and translations. By 1815, when Lewis sailed for Jamaica and started the journal later published as *Journal of a West India Proprietor,* abolitionists had accomplished their initial goal of abolishing the slave trade, passed by Parliament in 1807; however, the campaign to emancipate British slaves had yet to gather momentum. Lewis was both an abolitionist and a friend of prominent members of the Abolition Society, but he was no emancipationist.

Our fourth version of the planter picturesque was created not by a planter but rather by the artist and architect James Hakewill. After publishing *A Picturesque Tour of Italy* in 1820, Hakewill ventured to Jamaica, where he toured, sketched, and enjoyed "much kindness" from the "Resident Gentlemen." To these, he dedicated *A Picturesque Tour of the Island of Jamaica* – along with "The Noblemen and Gentlemen, Proprietors of Estates in the West Indies" and "The Merchants of the United Kingdom, connected with those valuable colonies." The book's contents, both images and text, are well calculated to oblige its dedicatees as well as to engage a metropolitan readership. A page or two of commentary accompanies each illustration.[9] I discuss Hakewill's version first because it introduces key features of the planter picturesque that I treat at greater length with reference to the three planter writers.

Between the end of the Napoleonic Wars in 1815 and George III's death in 1820, British abolitionist activity experienced a lull. The sugar colonies profited considerably during the long wars that followed the French Revolution. The implosion of the Caribbean's largest sugar producer, the French colony of Saint Domingue (i.e., present-day Haiti), boosted the output of sugar and other tropical staples throughout the British West Indies. After the peace, British humanitarians continued to watch the region, suspecting planters of violating the slave-trade ban instituted in 1807. In the face of planter outrage, they succeeded in implementing a system of registration of enslaved people beginning in 1817.[10] Continued low birth rates and high mortality convinced activists that they had been wrong to believe that slave-trade abolition would lead to better treatment of the enslaved. In 1823, therefore, they established a new organization: the Society for Mitigating and Gradually Abolishing Slavery Throughout the British Dominions.

The renewed campaign was fought in print as well as in Parliament: in the 1820s, veteran abolitionists William Wilberforce, James Stephen, and Zachary Macaulay each published a critical survey of conditions in the slave colonies. In 1825, *The Anti-Slavery Reporter* commenced publication; its editor, Thomas Pringle, later sponsored and edited Mary Prince's auto-biography (see Chapter 6). Popular response to the reorganized anti-slavery movement was gratifying, evidenced by the founding of local societies and the generation of petitions backing legislation to ameliorate conditions for slaves.[11] All of this put the West India Interest predictably on the defensive. As it had since the first stirrings of the abolitionist movement, the response included propaganda.

This is the point where Hakewill enters. His views of Jamaica illustrate how picturesque aesthetics functioned as part of the politics of place, vital to the abolition debate. He devotes his brief introduction primarily to defending slavery, although he begins by defining a picturesque tour as "any work intended to convey a general idea of the surfaces and external appearances of a country, without undertaking to develope its moral and political institutions."[12] This programmatic isolation of the visual from the political both belies and underwrites the ideological impact of Hakewill's images, which confer on the slave colony a seductive allure drawn from the influential style of the painter Claude Lorrain. The views in the book include two bridges (a favorite Claudean motif), one waterfall or cascade, and the Jamaican coast, along with prospects of or from a number of plantations and three towns.

The plantation scenes are pastoral, often dotted with cows or goats. Slaves are not shown working, except for three women washing laundry under one of the bridges. Neither are any of Hakewill's human figures, black or white, individualized; they are mere staffage – that is, human decora-tion – in the best picturesque tradition. Geoff Quilley writes of the pastoral plantation, with reference to the earlier Jamaican landscapes of George

Figure 1.1 James Hakewill, "Montpelier Estate St. James's," from *A Picturesque Tour of the Island of Jamaica* (1825). Courtesy of the National Library of Jamaica.

Robertson (William Beckford's protégé) that its depiction of lounging slaves "involves a double displacement: first, it sublimates the history of the slaves' enforced transportation from Africa, via the Middle Passage." Furthermore, the figures' inactivity "creates a separation between them and the reason for their enslavement, to be a labor force."[13] Hakewill's selective, stylized depictions of the colony – like those of the planter writers – persuade by what they do not show as much as by what they do.

"Montpelier Estate St. James's" (Figure 1.1) is typical of Hakewill's plantation views, with its verdant lawn dotted with livestock and pristine white buildings. Its composition follows the picturesque formula of receding planes, based on Claude Lorrain: on one side, a dark *coulisse*, or side-screen, shadows the foreground, the trees' foliage providing some of the "roughness" that Gilpin prized. The middle plane contains a large central feature – in this case, the plantation buildings.[14] In the distance, Jamaica's blue hills luminously recede into an even bluer sky. Also in the foreground is a gated wall, a feature prominent in several of the *Picturesque Tour's* plantation views (here, perforated by a bricked arch over a lazy stream, the outflow from a water-driven grinding mill). The gate and the gate-house, with the mounted white men (probably overseers), telegraph to viewers a sense of secure ownership and orderly management. If Hakewill's foreground is not very rough, his distance compensates for it with the "rich-ness" or "tenderness" of its "glowing tints," as Gilpin would describe it. The aquatint medium infuses the plantation with the famous "atmosphere" of a painting by Claude Lorrain. "Atmosphere is the technique of sustaining infinite light in finite space – of organizing color progression, contrast reduction, and variation in local color into a single scale of translucent haziness extending . . . from foregrounds of brown-green and chiaroscuro to backgrounds of spirit-hues and virtually no tonal contrast. Expressed as 'mood,' such atmosphere is repose direct."[15]

Not much is happening in this scene. Its serene stasis is evidence that, as Alan Liu states, the "repose of landscape art was really a recognition of labor finished or performed by others."[16] Hakewill shows us a plantation at rest, its parts poised in visual harmony, its buildings seemingly vacant of the laborers they existed to house. Hakewill's little book can be read as a special case of Liu's erudite argument that picturesque form, or formalism in general, arrests history, eliding narrative in favor of stasis or repose. "If form arrests motive [narrative] within the frame of a . . . pictorial text, there must be a larger, cultural context motivating and supervising the arrest."[17] The context in this case, of course, is the institution of slavery. Its history during the 1820s was by no means static but instead was moving in a direction that horrified Hakewill's planter friends. *A Picturesque Tour of the Island of Jamaica* marshals the formal resources of the picturesque tradition in defense of the planters' lifeline: the institution of slavery. Its placid plantation scenes try to "stop the clock," as it were, on British abolition by visually arresting Jamaica within the formalist conventions of the picturesque.

Thus far, we have glimpsed some of the ways in which Hakewill "improved" Jamaica's plantations. His rigidly formulaic visual version of the picturesque, with equally formulaic captions containing little more than statistics on acreage and encomia to the owners, betrays the exhaus-tion of an aesthetics approaching its end. Another of his images provides an apt comment on the demise of the planter picturesque: a tomb with a view. Entitled "Monument of the Late Thomas Hibbert, Esq., at Agualta Vale Penn, St. Mary's," the image shows a gentleman displaying Hibbert's massive, fenced memorial – an urn on a pedestal engraved with a coat of arms – to the faceless enslaved laborer holding his horse (Figure 1.2). In the background, scenic Agualta Vale stretches to the sea, with the buildings of

Figure 1.2 James Hakewill, "Monument of the Late Thomas Hibbert, Esq., at Agualta Vale Penn, St. Mary's," from *A Picturesque Tour of the Island of Jamaica* (1825). Courtesy of the National Library of Jamaica.

the pen (i.e., livestock farm) shown at the lower left. "On this spot," the caption reads, "as having yielded him many a happy moment, in the reflection of an amiable mind surveying his own creation of wealth and independence, for a long inheritance, [Hibbert] desired that his remains should be placed." The planter picturesque depicts land devoted to wealth creation through colonial agribusiness, growing a commodity crop destined to leave Jamaica's shores en route to the center of the empire. Hakewill underwrites that wealth with the fiction of independence, figured in "Montpelier Old Works Plantation" as the absence of the enslaved laborers on whom the island and its wealth depended. The massive edifice of Hibbert's tomb, looming over the valley, reifies the colonial presence: intensively cultivated land and coerced labor, transformed into this marble artifact of extracted wealth.

Reimagining Jamaican land according to a metropolitan aesthetic paradigm, the planter picturesque thus completes a circuit of commodification and exchange between colony and metropole: picturesquely packaged plantations circulated for British consumption along with refined West Indian sugar. Hakewill's version of the planter picturesque introduces some of its key features. The process of composing and framing land as landscape, viewed from a vantage point or station, sets the aesthetic subject apart from the place that he or she views. The epochal invention of pictorial perspective and the idea of landscape formed the essential historical foundation for the more specific set of conventions known as the picturesque. Organizing pictorial space as landscape allowed for the elision of narrative, or motive, in the long process that Liu traced through art history – a process recapitulated by the formal procedures of an artist such as Hakewill. The famous Claudean atmosphere of repose colludes in this aesthetic suppression of history, as shown in Hakewill's doggedly serene vision of Montpelier Plantation. Slaves, if included, should not work; if they do, their labor must be subsumed in the auxiliary aesthetic paradigm of the georgic.

A well-traveled artist such as Hakewill, or a planter familiar with European scenery and art, could apply these eminently portable means of place-making to "improve" Jamaica's landscape in aesthetically appealing and politically strategic ways. However, Hakewill's planter picturesque is also specific to its own historical moment. Earlier points in the history of British slavery generated versions that are related yet distinct, each arising from a discrete social and spatial location. I now examine these, beginning in the 1770s, when the importation of enslaved people to the West Indies was at its zenith and the abolitionist movement was not yet organized.

Ornaments of this country

Edward Long's 1774 *History of Jamaica* is an ambitious, encyclopedic work whose account of the island draws on an impressive range of discourses and disciplines, including political economy, aesthetics, natural history, agriculture, travel, and meteorology, as well as what we would now call history. All of these branches of Enlightenment learning collude to serve Long's polemical aims of defending slavery and promoting Jamaica's prosperity, as I argue in Chapter 3. Here, I focus on Long's use of one key Enlightenment discourse: aesthetics. The *History of Jamaica*'s second volume opens with a distinctive feature: a topographical survey of the island, parish by parish, or what we might today call a "virtual tour." Prominent throughout this section is the language of landscape aesthetics. We cannot actually call it a picturesque tour; Thomas West's best-selling guidebook to the picturesque Lake District did not appear until 1778, and Gilpin published his first picturesque tour in 1782 (although he penned the "Observations" contained in it in 1770). Nonetheless, this section of Long's book does take the form – later to become so popular – of an ambulatory survey of a region's visual attractions.

Long's virtual tour packages local sights in an obvious effort to present Jamaica's best face and to lure new settlers to help change the island's high ratio of black to white or enslaved to free. Set pieces of landscape description draw on the prestige of metropolitan high culture to confer aesthetic value on the island. In the following excerpt, Long describes Saint Elizabeth Parish:

> The prospects are finely variegated, and, from some stations, are extended . . . many miles: but one of the most pleasing scenes is, the spacious tract of open land, called Labor-in-vain Savannah, which appears partly of a vivid green, and partly of a russet color. One side of it is girt about with romantic hills and woods; the other, towards the South, is washed by the sea; the middle sweep is graced with scattered clumps of trees and under-wood; which objects all together combine in exhibiting a very picturesque and beautiful appearance.[18]

West famously used the term "stations" in his 1778 *Guide* to designate the exact locations from which the most picturesque views can be seen. Long's descriptive language, culminating with the catchall phrase "picturesque and beautiful," is general enough to apply to either Jamaican or English vistas. "Clumps" alludes to the trademark belts and clumps of the garden designer Lancelot "Capability" Brown, who remade many of England's great estates beginning in the 1750s. The colony as garden – Edenic in its beauty and capacity for exploitation – is, of course, a durable trope.[19]

The details of an earlier description, illustrated by one of Long's 16 plates, work through the tensions between Jamaica's New World, tropical specificity and the imperial civilization in whose image it was being remade. He honors one of the prime "sights" of the island, a 300-foot waterfall on the White River (Figure 1.3), with a lengthy description. The scene is "beyond the power of painting to express" but Long bravely tries, as follows:

> To complete the picture, the bason is ornamented with two elegant trees of the palm kind, which spring like strait columns out of the water, placed by the hand of nature at such even distance from the banks on each side, that art could not have done the work with more attention to propriety and exactness. The whole, indeed, has been executed by nature in a taste that surpasses either description or imitation. The late Sir Charles P–e, within whose territory it lay, would not suffer the least alterations to be made to it. . . . He preferred its natural beauties; and, in order to enjoy them, formed a club of gentlemen, and built a range of apartments on a pretty lawn just

Figure 1.3 Isaac Taylor, "A View of the White River Cascade," from Edward Long, *History of Jamaica* (1774). Courtesy of the National Library of Jamaica.

fronting the cascade. Here they had an annual meeting, which continued some weeks; during which, they took the diversion of shooting the ring-tail pidgeons, which in this part of the country are very numerous, and in great perfection at the proper season. If the lesser cascade [on the Rio Alto] is delicate and curious, this is grand and sublime. The former is contemplated with delight, and this with a pleasing and reverential wonder. The fall is said to exceed in grandeur that of Tivoli, or any other in Europe, though much inferior to that of Niagara.[20]

Again, Jamaican nature is elevated to the status of a work of art. The palm trees, a symbolic icon that has come to represent the entire Caribbean region – indeed, to signal any generic tropical zone – are likened to classical columns, the quintessence of European civilization. Delivering a lesson on the aesthetic categories of the beautiful and the sublime, Long flatters nature's taste and that of his readers. Cosmopolitan comparisons to Tivoli and Niagara draw the reader into a global system of aesthetic value that shadows and implicitly legitimizes the reach of British imperial influence. Yet local differences – although not emphasized – are quietly apparent in the palms, the ringtail pigeons, and (in the illustration) the enslaved attendant carrying the tourists' parasol. Long quietly asserts colonial difference in preparation for the key difference that the *History of Jamaica* sets out to defend: the institution of slavery.[21] A model of colonial identity emerges that asserts colonial dignity through metropolitan cultural paradigms, while simultaneously keeping intact the domain of cultural and political difference or autonomy that Long's approach to colonial governance throughout the *History* is determined to preserve.

Most remarkable in this description is its subordination of the sublimity of the falls to the aristocratic proprietorship of Sir Charles Price. Price tactfully declines to tamper with nature; instead, he forms a gentlemen's club and builds a shooting lodge to extract maximum enjoyment from his waterfall. Replicating the leisure activities of the English countryside in a colonial setting, Sir Charles displays the imperial drive to remake colonized territory in a metropolitan mold. Price's retreat in Saint Mary's Parish, The Decoy, "was the closest property in Jamaica to an English country estate," with "a deer park, a man-made lake stocked with wild duck and teal, and 'a very elegant garden.'" The latter phrase is Long's. The historian and booster of Jamaica appreciated The Decoy as "an outpost of burgeoning civilization.... Price had combined European fashion with Jamaican materials to transform a wild site into a place of cultivation – just as Long hoped would occur with Jamaican culture as a whole."[22] The civilizing process that the *History of Jamaica* describes and prescribes for the colony is English in character and aristocratic or hierarchical in structure.

Long's rhetoric in representing the planter class exploits the moral overtones lent to the aesthetic value of the "improved" country estate by a tradition of representation familiar in literature from Pope's "Epistle to Burlington" to Austen's *Pride and Prejudice*. The good taste displayed by the house and grounds both implied and advertised the good character of their owner.[23] We see this when Long calls the planter "Mr. F–n" of Clarendon Parish "worthy of being esteemed among the first ornaments of this country," conflating the aesthetic connotations of "ornament" with the moral aura of "esteem." Mr. F–n's great house, Long writes:

> commands [an] extensive prospect.... The beauties of nature that are displayed here are innumerable. In one place is seen a long, wavy surface, adorned with the lively verdure of canes, interspersed with wind-mills and other buildings. In another are beheld several charming lawns of

pasture-land, dotted with cattle and sheep, and watered with rivulets. In a third are Negroe villages, where (far from poverty and discontent) peace and plenty hold their reign; a crested ridge of fertile hills, which separates this parish from those contiguous on the North and East, distantly terminates the lanschape.[24]

Long composes the "lanschape" pictorially, bounded by a hilly horizon line, and positions the reader with the owner, in "command" of the building's aesthetic and practical value. As in the waterfall description, however, local details like the windmills (which were used to power cane-crushing machinery) and slave quarters vary the aesthetic pattern derived from pictures of the European countryside. Long's parenthetical aside shows him to be conscious of a growing suspicion of slavery among the metropolitan readers whom his propaganda targeted.[25] This comment highlights and at the same time dismisses the incipient contradiction of attributing contentment to enslaved workers. He betrays no awareness of the hardships of labor in Jamaica's cane fields and boiling houses.

Aesthetic theorists such as Gilpin actively discouraged traces of labor or cultivation in a landscape as incompatible with the aesthetics of the picturesque.[26] In view of this, Long's insistence on including these reminders of slavery is politically significant. Elsewhere in the book, he describes how sugar-cane fields "enliven every where the view with tints unspeakably beautiful." Tracing the "tint" at each stage of the young plants' growth, he continues, "Last of all appear the busy slaves, like reapers, armed with bills instead of sickles to cut the ripened stems; and teams of oxen in the field, to bring the treasure home; whilst the laborers chear their toil with rude songs, or whistle in wild chorus their unpolished melody." Long assimilates these sanitized figures to the georgic tradition best represented by Thomson's *Seasons*, in which the "meadows glow, and rise unquelled / Against the mower's scythe."[27] Long negotiates a delicate balance between metropolitan aesthetic paradigms and local, colonial needs; the conflation of picturesque with georgic representation in his Jamaican landscapes serves his rhetorical aims in a manner not achieved by either mode alone. The enslaved laborers need to be present, their presence not elided; he needs his readers to accept this, first aesthetically and then politically.

The man who delights in landscape

William Beckford, whose *A Descriptive Account of the Island of Jamaica* was published in 1790, likewise assumes the stance of an apologist for slavery and Creole culture. As a scion of Jamaica's richest planter clan, Beckford certainly had a stake in defending Jamaica to metropolitan readers.[28] However, he produced his *Descriptive Account* in circumstances very different from Long's. Both wrote in England, far from the island they described. Whereas Long was rich and independent, flush with sugar profits, Beckford was bankrupt – locked up, as his preface confides, in a "house of humiliation and misery." "There are but few men," he comments immodestly, "who could, like Cervantes, have added dignity to misfortune, and have taught the pen to charm in the confines of a gaol."[29] Owner of three plantations – Roaring River, Williamsfield, and Fort William – Beckford had taken out a mortgage in 1777 from his merchant cousin, Richard Beckford, in the amount of £20,967, secured by his land. In 1781, he owed his cousin more than £25,000. The series of hurricanes that hit Jamaica in 1780, 1781, 1784, 1785, and 1786 – an unprecedented five in seven years – seems to have finished off Beckford financially. When he went back to England in 1786 to see about his debts, bailiffs met his post-chaise and took him to London's Fleet Prison, where he spent much of the rest of his life.[30]

He devoted a good deal of his time in prison to writing in defense of the colony that he had left and the institution that sustained it. The 1787 founding of the Society for Effecting the Abolition of the Slave Trade (SEAST) helped to move abolition to the center of British politics. Propaganda and public opinion were essential elements of its attack. In 1788, Beckford published *Remarks upon the Situation of Negroes in Jamaica, Impartially Made from a Local Experience of Nearly Thirteen Years in That Island*. Trading on local knowledge for credibility, as his title suggests, the bankrupt ex-planter pitches his appeal to metropolitan readers of both sensibility and common sense. He advocates for needed humanitarian reforms in the slave trade and the practice of slavery, and assures his readers that, apart from isolated instances, Jamaica's enslaved workers are actually well cared for and contented – certainly better off than the metropolitan laboring class, soldiers, and sailors.

Histories of the anti-slavery movement, as George Boulukos points out, underemphasize amelioration – that is, the idea that the institution of slavery could and should be reformed rather than or prior to being abolished. At the point when SEAST made the strategic decision to pursue slave-trade abolition – at least at first – rather than outright emancipation, amelioration became "the goal, rhetorically at least, of both planters and anti-slavery activists." Of course, "visions of ameliorated slavery . . . would remain troubling if Africans were sincerely thought of as the equals of Europeans."[31] Like the planter-historian Bryan Edwards, discussed in

Chapter 3, Beckford makes amelioration the centerpiece of his defense of slavery.

If the enslaved are at the center of Beckford's first book, however, they are more marginal to his second. Beckford's *Descriptive Account* shares with Lewis's *Journal of a West India Proprietor* a seemingly willful quirkiness, an eccentricity of form as well as content. In both versions of the planter picturesque, compulsive aestheticizing and copious allusions to metropolitan high culture seem to be aimed at establishing a defensive distance from the troubling realities of the Jamaican slave society and economy. These realities presented conditions that might be expected to provoke a defensive response: the colony's frontier reputation compared with polished metropolitan culture; the precariousness of sugar agriculture, vulnerable to the vagaries of weather and markets; and, perhaps most threatening, the island whites' minority status, vastly outnumbered by their captive laborers.

Aesthetic distance – that is, separating the aesthetic subject from the object through formal procedures of framing, containing, and composing – is a key feature of the picturesque. In the colonial context, however, the formal distance between the aesthetic subject and object could serve as a trope for the geographical and cultural distance between colony and metropole. Negotiating that distance, as we saw with Long, additionally burdens the representation of colonial landscape. Moreover, where the picturesque assumes a static subject-object relationship, the planter picturesque is inescapably entangled with the dynamic relationship between the slave owner and his human property – precisely what it most desires to keep at a distance. In these versions of the planter picturesque, confronting "that which is radically other" brings out "the indeterminacy and self-contradiction within the discourse of the picturesque."[32]

However, the metropolitan picturesque already harbors an intercultural element. In the opening of Uvedale Price's *Dialogue on the Distinct Characters of the Picturesque and the Beautiful* (1801), three gentlemen on their way to a picture gallery come across a gypsy encampment, "a ruinous hovel on the outskirts of a heathy common."

> In a dark corner of it, some gypsies were sitting over a half-extinguished fire, which every now and then, as one of them stooped down to blow it, feebly blazed up for an instant, and shewed their sooty faces, and black tangled locks. An old male gypsey stood at the entrance, with a countenance that well expressed his three-fold occupation, of beggar, thief, and fortune-teller; and by him a few worn-out asses: one loaded with rusty panniers, the other with old tattered cloaths and furniture. The hovel was propt and overhung

by a blighted oak; its bare roots staring through the crumbling bank on which it stood. A gleam of light from under a dark cloud glanced on the most prominent parts: the rest was buried in deep shadow.

The "sooty faces" of these shabby, shady outcasts remind us that the encounter between Price's enthusiasts and the gypsies is a cultural confrontation on English soil.[33] It provokes disgust or repugnance, which is countered by a defensive aestheticizing response. The naïve Mr. Seymour is lectured by his sophisticated friends, who tell him how a scene that he finds merely ugly or disgusting can be transformed by the "abstracted and impartial attention" of a trained viewer into the pure visuality of the picturesque. For this to happen, however, one must disregard the "animal disgust and . . . nauseating repugnance of appetite" that would otherwise "drown and overwhelm every milder pleasure of vision."[34]

Price's tasteful gentlemen exhibit the willed obliviousness to the cultural connectedness between observer and observed to which Sara Suleri has called attention in the context of nineteenth-century India. Her comment on the "feminine picturesque" applies to the planter picturesque as well: "imperial anxiety . . . forces the act of cultural looking into narratives of profound unlooking." For Suleri, the "picturesque becomes synonymous with a desire to transfix a dynamic cultural confrontation into a still life, converting a pictorial imperative into a gesture of self-protection that allows the colonial gaze a license to convert its ability not to see into studiously visual representations."[35] The "pictorial imperative" emerges in Beckford's *Descriptive Account* and Lewis's *Journal of a West India Proprietor* as both a self-protective gesture and a transformative approach to potentially disturbing material. As Beckford remarks, "It is a known truth, that beauty may be copied from deformity."[36] Each writer cultivates the persona of an aesthete, his consciousness so steeped in metropolitan elite culture that picturesque tableaux and allusions to Virgil, Cervantes, or the London theater shape his representation of the sugar colony, helping him and his readers to overlook the violence of slavery.

Writing in the metropole, from memory, immobilized by the transatlantic credit economy in the darkness of the gaol, and separated from the island by a distance both physical and psychological, the bankrupt ex-planter takes readers on his own virtual tour of Jamaica's light-flooded vistas. "[W]herever you turn," he writes, "a new prospect delights the eye, and occasions surprise by the magnificence of the objects, by the depths of shadow or bursts of light, by the observation of gloomy dells or woody plains, of mountain-torrents, and of winding-streams; of groups of negroes, herds of cattle, passing wains; and by the recurrence of every rural object."[37] Here is the technical vocabulary of the picturesque on display, better codified and popularized by 1790 than when Long wrote in the 1770s: views and prospects, shadows and light, objects and groups. Beckford's planter picturesque, like Long's, puts aesthetics to work defending the slave colony and its stakeholders, enhancing its value through European comparisons and high-culture allusions.[38] However, several formal features of Beckford's book contribute to an effect rather different from that of Long's virtual tour. Written at the height of the propaganda war over slave-trade abolition, Beckford's eccentric contribution strives to paint Jamaica as a picturesque utopia, but it ultimately conveys a deeply dystopian view of colonial slavery.

The *Descriptive Account* is long: its two volumes total more than 800 pages. Although it is clearly intended as a defense of slavery and Creole culture, Beckford does not embark on his central argument – a desperate plea to forestall slave-trade abolition – until near the end of Volume II. The reader must wade through almost 700 pages of picturesque description, agricultural advice, and frequent, extended digressions before being treated to the author's opinion on "the uncertain situation in which the West-India islands at present stand."[39] We could read this postponed polemic as a deliberate rhetorical tactic, with everything else in the book intended to prepare readers – "soften them up," so to speak – for the main point. Conversely, we could read it as symptomatic: an ambivalent defender of slavery puts off his task until the last possible page. Beckford certainly displays considerable sympathy, whether strategic or truly felt, for the humanitarian concerns of the abolitionist movement. His defense of slavery is couched in a rhetoric of reform, or amelioration: he positions himself as a knowledgeable insider, sensitive and morally grounded, and qualified to offer advice on exactly which reforms could rehabilitate the slave trade.

Rather than psychologize, however, let us instead consider the *Descriptive Account*'s lop-sidedness as a formal feature. Beckford's book displays irregularity as well as variety, or we might even say intricacy – hallmarks of the picturesque as theorized by Gilpin and his successors, Uvedale Price and Richard Payne Knight. However, its drawn-out postponement of its rhetorical payoff also imitates the temporal structure of the transatlantic credit economy that finally caught up with Beckford and landed him in the Fleet Prison.[40] The irregularity, variety, and intricacy of the planter picturesque – in the form of the proliferating prospects and digressions that comprise the book's first 600-plus pages – function to stave off a final reckoning that, the author seems to suspect, may turn out just as badly as his personal balance sheet.

Beckford's version of the planter picturesque differs sharply from Long's in mood and tone. Whereas Long is restrained and impersonal, the gentlemanly mouthpiece of the planter class, Beckford is wildly subjective to the point of self-indulgence. The *Descriptive Account* emphasizes throughout the subjective experience or states of mind of its persona, whom we might call a planter-aesthete. This focal consciousness is well educated and well traveled, as was Beckford himself,[41] with a sensibility especially suited to Jamaican scenery: "The man . . . who can take delight in these objects of Nature . . . with a painter's eye, and is willing to treasure them up in his mind for future imitation, will hardly find a spot . . . upon the habitable globe, in which these objects may be studied with greater effect, than in the clouds, the fogs, and moon-lights of that Island." This sensibility is specifically picturesque. Such a man looks at nature and thinks about art (e.g., "representations" and "future imitation"), stocking his mind with collectible "beauties" capable of adorning a canvas. The *Descriptive Account* frequently invokes this projected consciousness, calling him "the contemplative man," the "reflective man," the "man who delights in landscape," and "a real enthusiast."[42]

The impact of Beckford's decision to make the planter-aesthete's subjective experience the central focus of the *Descriptive Account* is far-reaching. "Landscape might be seen," W. J. T. Mitchell writes, "as something like the 'dreamwork' of imperialism . . . folding back on itself to disclose both utopian fantasies of the perfected imperial prospect and fractured images of unresolved ambivalence and unsuppressed resistance."[43] Beckford's over-the-top picturesque effusions transform the productive terrain of colonial agribusiness into a dreamscape that is utopian in the word's root sense of being literally "no place."[44] This version of the colonial picturesque takes place, we might say, in the hypersubjective "no-place" of the jailed planter's mind. The style of his aesthetic reveries – extravagant and sometimes "hallucinatory"[45] – contrasts markedly with the sober tone of his agricultural advice. For example, "Where a piece [field] of sugar-canes is only meant to stand a first ratoon, or two cuttings, I would strongly recommend it to be rather highly worked than richly manured, and to be planted as thick as possible."[46] This stylistic disjunction has the cumulative effect of dis-placing Beckford's utopian fantasy of picturesque Jamaica. It seems to "float away" from the ratoons and manure of the material colony.

Beckford is somewhat self-conscious about his book's idiosyncratic form. He apologizes in advance for his digressions: "the fault is mine, if I have, for the elevated, mistaken the bombast." The book's self-indulgent quality, its seemingly compulsive excess, verges at times on self-parody – as when, early in the first volume, it ascends to the clouds: "what delightful appearances, or glowing with luster, or softened by shade, may not be imagined in the stationary, or lamented in the vanescent clouds of that warm and vapory region?" In one of these digressions, Beckford even claims to "fancy an exact resemblance, as given us in the prints, of the Island of Otaheite [Tahiti]."[47] Conjuring Tahiti from his fertile imagination – fueled by the most popular travel book of the century, the official account of Cook's first Pacific voyage – Beckford connects his account of Jamaica to a venture that combined imperial interest with tropical allure.

Most of Beckford's allusions and digressions, however, draw his reader's thoughts from the colonial periphery back across the Atlantic to the center of the empire. We are treated to his opinions on the madness and recovery of the "Patriot King," the works of Dr. Burney and his daughter, the French Revolution, and the "inimitable writings" of Samuel Johnson. The Grand Tour of Europe appears in repeated comparisons between Jamaican scenery and Continental beauty spots.[48] These references, of course, are consistent with Beckford's announced intention to consider the island scenery "in a Picturesque Point of View," given the roots of the picturesque in the history of the Grand Tour as the finishing touch on a young British aristocrat's education. Beckford's cosmopolitan comparisons, like Long's, assimilate Jamaica within an imperial system of aesthetic value.

However, the *Descriptive Account*'s mobile authorial consciousness differs subtly but importantly from Long's use of the virtual travelogue form. The *History of Jamaica* dwells on the aristocratic ownership of Jamaican land by elite planter families such as those of Sir Richard Price and Thomas Fearon. The view from Fearon's estate and Price's re-creation of English diversions draw Long's praise, in line with the branch of picturesque theory that Kim Ian Michasiw calls the "landowner picturesque." This is the doctrine of an improver such as Price or Knight, the "virtuosic landlord in whom . . . the picturesque and the drive to mastery intersect." Beckford's recurring fascination with clouds and other "vanescent" effects of light and shadow suggests a rather different relationship to colonial land. Other aspects of the *Descriptive Account* also connect it to a line of picturesque theory with a different "functional relationship to the landscape" in Michasiw's analysis: that is, Gilpin's picturesque tourist. Beckford's planter-aesthete recalls this "sensationalist nomad" in his acute consciousness of the "contingency and fragility of the picturesque order" – and the sugar planter's personal vulnerability.[49]

The Jamaica of Beckford's *Descriptive Account* is a beautiful and dangerous place. The bankrupt former planter is understandably preoccupied with the hazards of sugar cultivation. Early in Volume I, he devotes 13 pages to listing the enemies of sugar cane: drought, cattle, rats, ants, caterpillars, winds, and fire. A cane-field fire, he writes, exemplifies the "picturesque scenery of destruction"; its flames, the color of liquid lava, would delight the volcano-lover Sir William Hamilton.[50] However, another natural disaster transcends fire in its sublime horror: the hurricane of 1780, a devastating storm that flattened the island, causing widespread misery and sealing the financial ruin of Beckford and other planters. His description of the storm and its aftermath takes up another 50 pages. Its sheer destructiveness figures not just the French Revolution, in its early stages in 1790, but also the Saint Domingue insurrection, then on the horizon. Most important, the hurricane tropes the apocalyptic end of Creole culture that Beckford predicts if the British nation makes the mistake of freeing its slaves.

Trying to describe the "face of the country" on the morning after the storm, the *Descriptive Account* tellingly transposes the geography of the Atlantic Triangle. "The vallies and the plains, the mountains and the forests, that were only the day before most beautifully clothed with *every* verdure, were now despoiled of *every* charm... the whole prospect had the appearance of a desert, over which the burning winds of Africa had lately past."[51] Aesthetics and geography converge in this multivalent trope. The posthurricane prospect is emphatically anti-picturesque: stripped of vegetation and civilization, reduced to a desert the blankness of which figures the imaginary point of origin of enslaved Jamaicans – their supposed human emptiness before being civilized by their European captors. If Jamaica before the hurricane is like a picturesque Europe, Jamaica after the hurricane is like Africa before the Europeans' saving arrival. Nature, even natural disaster, colludes in Beckford's pro-slavery rhetoric. His politics of place imagines the routes of the modern network of transportation and trade that connected the British metropole with its sources of labor and raw materials suddenly severed – a prospect far more horrifying than a hurricane.

Much later in the book, and finally getting to his political point, Beckford explicitly compares slave-trade abolition to the various disasters that hit Jamaica in the 1770s and 1780s: drought, hurricanes, famine, and war. The West Indies are now threatened, he writes, with "a calamity superior to any above mentioned... which, if carried to further excess [through slave emancipation], will end in treachery, famine, or the sword." Emancipation would lead the formerly enslaved to "set fire to their houses, destroy their provisions, live in open war, and defiance of each other, and after having exterminated those of another color...extirpate those of their own."[52] Any survivors would starve. This bleak vision recalls Beckford's use of the African desert as a trope for Jamaica's posthurricane landscape. If the *Descriptive Account*, as Keith Sandiford argues, "implicates the picturesque in a very complexly constructed legitimation of Creole culture," then the politics of place that resonates through this series of apocalyptic tropes reinforces that case by negation.[53] Without Creole culture – that is, without slavery – Jamaica would revert to worse than African savagery, laying waste to productive land and demolishing the planter picturesque.

The book's final paragraphs return to the jailed planter-narrator's plight: "after having left a country in which slavery is established by law, I found myself a prisoner, unheard, and unarraigned, in one in which arrest is sanctioned, though contrary to the constitution, and in which I have found that a man, although born to freedom, may become a slave." Slavery, in Beckford's self-absorbed worldview, has followed him from colony to metropolis. Like the runaways in Jamaica's caves, he is stuck in a hole – immobilized, in pathetic contrast to the book's mobile persona.[54] This final reversal, turning the free man into a slave, recalls Long's dark threat that depriving colonists of their freedom to hold slaves will "enslave the principal state" – that is, damage British liberty at the center of the empire.[55] *A Descriptive Account of the Island of Jamaica* finishes not in Jamaica but rather in London, concerned not with scenery but instead with finance and law. The planter-aesthete's aesthetic distance has collapsed at the point when his geographical distance from his beloved island seems insurmountable.

The illusion of its effect

The pictorial imperative as self-protective gesture resurfaces a quarter-century later in *Journal of a West India Proprietor* (1834) by the Gothic novelist, poet, and dramatist Matthew Gregory Lewis. Unlike Long and Beckford, Lewis was no Jamaica insider. He set foot on the island for the first time on New Year's Day, 1816, having unexpectedly inherited two plantations and more than 500 slaves. Also unlike the earlier writers, Lewis was no pro-slavery propagandist. He was in favor of slave-trade abolition, enacted in 1807, but he was no emancipationist, as his *Journal* clearly states. The reforms he initiated (or tried to initiate) during two visits to his plantations earned him the wrath of neighboring planters.[56] Lewis thus occupies, with Beckford, the broad ameliorationist middle ground that was home to the majority of Britons. As a slave owner, the newly minted "West India proprietor" naturally had a vested interest in the survival of slavery as an institution, although he seems to have disagreed with his neighbors about the best means to that end.

The year that Lewis sailed for Jamaica, William Wilberforce put forward his Registry Bill, a Parliamentary bid for centralized recordkeeping, which was opposed with predictable fierceness by the West India lobby and colonial Assemblies. Across the Atlantic in Barbados, in early 1816, the anger of the enslaved workforce at the Assembly's resistance to this legislation – which some equated with a move toward emancipation – helped fuel an island-wide rebellion on Easter Sunday.[57] Yet, national politics seldom enters Lewis's *Journal*. Written between 1815 and the author's death at sea in 1818, it is largely a travel account, rendering an idiosyncratic outsider's perspective on colonial culture. The ways in which it aestheticizes Jamaica reveal – if unwittingly – the extent of the disjunction between colony and metropole. Lewis's record of his enslaved workers' voices and his interactions with them interrupts the account's self-indulgent aestheticizing.

This version of the planter picturesque is best approached through its relationship to two other key features of this idiosyncratic colonial text: its density of allusion to metropolitan high culture and its exaggerated theatricality. Lewis's use of allusions and the picturesque attempts to establish a defensive distance from the troubling realities of plantation life – in particular, from his interactions with his captive workers. When Lewis tries to impose the metropolitan perspective on the local colonial situation, the disparity between the normally static "frame" and the dynamic *agon*, or contest, between owner and captive gives the *Journal* an air of self-conscious artifice. This staginess, as we might call it, bespeaks Lewis's profound unease with his position as "Massa." Furthermore, it threatens to undo the picturesque frame and confound the formal distance, thereby opening the text to the voices of the enslaved workers whose own theatricality it imitates.

The language of performance that Lewis repeatedly uses to describe his interactions with his captive laborers further exaggerates the staginess of the *Journal of a West India Proprietor*. Scholars have analyzed a performative or theatrical dimension in the ongoing, day-to-day opposition of the enslaved to their captivity. Among the functions of Lewis's picturesque, critics suggest, might be defending against this subversive theatricality.[58] Such a defense is another way in which adaptation to local colonial circumstances significantly changes the metropolitan picturesque. The aura of naturalness associated with the picturesque – part of "the dominant cultural strategy that identified its own values and practices with nature"[59] – seems unable to coexist with the aggressive and defensive masking practices of Jamaican slave society. Lewis's record of one type of institutionalized performance – the Afro-Caribbean Christmas and New Year's festivities known as Jonkonnu – affords an evocative if enigmatic glimpse of enslaved workers' counterperspective on their masters' empire.

The verbal sketch or tableau is a prominent feature of Lewis's *Journal*, as in Beckford and Long. The following panoramic description of his Cornwall plantation is dated about a week after his arrival:

> On three sides of the landscape the prospect is bounded by lofty purple mountains; and the variety of occupations going on all around me, and at the same time, give an inconceivable air of life and animation to the whole scene, especially as all those occupations look clean, – even those which in England look dirty. All the tradespeople are dressed either in white jackets and trousers, or with stripes of red and sky-blue. One band of negroes are carrying the ripe canes on their heads to the mill; another set are conveying away the *trash*, after the juice has been extracted; flocks of turkeys are sheltering from the heat under the trees; the river is filled with ducks and geese; the coopers and carpenters are employed about the puncheons; carts drawn some by six, others by eight, oxen, are bringing loads of Indian corn from the fields; the black children are employed in gathering it into the granary, and in quarrelling with pigs as black as themselves, who are equally busy in stealing the corn whenever the children are looking another way: in short, a plantation possesses all the movement and interest of a farm, without its dung, and its stench, and its dirty accompaniments.[60]

Lewis's plantation is overtly, preemptively sanitized, retaining far less in the way of "dirty accompaniments" than Price's gypsy hovel. Why, however, we might ask – especially with all those oxen – would a plantation have less dung and stench than a farm? If Lewis is referring to English farms, we might take this as a gentleman planter's coded defense of colonial agriculture as a less dirty and hence more gentlemanly activity than metropolitan farming. Although purged by fiat of dirt and stench, however, Lewis's panorama is not purged of work, as the picturesque doctrine of Gilpin, for example, would have demanded. The figures that ornament the scene are neither idle nor static: they are emphatically busy, with a disciplined and productive activity that he will not often see his enslaved workers exhibit as the *Journal* continues.[61]

Lewis seems to enjoy a panoptic view from the Great House veranda. "In reality, though," comments Richard Burton on this passage, his "vision and power are as circumscribed as those of the slave children minding the pigs – indeed, perhaps more so because, on the evidence of the *Journal*, his

charges are engaged in all kinds of oppositional activities even as he looks
at them and they smile back at him."[62] Recent work on the *Journal of a
West India Proprietor* has begun to connect Lewis's colonial picturesque
with his anxiety about enslaved resistance.[63] To explore this connection
further, I begin in a section of the *Journal* that concentrates both scenery
and allusions. A recurrent allusion connects the picturesque to one especially vexatious aspect of labor management in the aftermath of slave-trade
abolition: the issue of reproduction. The fictional Yarico – who, in different
versions, is and is not a slave and a mother – opens a window into the
Journal's negotiation between aesthetic discourse and everyday plantation
life.

Lewis's cultivation of the picturesque surface is at its height during
his brief "excursion" from his Cornwall plantation to Kingston and back
about a month after his arrival. Scenic description, of course, was a long-
established convention of travel writing, suited to the traveler's superficial
acquaintance with the places he visits. Lewis's descriptive passages in this
section weave together local detail with metropolitan comparisons, as had
Long's writing several decades earlier:

> Though we had left the river, the road was still a narrow shelf of rock running
> along the edge of ravines of great depth, and filled with broken masses of
> stone and trees of wonderful magnitude; only that at intervals we emerged
> for a time into places resembling ornamental parks in England, the lawns
> being of the liveliest verdure, the ground rising and falling with an endless
> variety of surface, and enriched with a profusion of trees majestic in stature
> and picturesque in their shapes, many of them entirely covered with the
> beautiful flowers of 'hogsmeat', and other creeping plants.[64]

Alternating sublime ravines and picturesque meadows, Lewis displays his
command of the specialized vocabulary of landscape aesthetics with terms
such as "verdure" and "variety." This elevated diction accords with his
metropolitan reference point, those "ornamental parks." However, the
humble local designation, "hogsmeat," incongruously intrudes to highlight
the disparity between the metropolitan language of landscape description
and the colonial vernacular – here associated with labor, specifically feeding
the pigs.[65] Unlike Long's colonial georgic, which strives to elevate the traces
of plantation labor to the dignity of aesthetic discourse, Lewis's description
calls attention to the ill fit between metropolitan aesthetics and colonial
priorities.

The allusions in this section and elsewhere in the *Journal* assume a highly
literate, sophisticated reader:

Yesterday the only very striking point of view (although the whole of the road was picturesque) was "the Cove," situated between Bluefields and Lakovia, and which resembled the most beautiful of the views of coves to be found in "Cook's Voyages"; but our journey today was a succession of beautiful scenes, from beginning to end. . . . In particular, I was struck with the picturesque appearance of some wild fig-trees of singular size and beauty. . . . [A]s our cavalcade wound along through the mountains, the Spanish look of our sumpter-mules, and of our kittereens (which are precisely the vehicle in which Gil Blas is always represented when travelling with Scipio towards Lirias) gave us quite the appearance of a caravan; nor should I have been greatly surprised to see a trap-door open in the middle of the road, and Captain Rolando's whiskers make their appearance.[66]

Using the popular illustrated account of Cook's Pacific voyages as a reference point to describe a Jamaican view does not merely demand that readers be well read in the literature of exploration. The perspective that such an allusion assumes is not only metropolitan but also profoundly imperial, treating exotic landscapes as virtually interchangeable – seen from a London library. The *Gil Blas* allusion assimilates Lesage's picaresque Spain within this global collage while superimposing the Middle Eastern associations of the caravan. In the novel, the trap door leads to an underground robbers' cave, but the allusion also suggests a piece of machinery that might have been seen on the London stage – perhaps in one of Lewis's own successful melodramas.[67] These layers of allusion lend to his picturesque Jamaican landscape a patina of self-conscious artificiality.

This artificiality is especially clear in Lewis's description of Bluefields tavern. "It had a very pretty garden on the sea-shore, which contained a picturesque cottage, exactly resembling an ornamental Hermitage; and leaning against one of the pillars of its porch we found a young girl, who exactly answered George Colman's description of Yarico, 'quite brown, but extremely genteel, like a Wedgewood teapot.'"[68] Lewis's Jamaica is as self-consciously artificial as an "ornamental Hermitage," a fabricated prop in a lavishly designed estate garden of the previous century. He has already previously alluded in the *Journal* to the well-known story of Yarico. Both times, he connects her with the picturesque. Close attention to this repeated allusion may help us to trace the elaborate mechanism of defensive diversion through which Lewis's colonial picturesque distracts attention from problematic aspects of plantation life – but at the same time leads back to those stubborn realities.

The story of Inkle and Yarico, first published in Richard Ligon's 1657 *True and Exact History of the Island of Barbados*, probably reached its greatest readership in Richard Steele's 1711 *Spectator* version, republished throughout the eighteenth century and beyond. Shipwrecked in the Caribbean, the young English merchant Thomas Inkle is saved from death by Yarico, a beautiful Indian maiden. Inkle promises to marry her and take her to England. When rescued by a passing ship, however, the "prudent and frugal young man" sells Yarico into slavery – "notwithstanding that the poor girl ... told him that she was with child by him: But he only made use of that information, to rise in his demands upon the purchaser."[69] George Colman's 1787 comic opera, *Inkle and Yarico*, also became enormously popular. It was the most widely performed new play on the London stage during the last quarter of the eighteenth century and a favorite part of the English theatrical repertory well into the nineteenth century. Colman makes two major changes: he dispenses with Yarico's pregnancy and he substitutes for her sale a sentimental happy ending in which Inkle reforms and marries her. His prologue makes clear that he expects his audience to know the earlier version:

> Yet, you'll behold tonight – nor think it strange!
> Before the piece concludes some little change.
> A change not made to damp the glow of youth,
> But "To set passion on the side of truth."
> Here first, not following the stale narration,
> In Inkle's heart was wrought a reformation ...[70]

Lewis's somewhat garbled quotation about the teapot captures the blithely inane tone in which Colman's musical comedy approaches the issues of slavery and race. First staged in the year that SEAST was founded, Colman's revision sentimentalizes Steele's fable of capitalist callousness.

Also in 1787, the ceramics manufacturer Josiah Wedgwood, a committed abolitionist, brought out his black basalt-ware cameo of a kneeling black man in chains with the motto, "Am I not a Man and a Brother?" Frank Felsenstein construes Colman as alluding to this very popular item, which was inlaid in snuffbox lids and displayed on ladies' hairpins. Certainly, the moral momentum of Colman's goodhearted comedy runs against slavery, although in terms unsuited to modern sensibilities. Thus, Lewis's casual allusion to it could be taken as advertising the liberal (although not emancipationist) sympathies that gave rise to his reformist agenda for his plantations. Then why a teapot? At the time Colman wrote, Wedgwood also was producing a line of inexpensive unglazed earthenware, such as teapots, in a dark red to chocolate color, known as "rosso antico."[71] Comparing Yarico to a mass-produced teapot augments the abolitionist associations with something else: something associated with the mass reproduction and circulation of commodities, with domesticity and femininity, but also with the imperial trade that filled Wedgwood teapots with tea, taken with or without sugar. Although Colman's Inkle finally does not sell Yarico in Barbados, he almost does; the plot turns on his vacillation between his ingrained merchant's "prudence" and his newfound love. The simile manages to bring up both the status of the enslaved person as human commodity – bought, sold, and used like a teapot – and the connection between enslaved labor and domestic consumption, which would be made a political issue in 1791 by the abolitionist boycott of West Indian sugar.[72] Three decades later, with Colman's play still popular and slavery still in place, the allusion retained its currency.

The woman that Lewis casts as Yarico at Bluefields is not enslaved but rather is a Spanish refugee named Antonietta: "the handsomest creole that I have ever seen." The case differs, however, with the *Journal*'s previous allusion to Yarico. Three days after Lewis's arrival at Cornwall, on his way back from Montego Bay, he writes, "[A]bout a mile from my own estate, a figure presented itself before me, I really think the most picturesque that I ever beheld." This is an enslaved mulatta woman by the name of Mary Wiggins:

> [H]er air and countenance would have suited Yarico; but she reminded me most of Grassini in "La Vergine del Sole," only that Mary Wiggins was a thousand times more beautiful, and that, instead of a white robe, she wore a mixed dress of brown, white, and dead yellow, which harmonized excellently well with her complexion; while one of her beautiful arms was thrown across her brow to shade her eyes, and a profusion of rings on her fingers glittered in the sunbeams. Mary Wiggins and an old Cotton-tree are the most picturesque objects that I have seen for these twenty years.[73]

This Yarico is Lewis's own property; she also is a mother. Lewis reports that an overseer at a neighboring estate is to buy her freedom from him, along with "two little children, whom she had borne to him." Lewis has given the overseer permission to exchange Mary for another captive, but he has not yet found one "owing to the difficulty of purchasing single negroes."[74]

The most significant change in West Indian slave culture between Beckford's *Descriptive Account* and Lewis's *Journal* was the abolition of the slave trade in 1807.[75] When Lewis realizes how difficult it will be to furnish Cornwall with a new generation of captive workers, he will have cause to regret his generosity in this exchange of three – one a female of proven fertility – for only one. He institutes an elaborate program of rewards and perquisites for enslaved mothers whose children live past infancy. A mother receives a dollar for every child that survives its first 14 days of life. She also receives a scarlet girdle with a silver medal and then another medal for every additional child. Wearing these medals is supposed to provide the mothers with the first servings and bigger portions at holiday meals, forgiveness for minor faults, and "indulgence" when asking overseers for favors. Lewis even builds a new hospital for births and nursing mothers. Despite these incentives, however, "somehow or other . . . the children do not come." Typically, he blames the mothers: "I really believe that the negresses can produce children at pleasure."[76] He also repeatedly blames infant deaths on maternal neglect.

Clearly, the reproductive body of the enslaved woman is a site of intensive scrutiny and continual frustration for Lewis in his capacity as "West India Proprietor."[77] In his double description of Mary Wiggins as picturesque object and slave mother, his roles as proprietor and aesthete both intersect and diverge. His sketch of her is conventionally picturesque in its emphasis on color and light. The brown of her dress contrasts with its white and yellow, all in harmony with her mulatta skin. Her glittering rings add a variable lighting effect of the type prized by theorists of the picturesque, and her dramatic pose of one arm "thrown across her brow" arranges her as an ornament – the appropriate function for a human figure in a picturesque scene. Lewis comments, "I really think that her form and features were the most *statue-like* that I ever met with." Pygmalion in reverse, the owner verbally turns his human property to stone and then bids her to "tell her *husband* that I admire . . . his taste very much for having chosen her."[78]

This aestheticizing reaches its height with Lewis's rather incongruous comparison of his beautiful captive to a cotton tree. Old trees, of course, are among the most conventionally picturesque of natural objects. One page earlier, he describes a leafless cotton tree on the road from Montego Bay: "its wide-spreading bare white arms contributed nothing to the beauty of the scene, except where the wild fig and various creeping plants had completely mantled the stems and branches; and then its gigantic height, and the fantastic wreathings of its limbs, from which numberless green withes and strings of wild flowers were streaming, rendered it exactly the very tree for which a landscape-painter would have wished." As he petrifies Mary Wiggins into a statue, Lewis suggestively anthropomorphizes the tree, with its "bare white arms." It is not picturesque by itself, he specifies, but rather only in combination with its creeping vines. The suggestion of parasitism might be read in conjunction with his later remarks on "the *brown* females of Jamaica," who "seldom marry men of their own color, but lay themselves out to captivate some white person, who takes them for mistresses." Other writings on colonial Jamaica, such as Janet Schaw's journal, connect the mulatta (with conventional moral outrage) to the practice of abortion by traditional herbal means, which suggests further interconnections between Lewis's picturesque imagery and the vexed issue of slave fertility.[79]

The figure of Yarico, twice staged as a picturesque ornament to a palpably artificial Jamaican scene, both erases and preserves the connection to enslaved motherhood. Because Lewis and his readers would have known Steele's tragic Yarico as well as Colman's comic one, we can read these allusions as a double gesture. They concurrently highlight both the elaborate artifice of the *Journal's* picturesque palimpsest and a key source of the anxiety motivating its construction. In the metropolitan picturesque, human figures, usually of the laboring classes, become aesthetic objects – that is, staffage for a scene composed from an elite perspective in which aesthetic distance reinforces social distance. The process of "improvement" – that is, bringing real places into line with formal principles abstracted from painting – enacts the ownership or appropriation (symbolic for the tourist, material for the estate gardener) that is ideologically central to the picturesque. What difference does it make when the figure in the landscape is an actual piece of property, a human commodity? Lewis's colonial picturesque literalizes picturesque appropriation by decorating the scene with human figures that also are property. At the same time, however, he imbues his Jamaican landscape with a heightened artificiality, underscored by comparing Mary Wiggins to an Italian opera singer and Antonietta's cottage to an "ornamental Hermitage," not even a real one. The entire island, by extension, becomes a stage set for an opera or a landscape garden whose owner erects a faux hermitage to mime romantic solitude. It is as if the *Journal* compensates for straying too close to a tasteless literalism by taking aesthetic distance over the top – calling attention, as I argue, to the ill fit between metropolitan aesthetics and colonial priorities. The control that seems to be promised by picturesque conventions of framing and distancing loses its purchase, so to speak, when the frame tries to encompass the slippery dynamism of master–slave relations. Mary Wiggins as Yarico proves to be an untrustworthy ornament, eluding Lewis's frame, much as his enslaved women workers elude his attempts to turn them into tractable breeders.

The sense of the Caribbean island as too picturesque to be real has a postcolonial echo in Jamaica Kincaid's *A Small Place:* "Antigua is beautiful. Antigua is too beautiful. Sometimes the beauty of it seems unreal.

Sometimes the beauty of it seems as if it were stage sets for a play."
Kincaid's musings conclude a sarcastic diatribe that will not let the tourist-
reader imagine a beach without feeling the floating sewage "graze gently
against your ankle . . . for you see, in Antigua, there is no proper sewage-
disposal system."[80] Lewis's *Journal* gives Kincaid's postcolonial island an
apt nineteenth-century forebear: the labored artifice of its sanitized façade
uneasily concealing its rotten foundation.

Another type of allusion frequently appearing in the *Journal of a West
India Proprietor* may extend our understanding of the intractable disjunction between frame and picture, label and contents, at the unstable center of
Lewis's colonial picturesque. Captives often were given classical names. The
incongruity or disjunction between "civilized" appellations such as Plato or
Hercules and the perceived barbarity of their bearers was a long-standing
joke shared by the master class at their chattels' expense. As Orlando Patterson states, throughout the Americas, classical names served as a "badge
of inferiority and contempt" for the enslaved. Early in Lewis's visit to his
Cornwall plantation, he describes his negotiations with "*Venus* herself – a
poor, little, sickly, timid soul" who has purchased her freedom from him
but comes back to get her paperwork and demand a petticoat as a final
perquisite. "I . . . engaged to act the part of a second Vulcan by releasing
Venus from my chains. . . . I tried to convince her, that for Venus to wear
a petticoat of blue durant, or, indeed, any petticoat at all, would be quite
unclassical: the goddess of beauty stuck to her point, and finally carried off
the petticoat."[81]

Lewis's treatment of classical allusion differs from the allusiveness of
earlier writers on the West Indies, such as Long in his *History of Jamaica*.
Long's allusions earnestly accumulate cultural capital for the gentleman
planter as a man of taste, a fund whose major purpose seems to be to
distinguish the planter from his human property, to whom he denies the
"civilized" features that his own persona painstakingly displays (discussed
in Chapter 3). The gentleman planter's identity is defined against the
comprehensive negation that is the African character. Above all, Long
uses his cultural capital to defend racial distinction and to advocate for
slavery.

Lewis's rendition of his exchange with the sickly but tenacious Venus,
by contrast, can be read as satirical, highlighting the divergence between
the classical ideal represented by the Goddess of Beauty and the plantation setting represented by the "petticoat of blue durant." However, this
rather fragile satire, if such it is, cuts two ways. Lewis seems to be making fun of himself and his culture – ineffectual and irrelevant in the face

of such pressing demands – at least as much as of his slave's ignorance of the Roman gods. Unbeautiful and illiterate, immune to her "Massa's" erudite pleadings, Venus nonetheless gets what she wants. Casting himself as Vulcan – the lame blacksmith god who loses his wife to the handsome Mars – Lewis's self-deprecation registers a discomfort with his own role that recurs throughout the *Journal of a West India Proprietor*. The humor generated by the mock-heroic disjunction between "high" terms and "low" subject functions at the expense not only of the enslaved Venus but also of her owner. Although highly educated, Lewis portrays himself as slow to comprehend what is practically at stake as his illiterate charges successfully bamboozle him. This disjunction between label and contents, goddess and enslaved worker, London drawing room and plantation house, and colony and metropole is at the center of the profound unease that pervades the *Journal* and informs Lewis's version of the planter picturesque. The absentee owner, acutely aware of the irrelevance of his metropolitan experience in the day-to-day power negotiations of plantation life, obliquely conveys his deep discomfort with his role as "Massa" and his power over his captives at the level of style.

Lewis's persistent theatricality adds another dimension to the sense of dislocation or alienation that pervades this successful playwright's journal. He frequently represents his interactions with enslaved people in theatrical terms. With little Venus, he "act[s] the part" of Vulcan but cannot convince her to fulfill her assigned role. Shortly thereafter, several enslaved women refuse to carry away cane trash in what he jokingly terms a "petticoat rebellion." "Another morning, with the mill stopped, no liquor in the boiling-house, and no work done. The driver brought the most obstinate and insolent of the women to be lectured by me; and I bounced and stormed for half an hour with all my might and main."[82] "Massa" stages a strategic performance to counter what amounts to a labor action. A few days later, Lewis prepares to set out for Kingston. The women, "alarmed . . . with the idea that I was really going to put my threats into execution of leaving them for ever," stage a counterperformance. They "begged, and lifted up their folded hands, and cried, and fell on the ground, and kissed my feet – and, in short, acted their part so well, that they almost made me act mine to perfection, and fall to blubbering."[83] These mutual histrionics culminate in Lewis's dismissing an overseer about whom the women have complained – presumably the reason for their initial strike. Master and captives act out their roles in an economy of reciprocal artifice whose theatricality has the effect, in this case at least, of undercutting "Massa's" authority.

At Hordley, Lewis's second and larger plantation, which he visits only briefly, he describes himself berating a black driver for lying. "I blazed up like a barrel of gunpowder . . . volleying out in a breath all the curses that I ever heard in my life. . . . I stamped up and down the piazza, storming and swearing, banging all the doors till the house seemed ready to tumble about our ears, and doing my best to out-herod Herod." Shortly thereafter, having grilled the man again, "I was in such an imperial passion, as would have done honor to 'her majesty the queen Dolallolla.'"[84] The allusions to *Hamlet* and Fielding's burlesque *Tom Thumb* evoke not only theater but also a transparently exaggerated acting style that calls attention to its own artificiality. Significantly, it is at Hordley, the plantation that Lewis designates "a perfect hell," that he takes his theatrical interactions with enslaved people over the top. Told by his trustee before his visit "that Hordley was the best managed estate in the island" and "my negroes . . . the most contented and best disposed," Lewis arrives to find a "system of oppression" in which white overseers and black drivers have been allowed to treat enslaved workers with "atrocious brutality." As absentee owner, there seems to be little he can do. After firing one overseer (a second leaves voluntarily) and demoting the driver who had been the target of his theatrical rant, Lewis shows, in Judith Terry's words, "a clean pair of heels." He has stayed less than two weeks; his description of the visit takes up 5 of the original 408 pages of text.[85]

Does the allusive, overwrought style in which Lewis describes his performances at Hordley correspond to his sense of ineffectuality in the face of slavery's operational reality? One possible explanation for Lewis's overacting would be a racist assumption that such exaggeration was necessary to get his point across in the face of the enslaved workers' innate lack of intelligence: that is all "they" can understand. Although he certainly shows himself capable of generalizations about "the character of negroes," such an interpretation fails to account for the element of self-parody in Lewis's account of his performances at Hordley and at Cornwall. As in his interchange with Venus, the mode of representation highlights the distance – the palpable ill fit – between signifier and signified, frame and picture, and – by extension – metropole and colony. These three key elements of the *Journal of a West India Proprietor* – its insistent allusiveness, its recurrent theatricality, and its use of the picturesque – all contribute to this effect.

Yet, despite or perhaps because of the vast cultural distance that separates Lewis from his captives, the theatricality of their interaction emanates from both sides. "Massa's" near-hysterical performances respond to and even mirror those of his slaves. Maureen Harkin discusses the two-sided economy of the gaze on Lewis's plantation. As much as he tries to institute a one-sided, panoptical visibility, "regulating and policing space and the gaze," enslaved people invert the panopticon when they insist on looking back. When an old woman looks in through the "pervious" shutters of the "Temple of Cloacina" to curtsy and bid her master good day, or when a "negro Apelles" paints Lewis's portrait in a style that he humorously patronizes but that other enslaved people "consider . . . a striking resemblance," they assert "the power of a gaze, and of a representational practice other than that of the European."[86] Orlando Patterson's classic *Sociology of Slavery* analyzes performative slave opposition under the rubric of "Quashee," the profoundly ambiguous phenomenon in which the enslaved transform their masters' stereotypes into a self-fulfilling prophecy, playing on them for their own ends.[87] In Richard Burton's summary, "The whole point of 'psychological' resistance was to show and not show non-acceptance of the system and above all *not to be caught* in the act of maneuver, deception, or defiance. . . . [B]y voluntarily becoming the smiling, fawning dullard that Massa or Busha believed him to be, the slave could adroitly turn the stereotype against them, preserving an inner freedom beneath the mask of compliance."[88] In this analysis, everyday performance renders self-preservation into a mode of subtle subversion as well as an art form.

The critics Richard Burton and Lawrence Needham suggest that Lewis's picturesque functions in part to defend against this subversive theatricality. In pursuit of this suggestion, I turn to the first picturesque description of a Jamaican scene in the *Journal of a West India Proprietor*. Throughout the *Journal*, Lewis's use of the picturesque frequently has the obtrusively picture-like quality of a stage set. He makes this explicit when he remarks, "I never witnessed on the stage a scene so picturesque as a negro village." This staginess begins the moment he lands in Black River Bay:

> At length the ship has squeezed herself into this champagne bottle of a bay! Perhaps, the satisfaction attendant upon our having overcome the difficulty, added something to the illusion of its effect; but the beauty of the atmosphere, the dark purple mountains, the shores covered with mangroves of the liveliest green down to the very edge of the water, and the light-colored houses with their lattices and piazzas completely embowered in trees, altogether made the scenery of the Bay wear a very picturesque appearance. And, to complete the charm, the sudden sounds of the drum and banjee, called our attention to a procession of the *John-Canoe*.

Lewis's first Jamaican landscape, with the almost luridly colorful "illusion of its effect," serves as a backdrop for the loud, lengthy, and highly theatrical celebration of Jonkonnu. Disembarking to watch the parade, Lewis encounters an oddly familiar icon, which he describes in his characteristic tongue-in-cheek tone. It is "a strange uncouth kind of a glittering tawdry figure, all feathers, and pitchfork, and painted pasteboard, who moved most reluctantly, and turned out to be no less a personage than Britannia herself, with a pasteboard shield covered with the arms of Great Britain, a trident in her hand, and a helmet made of pale blue silk and silver."[89] The part of Britannia is played by an enslaved girl, shoved into line by her mistress, Miss Edwards, the owner of Lewis's hotel.

The obvious distance between the reluctant actress and her role echoes the distance – cultural as well as geographical – between colony and metropole: this Britannia is well out of her element. The debased icon refracts imperial power through Afro-Caribbean cultural appropriation. Seen from Jamaica, and seen as reconstructed by African captives and their descendants, Britannia looks tawdry indeed. If "Jonkonnu functioned as the core of the oppositional culture of Jamaican slaves," then juxtaposing it with picturesque scenery does more than lend the picturesque the self-evident artifice of the masquerade costume.[90] I argue elsewhere that looking at landscape in this period is "a paradigmatic mental exercise in ownership," interpellating the aesthetic subject in a position of domination or control.[91] In this case, Lewis is, in effect, setting a gentlemanly assertion of imaginative ownership side by side with a vision of a world upside down. This picturesque staging could potentially cut two ways: it could undercut gentlemanly aesthetic control, or it could recuperate the carnival as entertainment for "Massa" and for metropolitan readers.

From within Lewis's metropolitan culture, the artifice of the picturesque is a stabilizing, empowering position, able to support the ideologically potent designation of "natural." In this colonial environment, however – especially when confronted with this staged refraction of the "natural" sign of British nationhood – the picturesque no longer looks so natural. If Britannia looks tawdry through the lens of a raucous Caribbean aesthetics of assemblage, then picturesque nature, in this alienating mirror, looks downright unnatural – an obvious "illusion" or "effect."[92] For all of its efforts to recuperate Jonkonnu as a quaintly naive or primitive curiosity, Lewis's description betrays the destabilizing effect on "Massa's" assurance when the enslaved not only look back but also stage a counter-representation of colonial realities. At this point, the frame of the picturesque gaze simply falls apart.

Defacing the planter picturesque

I began this chapter by describing the picturesque as a placeless aesthetics of place, modern in its bifocal vision of the near through the lens of the far: presenting Jamaica, for example, according to compositional criteria and pictorial values derived from European models like the iconic landscapes of Claude Lorrain. Successive versions of the planter picturesque through the final decades of British slavery took part in a profoundly interested project of place-making. The Creole apologists Edward Long and William Beckford used Jamaican scenery to confer prestige on the colony and to negotiate its relationship to the metropole. Writing in England, for metropolitan readers, these planter propagandists tried to leverage the cultural capital of aesthetics toward colonial autonomy and away from slave-trade abolition. Their picturesque colony includes enslaved workers as staffage figures: parasol-holding attendants, georgic reapers, and decorative groups lounging on lawns in compositional balance with livestock. The formal architecture of Long's *History of Jamaica* counterposes the aesthetics of the cultivated colony to the barbarity of Africa to underscore the necessity of slavery. The irregular form of Beckford's *A Descriptive Account of the Island of Jamaica*, meanwhile, tries to fend off the uncertainties of colonial politics and Caribbean weather with aesthetic effusions.

Matthew Gregory Lewis's case is rather different. Not exactly an apologist, he wrote his account of Jamaica not across the Atlantic from the island but rather on it. He records his day-to-day impressions and interactions in a form, the journal, whose immediacy resists the distancing effect of the writer's aestheticizing strategies. The geographical and cultural distance between Jamaica and England enters the *Journal of a West India Proprietor*, I argue, as the disjunction between Lewis's roles of "West India Proprietor" and London aesthete; his allusive descriptions ward off his captives' competing vision of colonial reality. The novelist's peculiar sense of humor even made a joke of the colonist's worst nightmare. After recounting one enslaved man's attempt to seduce another's wife, Lewis dryly remarks, "some palates among them . . . require higher seasoned vices; and besides their occasional amusements of poisoning, stabbing, thieving, etc., a plan has just been discovered in the adjoining parish of St. Elizabeth's, for giving themselves a grand fête by murdering all the whites in the island."[93] The plot involved more than a thousand enslaved workers – putting it, if it had not been discovered, among the largest in the West Indies' long history of slave revolts.

Figure 1.4 Auguste Duperly, "Rebellion in the Island of Jamaica in January 1832. The
Attack of the Rebels on Montpelier Old Works Estate in the Parish of St. James's, the
Property of Lord Seaford." Courtesy of the National Library of Jamaica.

I conclude this chapter by examining a unique image in which the planter
picturesque directly encounters slave rebellion. In 1833, the engraver and
lithographer Adolphe Duperly performed a remarkable act of piracy on
an image taken from James Hakewill's *A Picturesque Tour of the Island of
Jamaica.* The year after the Western Liberation Uprising of 1831–2, Jamaica's
largest and last slave revolt, Duperly embellished Hakewill's view of the
Montpelier Old Works Plantation (discussed previously) by adding the
figures of the captives who fought there in a major battle of the rebellion
(Figure 1.4). Duperly's choice to deface Hakewill's picturesque plantation
may have been fortuitous, but the image that he produced powerfully
counters the planter picturesque. If Hakewill's image arrests history through
the pictorial device of stasis or repose, then eight years later – on the brink
of emancipation – Duperly resists that arrest.

In his lithograph, Hakewill's picturesque plantation is no longer static
and sleepy. It is the center of a war zone. Duperly's title, "Rebellion in the

Island of Jamaica in January 1832. The Attack of the Rebels on Montpelier Old Works Estate in the Parish of St. James's, the Property of Lord Seaford," encapsulates the historical narrative of the insurrection as an attack on property – on the physical plant of the Old Works and, more important, on Lord Seaford's property in the people who invade and set fire to the site of their captive labor. The Western Liberation Uprising of 1831–2, also known as the Baptist War, was the "largest and most widespread of all British West Indian slave uprisings, involving 60,000 slaves in an area of 750 square miles and resulting in the deaths of 540 slaves (and 14 whites)."[94] The revolt took place despite – indeed, partly because of – the rumors spreading throughout the island that emancipation was imminent or had already been passed across the Atlantic in the imperial metropole. It was planned as a work stoppage, similar to "Gandhi's . . . campaign of civil disobedience through non-violent resistance to unjust laws," although its organizers were prepared to meet force with force.[95] Organized under the cover of Baptist religious meetings, it was led by members of a Creole elite that included skilled workers. Its leader was Sam Sharpe, a Baptist deacon and now a Jamaican national hero.

The revolt took place during the week between Christmas and New Year's, traditionally a time when the "bonds of slavery [were] loosened" for a few days and the enslaved population celebrated Jonkonnu. By 1831, Jamaica's planters had spent eight years resisting the reforms mandated by the imperial government in George Canning's resolution of 1823. The planters and the colonial press were "fulminating against metropolitan liberals and local missionaries and petitioning the imperial government to hold the line against further concessions."[96] Reportedly believing that the planters planned to kill all enslaved men, the rebels decided to assert their claim to freedom by refusing to labor (a claim probably also sparked by the planters' refusal to give enslaved workers an extra day of rest because Christmas fell on a Sunday). The planned labor action rapidly spiraled out of control, with workers setting fire to buildings at several plantations, including Montpelier, and the planters calling out the colonial militia and imperial troops. It took two weeks to regain control of the affected areas. As always, the repression was bloodier than the uprising, with 200 rebels killed in the course of suppressing the revolt and more than 300 executed afterward.[97]

The battle that Duperly's image records took place on December 28, 1831. The "western interior militia [had] retreated from their barracks at Shettlewood to Old Montpelier estate. There . . . they confronted the rebels' military core, the Black Regiment, about 150 strong with fifty guns

Figure 1.5 Duperly, detail (slave rebels in foreground). Courtesy of the National
Library of Jamaica.

among them, assisted by slaves recruited from the surrounding estates and
under the command of the self-styled Colonel Johnson of Retrieve estate.
The militia was forced to retreat to Montego Bay."[98] Duperly commem-
orates the revolt by utterly transforming Hakewill's picturesque scene. He
wrecks its repose, populating its foreground with a miscellaneous, rambunc-
tious crowd: men and women, standing, squatting, or lying; holding guns,
knives, axes, torches, and clubs; carrying baskets, buckets, and wounded
comrades (Figure 1.5). The militia at left is a line of identical, barely
discernible figures in contrast to the highly individualized rebels, whose
uncontained energy overwhelms the plantation, disrupting its order and
destroying its facilities. (At right in the figure is the trash house in flames,
its smoke rising to join the other clouds ominously staining Hakewill's
Claudean atmosphere.)

The rebels' action and Duperly's both fit Michel de Certeau's description of "tactics": a model of action characteristic of the dominated element
in society, those who have no place they can properly call their own.
Seizing their opportunity, they manipulate events to their advantage on
another's terrain. Duperly's piracy resembles the everyday practices of consumer "poaching" that are de Certeau's main topic. He substitutes for
Hakewill's landowner picturesque an Afro-Caribbean aesthetics of carnival
or Jonkonnu. The women to either side of the arch in the wall who are
carrying branches of bananas on their head suggest the fantastic headdress

known as the Jonkonnu, a model of the plantation Great House mounted on the head of its wearer (see Figure 1.5) (although bearing burdens this way was, of course, standard in Africa). By this practice, Burton writes, the "order of the plantation is symbolically reversed, and the power of the Great House passes, as it were, into the model house the slaves have constructed."[99] Do these festive female figures adorning the plantation-turned-battlefield hint at the symbolic world upside down that the rebels, during carnival time, are working to make a reality?

Making Jamaica into a second Haiti does not seem to have been Sam Sharpe's dream. If we take him at his word (as attested by missionaries who knew him), he wanted to make the colony into a place more like England, where workers would be paid for their labor and could exercise freedom of religion.[100] Regarding the aims or desires of the rank-and-file rebels who crowd Duperly's lithograph, we can only speculate. By the time the image was published, Sharpe had died on the gallows and emancipation was truly in the offing. Of course, as we now know, that would not suffice to accomplish Sharpe's desire. The protracted aftermath of emancipation – the "withering [of] plantation society" – would encompass more violent interludes and painful times for Jamaica's formerly enslaved population.[101] Duperly, meanwhile, went on to establish a photography business in Jamaica in the early 1840s. In 1844, he published his own collection of Jamaican scenes: *Daguerian Excursions in Jamaica, Being a Collection of the Most Striking Scenery, Public Buildings and Other Interesting Objects, Taken on the Spot with the Daguerreotype and Lithographed in Paris*. His son and grandsons continued the family business into the twentieth century.

CHAPTER 2

Stedman's tropics
The mercenary as naturalist

Duperly's piracy makes graphic the contrast between picturesque aesthetics' ordering of colonial space and the rebels' carnivalesque invasion. However, slave resistance took many forms short of armed uprising. Running away – leaving the captive space of the slave colony to take refuge outside its bounds – began with New World slavery itself. Called "marronage," this practice soon led to communities of free Africans, or Maroons, living on the margins of Europe's New World colonies. Marronage began in the English colony of Jamaica, for example, soon after England took over the colony from Spain in 1655, and it continued until the government was forced to negotiate a treaty, which included freedom for the Jamaican Maroons, in 1739.[1] In Suriname, which was briefly an English colony before being ceded to the Dutch in 1667, enslaved workers escaped into the surrounding South American jungle, formed small communities, and raided plantations for supplies and women from early in the colony's existence. By the mid-eighteenth century, Maroon harassment caused planters to be afraid for their lives and at risk of losing their investments in sugar and enslaved laborers. In 1772, with the colony in crisis, the Dutch government sent a volunteer corps of 800 professional soldiers to Suriname to help the colonial government fight the Maroons.[2]

One member of this expedition was the impecunious, multitalented Scottish officer Lieutenant John Gabriel Stedman. Stedman also was an amateur artist and naturalist, and his years in Suriname afforded rich material for both pursuits. After his return to Britain, his journal of his experience and his numerous sketches of tropical landscapes, organisms, and people became the basis for a lavishly illustrated book, *Narrative of a Five Years Expedition against the Revolted Negroes of Surinam* (1796). Recounting its author's adventures, this sprawling tome draws a portrait of a place with an exotic appeal to readers. Like so much travel writing and colonial history, Stedman's book is formally heterogeneous, drawing on a diverse set of discourses or genres. Those that are discussed here include natural history – that is, identifying and describing tropical organisms – and military narrative, Stedman's account of working as a colonial soldier while trying desperately to acclimate to the tropics.[3]

As both soldier and naturalist, Stedman, I argue, was uniquely positioned to represent natural history's complex imbrication with colonialism. The fractured sense of place conveyed by his *Narrative* arises from his position on the cutting edge, so to speak, of both colonial domination and scientific research.[4] Colonialism and natural history were both transatlantic institutions, sustained by the flow of people, messages, money, specimens, and supplies over established networks of communication and trade. As colonial personnel, including the soldier-naturalist-author, worked to implement metropolitan European imperatives on tropical American ground, they encountered continuous resistance from both the place and its people – including those transplanted from elsewhere, the captives who comprised approximately 90 percent of the colony's population.

I examine two of the *Narrative*'s interwoven strands that represent the ways in which people in varying relationships to the colonial regime lived and worked in the forests of Suriname: Stedman's soldiering and the Maroons' life on the run from colonial slavery. I then consider the ways in which these diverse, incompatible ways of living in the same tropical place informed Stedman's practice as an amateur naturalist by analyzing one of his illustrations, which depicts the skinning of a giant snake. The violence of slavery emerges as latent content in Stedman's snake plate, I argue, through its visual echoes of some of his better-known images of slave torture. I connect this visual intersection to the soldier-scientist's complex, contradictory position, uneasily situated between the colonial machine and those whom it exploited. Stedman's encounter with the giant snake, as he represents it in his book, is both a military operation and an act of specimen collection – as well as (more speculatively) testimony to the soldier-scientist's implication in the systemic cruelty of the colonial slave society.

Natural history, colonialism, and place

The history of natural history is inseparable from that of European exploration and colonialism. The "sciences of collection and comparison," Michael Drayton observes, "depended on Europeans becoming exposed to the planet's physical and organic diversity."[5] Natural history's ambitious project of classifying the world's organisms depended on moving scientists to remote locations, often "piggybacking" on more profitable missions of colonization or trade. The geographer-theorist Bruno Latour proposed a model in which the materials collected in these far-flung areas – including maps, drawings, and descriptions, as well as actual specimens – were then processed in Europe's scientific zones, or what he calls "centers of calculation." Organizing and studying these materials helped to prepare for further expeditions by explorers and colonizers in what Latour terms "cycles of accumulation." Tim Fulford, Peter Kitson, and Debbie Lee expand Latour's insights by arguing that such "'centers of calculation' and 'cycles of accumulation' were all part of complex networks connecting scientific zones around the world."[6]

Building these networks was not driven by disinterested scientific curiosity alone. Natural history, Alan Bewell points out, was "integrally bound up with colonial economies."[7] Knowledge of nature – collected around the globe and processed in Europe's centers of calculation – was harnessed to the service of imperial expansion and wealth. Tropical nature was a source of accelerating agricultural profit, primarily from sugar but also from other crops, such as coffee, cotton, and indigo; the natural historian was a valuable contributor to this enterprise. Colonial personnel often pursued natural history in their spare time. The naturalists of the early British Caribbean, for example, often were physicians in the service of the colonial government or the area's planter-entrepreneurs. Later, it was not uncommon for military personnel and colonial administrators in places such as Australia and India to practice natural history as an avocation. Hans Sloane, for example, went to Jamaica in 1687 as physician to the Duke of Albemarle. While there, he catalogued some 800 species of plants and later published a two-volume account, parlaying his research into the presidency of the Royal Society.[8] Sloane's work also was typical in that the exotic specimens he collected included numerous organisms of potential use and profit to Jamaica's British proprietors.

Stedman spent much of his spare time in Suriname collecting and describing curious New World flora, fauna, and artifacts. He did not work at the scale or with the expertise of Hans Sloane; he had neither Sloane's training nor his elite connections. However, the potential profits of bioprospecting were quite possibly in the back of Stedman's mind.[9] His *Narrative of a Five Years' Expedition* mentions "my Little Collection of Natural Curiosity, which I . . . began to form some Idea of Exhibiting one Day to the Publick if I was Spared to return to Europe." This idea never became reality; however, in 1777, shortly after his return, he gave the Prince of Orange "for his museum" 18 wax figures of indigenous Surinamers that he had made himself. Much later, Stedman donated a number of items to the Leverian Museum in London.[10] However, the main form in which Stedman managed to disseminate and profit from his observations on the natural history of Suriname was his book, with its numerous illustrations. Of the 81 plates, 42 depict one or more animal, plant, or insect species, not counting the pictures of human inhabitants (e.g., Amerindians and Afro-Caribbeans) who were sometimes put under the rubric of natural history.[11]

Advertising the *Narrative*'s contents in his preface, Stedman puts natural history first: "no less than 30 Laboreous Chaptrs in which natural History is promoted – the Olive Indian admir'd – the sable negro slave Supported – & the black European expos'd to the naked eye, while the whole is Variegated with the most beautiful Landscapes, & the Account of my military wanderings through an unbounded forrest."[12] This capsule description bespeaks the author's canny sense of the prestige of natural history among Britain's reading elite (as well as the political importance of abolitionism in the early 1790s, when Stedman finished his manuscript). The half-pay officer's literary labor, as he strove to support his growing family, was in part a wager on the potential profit to be had from the "mushrooming... interest in natural history" during the later eighteenth century. John Gascoigne documents the steep rise in publications on botanical, horticultural, and related subjects from the 1760s to the turn of the century, and he notes the 1788 founding of the Linnaean Society as evidence of "the increasing self-confidence of natural historians and their conviction of the worth and utility of their discipline."[13] Stedman apparently lacked personal connections with credentialed naturalists. The subscribers to his book do not include Sir Joseph Banks, whose extensive networks picked up so much of the scientific activity of his day; most of Stedman's subscribers consisted of his military connections from Suriname and elsewhere. However, those who did read the *Narrative* found extensive first-hand data on the flora and fauna of a relatively unfamiliar tropical colony.[14]

Stedman's relationship with the metropolitan natural history establishment was vexed at best. At the time he wrote the book, living in England in the 1780s, he seems to have been fairly well informed about developments in the field. He frequently cites authorities from Linnaeus and Buffon to Edward Bancroft, author of a 1769 natural history of Guiana, and Maria Merian, the Dutch artist whose *Metamorphosis Insectorum Surinamensis* was based on her trip there in the 1690s. He also cites articles in periodicals including *European Magazine* and *London Review*. Despite his ostentatious familiarity with these writings, however, he positions himself in his text as an outsider. His preface imagines potential criticisms in order to refute them: for example, "Descriptions of Animals without so much as proper names." It is true that he seldom gives readers the Latin species name of an animal or plant, more often using English, Dutch, or Sranan common names. "That my plants fully prove I am nothing of a Botanist," he writes, "Guilty." He defends himself, pointing out that "the delicate investigation of Plants with Spectacles is not the work of one reader in one Hundred . . . besides having been debarr'd from a Classical Education and being next to a stranger in this Country [England], I have . . . had very little time . . . for Compiling this Laborious work."[15]

Stedman repeatedly positions himself closer to the common reader than to the bespectacled botanist, not "amongst the flycatching fraternity," "without the Smallest Pretensions to a Connoisseur in natural Philosophy." Nonetheless, he does not hesitate to correct the authorities, even Linnaeus himself, as well as both Buffon and Merian.[16] The colonial soldier's tense, self-conscious relationship to metropolitan science calls attention to the transatlantic networks that made possible natural history's production of knowledge. Lacking the personal connections through which more elite, better-educated travelers contributed to this process, Stedman aspires to democratize natural history to include relatively humble investigators whose contribution consists of first-hand empirical observations in inaccessible places.

His *Narrative of a Five Years' Expedition* imaginatively exploits the combination of military service with natural history. In line with his general tendency toward self-aggrandizement, he dramatizes his pursuit of natural history as a heroic endeavor. "As I have Undertaken to Describe All I Could of the innumerable Curious Animals & Vegetables that one Perpetually meets with in this Country – I am Determined Strenuously to Proceed with the Difficult Task . . . let me be in Whatever Situation I may, Fire, Watter, or the Clouds, no matter What, Providing I Can only keep above the Ground." Given the mortality rate among colonial troops, staying above the ground was no trivial affair. Natural history was not nearly as strenuous as the day-to-day effort of simply staying alive. At one point, slinging his hammock high in a tree, Stedman notices something odd – a leaf crawling up the bark. The leaf is actually an insect, which he describes in detail. "This must seem verry strange to many People," he remarks, referring "those who doubt" to an unpublished pamphlet by Dr. Richard Watson, Lord Bishop of Llandaff, in the November 1784 *European Magazine*.[17] The contrast between the harsh jungle conditions and the erudite citation exemplifies the incongruous synergy between metropolitan scholarship and colonial "boots on the ground" that shapes Stedman's natural history practice as presented in his book.

Scholars disagree on the significance of place to natural history as a discourse and a practice. Mary Louise Pratt's influential analysis characterizes the production of knowledge about nature as an ideological apparatus operating in tandem with colonization, which masks its violence through the benign figure of the "botanizer" with his innocent-seeming presence and minimal impact on non-European territory and people (she labels this trope "the anti-conquest"). Linnaean classification, she argues, following Foucault, was a knowledge-making project able to "subsume culture and history into nature. Natural history extracted specimens not only from their organic or ecological relations with each other, but also from their places in other peoples' economies, histories, social and symbolic systems"[18] – replacing them in a classificatory table bearing no relationship to their places of origin. This decontextualizing effect is reflected, for example, in the conventions of botanical drawing, which displays specimens on a neutral ground.[19]

More recent scholarship significantly qualifies this view. It may be true that taxonomy erases place, but location was important to the process through which natural history produced knowledge. This process took place, at least partly, on colonial soil. Although scientists working in metropolitan centers were indispensable to this process, so was the field-work of traveling naturalists and their assistants – local guides and helpers, often Indians or enslaved people. Colonials, male and female, also reported on local species, hoping that their contributions would boost the prestige of their colonial homes back in the center of the empire. Susan Scott Parrish's research exposes natural history's messier side as a transatlantic process of collaboration and negotiation. The "archive of colonial and transatlantic eighteenth-century natural history," she concludes, "reveals much more contentious, empirically embedded . . . cultures of knowledge-making" than later American nature writers – or scholars such as Pratt – were willing to acknowledge. Parrish's analysis accords to the colonial sites of natural history observation and collection – and the diverse individuals who performed it – an essential role in the character of the knowledge produced.[20]

Stedman's work as an amateur natural historian bears out this paradigm. His book embeds natural history – its practice as well as its product in the form of his descriptions and drawings of numerous tropical plant and animal species – in the colonial setting where his primary research took place. This procedure works to disclose natural history's complex connection to colonialism in various ways, which my argument attempts to unravel. Building on Stedman's sense of his book as "variegated," a "crazy quilt" of heterogeneous components with its seams showing, I put pressure on some of these juxtapositions to explore the diverse and often incompatible senses of place that inform the book's several strands. In this way, I hope to extend the analysis of natural history by Parrish and others as a hybrid knowledge profoundly shaped by its colonial origins. I turn first to Stedman's reason for being in Suriname: his work as a soldier.

The colonial soldier in the tropics

Soldiers, sailors, and the enslaved formed a motley group doing the dirty work of European imperialism. Mobile, often rootless citizens of the world, they were a multi-ethnic proletariat, a labor force for imperial trade and warfare, but also, on occasion, vectors for revolutionary ideas. Stedman describes Suriname's colonial troops as "a Composition of Scum – Composed of all nations – ages & shapes – and sizes & by chance wafted together from all the different Corners of the Globe, yet notwithstanding which they fight like little Devils."[21] Stedman's literacy and officer status made him more than a proletarian; he hovered on the lower fringe of the category of gentleman. Roving and uprooted he certainly was. He was born in 1745 in the Netherlands to a Scottish father and Dutch mother; as a child, he moved from post to post through the Low Countries with his father's regiment of the Scottish brigade of the Dutch army. As a young man, he followed his father into the brigade and its officer corps. In 1771, in debt and mourning his father's death, he signed up for hazardous duty across the Atlantic in the Dutch colony of Suriname.[22]

European soldiers posted to the Caribbean at that time could not reasonably expect to return. Alan Bewell's magisterial *Romanticism and Colonial Disease* documents the appalling number of lives lost in the "epidemiological contact zones opened up by colonial expansion" and the disturbing silence of metropolitan discourse about this. Normally, Bewell explains, mortality among soldiers and sailors was roughly twice that of civilians due to crowded quarters, poor hygiene, bad nutrition, typhus, scurvy, and sexually transmitted diseases. In the tropics, however, death rates were even higher due to tropical diseases such as malaria and yellow fever, to which Europeans had no immunity. Samuel Johnson understood this: "By incommodious encampments and unwholesome stations," he wrote, "where courage is useless, and enterprise impracticable, fleets are silently dispeopled, and armies sluggishly melted away."[23]

The metaphor of melting is one that Stedman uses repeatedly in writing about the losses among the volunteer corps with whom he arrived in Suriname. They landed in February; by April, they were burying five or six men a day and, by mid-May, a number of officers were sick as well. Suffering and death from such ailments as bloody flux, "frenzy fever," "lethargy," and dropsy form a doleful refrain throughout the book. At the end of June, Stedman reports, "our little Corps was already Melted from 530 able men to about 3 fourths of their number, by Death and Sickness, the Hospital being crowded by invalids of every kind." "Melting" suggests an invisible, irresistible force of nature assailing the troops, as if North Atlantic ice floes had been dropped into the Caribbean Sea. By the time Stedman left the colony in 1777, he estimates that of 1,200 troops sent there during the course of five years, 100 were returning, with perhaps 20 of those in good health, of whom he was fortunate to be one. The rest, he writes, were "sick; discharged; past all Remedy; Lost; kill'd; & murdered by the Climate, while no less than 10 or 12 were drown'd and Snapt away by the Alligators."[24]

Suriname's hostility to European bodies is a recurring theme in Stedman's *Narrative of a Five Years' Expedition*. Tropical nature formed a powerful threat to the soldiers trying to live and work within its malevolent reach. When Stedman and his troops were sent into the rainforest for a 10-week "campaign," we get a sense of Suriname beyond its small cultivated area as inaccessible and deeply threatening to Europeans. Colonists are starting to abandon plantations that have been destroyed by Maroon attacks. Somewhere out there in the "horrid and impenetrable woods" lurk the escaped captives, whose drums the soldiers hear at night. Stedman's orders are to cruise up and down the River Cottica in eastern Suriname on two barges that Stedman christens Charon and Cerberus (although calling them "sudden Death and willful Murder," he jokes bitterly, would be a better fit). The troops are supposed to keep the Maroons from crossing the river, capture or kill them if possible, and protect the plantations. A sympathetic planter predicts, "As for the Enemy . . . you may depend on not seeing one single Soul of them . . . But the Climate, the Climate will murder you all."[25] He is almost right on both counts.

The jumpy soldiers think they see enemies everywhere. One night, a sentinel announces he sees "a Negroe with a lighted tobacco pipe . . . in a Canoo." His panicky comrades leap out of their hammocks until a Surinamer explains that it is only a firefly. The soldiers are afraid to set foot on land, even to cook their meals, so they risk setting the barges on fire. "[A]ll the Elements," Stedman writes, "seem'd to oppose us." This sense of an active hostility in the place permeates his experience. The jungle terrain is nearly impenetrable; each officer is given a compass "by which we were to Steer like Sailors through a dark wood, where nothing is to be seen but heaven and Earth – as at Sea nothing appears but clouds and water." The maritime comparisons convey a sense of barely submerged panic at the pathless expanse. A march through the forest leaves marks on European bodies:

> We arrived at the Society Post . . . in a most shocking Condition, having waddled through Water and Mire above our hipps, Climb'd over heaps of fallen trees, creep'd underneath them on our bellies – Scratched and tore at by the thorns or macas that are here of many kinds, Stung all over by the Patat or Scrapat lice, ants, and *wassy-wassy* or wild bees, fatigued to death by marching in a burning Sun, and the last 2 hours in hells darkness, holding each other by the hand, and having left 10 Men behind, some with agues, some stung blind, and some with their feet full of Chigoes.[26]

The image of the soldiers holding hands in the dark suggests a deep need for comfort in the face of overwhelming physical and psychological threats.

Note Stedman's care to provide an exact designation of each nasty plant or bug, as if knowing which species stung you blind in the jungle made a difference. When he later launches into a catalog of the "many Plagues and Dangers, one is hourly Exposed to in the Woods of this Tropical Climate," the discourses of natural history and tropical medicine lose their scientific detachment as they designate threats to non-indigenous bodies: "*Prickly heat – Ringworm Dry-Gripes, Putrid fevers, Boyls, Consaca, Bloody-flux – Thorns, Briars – Alligators, Snakes* and *Tigers* &c . . . *Bush-worms, Large Ants, Locusts, Centipedes, Scorpions Bats & flying lice,* the *Crassy-Crassy Yaws, Lethargy, Leprosy,* and *Dropsy,* besides a Thousand other Grievances, that . . . for ever Keep'd us Company."[27]

The soldiers' extreme vulnerability to the combination of the tropical environment and their Maroon enemies is captured by another image to which Stedman returns several times in the book. He depicts it memorably in the plate entitled "March thro' a Swamp or Marsh in Terra-firma," engraved by Blake (Figure 2.1). He mentions a Lieutenant Lepper whose men are ambushed when they are up to their armpits in a swamp: "their black Enemies rushed out from under Cover and shot them dead at pleasure." Another illustration shows what became of Lepper and his men, their skulls impaled on stakes by the Maroons and their bodies left to rot. Following is Stedman's description of such a swamp march:

Figure 2.1 "March thro' a swamp or Marsh in Terra-Firma," from John Gabriel Stedman, *Narrative of a Five Years' Expedition against the Revolted Negroes of Surinam* (1796).

Col: Fourgeoud Preseded by a negro Slave as a Guide, to give Notice when the watter is too Deep, And followed by some of his Officers and Private Marines, Wading through the Marsh in a heavy shower of Rayn till Above Their Middles, and Carrying their Ammonition & their Accoutrements Above their Heads . . . While in the Offing may be seen . . . in What manner sometimes the rebel Negroes fire on the Troops, out of the Palm trees &c And which Situation of Marching is Certainly the most Dangerous in Surinam.[28]

Notice the forlorn look on the soldiers' faces, especially the man in the center, facing the viewer. The palm trees in the background bear the deadly fruit of Maroon sharpshooters who have shinnied up to an improbable height, creating a "vertical African axis" if, as Parrish suggests, the black guides sympathize with the insurgents. The "four soldiers in the foreground," she continues, are "penned in by the very tools of their technological superiority as Blake lines up their four rifles into a constrictive parallelogram." The plate deftly captures the imaginative merging so often suggested in the *Narrative* between the hostile jungle environment and the forest-dwelling Maroons.[29]

As a European soldier on the job, then, Stedman's sense of place – his relationship to his tropical workplace – developed in response to immediate, life-threatening pressure. Suriname's terrain and climate were unfamiliar, unpleasant, and dangerous, as were many of the flora and fauna – not to mention the human denizens, the Maroons. Tropical nature posed an intimate, ever-present threat, closing in on the soldier and overwhelming him with its host of "Plagues and Dangers." All of this the soldiers endured in the service of their employer, the colonial government, and its goal of bringing the troubled colony back to orderly, lucrative sugar production. The Maroons themselves remind Stedman of this in a conversation of sorts. He records this exchange, which took place in the aftermath of the only pitched battle that he fought against these elusive enemies in more than four years. Stedman's commander, Fourgeoud, shouts to the Maroons over the corpse-strewn battlefield, promising them "Life, Liberty, Meat, Drink, and All they Wanted, but they Replied With a Loud Laugh, that they Wanted Nothing . . . They Call'd to us that we were more to be Pitied than themselves, Who were only a Parcel of White Slaves, hired to be shot at, & Starved for 4 Pence a Day." The defiant fighters "Concluded by Swearing that *Bony* [the Maroon leader] Should soon be the Governor of All the Colony . . . fired a Volly gave three Cheers . . . And all Dispearsed With the Rising Sun" to the relief of their exhausted foes.[30] Indeed, soldiers and enslaved people had much in common as members of Caribbean colonialism's exploited, endangered workforce: expendable bodies vulnerable to disease, heat, hunger, overwork, and harsh punishment. The Maroons' analysis, delivered as a taunt, surely must have touched a nerve.

Being Boni

Stedman's Maroon antagonists live outside the boundaries of Suriname's colonial plantation society, in the wild South American forests and swamps. They have opted out of slavery, the cruelty of which Stedman's *Narrative of a Five Years' Expedition* copiously records and visually renders in his best-known illustrations. They seem to qualify as what Srinivas Aravamudan calls tropicopolitans. He defines a "tropicopolitan" as a "colonized subject who exists both as fictive construct of colonial tropology *and* actual resident of colonial space, object of representation *and* agent of resistance."[31] As fictive constructs in Stedman's text, the Maroons exemplify a relationship to tropical nature that radically diverges from both the planters' commodity agribusiness and the colonial soldiers' out-of-placeness, their miserable vulnerability. As the planter predicted, Stedman and his men seldom met a live Maroon. However, they did encounter material traces of the forest-dwelling escapees: the remains of temporary villages whose inhabitants had fled the soldiers' pursuit.

Destroying provision grounds was an important tactic used by colonial forces against the Maroons, whose life on the run the historian Wim Hoogbergen describes as "a constant battle."[32] Inspecting a recently abandoned site deep in the forest, Stedman writes admiringly, "Inconceivable are the many Shifts Which these People make in the Woods . . . Where in a State of *Tranquillity* [i.e., when not pursued by troops] they Seemed . . . [to] Want for Nothing – Being Plump and Fat at Least Such we found those that had been Shot." He goes on to catalog Maroon subsistence technologies: traps for fish and game; the barbecue (well known as a Caribbean contribution to good eating); forest agriculture, cultivating yams, plantains, rice, and cassava; and even seasonings, including butter made from pistachios or the fat of palm worms and salt from ashes – and, of course, "the *Palm tree Wine* they are never in Want of." Stedman describes Maroon methods of making soap, candles, pots, cups, brooms, hammocks, and ropes with a degree of detail that bespeaks a deep interest in Maroon life, implicitly contrasting their stripped-down yet (he imagines) comfortable life in the bush with the soldiers' forlorn existence. The Maroons make direct use of the forest plants and animals, in contrast to their former owners' participation in a transatlantic system of commodity production and exchange based on the exploitation of soldiers and slaves – a system that natural history, by identifying agricultural resources, also served.[33]

Stedman's fascination with his idealized version of the Maroons' forest life casts them as tropicopolitan "agents of resistance" to the colonial status quo: Suriname's fabulously productive sugar economy. However, his *Narrative of a Five Years' Expedition* elsewhere praises and defends this lucrative agribusiness. As was conventional in colonial histories or accounts, Stedman touts the colony's wealth and details the process of producing sugar (as well as cacao, coffee, cotton, and indigo), giving figures on cost and profit, which he estimates for 1771 at £200,000. He even presents the Maroons' lack of interest in "amassing Wealth by industry" as a reason why they should be re-enslaved. He does, however, make clear his deep ambivalence about slavery as it existed in Suriname, punctuating his account of the sugar-making process with graphic descriptions of its cruelties: an enslaved worker catching a finger in the cane rollers and having the limb chopped off with a hatchet kept ready for the occasion, or having his teeth knocked out for daring to taste "that Sugar which he produces by the Sweat of his Brow."[34] Stedman obviously deplored such treatment but he nonetheless defended slavery as an institution. In fact, he owned one enslaved person, the boy Quacoo (whom he took with him back to Europe and later gave to the Countess of Rosendaal as a gift). His attempts to purchase a second – his concubine, or "Suriname wife," Joanna – did not succeed.

This heterogeneous, self-contradictory book thus alternately praises incompatible ways of living in and from tropical nature: the stripped-down self-sufficiency of the itinerant Maroons and the slave-driven commodity production of the colonial machine. Stedman's role as a soldier, in the pay of the colonial government but working outside of the colony's cultivated area – occupying the same wild space as the fugitives he hunted – positioned him to develop such a bifocal vision of colonial Suriname.[35] The *Narrative*'s long section on Suriname's sugar production concludes with a surprising comment: "Independent of the great Wealth that the West indies in general afford, it shall ever [be] my opinion, that the Europeans could live as Comfortably without them, if not more healthy, where the want of Sugar, Coffee, Cotton, Cacaw, indigo, rum, and Brazil-Wood, can be amply supplied by honey, Milk, Wool, geneva [gin], ale, English-Herbs, British-Oak &c." Transposing the idea of locally based subsistence living into British terms, Stedman almost seems to suggest that Britain should drop out of the colonial commodity economy. Written during the first wave of abolitionist agitation, which included a sugar boycott, the passage may have given liberal British readers food for thought. The image of the oak, a familiar national symbol that Stedman elsewhere calls "the natural produce of the Soil" in a "Land of Liberty," adds a patriotic flavor to this radical idea; the *Narrative of a Five Years Expedition*, however, does not pursue it further.[36]

The Maroons, those intrepid tropicopolitans, thus emerge as migrating sites of discursive disruption in Stedman's text. One Maroon in particular gets Stedman's attention: he forms an imaginative relationship to the notorious Maroon leader, Boni. Introduced as a conventionally primitive, bloodthirsty savage, Boni unexpectedly morphs into what we might call Stedman's alter ego. He enters the *Narrative* during Stedman's account of his "Second Campaign" in November 1773. Joining his commander, Colonel Fourgeoud, in the jungle, Stedman is briefed by the Rangers on their recent achievement of taking three Maroon villages and destroying the nearby rice fields "after driving the Rebels to flight, who were commanded by one *bony* a relentless Mullatto, who was born in the forest." Boni is a leader, he is relentless, and he was born in the forest. In the first of these descriptions, he resembles Captain Stedman; the other two predicates, however, position him as Stedman's opposite. The mercenary is concerned to portray himself as a man of feeling, kind and sensitive, sometimes to a fault.[37] He elaborates, in contrast, on Boni's reputation for cruelty: a woman prisoner has told the Rangers that Boni had white male prisoners stripped and flogged to death "for the recreation of theyr [the Maroons'] Wives and their Children." His earlier description of Lieutenant Lepper's death concludes by describing how Boni's Maroons impaled the dead soldiers' skulls on stakes. An illustration depicts Stedman coming upon this grisly display, his melancholy expression conveying how much it shocks his civilized sensibility. At this point, Stedman presents the rebel commander as a stereotypical non-European Other, a savage denizen of the South American bush.[38]

Information about Boni from other sources supplements – and occasionally contradicts – Stedman's account. Suriname had several different Maroon groups; the one eventually led by Boni first formed in the swamps east of the Cottica River, probably around 1712. Born in the forest about 1730, Boni was the son of a woman who had escaped from the plantation Barbakoeba, or Annaszorg, and a father who was probably Amerindian (Stedman's story that Boni's father was a planter who raped his enslaved mother contradicts most records). He had at least two brothers and one sister among the Maroons. An excellent blacksmith, he was able to repair guns and forge axes and picks.[39] Boni assumed the leadership of his Maroon group around 1768 along with another man, Aluku.

According to Hoogbergen, Boni was a good strategist, knew guerrilla tactics, and "loved spectacular actions" – such as the raid on the plantation Nieuw-Roosenbeek, at which the Maroons stayed for several hours and made a racket heard for miles, rather than take their loot and leave before soldiers arrived. (This leisurely pace resulted in their having to leave behind most of the goods they had packed, but the psychological effect of such daring may have been worth it.) Sending a released prisoner back to the colonists, Boni instructed him to have them sue for peace immediately – but, if not, to send three shiploads of Rangers, because it would take at least that many to defeat him. Besides being a military leader, Boni was honored among the Maroons as *krutu*, meaning "spokesman" or "judge," an important function in the early stages of a Maroon tribe whose members consisted of African-born escapees of various ethnicities and Creoles from a number of different plantations. As Hoogbergen states, "It was extremely difficult to make a coherent society out of this melting pot of desperados."[40]

Boni's next appearance in the *Narrative* is metonymic. Stedman cathects with the Maroon leader via a made object, the product of a Creole technology that the European soldiers had been imitating to good effect. The soldiers had learned a local method of building huts in the forest using palm fronds and vines so as not to have to carry tents. One evening, after a long march in the forest, Stedman and his men found that they need not put up huts: "we found our Quarters ready made, loging in the *wigwams* or huts that were left standing when the Rice-Country had been demolished, and Bony with his Men drove to flight . . . Bonys own house . . . was a perfect Curiosity, having 4 pretty little rooms, and a Shade or piazza inclosed with neat Manicole [palm] Palisades." His choice of words is significant: "curiosity" invokes the language of natural history, linking the Maroons' deserted village to the tropical flora and fauna – including human natives – that were the object of the natural historian's curious gaze.[41] To apply the term "curiosity" to Boni's house was to incorporate the Maroon leader into the powerful European discourse of place that was natural history. He becomes an object of scientific regard, a curiosity to be collected and displayed in the pages of Stedman's book. The adjectives "pretty," "little," and "neat" combine to miniaturize the Maroon warlord into the metonymic form of an "inclosed," controllable artifact.

Such discursive containment proves predictably unstable. When Boni reenters the *Narrative*, it is in a quite different relationship to its protagonist, who meanwhile has undergone a dramatic change of his own. Stedman's tropical seasoning – his Creolization or transculturation[42] – is a significant theme of his book, involving personal transformation at an intimate level in response to the very real pressures and dangers of his service in the South American jungle. Stedman's response is rather different from those of his peers. A few months after his arrival, when his fellow soldiers begin to get sick and die, he asks "the advice of an old Negroe – 'Cramaca /said I/ what do you do to keep your health[?]'" Paying attention to enslaved people's medical knowledge (linked to African religion, or obeah, and American Indian herbal lore) was fairly common in the Caribbean colonies. This type of knowledge also made slaves and Indians useful informants for natural historians. Reaching out to a long-time resident whose age suggests his advice on preventive medicine is worth taking seriously, Stedman assimilates Creole practices into his daily routine. Cramaca tells him to go swimming twice a day (keeping an eye out for piranhas, or "P[ric]kbiters" as Stedman's diary vulgarly calls them); go barefoot to toughen his feet; and dress lightly, which Stedman takes quite seriously. "There is a kind of pleasure," he remarks, "in rambling naked when the occasion will permit it, which I always envied the Indians and Negroes."[43]

Much of the credit for Stedman's unlikely survival is due to what we might call his human health insurance – his enslaved concubine, Joanna. In addition to her sexual service, she was his housekeeper and nursed him when he got sick. The institution of concubinage was common in the colonial tropics and in European slave societies generally, as Jenny Sharpe notes. Women of color took on white women's usual domestic role for colonial men who were handicapped by the shortage of white women in these areas. Highly convenient for men, this arrangement could benefit the women, as well, and often their entire families, who shared in the cash, gifts, and prestige they gained from their white lovers. The benefits to men like Stedman were clear. Sexual service was probably less important, at least at times, than preserving health – nurturing men with good cooking and household hygiene and nursing them when they fell ill, as Joanna did for Stedman. Psychologically, as Sharpe observes, "Joanna, and the domestic space she occupied, served as a point of stability during Stedman's long military campaigns against the rebels. The knowledge that he had a wife awaiting his return helped him to survive the despairing conditions of life in the bush."[44] However, his liaison with Joanna also connected him – by family ties, as many of the enslaved also were connected – to his Maroon enemies. Her mother's protector (one of Stedman's in-laws, so to speak) was the prominent Maroon military leader Jolicoeur.

During his jungle campaigns, Stedman continued to imitate Creole practices, eating fresh food and encouraging his men to do likewise – unlike his commander, Colonel Fourgeoud, who thought soldiers should live on imported salt meat and hard biscuit. Stedman tells of sampling local delicacies such as fat, juicy palm worms. "Delicious," he says, "I never Made a Better Supper." His pragmatic mimicry of the natives extends to carrying a calabash as a food bowl and eating "with a folded leaf in imitation of the Slaves." The native method of putting up huts in the forest also played a vital role in colonial military success in Suriname, such as it was. (Although few Maroons were ever captured or killed, the troops' harassment eventually drove them over the border into present-day French Guiana.) Changing his dress, diet, and hygiene, and living intimately with a Creole woman, the soldier of fortune ran a risk that inspired anxiety in colonials throughout the Americas.[45] The tropics had begun to transform him, as became evident in a dramatic confrontation that takes place, appropriately, in yet another swamp.

In March 1775, Stedman was stationed at Magdenburgh, site of an abandoned plantation. One day, as he tells it, "I had nearly Lost my own Life by an Accident." He went hunting with two slaves and got caught in heavy rain. To reach shelter, they had to cross a deep marsh. They waded in up to their armpits and started to swim when Stedman, weighed down by his musket, sunk "like a Stone." One of the slaves dove down to retrieve the gun.

> But we were Scarcely again Sat a Swimming when a Thundering Voice Called out through the Thisket *"Who som ma datty"* and another *"Sooto Sooto da Bony Kiry da Dago"* – who is there, Fire, Fire, it is Bony kill the Dogue [–] and Looking up we saw the Mussels of 6 Muskets Presented upon us, at a Very Little Distance, I instantly dived, but Philander Answering we Belong'd to Magdenbergh, we were Permitted to come a Shoare, one by one, at the Jacob [a plantation], where the Trusty Negroes having heard a Flouncing in the Water, and Seeing Three Armed Men in the Marsh, they took it for granted the rebels were Coming Headed by Bony Himself for when [whom] they had taken me, Being Almost quite Naked, and so Much Sunburned, besides my Hair Being Cut Short and Curly, that I Absoluetly Look'd like a Mulloto.[46]

The plantation guards' near-fatal mistake is a predictable product of guerrilla war. Everyone is continually on edge and it is difficult to determine who is on which side. It is a moment of acute danger for Stedman, to be sure. It also brings home the dramatic changes he has undergone in two years of colonial service – the outward signs of his transculturation. His dress, his hairstyle, and even his skin color now diverge from European norms. To say he looks like a mulatto is to place himself, by implication, between the warring groups, as well as to align himself with his "Suriname wife" Joanna, whom he occasionally calls "my Mulatto."

Indeed, Stedman is in between in significant ways, including the Maroon family ties he has acquired through his relationship with Joanna. He interacts easily with Creole Afro-Surinamers. Adept at languages, he understands the local patois, Sranan, as we notice when he easily translates the "thundering" call. Living for two years under the pressure of Suriname's tropical, colonial environment, the multitalented mercenary indeed has lost, in an important sense, his own – European – life. It has been misplaced, so to speak, in the "Thisket," the tropical rainforest and the colonial slave society, to both of which he has been forced to adapt or literally lose his life. How does he feel about being mistaken for Boni? He does not say. However, if we read his narration of this tense encounter alongside his earlier description of Boni's house as a "Curiosity," we notice a movement from outside to inside: from the natural historian's self-conscious, self-protective detachment to almost inhabiting Boni's skin, looking enough like him to be mistaken for him in a life-and-death situation. The plantation guards' reaction reflects back to the Creolized European the distance he has come in two years of immersion in the tropical environment and the colonial slave society, bringing home to Stedman and his readers that he now inhabits the same space – literally and figuratively – as his Maroon antagonists.

Stedman's account of his work as a soldier and the presence of the forest-dwelling Maroons weave into his *Narrative*'s "variegated" text diverse and mutually incompatible types of relationships to colonial Suriname's tropical terrain. Readers experience Stedman's tropics from multiple perspectives, serially and even simultaneously. One striking visual instance of this multi-perspectival effect is Stedman's frontispiece, engraved by the Italian master Bartolozzi. The plate depicts a youthful, melancholy Stedman standing over the supine, bleeding corpse of a Maroon (Figure 2.2). In the background burns the Maroon village of Gado-Saby, in the aftermath (we learn from the narrative) of the only real battle that Stedman fought during his years in Suriname.

Figure 2.2 Francesco Bartolozzi, frontispiece, from John Gabriel Stedman, *Narrative of a Five Years Expedition against the Revolted Negroes of Surinam* (1796).

At first glance, the image is organized by a series of oppositions: between light and dark skin; between the standing and the supine figure, respectively clothed and naked except for a breechcloth; and, of course, between living and dead. The verse caption, however, complicates the relationship between the colonial soldier and the slain Maroon, presenting it as an interchange, almost a merging, catalyzed by violence and pain:

> "From different Parents, different Climes we came,
> At different periods"; Fate still rules the same.
> Unhappy Youth while bleeding on the ground;
> 'Twas **Yours** to fall – but **Mine** to feel the wound.[47]

Stedman and Bartolozzi's plate captures the peculiar, claustrophobic intimacy of colonial violence in a Manichean image. The men's contrasting skin colors bind the composition as the faint, aestheticized flames and smudgy smoke transpose warfare into an almost dreamlike register. The caption frames the act of killing as the catalyst of a breakdown of boundaries between selves that allows Stedman to claim the dead man's pain as, in some sense, indeed his own – although subject to the unequal division of labor that the verse proposes: "'Twas **Yours** to fall – but **Mine** to feel the wound."

Marcus Wood is correct to point out that Stedman, writing the *Narrative of a Five Years' Expedition* after his return to Europe, sometimes imposes the fashionable discourse of sensibility on his colonial material. He even describes himself during the battle, ludicrously, as shooting with his eyes closed, unable to bear the pain he must inflict.[48] However, the imaginative identification with Boni that we have noticed elsewhere in the *Narrative* suggests a rather different relationship to bloodshed. Being Boni in moments of imaginative identification opens the door to the idea that Stedman is just as capable of inflicting pain as the "relentless" guerrilla leader, his opposite number in the forest. The image presents him as a victorious killer standing over his victim: the Maroon becomes a trophy – a specimen of an elusive forest species, captured on paper, and displayed as a curiosity to Stedman's readers.

The caption's apostrophe to the dead man, however, runs counter to this visual impression. Addressing the "Unhappy Youth" as a fellow subject – a human being, although native to a "different Clime" – Stedman takes up the problem of place with which so much of the *Narrative* is engaged. The trope of apostrophe refigures the protagonist's relationship to his tropicopolitan opponent as the play of sameness and difference structures the verse. Both Stedman and the Maroon have come from elsewhere: Europe and Africa, respectively. Arriving in the New World from "different Climes," they now occupy the same South American "ground." The earth beneath the soldier's feet, soaking up the dead man's blood, is the same tropical earth that has buried so many of Stedman's fellow sol-diers – murdered by the climate, as the planter foresaw. Gesturing toward the parallel place – figuratively speaking – of soldiers and the enslaved in the colonial-exploitation machine, Stedman's sentimental tribute to his dead enemy stands in irresoluble tension with the visual image of a vic-torious killer standing over his victim – a tension organized by the dis-courses of place that structure the "variegated" *Narrative of a Five Years' Expedition.*

Tropicalizing natural history

I turn now to another image existing at the intersection of natural history, slavery, and colonial militarism. "The skinning of the Aboma Snake, shot by Cap. Stedman," engraved by William Blake (Figure 2.3), is unlike the book's other natural history plates in that it renders visible the violence involved in turning an animal – especially one this big – into a scientific specimen. The art historian Kay Dian Kriz argues that the images that European visitors created of the plants, animals, and human artifacts found in a tropical colony could help "articulate . . . fraught relationships under construction in the Atlantic world." In Hans Sloane's illustrations of Jamaican organisms and artifacts in his 1725 natural history of Jamaica, for example, the "fear of . . . violence, emanating from the entire Jamaican ecosystem of plants, animals, and humans, surfaces as latent content in the realm of the visual."[49] In Blake's rendering of Stedman's giant snake, the violence of the interaction between humans and tropical megafauna is quite blatant – the connection to the human-on-human violence of the slave society somewhat more subtle.

Natural history illustrations, in Stedman's lifetime and thereafter, gener-ally included little, if any, natural and no human context. Botanical drawing conventionally displays specimens on a neutral ground (usually cut into parts, such as leaf, fruit, and reproductive organs). Zoological illustrations by Stedman's contemporaries more often – although by no means always – place the animal in a setting suggesting its connection to a geographical area or region. The illustrations in the 1780 English translation of Buf-fon's massive natural history, for example, which Stedman knew, show the dromedary with a pyramid in the background and the "Buck of Juda" with

Figure 2.3 William Blake, "The skinning of the Aboma snake, shot by Cap. Stedman,"
from John Gabriel Stedman, *Narrative of a Five Years Expedition against the Revolted
Negroes of Surinam* (1796).

a Middle Eastern cityscape in the distance. Most of the plates, however, put the animal in a minimal, generic setting or on a neutral ground (snakes in the latter).

Stedman's practice is similar. Of his numerous natural history plates, only four in addition to "The skinning of the Aboma Snake" include human figures. Two of these, "Manicole and the Cocoa Nut Tree" and "The Mountain Cabbage and Maureecee Tree," depict palm trees similar to those in the background of "March thro' a Swamp" (discussed previously), decorated with tiny figures presumably representing Afro-Surinamers. One of the figures in "Manicole" wields a machete and one in "Mountain Cabbage" shinnies high up the trunk of the palm tree. However, "The skinning of the Aboma Snake" fully displays the exotic creature in the context of the slave society. Suspended on a rope held by two black men, it is skinned by a third in an embrace of intimate violence, supervised by the uniformed figure of Stedman himself. Thus, Stedman's snake uniquely epitomizes the *Narrative*'s richly textured rendering of the colonial practice of natural history in the tropical slave colony by an amateur naturalist who was also a soldier.

The Aboma snake, as Stedman represents it visually and verbally, also exemplifies the multi-sitedness of natural history: it refuses to stay in one place. The gigantic reptile occupies several categories at once: its capture is a military conquest, an epic battle against an opponent that Stedman and his men at first mistake for one of their Maroon enemies. Its subsequent flaying, depicted in the plate, mimics some of the punishments meted out to slaves in this cruelest of sugar colonies as depicted by Stedman in other illustrations. Moreover, the products of this bloody process are disposed of in ways that epitomize the uses of natural history as both metropolitan entertainment and colonial utility.

Stedman's narrative of killing the snake is embedded in the texture of military life on rainforest patrol. He starts out by mistaking it for one of his Maroon enemies, something the nervous soldiers did fairly often (e.g., recall the innocent firefly mistaken for a rebel's lit pipe). Another time, the soldiers hear monkeys "Knocking Large Nuts / of what Species I Know not / Against the Branches of the Trees, to Break them . . . which Sound of *Tuck, Tuck, Tuck* we had Mistaken for the rebel negroes Cutting Wood with an Ax." This link between tropical fauna and Maroons recurs in the incident of the snake. Stedman is lying in his hammock on his patrol boat when a "Sentinel call'd to me that he had seen and challenged Something black and moving in the brushwood on the beach which gave no Answer and which from its thickness he concluded must be a Man." They got in a canoe and rowed ashore. "I suspect[ed] this to be no other than a rebel Spy," Stedman declares, "when one of my Slaves named David declared it was no Negroe, but a large amphibeous Snake."[50]

In David, we meet another tropicopolitan: one more of the ambiguous Creole figures who mediate Stedman's relationship to tropical nature, along with old Cramaca; Stedman's "Suriname wife" Joanna; and, of course, Boni and the Maroons. The enslaved man invites Stedman to shoot the creature. When he declines, David asks permission to shoot it himself. "[T]his Spirited me so much," Stedman writes, "that I determined to ... kill it myself, providing he was to point it out to me, and bail the hazard by Standing at my Side, from which I Swore that if he dared to move I should level the piece at himself, and blow out his brains without Judge or Jury." His threat of violence swerves from snake to human captive and back again, linking the two as targets of his fear-fueled rage. Of course, in the Suriname slave society, Stedman could have carried out his threat of murder with impunity, as David would have been well aware. Colonial masculinity cuts an ironic figure, exploding with threats but in need of a helper to "bail the hazard" – and even to spot the prey: "he call'd out, *me see Snakee*, viz, that he saw the Snake coild under the fallen leafs & rubbish of the trees. 'D[am]n you rascal / said I / then stand before me till I also see him or you are dead this instant,' and this he did."[51] Unnecessarily translating David's Sranan, Stedman inserts the capable hunter's voice and vision into his narrative – the other man's taciturnity a cool contrast to the blustering soldier's near-hysteria.

The battle goes on for a couple of pages; the illustration shows its endgame (see Figure 2.3). The snake is suspended by a rope slung over a high branch and held by two naked, undifferentiated male figures. David, who first spotted the beast, is doing the skinning. Here, an enslaved man inflicts violence; enduring it is the anthropomorphized snake, which seems to eye its tormentor reproachfully. Stedman, his bayonet propped against the tree, supervises the procedure. The contrast between his fully clothed figure and his helpers' nakedness implicitly aligns the latter with the beast, as does the violent embrace in which David holds the huge reptile. "David with a sharp knife between his teeth now left the Tree, and clung fast upon the Monster which was still twisting, and began his Operations by ripping it up and stripping down the Skin as he descended, which though the Animal could now do him no hurt; I acknowledge had a terrible appearance, viz, to See a Man Stark naked, black and bloody, clung with Arms and legs around the Slimy and yet living Monster."[52] As the men's labor actively transforms the spectacular beast into a specimen, natural history is brought into contact – even implied complicity – with the violence of the slave society.

A "Man Stark naked, black and bloody" would not have been an unfamiliar sight in this, one of the most brutal of the New World slave colonies. This bleak association is reinforced by the visual echoes between this plate and two of the book's grisliest images of slave torture, both engraved by Blake, in which suspension – bodies hanging from posts or trees – also plays a role. In "A Negroe Hanged Alive by the Ribs to a Gallows," the victim of this grotesque torture has his arms tied behind him so as to appear virtually limbless – like a huge snake. The composition of another plate, the well-known "Flagellation of a Female Samboe Slave" (Figure 2.4), is remarkably similar to that of the snake plate.[53] In both, we see Stedman, viewed from the back, in the lower left corner. He even has his right arm raised in both pictures, although his stance in "Flagellation" is different and his other arm, raised to his head, suggests distress at the woman's plight. On the other side is the overseer who has ordered her whipping, with a pointing gesture similar to Stedman's in the snake plate, accompanied by two naked black men armed with whips. The curves of the suspended woman's body echo those of the snake's. This visual echo refuses to let us separate Stedman's scientific avocation from the reason that he is in the jungle – the violence of Suriname's decadent slave society.[54]

The connection is strengthened when we find out what becomes of the products of this bloody process. They end up in two places, as Stedman reports. He sends 4 gallons of clarified snake oil to the army hospital, "it being deem'd particularly for Bruises, a verry excellent Remedy." Tropical nature is processed into a commodity in support of colonial militarism. The snake's skin, which Stedman carefully dries on the bottom of a canoe, is "sent to Holland as a Curiosity" – arriving at the imperial center via natural history's global network of specimen transportation, presumably carried on a military vessel.[55] The image of "The skinning of the Aboma Snake," with Stedman's narrative of the incident, renders a rich, multifaceted account of natural history as colonial science, one made possible by its creator's dual roles as soldier and scientist, mercenary and natural historian. Stedman's tropics are the site of planter exploitation and Maroon evasion, the naturalist's paradise and the soldier's grave. Colonial Suriname emerges from his "variegated" book as a node in transatlantic networks of commodity production and specimen transportation but also as a place that – like the Maroons – persistently eludes containment by those networks.

Figure 2.4 William Blake, "Flagellation of a Female Samboe Slave," from John
Gabriel Stedman, *Narrative of a Five Years' Expedition against the Revolted Negroes
of Surinam* (1796).

Return

Near the end of Stedman's *Narrative of a Five Years' Expedition*, we encounter what we might call an irony of place. His colonial service, as previously discussed, led to a personal transformation so extreme as to leave him outwardly resembling his Maroon antagonist, Boni: dark-skinned, weathered, wading in Suriname's swamps wearing little except a gun. The subjective consequences of his tropical seasoning emerge most starkly on his return to European civilization. Arriving on the shores of Holland after five years of guerrilla warfare, he sketches a picture of ordinary Europeans worthy of Swift's Gulliver. The

> *inhabitants* who Crowded About us for Curiosity to see us appear'd a Pack of the uglyest & nastyest tatterdemalions that I ever Behel'd, Since I had been Accustomed to live amongst the indians & Blacks –
>
> Theyr Eyes seem'd to be like those of a pig – theyr Complexion like that of Foul Linnen, they seem'd to have no Teeth & to be Cover'd over with Rags Dirt & Vermin . . . Compared to the Sparkling eyes ivory Teeth, the Shining skin and Remarkable Cleanliness of those I had left Behind – But the most Laughable was, that during all this we never Considered the truly Contemptible Figure that we exibited *our selves* . . . being . . . so much Sunburnt . . . that we look'd exactly like tann'd Leather or dried Parchment, while our hair was mostly become Gray by heat and Fatigue & we were so thin that our Backs seem'd to Stick fast to our Bellies . . . we had perfectly the appearance of Wild people.[56]

Stedman presents not only the "tatterdemalion" Dutch but also the returning soldiers, himself among them, as grotesque, filthy "Wild people" in comparison to Suriname's clean and healthy "indians & Blacks." Dirt, as Mary Douglas's classic anthropological study informs us, is matter out of place. Stedman is once again out of place, now alienated by the European culture that had been his home. The dirt in this passage is clearly intended to carry moral force, the Creoles' cleanliness implying an idealized innocence and closeness to nature. Figuring his own skin as leather or parchment – commodities produced from once-living skin – Stedman reverses the commodification imposed on Suriname's African population. The description's grotesque reversals convey the psychological effects of his return. More than this, however, they mount a satirical critique of a system of relationships among places and people that consumes, commodifies, and sullies all of its participants.

Advocate of slavery but outspoken critic of its cruelties; sympathizing and even identifying with the rebel Maroons as he does his best to wipe them out of existence; cataloguing the riches of colonial capitalism as he admires the virtues of subsistence living – Stedman presents these outrageous self-contradictions in a narrative that is at least as much an account of a cathartic transformation as it is an ideological mystification in the service of the colonial project. The combination of a radically unfamiliar physical ecology and a colonial society in crisis has given us this deeply divided text, almost willfully inconsistent with itself, with its equivocal projections of a European identity struggling to detach from the consequences of its own commitments. A member of colonialism's expendable corps of enforcers, returning alive against all odds, Stedman delivers a disturbingly incoherent glimpse into the human cost of Europe's imperial projects.

CHAPTER 3

Colonial history and Atlantic geography

Natural history informs Stedman's portrait of colonial Suriname as a captive space, made and marred by slavery, the corrosive violence of which pervades even a drawing of a giant snake. Natural history and geography are closely connected as Enlightenment enterprises concerned with place: place as literal habitat and as metaphorical "symptom of rationalizing order," with taxonomy and mapping as parallel ways of putting the world and its creatures in place. Explorers collected new places as naturalists collected new species, but geography served other ends as well. Building and maintaining empires, of course, involves a "struggle over geography," as Edward Said reminds us. Just as important as the "actual geographical possession of land," as postcolonial criticism has long known, is imaginative geography: that is, what Said calls "the accumulation and differentiation of social space."[1]

This chapter traces the struggle over the imaginative geography of the Atlantic Triangle – that is, the nodes of the imperial network that supports Caribbean slavery – through an eventful period in its history. My main texts are influential exemplars of the prose genre of colonial history, a product of what we might call "the colonial Enlightenment." The authors, Edward Long and Bryan Edwards, rank alongside Thomas Jefferson and Moreau de Saint-Méry as what David Brion Davis calls "*philosophes* of the Caribbean" – in other words, "men of the Enlightenment who looked to plantation slavery as the basis of their livelihood." Colonial histories are portraits of places. They consist less of what we would call "history" – a narrative of past events – than of other types of documentation about colonies, including such matters as "geography, meteorology, ethnology, and political economy."[2] Colonial history as a genre has a distinctive agenda. It touts and naturalizes colonies' creation of various types of value, their contribution to the "mother country": economic or financial value, tallied in cultivated acreage and production of tropical commodities, but also aesthetic, scientific, and moral or civilizational value.

Vital to colonial history's work of justifying the colony's value to the nation is imaginative geography: that is, mapping the nodes of the Atlantic Triangle and the relationships among them. These include the fraught relationship between colony and metropole, which looks quite different from Jamaica than from London. The controversial third term in this relationship is, of course, Africa – the source of shiploads of captive laborers who were indispensable (as pro-slavery advocates argued) to colonial prosperity. Building on the long-standing body of work that documents eighteenth-century Britons' knowledge of Africa,[3] I explore colonial historians' creative formal and discursive tactics for justifying the colonies' existence as captive spaces: sites whose topographical, demographic, and cultural configuration served the needs of slave labor and tropical-commodity production.

The terms of this justification shifted with the march of events in those eventful years. Long's *History of Jamaica* defends slavery in 1774 with a confidence, even arrogance, no longer available to Edwards's *History of the West Indies* in 1793, when the abolitionist movement was publishing copious propaganda of its own. Later in that turbulent decade, Edwards published a second and decidedly different book: *A Historical Survey of the French Colony in the Island of St. Domingo* (1797). Here, he records and responds to the event that Davis compares to "the Hiroshima bomb" as a "turning point in history": the massive, bloody insurrection of enslaved Africans that led to the 1804 founding of the Republic of Haiti.[4] This was the planters' worst nightmare come true, and it inevitably transformed British discourse about slavery.

Edwards views the Saint Domingue uprising as a threat and a warning to all white inhabitants of the Caribbean. However, there is one conclusion that he refuses to draw. The insurrection cannot be attributed, he writes, to "the impulse of human nature, groaning under oppression" – that is, to the human agency of the rebels themselves. It was caused, rather, by unwarranted metropolitan interference in colonial affairs: "those hot-brained fanaticks, and detestable incendiaries, who, under the vile pretence of philanthropy... preach up rebellion and murder to the contented and orderly negroes." Blaming the abolitionists (in this case, the French Amis des Noirs), the planter-historian stoutly persists in denying the humanity of his and his fellow planters' human property.[5]

Meanwhile, Toussaint Louverture and his black army proceeded to liberate the richest piece of the colonial Caribbean, opening a space of freedom in the midst of enslavement. The third historian I discuss, Marcus Rainsford, visited Saint Domingue around the time that Edwards's second book was published; he wrote *An Historical Account of the Black Empire of Hayti*

(1805). An Anglo-Irish soldier with a British West India regiment, Rainsford draws a different set of lessons than Edwards from the emergence of the "Black Empire of Hayti." For this soldier-author, "African nature" is not fundamentally different than human nature in general. Postrevolutionary Haiti emerges as a laboratory in which human nature of all complexions has the chance to unfold to its full potential in what Rainsford admiringly calls "a real system of equality."[6]

Slavery and the politics of place to 1772

Before the 1760s, Britain – like the rest of Europe – saw no real public debate over slavery. It was accepted by authoritative opinion in both Europe and the New World, although this acceptance coexisted with a long-standing popular consensus "that the condition of the slave was odious and that slaveholding menaced the liberties of the free-born."[7] This state of affairs persisted throughout the Anglo-American world in the century from 1660 to 1760, as Atlantic slavery and the colonial plantation economy rapidly expanded, generating increasing wealth and power for individuals and the nation. British subjects' sense of themselves as exceptionally and distinctively free had a long history. England, most believed, was ruled by an ancient constitution and a body of common law that accorded each subject due process. Liberty was a national inheritance that the English (and, since 1707, the British) possessed as a highly civilized nation but did not necessarily share with less advanced peoples.[8]

Their need to see themselves as a people uniquely devoted to liberty made it difficult at times for the British to be entirely complacent about slavery in their overseas colonies. However, as Christopher Leslie Brown points out, these very real reservations were not sufficiently compelling to motivate individual or collective action against the institution except in isolated cases. In other words, the powerful private and public interests supporting slavery were not concretely threatened by the traditional British bias in favor of freedom. The "metropolitan investment in the idea of English liberty and the extensive material investment in the institution of slavery" thus existed in continuing tension.[9]

For the metropolitan British, slavery helped to define the difference between America and Europe. Natural history provided a paradigm with its drive to assign each creature to its proper place and to characterize places by their indigenous creatures. "Like the distinctive topography, flora, fauna, and peoples, the institution of human bondage made the New World new," Brown writes. Slavery took hold in the New World well before England gained a colonial foothold there. Therefore, it would have been surprising had English colonists in the Caribbean not imitated their Spanish, Dutch, and French neighbors and used slave labor to cultivate colonial land. Colonial laws relating to slavery, argues Eliga Gould, also contributed to an "image of Britain's Atlantic periphery as a region 'beyond the line,' a zone of conflicting laws where Britons were free to engage in forms of violence that were unacceptable" in Britain proper or the rest of Europe. Although British institutions followed settlers wherever they went, slavery was one of the areas in which the legal pluralism arising from imperial decentralization and colonial autonomy was most pronounced.[10]

The Mansfield Decision highlighted this state of affairs. The events leading up to this legal verdict are fairly well known. After being brought to England and cruelly abused, an enslaved man named James Somerset ran away from his owner. The owner, Charles Stewart, tried to repossess his human property and ship him back to the Caribbean, whereupon the anti-slavery activist Granville Sharp brought suit on Somerset's behalf. In 1772, Lord Mansfield, Chief Justice of the Court of the King's Bench, issued a ruling interpreted by many (despite its ambiguous terms) as declaring slavery illegal on English soil.[11] Up to and including this ruling, attempts by slavery's isolated opponents to limit its effects tended to be spatially defined. Champions of liberty including Sharp showed little interest in challenging the slave system as a whole – the transatlantic network encompassing the merchants and bankers in the British Isles who funded the slave trade, the British manufacturers whose goods slave traders bartered for captives in Africa, and those directly exploiting the enslaved: that is, the planters and merchants in the colonies. Instead, isolated initiatives sought to discourage the expansion of slavery or expel it from a particular jurisdiction. One example is the colony of Georgia, chartered in 1732, whose founder, James Oglethorpe, secured in 1734 a Parliamentary ban on transporting new captives to the colony.[12] The experiment failed but the principle of "not in my backyard" (NIMBY) – as opposed to challenging the entire institution of slavery – retained a lasting appeal.

The planter-historian Edward Long was among those who condemned the Mansfield Decision in print. His *Candid Reflections upon the Judgement Lately Awarded by the Court of the King's Bench, in Westminster-Hall, on What is Commonly Called the Negroe-Cause, by a Planter* appeared later in 1772. The politics of place informed both the court proceedings and Long's scathing response. The strategies used by the defense team that argued Somerset's case and by Long in protesting the Court's decision turn on the NIMBY principle. With the growth of Britain's black population by the 1760s and 1770s, the legality of slaveholding in England became an issue of public controversy. Blacks "made slavery an issue by making themselves a nuisance." Individual captives tried to get out of slavery by being baptized, marrying a free person, or (in the absence of a fugitive-slave law) simply leaving their owners.[13] Unlike colonists, who had the backing of colonial governments in exercising private authority over enslaved people, owners who brought their human property to England could assume no such support. In 1767, Granville Sharp began to make himself a nuisance by assisting enslaved people whose owners – after the captives decamped (or, in one case, after an owner beat and discarded one) – recaptured them, intending to take or send them to the West Indian colonies. Sharp sought a judicial ruling on the status of the enslaved in England; five years later, in the Somerset case, he received it.

The learned members of Somerset's defense team asserted repeatedly, in various ways, that colonial law was not the law of England, and they implored Lord Mansfield to guard the liberty that distinguished England from its overseas possessions. Slavery, they argued – wherever it took place – was merely local, not portable. What if a boatload of wretched galley slaves were to wash up on English shores? Would their owner be allowed to reclaim them? Assuredly not! Mansfield's ruling, when it came, did not exactly clarify the status of slaves on English soil; Brown terms it "Delphic." Contrary to the persistent misconception that the decision abolished slavery on English soil, its applicability was narrowly limited to cases resembling Somerset's. It was now impermissible to take an enslaved person out of England against his or her will. However, the context of the ruling – that is, public concern about the growing number of black people in England – lent credence to its interpretation as an attempt not only to assert English liberty but also to discourage more owners from bringing enslaved people to the British Isles.[14]

One trope turns up repeatedly in the proceedings. A man brought an enslaved person with him from Russia "and would scourge him; for this he was questioned, and it was resolved, That England *was too pure an air for Slaves to breathe in.*" Sergeant William Davy, arguing Somerset's case, rejoins, "That was in the 11th of Queen Elizabeth. . . . I hope, my Lord . . . the air does not blow worse since. But unless there is a change of air, I hope they will never breathe here; for . . . the moment they put their foot on English ground, that moment they become free."[15] Air, as a metonym for climate, draws on medical discourse – in particular, tropical medicine, which cast air as the fundamental medium for fevers. Disease was understood as a geographical phenomenon, integral to the climate or environment of a particular place. Hence, invalids, for example, were prescribed a change of air.[16] In the King's Bench courtroom, however, air metaphorically assumes an ethical dimension: the purity of English air figures England's freedom from the moral pollution of slavery.

Davy makes the medical association explicit when he revisits the trope on the fourth day of arguments (several months later), rebutting the case made by a Mr. Dunning, counsel for Somerset's owner, Charles Stewart. "The air of England, I think . . . has been gradually purifying ever since the reign of Elizabeth. Mr. Dunning seems to have discovered so much, as he finds it changes a slave into a servant; though unhappily he does not think it of efficacy enough to prevent the pestilent disease reviving, the instant the poor man is obliged to quit this . . . country." As a "pestilent disease," slavery belongs, Davy implies, in the colonial tropics, not in temperate England. His argument draws on the geopolitics of climate, the powerful symbolism of which persisted well into the nineteenth century.[17]

One way to address disease is through quarantine. Granville Sharp and Edward Long did not agree on much, but on this they were of one mind: the fewer enslaved people in England, the better. In his first anti-slavery treatise, *A Representation of the Injustice and Dangerous Tendency of Tolerating Slavery, or of Admitting the Least Claim of Private Property in the Persons of Men, in England . . .* (1769), Sharp writes that enslaved people in England are "already much too numerous" and that "the public good seems to require some restraints on the unnatural increase of black subjects." In a 1786 letter, he describes the Mansfield Decision as keeping owners from "bringing with them swarms of Negro attendants into this island."[18] Long is more specific about his reasons for wanting a *cordon sanitaire* around the British Isles. With the influx of enslaved blacks, he writes, "in the course of a few generations . . . the English blood will become so contaminated with this mixture . . . till the whole nation resembles the *Portuguese* and *Moriscos* in complexion of skin and baseness of mind." Such miscegenation, to him, is "a venomous and dangerous ulcer," an "infection" that every family in Britain will eventually contract if some action is not promptly taken. Samuel Estwick, also writing to protest the Mansfield Decision, suggests that Britain should block the importation of enslaved people, as France had done, to "preserve the race of Britons from stain and contamination." Writers on both sides of the issue of slavery can agree, at this point, on a spatial or territorial approach: slavery and the enslaved belong across the Atlantic, safely distant from British soil.[19]

However, Long seems unwilling to separate the colony simply or absolutely from the metropole. His goals require a more complex delineation
of the relationship, balancing continuity with separation. Like Estwick, he
maintains that the law understands the enslaved as not people but rather
property. The "laws of *meum* and *tuum* are alike," he declares, on both
sides of the Atlantic. In this regard, "it is the same as if the lands of both
[Britain and the West Indies] were in one continuity." Rather than prevent
an owner such as Stewart from reclaiming his human property by judicial
fiat, the state ought to buy Somerset and, thus, "by a fair purchase, rather
than I know not what strange efficacy of the English air, redeem his Negroe
from bondage." Long ridicules the defense counsel's trope. Can pure air,
he asks incredulously, really separate a man from his property? Elsewhere
in the pamphlet, however, he asks readers to take seriously the contrasting
climates of Britain and its Caribbean colonies. He argues at length that slavery is necessary in the latter because Europeans cannot labor in a tropical
climate without grave danger to their health. For the defense's inspirational
symbolism, Long substitutes a scientific argument, supplemented with an
economic argument. Because Europeans cannot safely labor in the tropics,
Britain must either give up her colonies and the immense wealth they
generate or allow slavery there.[20]

The gentleman planter and the metropole

The Mansfield Decision – cryptic though it was – seemed to be taking a
spatial approach to the national problem of slavery: it may be acceptable
across the Atlantic but not at home in the British Isles. Long's response
in *Candid Reflections* was to agree with the principle of excluding enslaved
people from Britain but disputed Mansfield's means of achieving that end.
The History of Jamaica, published only two years after the Court's decision,
expands the pro-slavery argument first developed in *Candid Reflections*.
In three lengthy volumes, it polemically describes the island colony in
its relationship to Britain, its "mother state," and Africa, the source of
its planters' human property. Long's opus has much to impart about the
importance of place to the slavery debate.

The *History* is mentioned most often today in connection with race.
Roxann Wheeler analyzes Long's book in her important study of theories
of human variety as they developed in the course of the eighteenth century,
The Complexion of Race. Only late in the century, she demonstrates, was skin
color reified as the primary register of human difference. Wheeler views
the 1770s as a turning point in this process of "refining an increasingly

racialized British identity," and she presents Long as "one of many 1770s texts that contributed" to this process. The biological racism for which the *History* is most notorious, she points out – including polygenesis, the belief that black people were a different species from whites – was a fringe view. It was rejected by most of Long's contemporaries as "improbable – or at least too impolitic to print" – not to mention blasphemous, contradicting the Christian belief in a single creation of humankind.[21]

Wheeler sees this emergent racial ideology, which was to gain increasing traction in the Victorian era, as coexisting in the *History* with a different type of racial ideology. This is Scottish Enlightenment stadial theory, which categorizes peoples or nations by what they do and how they live: the mode of production, from hunting and gathering through modern commercial markets, and the structure and complexity of the society. *The Complexion of Race* makes the initially surprising choice to compare Long to his contemporary Samuel Johnson, whose *Journey to the Western Islands of Scotland* similarly "engage[s] discourses of savagery, consumerism, literacy, and labor" to position Scotland's various populations "in relation to each other and to England," as Long does with the various groups populating Jamaica. Bringing together these two "conflicting views of human differences," Long comes close to contradicting himself on a central point.[22] Are Africans, or "Negroes," essentially different from and inferior to Europeans? Or can their inferiority be remedied through extended contact with members of a superior civilization? Read in light of this "tension between ideologies of skin color and of civil society in the 1770s," Long's *History* offers rich insight into a pivotal moment in the trajectory of racial ideology in imperial Britain.[23] It is not this aspect of his work, however, that is central to my argument.

It is important to remember that the *History* contains much more than its notorious vilification of Africans. It was accepted well beyond its author's lifetime as the standard work on Britain's largest Caribbean colony. Elsa Goveia's historiographical survey concludes, "Long's book is not merely a mine of information. It possesses distinction as historical literature, brilliance as polemical writing, and unsurpassed importance as one of the most interesting social documents left to posterity by any single historian of the British West Indies."[24] This sprawling, encyclopedic work marshals a wide range of information in support of its goals of promoting Jamaica's prosperity and defending slavery. What we would now call "history" takes up comparatively little space. Jamaica's history as a British colony was fairly short, beginning with England's takeover of the island from the Spanish in 1655. The remainder of the *History*'s three volumes presents a comprehensive account of the current state of the colony, showcasing Long's command of the various branches of Enlightenment knowledge from political economy and meteorology to aesthetics (see Chapter 1) and natural history.

All of these disciplines and discourses collude in the service of the author's polemical aims. They do so partly through their careful arrangement in a structure that is part of Long's argument. That argument revolves around the politics of place. The *History*'s representation of the corners of the Atlantic Triangle – Britain, Africa, and Jamaica – and the relationships among them forms the foundation of Long's case in defense of slavery. Should enslaved people be allowed in Britain? Why or why not? Why do the British Caribbean colonies absolutely need enslaved labor to flourish, and why are Africans most suited to perform this labor? Answers emerge from the *History*'s careful characterization of Britain and Africa, as well as Jamaica, deploying Long's broad knowledge in the service of his polemical aims. In this way, *The History of Jamaica* is a prototypical colonial history: it builds a portrait of a place in terms that specify that place's relationships with other places of the Atlantic network.

Britain's presence pervades the *History* as political model, home of liberty – a key concept that Long interprets somewhat idiosyncratically – and cradle of advanced civilization, forming cultivated gentlemen like its author. The *History* presents the island as dependent on the parent state and existing primarily to support it. The first 200 pages detail Jamaica's governmental institutions, based on the British model: governor, council, legislative assembly, courts, public offices, and, importantly, militia. He later presents a "Plan . . . for assimilating the frame of the Legislature in this Colony, nearer to that of *Great-Britain.*" Potential settlers, therefore, could "even in this remote part of the empire, enter into full enjoyment and inheritance of a compleatly British form of government." The more like the metropole the colony becomes in its institutions of government, the happier colonists will be.[25]

Of course, the property they can enjoy there includes other human beings. Long is concerned to preserve for Jamaica and the rest of the West Indies one key area of autonomy: the institution of slavery. To this end, he again argues spatially. He defines liberty – central to British political discourse – as geographically and ethnographically differential. Long's introduction performs an adroit sleight of hand, pivoting between the two types of governance that the *History* tries to balance: Britain's governance of its colony and Jamaican planters' governance of their human property.

When the planters have complained of violations done to their liberty, the enemies of the West-India islands have often retorted upon them the impropriety of their clamoring with so much vehemence for what they deny to so many thousand Negroes, whom they hold in bondage. "Give freedom" (say they) "to others, before you claim it for yourselves." – Servitude, restricted to a particular class of persons, was tolerated both by the *Romans* and *Athenians*: yet no people were ever more jealous of their own liberty; nor did they find their own enjoyment of it at all incompatible with the exclusive obligation to labor imposed on others within a certain limit.

Long's careful wording – "within a certain limit" – and classical references to the Athenians and Romans project a measured, reasonable, respectable version of slavery. Servitude, he continues, "may be permitted with the least disadvantage, both to the master and vassal, in those parts of the world, where it happens to be *inevitably* necessary" (i.e., the tropics). It is this premise that the *History*'s diverse components work so hard to support throughout three volumes. Even in these places, steps must be taken to limit slavery so that it does not "enslave the principal state" by depriving slave owners of the full extent of their British freedom.[26] For the parent state to remain free, in other words, colonists must be as free as possible; however, their most prized freedom is their right to keep thousands enslaved. This argument appears convoluted unless we accept Long's central premise about the geographical necessity of slavery in certain parts of the world.

Long's rhetorical strategy in this passage is compatible with the gentlemanly persona he projects. This persona, or *ethos* – that is, the author as colonial gentleman – is absolutely central to the book's polemical aim of defending slavery.[27] Some conventional elements of Long's ethos are set up in his introduction: modesty, for example, and public spirit. More significant, however, is the breadth of knowledge displayed throughout the book. Its encyclopedic format shows off a multifaceted intellect, or at least an ability to comprehend and compile knowledge of diverse kinds. As important as broad knowledge to Long's gentlemanly ethos is taste – that is, the ability to appreciate beauty and art – demonstrated in the *History*'s "virtual tour" of the island's scenic beauties. Also showcased is the time it takes to produce these massive volumes: the leisure that Long enjoyed in England for the last four decades or so of his life, funded by the vast acreage and numerous enslaved people owned by his planter clan. By displaying his laboriously assembled, multidisciplinary knowledge about the island and his elite education and exquisite taste, the author of the *History of Jamaica* bids for credibility and prestige as the epitome of the gentleman.

Born in Cornwall, England, in 1734, Edward Long was educated at Bury St. Edmunds School before entering Gray's Inn to study law in 1753. He spent only 12 years on the island of Jamaica, from his father's death in 1757 until 1769. His marriage to the heiress Mary Ballard Beckford, widow of John Palmer, connected him to the fabulously wealthy Beckford-Ballard-Palmer family group, which in 1750 owned at least 44,670 acres of Jamaica (as of 1775, approximately one million acres of the island were cultivated). Long served as Chief Judge of the island's Vice-Admiralty Court; was elected a member of its Assembly for the Parish of Saint Ann in 1761, 1765, and 1766; and served briefly as Speaker in 1768. The remainder of his life he passed, according to his tombstone, "in literary retirement" in England with his wife, children, and grandchildren.[28]

It was England, not Jamaica, where Long wrote his *History*. Commentators agreed that Jamaica "was not a propitious environment for cultivating the life of the mind." Anglo-Jamaicans were indolent by nature, more inclined to the pleasures of the table (and the bed) than those of the intellect.[29] In his introduction, Long writes sarcastically:

> They who in general visit this island do not emigrate for the purpose of compiling histories, but avowedly that of accumulating money; which being their chief employment while they continue to reside in it, we cannot expect that any one person should of himself find leisure sufficient for bringing together the many things required to form so perfect a structure; or that he can reap much assistance from others, who regard it only as a temporary abode, and have no incentive to know any thing further about it, except in what relates to their immediate occupation.[30]

The comment invokes the discourse of civic humanism, for which hands-on, day-to-day involvement in one specialized occupation disqualifies a man from achieving the detached perspective needed to form valid political judgments.[31] Only property-owning, educated, leisured gentlemen can achieve such a perspective and thus are qualified to govern. They are found, Long implies, "in general" not in Jamaica but rather in England, where he resided when he wrote his book. Planters made money in the colony so that they could return to the British Isles and enjoy their leisure with access to types of culture unavailable – or at least scarce – in Jamaica. One could be a Jamaican patriot, as Long certainly was, from across the Atlantic.[32]

Britain, then, appears in the *History of Jamaica* as the locus of higher learning, model of political organization, and home of liberty. The book's deferential attitude to the "mother state" is tempered by its learned author's insistence on slavery as the basis of Jamaica's contribution to that state. If the "enemies of the West-India islands" attack slavery, Long is prepared to support it, using cutting-edge economic and scientific information. Patriotically taking stock of a prized colonial possession with a view to preserve and improve it, the *History* surveys its institutions, topography, and population. In pursuit of his aim, the historian mines the discursive resources of Enlightenment knowledge.

"Guiney, or Negro-Land"

Prominent among those resources was natural history. This colonial science, as discussed in Chapter 2, was essential to tropical agribusiness. Bioprospecting botanists identified potential cash crops so that specimens could be transported to botanical gardens for propagation and experimentation. Long, always the booster, used his *History* to promote the imperialism of improvement. Jamaicans were making a collective effort to improve their colony: in 1767, they organized "a patriotic society, for improving the productions and commerce of the island, and extending the cultivation of its lands." A book like "Mr. Home's useful little tract upon soils," Long writes, may "shew the necessity of rescuing this art [agriculture] from . . . the shackles of antiquated prejudices; it may also prove how much this pursuit stands in need of the aid of natural philosophy, chemistry, and some other branches of polite science, to bring it still nearer towards perfection." Aligned with science and progress against ignorance and prejudice, the historian of Jamaica advocated for practical Enlightenment in a colonial setting.[33] Indeed, most of the *History*'s third volume is taken up by "*A SYNOPSIS of Vegetable and other Productions of this Island, proper for Exportation, or Home Use and Consumption. Of Exotics, cultivable for one or other of these Purposes; and of its noxious and useful Animals, &c.*" This exhaustive list of Jamaica's plant and animal species begins, of course, with the most profitable: "SUGAR CANE – *Arundo Saccarifera.*"

"Polite science" succinctly yokes Long's scientific pursuits to the gentlemanly persona he cultivates. As natural history gradually moved from courts and noblemen's curio cabinets into the salons, coffeehouses, provincial academies, museums, botanical gardens, and government-sponsored expeditions of the eighteenth century, the meaning of polite science shifted toward the application of natural knowledge to national improvement. This took networks of scientific communication and specimen transport – networks to which Long's *History* also aimed to contribute. Volume 3 provides "useful directions for the transportation of plants and seeds from one country to another" – transcribed from a pamphlet by John Ellis, Esquire,

Fellow of the Royal Society – and recommends that Jamaica establish its own botanical garden, which it did not long after the *History* was published. Long's contemporary, Sir Joseph Banks – who accompanied Cook as a naturalist on his first voyage (1768–71) – became a pioneer in transporting flora and fauna among far-flung parts of the empire. As President of the Royal Society (1778–1820), Banks was the "shadowy impresario of Britain's colonial expansion," dispatching explorers and collecting, classifying, and disseminating data and specimens. Perhaps the most famous example is the Bligh expedition that brought breadfruit from the Pacific to the Caribbean on the second attempt (the first was foiled by an inopportune mutiny).[34] Banks's career epitomizes the imperial enterprise of which Long's *History* aspired to be a part.

Yet the most crucial purpose to which Long turns natural history is the defense of slavery. His detailed ethnography of the island's inhabitants demands that he leave Jamaica, taking readers on a virtual journey across the Atlantic. The destination is "Guiney, or Negro-Land"; the underlying assumption is that Africans' nature is tied to their habitat or place of origin. Therefore, they can be characterized by relying on travel writers, who have observed them on their native ground, and natural historians, who have inserted these data into taxonomic schemes. This chapter is the most erudite of the *History*, replete with citations to travel writers on Africa and other areas – including India, China, and North and South America – and thinkers such as Monboddo, Montesquieu, Beattie, and Hume.

If Long's expansive display of learning contributes to his ethos or persona, the foil to that self-image is the image of Africans that he projects. He denies to Africans everything that Europeans value most about themselves. Africans, he asserts, lack "genius," "civility," "science," "moral sensations," self-discipline, and the ability to appreciate beauty. "Their houses are miserable cabbins. They conceive no pleasure from the most beautiful parts of their country, preferring the more sterile."[35] Most damning of all, Africans lack taste – the crowning ornament of Long's gentlemanly persona. Here, we have identity construction as the political process of drawing boundaries around a group by contrasting it with another group. The gentleman planter's identity is defined against the comprehensive negation that is the African character.

Following this broad denunciation, Long turns to natural history to support his belief that Africans are a different species of the same genus as Europeans.[36] His next move is explicitly spatial: mapping the variation in human intellect – those "gradations" crucial to his version of the Chain of Being – onto the African continent by taking his readers on a virtual tour of Africa, mirroring the much fuller tour of Jamaica in Volume 2. We move from north (closest to Europe) to south (farthest away). In the north, we meet "the Moors, a race of tawny men, who possess many vices, and some virtues; they are acute, industrious, and carry on trade and manufactures." Descending the west coast, we pass the "Jaloffs [Wolofs or Oulofs], Phulis, and Mandingo Blacks," thought by some travelers to be "amiable," less so by others. Moving southward through the grain, ivory, gold, and slave coasts, occupied by "petty Negroe states, whose character is nearly uniform, and who scarcely deserve to be ranked with the human species," we finally reach Angola and Benguela. These regions, Long reports, are populated by the Giagas, whom he compares to "the Goths and Vandals of Europe": a "barbarous race, hardened in idolatry, wallowers in human blood, cannibals, drunkards, practiced in lewdness, oppression, and fraud; proud and slothful, cursed with all the vices that can degrade human nature, possessing no one good quality, and in short more brutal and savage than the wild beasts of the forest." Moralizing geographical space, Long surveys the map of Africa in support of his contention that Africans – at their worst – are the absolute opposite of civilized Europeans.[37]

Lurid reports of African cannibalism would be useful to Long's heirs in the slavery debates of the 1780s and 1790s, in which pro-slavery propaganda occasionally took the form of travel writing.[38] The defense of the slave trade as a rescue operation – that is, relocating Africans from their barbarous home to the New World and "a condition comparable with the peasantry of Europe" – was standard throughout the first half of the eighteenth century, and Long uses it as well. However, his sources on the man-eating Giagas were severely dated: secondary works that rely on Battell's sixteenth-century and Ogilby's seventeenth-century accounts, without modern corroboration. Moreover, even if we concede the existence of cannibalism in Africa, its pertinence to Long's case for slavery would depend on another premise that sits uneasily with his central natural-historical argument about the gradation of species.[39]

If blacks were a different and inferior species, then their improvability – their potential for moving from savagery to civilization – should be quite limited if, indeed, they were improvable at all. However, justifying slavery as rescue seems to depend on Africans' potential to change or improve – that is, their mental and moral capacity. In Africa, Long asserts, "they remain at this time in the same rude situation in which they were found two thousand years ago." Brought to Jamaica, however, Africans' "savage manners" can mend through contact with a more civilized people, especially if they are "imported young." Their island-born progeny benefit even more. "Negroes . . . born and trained up" in the colonies "have appeared more humanized than their ancestors."[40] By introducing Africans to civilized society, Long suggests, slavery initiates a process of cultural change. However, this casts doubt on his assertions of static racial difference elsewhere in the *History*. Long's book is subject to charges of self-contradiction on this key point, although he does posit inherent limits to black attainment (e.g., in his sneering sketch of that Enlightenment "guinea pig," the Jamaican schoolmaster and poet Francis Williams).[41]

Goatish embraces

At the third corner of the Atlantic Triangle – Jamaica – Britain and Africa meet in the colonists and their slaves. Long's entire opus is devoted to substantiating the colony's value for the mother country through multiple registers: topographical, aesthetic, scientific, agricultural, and – above all – economic. His greatest challenge is attempting to describe the coexistence of these deracinated populations in Jamaican slave society. A more recent commentator, Edward (Kamau) Brathwaite in *The Development of Creole Society in Jamaica* (1971), views white racism as the central obstacle to the emergence of a new society creatively adapted to its New World setting:

> Here, in Jamaica, fixed within the dehumanizing institution of slavery, were two cultures of people, having to adapt themselves to a new environment and to each other. The friction created by this confrontation was cruel, but it was also creative. [W]hite . . . institutions . . . reflect one aspect of this. The slaves' adaptation of their African culture to a new world reflects another. The failure of Jamaican society was that it did not recognize these elements of its own creativity.[42]

Long's refusal of creative Creolization appears most emblematically in his uncomfortable handling of interracial sex. White and black, he writes, are "two tinctures which nature has dissociated, like oil and vinegar." As he catalogs the island's inhabitants, Long praises the planters for their spirit, charm, and hospitality. However, he cannot conceal their faults, including laziness and self-indulgence, particularly in the area of sex. They are not always, he tactfully admits, "the most chaste and faithful of husbands." More alarming, when they stray, it is almost always across the color line that is so central to the *History*'s ideological agenda. Men "of every rank, quality and degree here," he writes, "would much rather riot in these goatish embraces, than share the pure and lawful bliss derived from matrimonial, mutual love." He rationalizes his instinctive revulsion against interracial sex, apparent in this bestial figure, with forthright argument. It would be better for both England and Jamaica, he opines, if white colonial men would leave the black women alone and marry white ladies. The colony would not be burdened with "spurious offspring of different complexions," a "tawney breed."[43]

More to the point (Long was, after all, a lawyer), with less interracial sex, planters would not have illegitimate half-caste children to whom they could leave property. "A subject . . . in Jamaica ought not to bequeath his whole personal estate which may be very considerable, to a slave; and, if he should do so, it is easy to conceive that it would be utterly repugnant to the civil policy of that island." Interracial sex leads to the interracial transfer of property and power: alarming, indeed. "It is a question easily answered," Long declares, "whether . . . it would be more for the interest of Britain, that Jamaica should be possessed and peopled by white inhabitants, or by Negroes and Mulattos?"[44] One of the *History*'s main aims, as a piece of colonial propaganda, was to attract more white settlers to an island the population of which was seen as dangerously out of balance (i.e., enslaved black people outnumbered whites by as many as ten to one at the time that Long was writing).

Reluctantly acknowledging the prevalence of interracial sex in the colony, Long warns white Jamaican men against the long-term consequences of acting out their masculinity through sexual mastery. However, as Wheeler diplomatically states, "inserting planters into acceptable notions of English masculinity proved difficult."[45] Sexual activity and the subordination and possession of women certainly formed part of one enduring model of masculine identity. However, the control of passion – in particular, sexual self-control – defined a competing model of masculinity increasingly prevalent in the eighteenth century.[46] Long tries to blame interracial sex on the "cajolements" of the "African mistress," using the stereotype of the oversexed African woman to shift attention away from planters' misbehavior.[47]

However, he does not blame only the concubines. He also cites the deficient attractions of white Creole women, due to their "constant intercourse from their birth with Negroe domestics, whose drawling, dissonant gibberish they insensibly adopt, and with it no small tincture of their aukward carriage and vulgar manners." White women who are "negroefied" by too much social "intercourse" with the enslaved cause white men to turn from them to another kind of intercourse with theirs.[48] Sexual and cultural intermixture – the hybridity that for many theorists typifies the Caribbean region – causes Long great difficulty in his efforts to rationalize the colonial social order. His pro-slavery politics of place drives him to present the colonists as fundamentally British and their captives as African: different species, at home in widely separated regions, able to coexist on the island only in a strict hierarchy. However, interracial intercourse disturbs this coexistence, putting the "traditional sexual prerogative of ruling-class men . . . at odds with good governance and island security," revealing the white Creoles' difficulty in governing themselves as well as others.[49]

Black and white Jamaicans, after all, are not fundamentally opposite. Both groups enjoy sex in ways that impede Long's aspirations for the colony. Elsewhere, however, as Wheeler points out, the *History* proposes ways to integrate the products of the planters' "goatish embraces" into a thriving colonial society. Mulattos should be enfranchised at birth, educated, and enlisted in the island militia as "orderly subjects, and faithful defenders of the country." In this vision, mixed-race Jamaicans would function as a "model minority," a "buffer group" to help contain and regulate colonial heterogeneity. They should even be freed: "I can foresee no mischief . . . from the enfranchisement of every mulatto child." Apprenticed to trades, paid a modest wage, mulattos and free blacks "will gradually strive for conveniencies, and . . . even for superfluities." Selling services and consuming goods, contributing to the island economy and to its defense, they would share – as subordinates, of course – in British civility. "This dynamic vision of Creole inhabitants," Wheeler observes, "contradicts the static conception of race" evident in assertions such as Long's implausible claim that two mulattos, like mules, will fail to reproduce.[50]

As the *History of Jamaica* elaborates the imaginative geography of the Atlantic Rim in the service of slavery, it builds on spatial strategies deployed by both sides early in the slavery controversy. As previously discussed, Long runs into problems at each corner of the Atlantic Triangle. Striving to reconcile slaveholding with British liberty, to present Africans as redeemable barbarians, and to come to terms with colonial racial intermixture, the planter-historian becomes tangled in successive contradictions. A stop on Volume 2's "virtual tour" of the island figures the difficulties that plague Long's politics of place.

One "celebrated curiosity" he visits is a cave. Many writers on Jamaica mention caves as a characteristic topographical feature of the island, often as the retreat of runaway slaves. William Beckford's *Descriptive Account of the Island of Jamaica*, for example, calls caves "the refuge and asylum of runaway negroes." Like forests, swamps, mountains, and Jamaica's rugged cockpit country, caves were regarded (with good reason) as havens for rebellion. "Runaways . . . mastered these natural retreats in a way that colonial authorities, and even their black rangers, could not."[51] In Stedman's narrative, Suriname's forests are a natural refuge for the Maroons, and the swamps provide a tactical advantage over their pursuers. The Virginia planter William Byrd writes similarly of North America's Great Dismal Swamp, as does the planter-historian Bryan Edwards of Jamaica's mountains. These are places that stubbornly elude colonial control, allowing runaways to hide, regroup, and – on occasion – strike back.

To tame this threatening space, Long's tactics include repeated allusions to European high culture. The arched cave entrance recalls Gothic architecture, with a niche perfect for a Madonna and a font for holy water. Crawling into an inner chamber, he turns from geology to aesthetics: the walls and ceiling, "covered with stalactic and sparry matter," reflect the torchlight in a "rich and splendid appearance." A stalagmite reminds him of a hermit; he draws a face on it with a bit of charcoal, comparing his style (tongue in cheek) to that of "Roubillac, the rival of nature." Theseus's labyrinth makes a predictable appearance, but the master trope is, of course, the epic visit to the underworld. Long turns from citing Virgil – "*Spelunca alta fuit* [deep the cavern lies]" – back to science: the soil is "a *congeries* of bat dung" most likely "impregnated with nitre" (i.e., fertilizer for the improving planter). This sequence, which showcases Long's erudition, ends with another Gothic image: "it is supposed that run-away Negroes were not unacquainted with so convenient a hiding-place."[52] Insubordination by the enslaved haunts the *History* even at its most erudite moments. If colonialism turns on the control of space, Jamaica's caves symbolize the ways that New World topography helps captive Africans to elude and resist such control. *The History of Jamaica*'s imaginative map of the Atlantic Rim cannot fully assimilate this stubbornly local feature.

Long's encyclopedic work opens Britain's decades of bitter debate over slavery with a comprehensive rhetorical strategy. The gentleman planter orchestrates key sectors of the new Enlightenment division of knowledge – aesthetics, natural history, and geography – as facets of his formidable erudition. The *History of Jamaica* needs the distorted account of Africa at its center (presented as cutting-edge science) to offset the display of colonial civilization in the remainder of the book. Couching the contrast between civilization and barbarity in spatial terms, the pro-slavery propagandist renders the transatlantic economic network as a moralized map. Abolitionist writers, needless to say, saw matters differently.

Abolitionist geography

Much changed for Britain and its Caribbean colonies in the two decades between the publication of Edward Long's and Bryan Edwards's colonial histories. The loss of the American colonies, which Long had feared, severed Jamaica's trade connections to most of North America, forcing the colony into greater self-sufficiency but also causing widespread starvation among enslaved people throughout the West Indies, whose owners had not prepared for this contingency. The 1780s also saw the founding of SEAST in 1787. Its members, among them the redoubtable Granville Sharp, included Quakers and others with evangelical leanings. The Quakers petitioned Parliament against the slave trade in 1783, supported by the reformist Society for Constitutional Information. Sharp, alerted by Olaudah Equiano, also called public attention to the horrific proceedings aboard the slave ship *Zong*, whose captain ordered 133 captives thrown overboard and drowned so as to collect insurance on the lost "cargo."[53]

With the founding of SEAST, slave-trade abolition "moved to the center of British political life and set the pattern for a novel type of reform movement."[54] Extra-Parliamentary participation included the massive nationwide petition drives that helped to expand the bounds of the political nation.[55] Other tactics ranged from public lectures by abolitionists (including Equiano's book tour of the British Isles) to the sale of medallions, jewelry, and other items (e.g., Wedgwood pottery) displaying the famous icon of a kneeling man in chains. A campaign to abstain from slave-grown sugar drew widespread support, particularly by women turning their power over the domestic sphere to political use.[56] Books and pamphlets, of course, were central to abolitionists' massive effort to educate and persuade their fellow Britons. Along with the writings of formerly enslaved authors, including Equiano and Ottobah Cugoano, and former slave traders such as John Newton, the abolitionist movement reissued the American Quaker Anthony Benezet's *A Short Account of that Part of Africa, Inhabited by the Negroes* (1762) as *Some Historical Account of Guinea* (1788). Another influential entry was Thomas Clarkson's *Essay on the Slavery and Commerce of the Human Species* (1788). With these publications, the anti-slavery movement embraced the politics of place.

Long's moralized map of the Atlantic Rim presented Britain as the height of civilization, Africa as its barbaric opposite, and the Caribbean colonies as the triumphant spread of British culture across the seas. Benezet and Clarkson also made rhetorical use of Atlantic geography but in a decidedly different way. Their mental map contradicts that of slavery's defenders, correcting their skewed view of Africa: rather than draw them closer, it aims to separate the colonies and their slaveholding inhabitants from metropolitan British subjects. The abolitionists' account of the Atlantic Triangle is a spatiotemporal schema in which geography and history intersect: Britain and Africa occupy different points on the same historical track of progress toward higher civilization. The ancestors of the British were savages who, as Benezet states, "brother with brother, and parents with children, had wives in common . . . [a] greater barbarity than any heard of amongst the Negroes." Since then, of course, Britain has reached the height of civilization, and Africans are capable of doing likewise in the fullness of time. They are already industrious, honest, and strict in their morality.[57]

In essence, Benezet's book was a compilation from the fairly extensive archive of travel accounts circulating by mid-century in collections by Churchill (1704, 1744–46) and Astley (1745–47). Written by men who had been there, such as slave traders, sea captains, physicians, and naturalists, these books document in abundant detail African agriculture, trade, material culture, family life, social and political organization, and religion.[58] Of course, anti-slavery writers were selective in their use of these sources. Benezet's pastoral vision emphasizes the "innocent simplicity" that Africans retain, despite the bad influence of intruding Europeans. Africans' improvability – their susceptibility to positive influence and capacity for progress – is a tenet shared (as I have noted) albeit ambivalently, by Long's otherwise contrasting vision of the continent.

The only impediment to Africans' development, from the abolitionists' perspective, is slavery, the renewal of which (after the abolition of medieval European serfdom) puts the progress of civilization at risk. Clarkson's dramatized rendering of coastal Africa in the age of the slave trade "came to dominate representations of Africa and the slave experience in the poetry, novels and political literature" of the 1780s and 1790s.[59] He asks his readers to imagine watching a "train of wretched slaves," chained together in pairs, pass by on their way to the waiting ships. In Clarkson's scenario, a "melancholy African" narrates "the history of some of the unfortunate people" – their homes, their families, and the misfortunes that landed them in captivity. However, it was not only Africa – in the abolitionist scheme of things – that was damaged by the slave trade. Slavery, writes Benezet, threatened to "reduce those countries which support and encourage it, but more immediately those parts of America which are in the practice of it, to the ignorance and barbarity of the darkest ages." The Caribbean colonies appear in his book as degenerate zones the sinfulness of which puts them outside the normal scheme of progress and at risk of reversion to savagery.

Avarice perverts the rule of law and depraves the white masters, making them idle and debilitated as well as cruel.[60]

Both Benezet and Clarkson do their best to obscure the connection between colony and metropole and the constant circulation of resources and people that sustains it. Their abolitionist rhetoric, dependent on an ideal of British liberty, needs to posit colonial slavery as an aberration and distance it spatially as well as morally from British soil. Benezet poses it as a conundrum: "It is a matter of astonishment how a people, who as a nation, are looked upon as generous and humane, and so much value themselves for their uncommon sense of the benefit of liberty, can live in the practice of such extreme oppression and inhumanity, without feeling the inconsistency of such conduct, and feeling great remorse."[61]

Clarkson dramatizes the paradox in an imaginary dialogue between the author and an "intelligent African." "What is *Christianity*," asks the African rhetorically, "but a system of *murder* and *oppression?*" Clarkson replies:

> [T]he people against whom you so justly declaim, are not *Christians*. They are *infidels*. They are *monsters*. They are out of the common course of nature. Their countrymen at home are generous and brave. They support the sick, the lame, and the blind. They fly to the succor of the distressed. They have noble and stately buildings for the sole purpose of benevolence. They are in short, of all nations the most remarkable for humanity and justice.[62]

To deny slavery's economic and cultural integration into the mainstream of British life is to make it easier for the British people to renounce it and feel good about themselves for doing so. The abolitionists thus re-drew Long's map of the Atlantic, asserting metropolitan British subjects' moral distance from the slaveholding colonists whose livelihood they attacked.

Meanwhile, political agitation gathered momentum in and outside Parliament. In 1788, Sir William Dolben successfully sponsored a bill to regulate the slave trade by limiting the number of captives a ship could transport in proportion to its total burden – possibly a tactic to derail abolitionist agitation. The next year, Wilberforce introduced his first resolution against the slave trade, but his opponents obtained a postponement of the vote until Parliament could hold more hearings. The disadvantage for the pro-slavery faction was the publicity that the hearings generated for evidence about the slave trade presented by SEAST and others. The "West India interest" in the House of Commons was robust, however, and the slave trade had powerful backers in the House of Lords and at court, including George III and his brother, the Duke of Clarence (later William IV).

Debate finally resumed in early 1791, with Prime Minister William Pitt speaking in favor of the bill, although he declined to make it a government measure. The bill failed, 163 to 88.[63]

Nationwide abolitionist activity continued, with stacks of petitions delivered to Parliament: a total of 519 from England and Scotland in 1792, which contained between 380,000 and 400,000 signatures (only adult men could sign). "The parliamentary debates on abolition in 1789 and 1791 had appeared to open a breach in the stony façade of the ruling oligarchy," in Blackburn's words; "radicals and reformers of all descriptions sought to press the advantage." Meanwhile, however, the French Revolution had Britain's imperial rival in turmoil. France's most profitable colony, Saint Domingue, was in the grip of a massive slave revolt beginning in 1791. The argument that slave-trade abolition would strengthen competitor nations became less persuasive. It was in no one's interest, abolitionists could urge, to bring increasing numbers of "raw and hostile captives" from Africa, further destabilizing Caribbean slave societies. The international situation was growing more hospitable to abolition, although this sentiment would not last. As the French Revolution gathered momentum, conservatives increasingly could present any type of reform initiative as "tantamount to a threat to stability and the preservation of civilized life in Britain."[64]

"I have been myself an eye-witness"

Bryan Edwards was at work on his *History, Civil and Commercial, of the British Colonies in the West Indies*, published in 1793, during the most eventful years of the abolition debate. Like Long's *History of Jamaica*, Edwards's *History* had as a central aim the defense of the sugar colonies and their political interests to metropolitan readers. However, times had changed substantially in two decades and Edwards crafted his appeal accordingly. The moderate, "enlightened" tone of his *History* is unquestionably more typical of mainstream pro-slavery opinion than the extreme white-supremacist views represented by Long. Like the majority of writers on both sides of the slave-trade debate, Edwards was an ameliorationist, who urged gradual reform rather than precipitous abolition of the trade, much less emancipation.[65] As a spokesman for the plantocracy, he is pragmatic, mindful that the upsurge of humanitarian sympathy for the enslaved had put slave owners on the defensive. According to Goveia's *Historiography of the British West Indies*, Edwards also was genuinely humane, possessing "independence of mind," "intelligence and integrity," and a surprising degree of objectivity. None of this changed his need to rationalize slavery and to harness a prevalent mythology of "African character" to that end.[66]

Also like Long, Edwards embedded his defense of slavery in an impressive intellectual edifice. The "scope of his work is large, and much of it not directly concerned with the matter of enslavement."[67] In addition to narrating what we would now call "history," Edwards intervened in an important debate in natural history, weighing in on the impact of environment on animals, people, and cultures. He disagreed with the famous French naturalist Buffon's claim that the New World produced inferior, degenerate animals and humans. He argued his case using detailed information on the physical geography of the islands – the size of trees, the variety of birds and exotic fruits – and challenged the idea that the American environment produced fewer species than the Old World. In 1774, Edwards was elected a Fellow of the American Philosophical Society, based in Philadelphia – a credential proudly inscribed on the title page of his *History*. Its publication resulted in his election as a Fellow of the Royal Society, proclaimed on the title page of the second edition.[68]

David Brion Davis's classic *The Problem of Slavery in the Age of Revolution* groups Edwards with Thomas Jefferson and Moreau de Saint-Méry of Saint Domingue as "Philosophes of the Caribbean": "the pre-eminent statesmen-intellectuals of their respective slaveholding societies," "cosmopolitan men of the Enlightenment." Intensely curious and well read, the three shared "a passion for measurement and for specific information on geography, meteorology, ethnology, and political economy." Olwen Blouet summarizes the similarities between Edwards and Jefferson: "Although sharing a humanitarian sensibility, they ultimately protected the institution of slavery.... They hoped slavery would wither away."[69] Edwards's persona in his *History*, like Long's in his, is the colonial gentleman: highly educated, tasteful, and public-spirited, celebrating his beloved colony in terms calculated to impress the metropolitan elite.

Edwards was a Creole, spending most of his adult life in Jamaica. His father's death in 1756 left his mother a widow with six children. A wealthy uncle, Zachary Bayly, invited the teenager to help him manage his sugar plantations. He arrived in Jamaica in 1759, immediately before one of the island's bloodiest slave uprisings: Tacky's Revolt, in which 30 to 40 whites were slaughtered – events that Edwards dramatically narrates in the *History*. It was clearly a formative experience. The rebellion started on the plantation next to his uncle's; Bayly was central in mobilizing island whites to fight back, as Edwards notes in an emotional tribute. Edwards later entered local politics, joining the Jamaican Assembly in 1765. On Bayly's death in 1769, he inherited several plantations and became one of the richest men on the island, owning approximately 1,500 enslaved people.[70]

Edwards went on to contest colonial politics in the metropole, beginning with a trip to London in 1774 to try to persuade the Board of Trade to allow the Jamaican Assembly to regulate the slave trade (he failed). He joined forces with the West India Committee, the planters' and merchants' lobby. His next sojourn in England began in 1782, when he tried to get elected to Parliament (he failed) and protested the imperial prohibition on trade between the West Indies and the United States. These experiences taught Edwards "that London did not understand the needs of distant colonies."[71] Back in Jamaica in the late 1780s, he faced the planters' next major political fight. The anti-slavery movement was on the rise, promoting slave-trade abolition. A speech that Edwards made in 1789 to a joint conference of the Jamaican legislature colorfully responds to "Mr. Wilberforce's Propositions in the House of Commons, Concerning the Slave Trade." He begins by conceding that Wilberforce's account of the slave-trade's effects on Africa is correct. "Sir, the whole, or greatest part, of that immense continent is a field of warfare and desolation; a wilderness, in which the inhabitants are wolves towards each other." However, the abolitionists' solution is the wrong one. Protesting that "I am no friend to slavery in any shape, or under any modification," Edwards nonetheless maintains that abolishing the slave trade would not help Africa and would squander "the vast advantages which have accrued to the trade, navigation, and revenues of Great Britain, from the settlement of this and the rest of the sugar islands."[72]

At the center of his case is geography. Edwards attacks the abolitionists for combining ignorance with arrogance, purveying inaccurate information about places they have never been. "Mr. Clarkson, a Clergyman of the Church of England . . . though he has never visited either Africa or the West Indies, professes to have acquired a more extensive and intimate knowledge both of the manner in which the Slave Trade is conducted on the Coast, and of the treatment which the negroes meet with at sea and in the Sugar Islands, than is possessed either by the African merchant, or the West-Indian planter," Edwards sneers. Clarkson's information, he argues, is ludicrously out of date, drawing on Anthony Benezet and Granville Sharp, who in turn cite Hans Sloane's account, published in 1707 and 1727 but based on travels in the previous century: "the stale crimes and violences of lawless men in the days of Charles II are cited as a just representation of our present laws, manners, and dispositions. . . . Does Mr. Clarkson mean to charge the present inhabitants with the guilt of the Buccaneers?" In the course of a century, Edwards claims, West Indian manners – in particular, the treatment of the enslaved – have changed and continue to change for the better.[73]

Amelioration is a central theme in Edwards's *History* as well. The chapter on slave life in the West Indies (ornamented with Agostino Brunias's picturesque "Negro Festival . . . on the Island of St. Vincent") gives an optimistic picture of plantation conditions. The slave quarters, or "cottages of the Negroes," he writes, "sometimes exhibit a pleasing and picturesque appearance." They may not seem like "very tolerable habitations" to an "untraveled Englishman," but "they far excel the cabins of the Scotch and Irish peasants, as described by Mr. Young, and other travelers." Edwards cites recent acts by colonial legislatures in Jamaica and Grenada, creating a "*council of protection*" and "*guardians of the slaves*," respectively. He continues by presenting his own "schemes . . . for further meliorating the condition of the slaves," including setting work quotas, paying workers for extra labor, and "instituting a sort of juries among them for the trial of petty offences." The latter, he opines, would "operate powerfully toward their civilization and improvement." Edwards's tone is humane and condescending – in the positive eighteenth-century sense of the word – generously deigning to take an interest in the welfare of those of a lower station. He is at pains to present slavery as part of a global civilizing process in which Britain plays an important role. The "age itself," he proclaims, "is hourly improving in humanity: and . . . this improvement visibly extends beyond the Atlantick."[74]

The rhetoric of the *History* is conciliatory, sensitive to the growing power of Edwards's abolitionist opponents. The "Preliminary Observations" to his chapter "Of Negroes in a State of Slavery" concede a great deal to the abolitionist position. He begins:

> The progress of my work has now brought me to the contemplation of human nature in its most debased and abject state; – to the sad prospect of 450,000 reasonable beings (in the English islands only) in a state of barbarity and slavery; of whom – I will not say the major part, but – great numbers assuredly, have been torn from their native country and dearest connections, by means which no good mind can reflect upon but with sentiments of disgust, commiseration, and sorrow![75]

To call the enslaved "reasonable beings," even if currently "in a state of barbarity," distances Edwards from a polygenist position like Long's. On the matter of race, the *History* is equivocal, happy to "blur the border between cultural and essential difference." The "good mind" that reflects on this unfortunate state of affairs is both Edwards's and the (metropolitan) reader's; together, they occupy the ethical high ground on the issue of slavery. In Boulukos's words, "Whatever the guilt of slave traders, planters are left to deal with the reality of slavery, and their efforts toward amelioration show the properly moral approach."[76]

Edwards continues by more specifically addressing the current political controversy over the slave trade:

> I am not unapprised of the danger I incur at this juncture *(a)* in treating the subject of African Slavery, and the Slave Trade. By endeavouring to remove those wild and ill-founded notions which have been long encouraged by misinformed writers in Great Britain, to the prejudice of the inhabitants of the British Sugar Islands, I am conscious that I shall be exposed to all that "bitterness and wrath, and anger and clamour, and evil-speaking and malice," with which it has long been popular to load the unfortunate slave-holder: yet nothing is more certain than that the Slave Trade may be very wicked, and the planters in general very innocent. By far the greatest part of the present inhabitants of the British West Indies came into possession of their plantations by inheritance or accident.[77]

The footnote reads, "*(a)* Alluding to the petitions depending in parliament (1791) for an abolition of the Slave Trade." Although the anti-slavery movement is "popular," its leaders are "misinformed," spreading "wild and ill-founded notions" that harm "innocent" planters. The planters and the British public, Edwards implies, actually share the same interests. Were it not for the misinformation spread by agitators, the two groups would be able to agree on a solution to the problem of slavery. Britain and the West Indies – at least their white colonists – form an axis of civility on Edwards's pro-slavery map.

Edwards's own contribution to the slavery debate, he emphasizes, is place-based. To readers in Britain, ignorant of the colonies (e.g., the risibly ill-informed judge who thought molasses was the "unconcocted juices extracted from the cane"), he offers the fruit of "personal knowledge and actual experience." However, his insider knowledge is not only of Jamaica where, unlike Long, he lived while writing his book. Edwards also claims privileged access to "the manners and dispositions of the native Africans": knowledge gained from enslaved people, newly imported from Africa, on his own Jamaica plantations.[78] The geographer David Lambert studied the use of such "captive knowledge" by a later defender of slavery: the armchair geographer and pro-slavery propagandist James MacQueen. MacQueen's interest in the geographical problem of the course of the river Niger dated to his stint as an overseer in Grenada in the late eighteenth century. Noticing an "intelligent boy" listening attentively while he read aloud from Mungo Park's *Travels*, MacQueen's "imagination was . . . taken captive by the mystery of the Great River," his obituary recounts. The overseer pumped the young African, "a Mandingo, born in the country of the Upper Niger," for information that the geographer later used in writing his *Geographical View of Northern and Central Africa* (1821).[79]

Lambert's moving meditation on this use of captive knowledge makes clear the exploitative character of MacQueen's research. How might the unnamed "negro boy" have experienced this incident? Despite postcolonial criticism's injunction to beware of speaking for the subaltern, we can speculate that "Joliba" – the Mande name for the Upper Niger – may have represented to this young man a lost home. "Hence, what MacQueen regarded as a source of geographical expertise may have been an emotional moment of recall, nostalgia, loss, sorrow, or anger for the displaced and enslaved 'negro boy.'" Lambert characterizes this moment on the Grenada plantation as what Saidiya Hartman calls a "scene of subjection." Slavery's profound harm, Hartman proposes, is best understood not by studying incidents of overt, shocking violence but instead through everyday interactions like the one described in MacQueen's obituary. She probes "the savage encroachments of power that take place through notions of reform, consent and protection." The "barbarism of slavery," she maintains, "did not express itself singularly in the constitution of the slave as object but also in the forms of subjectivity and circumscribed humanity imputed to the enslaved." Although crediting the boy with intelligence and valuing the information he provides, MacQueen compels him "to speak of his lost home in a manner that would propel MacQueen's geographical career and facilitate the penetration of West Africa by British commercial networks."[80]

Lambert is interested in locating the quotidian violence of slavery at the foundation of geographical knowledge. The knowledge of place that Edwards packages in his *History of the West Indies*, with its polemical pro-slavery edge, also incorporates involuntary or quasi-voluntary contributions from enslaved people. A number of comparable "scenes of subjection" went into the making of the *History*, providing the historian with information that he uses to build his case against abolishing the slave trade. Edwards relegates much of this material to footnotes. Faced with contradictory evidence from different witnesses in the House of Commons and Privy Council hearings concerning how many of the Africans sold in the Atlantic slave trade had already been enslaved in Africa, he writes, "it occurred to me, during my residence in Jamaica, to examine many of the Negroes themselves." He makes a point of his rigorous methodology:

I enquired of many young people, from different parts of Africa, concerning the circumstances of their captivity and sale, and having reduced their information to writing, I interrogated many of them again on the same subject, after an interval of several months. If the same account precisely was given by the same people a second time, I commonly considered it as grounded in truth. On other occasions, I have examined brothers and sisters apart. If their information agreed in minute particulars, I could have no reason to suspect them of falsehood.[81]

These elaborate precautions guard against the presumption that Africans are inclined to lie, especially about this issue. They are not in Jamaica long, Edwards explains, before they observe "the privileges which attach to freedom in the West Indies," and they are tempted to claim that they used to be free as well.[82]

The *History*'s main text summarizes the results of the planter's "interrogations." Of 25 subjects, 15 admitted to being born into slavery, 5 claim they were kidnapped, and 5 were prisoners of war. By no means, Edwards frankly admits, do these statistics prove the slave trade acceptable: "it cannot surely be a question, amongst a humane and enlightened people, concerning the injustice of a traffick thus supported." Yet, he nonetheless claims that those who were enslaved in Africa (i.e., the majority) "are, by being sold to the Whites, removed to a situation infinitely more desirable, even in its worst state, than that of the best and most favored slaves in their native country" – that is, the familiar pro-slavery view of the Atlantic slave trade as a rescue operation. Enslaved people in Africa, Edwards reports, can be sold or slaughtered at their owner's whim. He emphasizes the wanton slaughter of "old and infirm" prisoners of war and cites funeral sacrifices, including one of "upwards of one hundred people," that his captives in Jamaica describe. These displaced Africans – his human property – have thus (under at least implicit compulsion) provided the planter-historian with information that he could use to defend the slave trade that tore them from their homes and thrust them into exile and servitude.[83]

Edwards relegates the details of his interviews with his enslaved informants to lengthy footnotes. Focusing attention on this marginal, paratextual material follows a strategy familiar to postcolonial criticism.[84] We can read Edwards's footnotes as miniature slave narratives: vignettes of individual Africans, each narrating how he or she got caught up in the Atlantic slave trade. The first bears similarities to the story (possibly fictional, we now know) of Gustavus Vassa or Olaudah Equiano:

Adam (a Congo) a boy as I guess about fourteen, his country name *Sarri*, came from a vast distance inland, was waylaid and stole [sic], in the path about three miles from his own village, by one of his countrymen. It was early in the morning, and the man hid him all day in the woods, and marched him in the night. He was conducted in this manner for a month, and then sold to another Black man for a gun, some powder and shot, and a quantity of salt. He was sold a second time for a keg of brandy. His last-mentioned purchaser bought several other boys in the same manner, and when he had collected twenty, sent them down to the sea-coast, where they were sold to a captain of a ship. He relates further that his father, *Scindia Quante*, was a chief or captain under the king, and a great warrior, and had taken many people, whom he sold as slaves.[85]

Pushed to the margins of the *History*, this youthful African Adam is individualized by both his enslaved name and his "country" or African name, both italicized in Edwards's text. Elided is the power by which his current owner, Edwards (or an employee), replaced the latter name with the former. Readers of Equiano will recall his futile protest against his rechristening by his owner, Pascal, and his initial refusal to comply, which earned him a beating.

Also not included in Edwards's concise, matter-of-fact redaction is any trace of the boy's emotional response to his violent, presumably traumatic enslavement and its aftermath – or to being required to tell his owner about it. We can imagine Sarri going before the master, the powerful owner of 1,500 other human beings, to be "examined" or "interrogated" – not once but twice. Silence would not have been a realistic option. This quite possibly may "have been an emotional moment of recall, nostalgia, loss, sorrow, or anger for the displaced and enslaved . . . boy," as when that other boy told the overseer MacQueen about the River Joliba. We can assume that Sarri told his story through an interpreter, at least the first time, given Edwards's insistence on examining "Negroes newly arrived from Africa" because he thought those familiar with the West Indies were more likely to lie. The boy's words are thus mediated for readers by both the interpreter (presumably another "Congo" slave) and Edwards's crisp summary. What did the historian "prune" from Sarri's autobiographical snippet as irrelevant – or potentially damaging – to his ends? We will never know.[86]

Edwards's next vignette is the only one of the six in this very long footnote (occupying the feet of three pages) where an interaction from the interview itself – the "scene of subjection" – makes it onto the page:

> *Quaw* and *Quamina* (brothers) from the Gold Coast, one of them, as I guess, about twenty years old, the other eighteen, were born slaves to a man named *Banafou*, who had a great many other slaves, and sold these two to the captain that brought them to Jamaica. On being asked for what cause

their master sold them, they supposed the question implied a charge against them of misconduct, and one of them replied with great quickness, that they were not the only slaves that were sold in Guiney without having been guilty of any crime: their master, they said, owed money, and sold them to pay his debts.[87]

The two brothers' defensive reaction hints at consequences in the present if their master were to learn of past misdeeds. In an eighteenth-century gentleman, such sensitivity to reputation would bespeak a keen sense of honor. In an enslaved person, it smells of fear, masked by subtle impertinence. This, the only vignette with emotional content, suggests the flavor of the interaction that produced this quantum of knowledge for Edwards's opus.

The long footnote opens, "Perhaps the reader will not be displeased to be presented with a few of these examinations, as they were taken down at the time, and without any view to publication."[88] The litotes ("not...displeased") coyly brackets any suggestion of pleasure in reading about enslavement. Offering these vignettes of barbarity without being tainted by them depends on Edwards's adamant separation of Jamaica from Africa, innocent planters from wicked slave traders. With this separation taken for granted, the planter's interest in the lives of his captives may even enhance the humane, enlightened persona that the *History* projects. Poignantly, those "interrogated" are youthful, the majority in their teens. This is the type of thing that happens in Africa, Edwards telegraphs to his readers: this is why these young people were fortunate to get out of there and land in the West Indies (although they may not have felt fortunate at the time). Captive knowledge extracted from his human property thus contributes to Edwards's pro-slavery map of the Atlantic Triangle, contrasting a barbaric Africa with a civilized and civilizing West Indies, British in its values.

Elsewhere in the *History*, Edwards brings up cannibalism, which by 1793 was a well-worn topos of African savagery. He is describing natives of the Bight of Benin, "called in the West Indies *Eboes*." Although timid and melancholy rather than "frank and fearless" like those from the Gold Coast, Eboes are "more truly savage" than the latter because they are "accustomed to the shocking practice of feeding on human flesh." Edwards's source is "an intelligent trust-worthy domestick of the Ebo nation, who acknowledged to me, though with evident shame and reluctance, (having lived many years among the Whites), that he had himself, in his youth, frequently regaled on this horrid banquet." This report performs double duty for Edwards's case, illustrating both African barbarity and the civilizing power of life "among the Whites."[89]

Knowledge gained from enslaved people on Edwards's plantations also helps to illustrate the "savage and sanguinary" manners of the notorious "Koromantyn, or Gold Coast Negroes." A funeral sacrifice highlights the testimony of "*Clara*, a most faithful well-disposed woman, who was brought from the Gold Coast to Jamaica the latter end of 1784." Born into slavery and sold on her owner's death, Clara reports "*[t]hat twenty others were killed at his funeral.*" Edwards asks, "which country she liked best, Jamaica or Guiney? She replied that Jamaica was the better country, '*for that people were not killed there, as in Guiney, at the funeral of their masters.*'" Italicizing salient points, Edwards commends his human property for a job well done. By telling her master what he wants to hear, Clara earns his approval as she unwittingly contributes to his political project of defending enslavement. However, another item from Clara's testimony does not square quite as well with Edwards's picture of a barbaric Africa. "She informed me also, in answer to some other enquiries, of a remarkable fact (i.e.) that the Natives of the Gold Coast give their children the *yaws* (a frightful disorder) *by inoculation*," which prevents them from contracting it later in life. African medicine, in this and other respects, often could be more effective than the European medical practice of the day.[90] The *History*'s paratextual margins thus yield insight into the strength and practical efficacy of African culture, aspects not dwelt on in Edwards's text.

Theater of anarchy and bloodshed

Edwards's *History* was of its moment, the early 1790s, in its moderate tone. Its contrast with Long's earlier, more extremist rhetoric reflects the growing influence of the abolitionist movement as well as the author's pragmatic bent. However, the political climate changed rapidly in that tumultuous decade, as the French Revolution went from bourgeois reform to Jacobin terror and France declared war on Britain – a war that would last, with one brief interruption, for more than 20 years. The colonial Caribbean, meanwhile, was the scene of another revolution just as epochal as the one in France. The most profitable of Europe's sugar islands was the French colony of Saint-Domingue, present-day Haiti: "its private luxury, and its public grandeur, astonished the traveler; its accumulation of wealth surprised the mother country; and it was beheld with rapture by the neighboring inhabitants of the islands of the Antilles."[91] Yet, all of this wealth rested on a shaky foundation.

Burgeoning colonial profit helped to destabilize France's *ancien régime*. When the Revolution came, its politics played out in the slave colonies in ways shaped by preexisting tensions. If it could not have happened without the wealth and power of France's maritime bourgeoisie – that is, mercantile fortunes in places like Bordeaux and Nantes, deeply involved in the slave trade and tropical commodities – the implications of revolutionary ideology nonetheless spelled trouble for colonial slavery, the basis of those fortunes. The Haitian Revolution was "the most concrete expression of the idea that the rights proclaimed in France's 1789 Declaration of the Rights of Man and Citizen were indeed universal."[92] The colonies were an intractable problem for the French Revolution. However, the Revolution posed a grave threat for slaveholding colonists in the Caribbean holdings of all European nations, particularly Britain, whose most lucrative sugar island, Jamaica, was situated much too nearby as Saint Domingue erupted.

The Caribbean had been a multinational colonial enterprise almost from the beginning. Christopher Columbus occupies a place of honor in the colonial histories of Long and Edwards (and Rainsford's history of Haiti). Hispaniola, the island split between French Saint Domingue and Spanish Santo Domingo, was "the ground zero of European colonialism in the Americas" – site of the "brutal massacre and bewildering decimation of indigenous people" that soon followed Columbus's landing.[93] The French, the British, the Dutch, and even the Danish followed the Spanish in exploiting the tropical islands, especially after the "Sugar Revolution" of the mid-seventeenth century blossomed into the "economic miracle of the eighteenth century." The sugar colonies "both depended on and drove the expansion of the emerging capitalist system of the Atlantic world." It was a system fueled by the sweat of many thousands of captives. The European empires colonized, cultivated, enslaved, exploited, profited, and fought in the Caribbean over the centuries. It became a theater of imperial warfare, with colonies as prizes, ceded back and forth as the fortunes of each great power waxed and waned.[94]

The onset of the Revolution saw French planters and merchants divided between those with primary loyalties to the metropolis and others who set their sights on greater colonial autonomy, or even independence. The colonial politics of this period are much too complex to review in detail here.[95] The threat of insurrection loomed over the tense deliberations about who should be granted political participation. Were free people of color (many of whom owned property and enslaved people) essential allies against the insurgent laborers, or was granting them rights a "slippery slope" to be avoided at all costs? The question was debated in Paris and in Saint

Domingue (as well as in France's other Caribbean colonies, Guadeloupe and Martinique). The enslaved population, meanwhile, held their own deliberations. In August 1791, they launched the impressively concerted and sustained insurrection that would culminate, after many twists and turns, in the founding of the Republic of Haiti on January 1, 1804.

The Saint Domingue revolt happened before the 1793 publication of Edwards's *History of the West Indies* and is briefly mentioned in that work. Edwards visited Saint Domingue in late 1791 with a delegation sent by the governor of Jamaica to the white victims of the slave rebellion – a visit he dramatically describes in his next book, *An Historical Survey of the French Colony in the Island of St. Domingo* (1797). He had planned, he writes in the preface, to do "a general account of the settlements made by all the nations of Europe in that part of the New Hemisphere, but more particularly the French, whose possessions were undoubtedly the most valuable and productive."[96] Unable to accomplish this, he focused instead on the site of the 1791 revolt. Its human tragedy presents the pro-slavery propagandist with an irresistible opportunity.

The British political climate of the deeply reactionary late 1790s differed from that during the French Revolution's moderate early stages, when Edwards was writing his *History of the West Indies*. There now was no more need for the painstaking moderation Edwards had cultivated in that work. *An Historical Survey* cannily aligns the planters' cause with the national mood of counter-revolution, producing a polemical document with striking similarities to Edmund Burke's prescient counter-revolutionary manifesto, *Reflections on the Revolution in France* (1790). Similar to Burke's *Reflections*, *An Historical Survey* paints revolutionary atrocities in shamelessly purple prose and celebrates the *ancien régime* in aestheticized language. Also like Burke's book, Edwards's condemns the extremist "philosophers," whose radical ideas they both see as the source of the bloodshed. His particular villains are the Amis des Noirs, the French abolition society.[97] Programmatic, precipitous reform – like that advocated by the radical Jacobins for France and the Amis des Noirs for the colonies – brings disaster, according to *An Historical Survey*. One cannot "correct . . . *by force*" long-standing, deep-rooted "prejudices of habit, education, and opinion."[98] The immediate context of this Burkean language in *An Historical Survey* is the granting of political rights to free people of color.

A footnote highlights Edwards's role as the colonial insider interpreting Caribbean politics for "the mere English reader." He makes the analogy with the British colonies: "supposing the English parliament should pass a law declaring, for instance, the free mulattoes of Jamaica to be eligible into the assembly of that island, such a measure would prove there, as it proved in St. Domingo, the declaration of civil war."⁹⁹ Metropolitan observers need to take colonial culture – crucially differing from their own – into consideration. Edwards's conclusion makes the lesson clear:

> To Great Britain I would intimate, that if, disregarding the present example [the Saint Domingue revolt], encouragement shall continue to be given to those hot-brained fanaticks, and detestable incendiaries, who, under the vile pretence of philanthropy and zeal for the interests of suffering humanity, preach up rebellion and murder to the contented and orderly negroes in our own territories, what else can be expected, but that the same dreadful scenes of carnage and desolation, which we have contemplated in St. Domingo, will be renewed among our countrymen and relations in the British West Indies?¹⁰⁰

Harnessing the pro-slavery cause to the wartime climate of counter-revolution, Edwards uses the violence of the uprising to argue against metropolitan interference in colonial affairs. The conclusion of *An Historical Survey* advocates a gradual end to the slave trade because "barbarous men" fresh from Africa threaten the good order of the colonies. Edwards emphasizes, however, that the "Colonial Legislatures, by their situation and local knowledge, are alone competent to this great and glorious task" – not the British Parliament.¹⁰¹

The extreme violence that *An Historical Survey* graphically describes supports an imaginary geography that harks back to Long's. In his polygenist paradigm, Africans are a different species, lacking everything that makes Europeans civilized people. Edwards, although no polygenist, is what we might call a "culturist." He prefaces his litany of horrors with a telling simile. "Upwards of one hundred thousand savage people, habituated to the barbarities of Africa, avail themselves of the silence and obscurity of the night, and fall on the peaceful and unsuspicious planters, like so many famished tygers thirsting for human blood." Comparing them to wild animals, Edwards dehumanizes the insurgents. On this devastated island, no "condition, age, or sex is spared" among the rebels' victims. "All the shocking and shameful enormities, with which the fierce and unbridled passions of savage man have ever conducted a war, prevail uncontrolled." *An Historical Survey* regales readers with sensational vignettes: white women raped "on the dead bodies of their husbands and fathers"; a white infant's body impaled on a stake, carried by the insurgents as a "*standard.*"¹⁰² The quotidian violence of colonial slavery, of course, appears nowhere in Edwards's book.

Yet, the sensational content of *An Historical Survey* is not wholly discontinuous with Edwards's portrayal of African culture in his earlier, more measured work. The *History*, as discussed previously, narrates an earlier Jamaican slave revolt with some similarity to the Saint Domingue uprising, although more limited in scope and quickly subdued. This is Tacky's Revolt (1760), which Edwards lived through as a teenager newly arrived in Jamaica. Significantly, he inserts his eyewitness account of the rebellion into his ethnographic catalog of "predominant features" of "several . . . African nations" where West Indian slaves are captured. Its place in the structure of the *History* renders Tacky's Revolt a testimony to African cultural or racial essence. "Koromantyns," or "Natives of the Gold Coast," represent for Edwards the "genuine and original unmixed Negro," possessing "firmness both of body and mind; a ferociousness of disposition; but withal, activity, courage, and a stubbornness, or what an ancient Roman would have deemed an elevation, of soul, which prompts them to enterprises of difficulty and danger; and enables them to meet death, in its most horrible shape, with fortitude or indifference."[103]

These traits, which Edwards presents to his readers with ambiguous admiration, led 100 or so saltwater Koromantyns in 1760 Jamaica to make a violent bid for freedom. After describing how they "butchered . . . Whites and Mulattoes, not sparing even infants at the breast" and "literally drank their blood mixed with rum," Edwards notes the stoicism with which captured rebels endure their punishment. "The courage, or unconcern, which the people of this country manifest at the approach of death, arises doubtless, in a great measure, from their national manners, wars, and superstitions, which are all, in the highest degree, savage and sanguinary." He documented these "sanguinary" customs through captive knowledge of the type discussed previously: interviews with his captives, including Clara's report of funeral sacrifices on the Gold Coast. Another captive, Cudjoe, tells of one such sacrifice reportedly claiming more than 100 victims. The *History* mainly deploys such captive knowledge to defend the slave trade as rescuing Africans from the "sanguinary" culture of their home. This brief but intense narrative of the 1760 revolt graphically illustrates what enslaved Africans are capable of, absent sufficient restraint.[104]

The marked difference in rhetorical strategy between Edwards's two books, published only four years apart at different points in the turbulent 1790s, should not distract from the underlying continuity in their characterization of the enslaved. Like Long, Edwards considers Africans to be basically savages. Also like Long, he sees them as capable of "improvement" up to a point – a key tenet of his case in support of slavery. "This contempt of death, or indifference about life, they bring with them to the West Indies; but if fortunately they fall into good hands at first, and become well settled, they acquire by degrees other sentiments and notions." Edwards illustrates with the improbable anecdote of a sick Koromantyn whose owner tries to cheer him up. The enslaved man seems "ashamed of [his] own weakness . . . *Massa*, said the Negro (in a tone of self-reproach and conscious degeneracy) *since me come to white man's country me lub (love) life too much!*"[105] The apologist for slavery trades on Africans' supposedly malleable nature, mixing patronizing humor with self-congratulation – on our plantations, the enslaved love life.

An Historical Survey takes this in a different direction. When enslaved Africans reject the civilizing influence of their owners, as in the Saint Domingue revolt, they revert to savagery, according to Edwards. This is what he predicts for Saint Domingue's future if the self-emancipated slaves take over. "Experience has demonstrated," he writes:

> that a wild and lawless freedom affords no means of improvement, either mental or moral. The Charaibes [Caribs] of St. Vincent, and the Maroon negroes of Jamaica, were originally enslaved Africans; and *what they now are*, the freed negroes of St. Domingo *will hereafter be*; savages in the midst of society – without peace, security, agriculture, or property; ignorant of the duties of life, and unacquainted with all the soft and endearing relations which render it desirable; averse to labor, though frequently perishing of want; suspicious of each other, and towards the rest of mankind revengeful and faithless, remorseless and bloody-minded; pretending to be free, while groaning beneath the capricious despotism of their chiefs, and feeling all the miseries of servitude, without the benefits of subordination![106]

This echoes the relentless negation with which Long describes African "negroes." Yet, the earlier historian's erudite redaction of travel writing and natural history pales in comparison to the visceral fear and fury that drive the narration of *An Historical Survey*. This makes more sense when we realize how quickly word of the Saint Domingue uprising spread to the neighboring island. Barely a month after it began, the governor of Jamaica reported that Jamaican slaves were composing songs about it. The reaction of white colonists throughout the hemisphere was intense and lasting. "The awesome scale of the events in Saint Domingue instilled a sort of permanent panic in the minds of New World slave owners."[107]

The Saint Domingue insurrection stalled the British abolitionist movement for several years. It also shifted the parameters of Edwards's imaginary geography of the Atlantic Triangle. In *An Historical Survey*, the "voice of the plantocracy" takes on a newly bellicose tone. The moderate tactician of the

1793 *History of the West Indies* emerges in 1797 as a Caribbean Cassandra, watching Saint Domingue degenerate into a new Africa populated by feral subhumans. Where he was earlier concerned to emphasize the common ground between colony and metropole, now Edwards warns London to back off: if ignorant parliamentarians and abolitionist ideologues cannot refrain from meddling in colonial affairs, Jamaica will be the next Saint Domingue.

Edwards admits that he cannot predict the eventual outcome of this seismic shift in imperial geopolitics. If the insurgents remain free, "all other reflections must yield to the pressing consideration how best to obviate and defeat the influence which so dreadful an example of successful revolt and triumphant anarchy may have in our own islands." Conversely, if France succeeds in "reducing the vast body of fugitive negroes to obedience" and wresting the other half of the island from Spain, Edwards predicts a decidedly different outcome. Planters from all over the Caribbean will flock to the fertile island: "a West Indian empire will fix itself in this noble island, to which, in a few short years, all the tropical possessions of Europe will be found subordinate and tributary." Hispaniola's strategic location, combined with its fertile soil, will bring even Mexico under its sway. This vision of a consolidated Caribbean as a mighty New World empire includes a dramatic shift in the European balance of power, leaving a "humbled Spaniard" and a rueful Great Britain to reflect on what might have been.[108] Either way, the geopolitical impact that the planter-historian foresees for the Saint Domingue captives' unprecedented self-emancipation is huge.

A real system of equality

I conclude this chapter by discussing a different type of history: not a colonial history but rather that of an independent Caribbean state. The Anglo-Irish officer Marcus Rainsford served in the Caribbean in the 1790s and spent several months in Saint Domingue in 1797–98.[109] After retiring from active duty, he took advantage of public interest in the beleaguered ex-colony and expanded his memoir into a full-scale *Historical Account of the Black Empire of Hayti* (1805). For the historical portion of the book, he did extensive research by consulting a number of sources, including Edwards's *Historical Survey*. There exists, Rainsford's introduction claims, "no correct or comprehensive account" in English "of this interesting country." Recently republished for the first time since 1805, the book is valuable, its modern editors point out, as a glimpse of a genuinely new kind of New

World society – the "ethnography of a people on the verge of birth," "both the celebration of a world to come and an elegy for a world that never arrived."[110] Rainsford's portrait of the emerging free black society stands in striking contrast to Edwards's inflammatory focus on the violence and victims of the slave revolt. *Black Empire* reverses the conventional binary asserted by both Edwards and his predecessor Long: that is, white Europeans as possessing a monopoly on civilization, black Africans as essentially savage. In a free Haiti, Rainsford suggests, the majority-black society has rapidly evolved into an eminently civilized one. Haiti is a laboratory in which African nature, no longer enslaved, is able to unfold its full potential in what Rainsford calls "a real system of equality."[111]

As a soldier, Rainsford, like John Stedman, is positioned uneasily between the colonial machine and those whom it exploited. Soldiers like Rainsford were the expendable fodder of the British Empire's insatiable drive to expand: witness the tens of thousands who gave their lives in Britain's failed takeover of Saint Domingue between 1793 and 1798.[112] Like Stedman as well, Rainsford was an artist; his illustrations for *Black Empire* were perhaps its "most influential aspect." Another interesting point of similarity with his Scottish contemporary is the incipient contradictions that mark the Irishman's presentation of the slave colony. *Black Empire* is marked (or marred) by intrusive disclaimers distancing the author from British abolitionists, doubtlessly driven by the still conservative cultural climate of the early 1800s. Rainsford even suggests – faintly echoing Edwards – that a reformed slavery might have avoided upheavals like those in Saint Domingue. An appendix cites the French planter de Charmilly's "judicious ideas of negro amelioration," with which Rainsford agrees, including an extensively regulated but still legal slave trade with Africa.[113]

Despite his nonprogressive stance on political issues, however, Rainsford's brief portrait of post-emancipation Haitian society contravenes the fundamental assumptions of pro-slavery writers such as Edwards and Long. For him, African nature is not fundamentally different than human nature in general, as becomes clear with slavery abolished. His arrival in Saint Domingue is accidental. The Danish schooner on which he is en route from Jamaica to join his regiment in Martinique is disabled by a storm, washing up at the colonial capital, Cap Français. The little ship and its occupants "await the relief of the brigands, an appellation which the superior policy that already appeared in this extraordinary republic, had not yet obliterated from its members."[114] The derogatory "brigands" was a stock epithet for the insurgent slaves, which Rainsford foregrounds at the same time as he undercuts it. We are about to tour an "extraordinary republic" with a "superior policy," not a haven of brigands or outlaws.

The memoir proceeds to thwart the expectations of Rainsford's contemporaries with first-hand observations about the ways that Haitian society has evolved in the years since the French government proclaimed emancipation in 1794. He poses as an American to avoid well-grounded suspicions of the British, who had invaded the island in 1794 and occupied parts of it until 1798. Sojourning in Cap Français, he seeks out the Hotel de la Republique, "an edifice of rather elegant appearance." On his way there:

> except the preponderancy of Black complexion, [he] perceived but little difference from an European city. On entering the house, however, he immediately perceived that the usual subordinations of society were entirely disregarded, and that he was to witness, for the first time, a real system of equality.
>
> Here were officers and privates, the colonel and the drummer, at the same table indiscriminately; and the writer had been scarcely seated at a repast . . . when a fat negro, to initiate him in the general system, helped himself frequently from his dish, and took occasion to season his character by large draughts of the wine, accompanied with the address of "Mon Americain." The appearance of the house, and its accommodations, were not much inferior to a London coffee-house, and on particular occasions exhibited a superior degree of elegance.[115]

For the military man, used to a strict hierarchy of rank, and the colonial soldier, used to racial hierarchy, this is a novel social experiment. Retaining the elegance of metropolitan Europe, the society of "the Cape" sets aside its invidious distinctions – in ways that could be off-putting at first, as Rainsford's humorous treatment of his table companion suggests. The work of running the new society is likewise color-blind: "Negroes, recollected in the lowest state of slavery, including Africans, filled situations of trust and responsibility; they were, likewise, in many instances, occupied by those who had been in superior circumstances under the old regimen, free negroes, and mulattoes."[116]

The city, of course, is deeply scarred by war, its "spacious streets" marked by "desolation" and "magnificent ruin." Leaving the ruins of the capital as they are, at least for the present, constitutes for Rainsford a sign of the ex-slaves' civilized nature: "with an ardent sensibility . . . they appeared to shrink from reinstating it, as if in rebuilding their former residences, they should create new masters." The visitor mingles with the Haitians and enjoys their hospitality, from the "superior order" to the "negro hut." The good taste and refinement of the former impress him: "In many instances the writer has heard reasoning, and witnessed manners of acuteness and elegance, the relation of which would appear incredible, from those who were remembered in a state of servitude, or whose parents were in situations of abject penury; while sallies of wit, not frequently surpassed, have enlivened many an hour." Public culture, he reports, remains eminently civilized. "The drama, that source of rational delight, always so prevalent in St. Domingo, existed, in more strength and propriety than it had done before [.]" French actors share the stage with "black performers, who . . . were not behind in talents; the writer saw a play of Molière's performed with an accuracy that would not have disgraced the first theatre in Europe." Music and art, he observes, still flourish as well.[117]

Even the humblest members of this new society participate, Rainsford suggests, in the new manners made possible by emancipation. "Those qualities conspicuous in the negroes under their worst circumstances, their regard for all the relations in life, and tendernesses to each other, seemed expanded with their freedom." He visits "the cottage of a black laborer" with three wives and thirteen children, whose family he dubs "a well regulated kingdom in miniature." "Every thing convenience required was to be found on a small scale, and the whole so compact, and clean, with such an air of *properté* throughout as was absolutely attractive." The humble patriarch is literate as well, keeping "a mass book, and a mutilated volume of Volney's Travels" on "a neat shelf."[118]

Rainsford also describes the quasi-utopian agricultural "productive system" that has replaced plantation slavery in this part of the island:

> Every individual employed a portion of his time in labor, and received an allotted part of the produce for his reward, while all took the field, from a sense of duty to themselves. A perfect combination appeared in their conduct, and every action came directly from the heart. . . . Little coercion was necessary, and punishment was chiefly inflicted by a sense of shame produced by a slight confinement, or the like. Labor was so much abridged, that no want of leisure was felt; it would be a great gratification to the feeling heart, to see the peasant in other countries with a regulated toil similar to that of the laborer in St. Domingo.[119]

Agricultural production was a troublesome issue for the relationship between the revolutionary French and their former colonies. Liberty in the abstract, of course, had tremendous appeal. Granted total freedom, however, the formerly enslaved (or "cultivators," as they were

euphemistically called) often would choose not to continue doing plantation labor, with its demanding work regime. They preferred subsistence
farming, when they could obtain small plots of land. However, as the historian Carolyn Fick points out, "liberty and citizenship . . . had its limitations,
and in Saint Domingue, although slavery was abolished, colonialism was
not." The revolutionary nation, at war with the rest of Europe, desperately
needed the profits of the plantation complex. Rebel leaders, including
Toussaint Louverture, instituted authoritarian work regimes that tied the
formerly enslaved to their plantations. Their "regulated toil" may have
appeared to be self-motivated to Rainsford as an outside observer; however, in reality, agriculture was militarized and individual liberties were
severely restricted.[120]

This brings up the distance between Rainsford's observations and the
perspective of the newly emancipated Haitians themselves. He compli-
ments them for achieving aspects of "civilization" on a European model –
being tidy, being witty, performing Molière. Yet, what would utopia look
like to members of the majority of newly freed Afro-Caribbeans, who were
mostly plantation laborers? Given the rarity with which their voices enter
the historical record, we may never know for certain. Fick's groundbreaking
Making of Haiti argues that the behavior of the newly emancipated Haitians
repeatedly indicates what they wanted was "freedom to till their own soil":
an "independent relation to the land, African in outlook," amounting to
"agricultural egalitarianism."[121] Rainsford, so unlike his British contemporaries in his view of black Haitians and their society, is still far from being
able to speak for their aspirations.

Rainsford's introduction opens with a reflective passage the insights of
which are worth quoting at length:

> It has frequently been the fate of striking events, and particularly those which
> have altered the condition of mankind, to be denied that consideration by
> their contemporaries, which they obtain from the veneration of posterity.
> In their vortex, attention is distracted by the effects; and a distant society
> recedes from the contemplation of objects that threaten a violation of their
> system, or wound a favorite prejudice. It is thus that history, with all the
> advantages of calm discussion, is imperfect; and philosophy enquires in vain
> for the unrecorded causes of astonishing transactions. . . .
>
> The rise of the Haytian empire is an event which may powerfully affect the
> condition of the human race; yet it is viewed as an ordinary succession of
> triumphs and defeats, interrupted only by the horrors of new and terrible
> inflictions, the fury of the contending elements, and destructive disease,
> more tremendous than all. . . .

It is on ancient record, that negroes were capable of repelling their enemies, with vigor, in their own country; and a writer of modern date has assured us of the talents and virtues of these people; but it remained for the close of the eighteenth century to realize the scene, from a state of abject degeneracy: – to exhibit, a horde of negroes emancipating themselves from the vilest slavery, and at once filling all the relations of society, enacting laws, and commanding armies, in the colonies of Europe.

The same period has witnessed a great and polished nation, not merely returning to the barbarism of the earliest periods, but descending to the characters of assassins and executioners; and, removing the boundaries which civilization had prescribed even to war, rendering it a wild conflict of brutes and a midnight massacre.[122]

The "veneration of posterity," in the case of the Haitian Revolution, has yet fully to arrive. Recent work by a few historians and cultural critics both asserts its importance, ranking it alongside the American and French Revolutions as a turning point of Western modernity, and documents its systematic and continuing neglect by prominent historians and philosophers. Apparently, the "prejudices" that Rainsford cites still prevail. Their cumulative effect is by now impossible to untangle from the other factors that drove Haiti's troubled history in the nineteenth and twentieth centuries.[123]

The reversal that Rainsford satirically describes plays on British readers' deep-seated prejudice and wartime animus against their perennial enemies, the French, whose revolutionary excesses were proverbial by 1805. This becomes a springboard for him to attack the entrenched binarism at the center of the imaginative geographies that this chapter surveyed: the contrast between "polished" civilization and frightening "barbarism." Edward Long mapped the Atlantic Triangle based on this fundamental divide, posed in terms of plenitude versus lack. Genius, civility, science, moral sensation, self-discipline, and taste – the defining attributes of Enlightenment civilization – present in Europeans are absent, Long asserts, in "Negroes." Sub-Saharan Africa appears on his mental map as a chaotic wasteland populated by subhuman barbarians.[124] Bryan Edwards's *History* documents this with "research" conducted among captives on his plantations. Absent European domination, the freed Africans of Saint Domingue revert to savagery, striking fear into white settlers hemisphere-wide.

Rainsford's introduction mounts a trenchant riposte to the planter-historians' imaginary geography. Civilization and barbarism are not geographically tied (nor, he implies, race-based). Europeans can fall into barbarity; Africans – in a remarkably short span of time, in this case – can advance toward higher civilization. The new nation of Haiti, in this optimistic view, is poised to fulfill the full promise of the Age of Revolution. Alas, as we now know, in a hostile hemisphere packed with slave-owning nations, it did not happen that way.

CHAPTER 4

Equiano's politics of place
From roots to routes

The Haitian Revolution tore through the captive spaces of the colonial Caribbean, opening a fragile space of freedom through collective, violent action. The anonymous rank-and-file of the rebel armies did not record their view of these epochal events; few enslaved people had access to literacy, much less to print. Those who did were privileged individuals, unrepresentative of the masses of their fellow captives. Nevertheless, writings by the enslaved or formerly enslaved have much to tell us. For my purposes, so-called slave narratives offer unique perspectives on the politics of place. The relationships of the enslaved or formerly enslaved to the sites of slavery – the nodes of the Atlantic system – differ in significant ways from those of free people. This emerges most clearly when we read slave narratives as travel narratives. I treat the two formerly enslaved authors in this study, Olaudah Equiano and Mary Prince, as travel writers.

A diverse range of labels is applied to geographical movement, largely according to who moves. The word "travel," James Clifford points out, carries "a history of European, literary, male, bourgeois, scientific, heroic, recreational meanings and practices."[1] Even bourgeois women were seldom taken seriously as travelers, much less women and men of the laboring classes. A "traveler" has been defined (or mythologized) as someone with the security and privilege to move around with few constraints.[2] By this narrow definition, Olaudah Equiano and Mary Prince do not qualify as travelers. Yet, travel – even by the least privileged individuals and under the harshest conditions – has proven to be a source of power and knowledge of a different type from that which lends prestige to more traditional travelers.

Rich and complex "cultures of displacement and transplantation" – notably the black diaspora cultures of Britain, the Americas, and the Caribbean – were forged by specific and often violent histories, such as the history of transatlantic enslavement, which involved the geographical movement of entire populations. These histories generate what Clifford calls "discrepant cosmopolitanisms," a term that sets aside "the notion that certain classes of people are cosmopolitan (travelers) while the rest are local (natives) . . . as the ideology of one (very powerful) traveling culture."[3] In this sense, Olaudah Equiano is indeed cosmopolitan: learning and growing through his travels, including involuntary travels; each journey moving him closer toward the sense of self that will enable him to narrate his life story for publication.

Amid the extensive scholarship on Equiano's now canonical *The Interesting Narrative of the Life of Olaudah Equiano, or Gustavus Vassa, the African*, a relatively recent strain treats him as a denizen of the Black Atlantic. Reading him and other African diaspora writers in this way has both "widened the focus, substituting capitalism and empire, for example, for nation and ethnicity as master terms, and narrowed it to the manifold ways in which selves – racial, gendered, ethnic, national, and diasporic – are pieced together in communicative acts."[4] Within this widened analytical focus, however, nation and ethnicity still function as powerful signifiers. I begin my investigation of *The Interesting Narrative* by surveying its rhetorical use of nation and ethnicity and the established contexts that shaped this rhetoric, some of which were introduced in the previous chapter. Like his fellow activists in the abolitionist movement, Equiano resisted the politics of place represented by pro-slavery colonial historians, including Edward Long and Bryan Edwards. It is not surprising that his imaginary geography of the Atlantic Triangle is broadly congruent with that of white abolitionists. Less obvious are the ways in which Equiano subtly challenges his white allies with nuanced, occasionally sarcastic interventions in the ongoing contest over the character and relationships of the captive spaces of the colonial Atlantic.

Formal features of *The Interesting Narrative* – in particular, its famously elusive narrating persona or voice – complicate its representation of Atlantic geography. As Equiano's narration both constructs and dismantles the relationships between identity and place, person and nation, his persona evolves from "roots" to "routes"[5]: from the geographically defined characters of African native, Caribbean slave, and black British subject to the cosmopolitan roles of sailor and diasporan activist. To notice this shift is to recognize *The Interesting Narrative*'s status as travel writing, a genre devoted to geographical mobility and equipped for cultural critique. Equiano, the anti-slavery polemicist, skillfully uses abolitionist geography to advance his political ends. Equiano, the traveler and travel writer, I conclude, finally departs from that spatial schema, with its rhetorical separation of colony from metropole. The two are systemically connected: Equiano, the discrepant cosmopolitan, tacitly affirms this fact by living it.

It is no longer possible to discuss Equiano without engaging the still accumulating fallout from the 1999 publication of evidence found by Equiano's editor and biographer, Vincent Carretta, which suggests that Equiano may not have been born in Africa, as he claimed, but instead in North America. Was he African? Will we ever know for certain? Does it even matter?[6] Before the emergence of these admittedly inconclusive data, critics already were divided over how to interpret Equiano's self-presentation.[7] My contribution to this ongoing debate is a result of analyzing *The Interesting Narrative*'s construction of the sites of slavery – that is, the corners of the Atlantic Triangle: Africa, England, and the Caribbean – and asking how each bears on the book's complex, conflicted representation of "Olaudah Equiano, or Gustavus Vassa, the African . . . Himself."

Abolitionist geography

We begin with Africa. Even before Carretta's recent discoveries, it was obvious that *The Interesting Narrative*'s representation of its author's purported birthplace is a rhetorical construction, at least in part. In 1982, S. E. Ogude presciently remarked, "Equiano's account of his early life cannot bear close scrutiny." If he was in fact kidnapped into slavery, it happened at a tender age: ten according to Equiano himself, seven or eight by his biographer's calculations. "Even with the best of memory," Ogude notes, "there were bound to be some problems" with reconstructing such early experiences several decades later.[8] Equiano based his patchwork ethnographic portrait of the Igbo people on widely available materials, including the Philadelphia abolitionist Anthony Benezet's *Some Account of Guinea*, as well as on his own purported experience. He indicates early in *The Interesting Narrative* his familiarity with the imaginary geography described in Chapter 3, known to his readers from the influential writings of Benezet, Clarkson, and other abolitionists.

This spatiotemporal schema – which polemically challenges slavery's defenders – presents an Africa capable of progress, although far less advanced than Europe. This potential for advancement is endangered by the slave trade, which skews the path of history, threatening to plunge both Africa and Europe back into "the ignorance and barbarity of the darkest ages."[9] Europe's Caribbean colonies feature on this moral map as degenerate zones where base passions endanger the enslaved as they corrupt their owners. Abolitionist geography took great pains to distinguish colonies from metropole, the sugar islands from the British Isles – strategically absolving metropolitan readers' guilt while urging them to take action for change.

The Interesting Narrative clearly shares white abolitionists' political agenda. Whereas Equiano's representation of the corners of the Atlantic Triangle generally follows his allies' lead, however, significant nuances inflect this established geographical schema.

George Boulukos analyzed in detail the eighteenth-century debate on Africa that forms the context for its representation by Equiano and his fellow abolitionists as well as pro-slavery writers.[10] *The Interesting Narrative* strives to combat common pro-slavery stereotypes of Africans. For example, Equiano portrays Igbo women as "modest to a degree of bashfulness" and never "incontinent" before marriage, fighting the popular idea of African women as sexually voracious. Like Benezet, he emphasizes the Igbos' industriousness – "we are all habituated to labor from our earliest years" – against the stereotype of the lazy savage in such pro-slavery publications as Long's *History of Jamaica* (1774) and Matthews's *Voyage to the River Sierra Leone* (1788).[11] Similar to the planter-writers discussed in Chapter 1, *The Interesting Narrative* also enlists the cultural prestige of aesthetics: Equiano uses it to rebut pro-slavery libel of Africans, such as Long's. Among the civilized qualities that Africans lack, according to Long (see Chapter 3), is taste, or the ability to appreciate beauty. Equiano presents the Igbo as "almost a nation of dancers, musicians, and poets." Creators of art, they are beautiful people as well: "Deformity is indeed unknown amongst us, I mean that of shape . . . for, in regard to complexion, ideas of beauty are wholly relative." Equiano thus attacks the Eurocentric assumptions that historically structured aesthetic discourse.[12]

At a few points, *The Interesting Narrative* does more than merely rebut European superiority. In Kerry Sinanan's words, Equiano "situate[s] his account of the Ibo within the tensions occasioned by the doubts a supposedly civilized West was having about itself."[13] His Rousseauist emphasis on the simplicity of Igbo life – with little commerce, few wants, few manufactures, and few luxuries – presents this civilization as something approaching a golden age, in which people live together sociably yet without the degeneracy and corruption that plague more complex societies.[14] His language in this section hints at unfavorable comparisons with modern Europe: the "natives are unacquainted with those refinements in cookery which debauch the taste." Such comparisons invoke the powerful discourse against luxury that was current in British thought throughout the eighteenth century.[15] The Igbos, Equiano notes, "were totally unacquainted with swearing, and all those terms of abuse and reproach which find their way so readily and copiously into the languages of more civilized people."[16] Here, "civilized" takes on a sarcastic edge. The sarcasm is more pronounced when he writes of "the enlightened merchant" who foments war between one African district and another to facilitate obtaining more slaves, a charge that echoes Benezet and Clarkson.[17] Far from the abject savagery portrayed by pro-slavery writers, *The Interesting Narrative* presents a version of African civilization morally superior, in important respects, to that of the British.

Chapter III of *The Interesting Narrative* again compares Britain with Africa. The young Equiano's mixed first impressions of England, landing at Falmouth in 1757, exploit the fallible narrating voice associated with this period of his life. After a comic encounter with snow, he goes to church with his friend Dick Baker, a white Virginian, who interprets the ceremony for him:

> And from what I could understand by him of this God, and in seeing these white people did not sell one another, as we did, I was much pleased; and in this I thought they were much happier than we Africans. I was astonished at the wisdom of the white people in all things I saw; but was amazed at their not sacrificing, or making any offerings, and eating with unwashed hands, and touching the dead. I likewise could not help remarking the particular slenderness of their women, which I did not at first like; and I thought they were not so modest and shame faced as the African women.[18]

These comments cut two ways: fighting pro-slavery stereotypes of Africans, they subtly undermine the image of Britain as a supremely civilized nation. The naïve boy's observation that "white people did not sell one another, as we did" intervenes at a sensitive point in the abolition debate. That Africans did, in fact, sell one another to other Africans, as well as to Europeans, was an argument often advanced by pro-slavery writers. Matthews, a slave trader, asserts that "the practice of making, buying, and selling slaves, was in use in Africa long before our knowledge of it" and that "slavery can never be abolished in a country like Africa . . . where the people are of a vindictive and revengeful spirit, and where the laws make every man a slave who is convicted of the most trifling offence." Equiano's account of African slavery decidedly differs from Matthews's account. He does not conceal the fact that some Africans deal in slaves strictly for profit; however, the Igbo, he maintains, sold "only prisoners of war, or such among us as had been convicted of kidnapping, or adultery, and some other crimes which we esteemed heinous." Neither was their treatment of those they enslaved brutal compared to the practices of European slave owners: "[H]ow different was their condition from that of the slaves in the West-Indies!"[19]

To write that the British "did not sell one another" in a book marketed principally as a polemic against the slave trade is deeply ironic in its deliberate obtuseness. The contradiction between Christianity and the slave trade was at the heart of the abolitionist case. Commending the British for not selling one another while conspicuously omitting the nation's massive involvement in the buying and selling of Africans, Equiano uses the young boy's fallible voice to call attention to the latter. White people were obviously fortunate not to be sold, although what this has to do with God is left unclear. Comparing Africa with Britain, Equiano both echoes and perceptibly shifts the geographical schema he inherited from earlier abolitionist writers. As it works to refute pro-slavery slurs – a daunting task in 1789 – *The Interesting Narrative* subtly reassesses the self-congratulatory version of Britishness that infused abolitionist rhetoric.

At key moments, nonetheless, Equiano succumbs to overt flattery of his metropolitan British readers. However, such displays of patriotism also can lead to self-contradiction, as in the book's dedication:

> To the Lords Spiritual and Temporal, and the Commons of the Parliament of Great Britain.
>
> My Lords and Gentlemen,
>
> Permit me with the greatest deference and respect, to lay at your feet the following genuine Narrative; the chief design of which is to excite in your august assemblies a sense of compassion for the miseries which the Slave Trade has entailed on my unfortunate countrymen. By the horrors of that trade I was first torn away from all the tender connexions that were dear to my heart; but these, through the mysterious ways of Providence, I ought to regard as infinitely more than compensated by the introduction I have thence obtained to the knowledge of the Christian religion, and of a nation which, by its liberal sentiments, its humanity, the glorious freedom of its government, and its proficiency in arts and sciences, has exalted the dignity of human nature.[20]

If becoming British and Christian has "more than compensated" Equiano for being enslaved, an assertion also found in writings by black contemporaries such as Phillis Wheatley; if, as pro-slavery advocates argued, bringing Africans to Europe was actually doing them a favor, then the slave trade and slavery cannot be unambiguously labeled evil.[21] Thus, this elaborate compliment to the British nation actually undermines Equiano's case against "the horrors of that trade." In line with common abolitionist strategy, the dedication's extravagant deference takes pains to separate the crimes of slavery from the glories of the British nation. However, the doubt lurking in "ought to" undercuts the conventionally effusive praise.

Intervening in the high-stakes debate on the slave trade, *The Interesting Narrative* pursues a politics of place broadly congruent with that of most white abolitionists, but it is calibrated in ways that subtly set Equiano apart. This appears in his well-researched "memories" of West Africa as well as the terms in which he compares Africa with Britain or Europe. Yet, the place in whose representation the formerly enslaved writer seems to be most emotionally invested is the Caribbean. *The Interesting Narrative* presents, in most respects, the Caribbean of standard abolitionist rhetoric: an aberrant region where cruel colonists, unrestrained by morality or law, mistreat the enslaved with impunity. Equiano's travels brought him into contact with the British abroad, from the "white men with horrible looks, red faces, and long hair" who ship him off from Africa as a boy, to those who buy, sell, and abuse Africans in the Caribbean, where he experiences colonial slavery in practice.[22] Like earlier abolitionist writings – and emphatically unlike pro-slavery propaganda (e.g., the colonial histories discussed in Chapter 3) – *The Interesting Narrative* works to maintain the distinction between slave-owning colonists and the metropolitan British.

The four chapters at the center of the book (Chapters V through VIII), which recount Equiano's experience in the West Indies as an enslaved man, are its most anthologized section, the material that justifies assimilating it to the genre of the "slave narrative."[23] Sold without warning by his master, Lieutenant Pascal, the young slave is shipped to what he labels "this land of bondage." He hates the place and cannot wait (he says) to leave it forever. To set the scene, he quotes Milton's description of Hell, and Thomas Day and John Bicknell's popular sentimental anti-slavery poem, "The Dying Negro" ("Now dragg'd once more beyond the western main, / To groan beneath some dastard planter's chain"). This section of *The Interesting Narrative* contains its most concentrated tirades against the slave trade and slavery, supported by eyewitness evidence of brutality and degradation. "Such a tendency has the slave trade to debauch men's minds, and harden them to every feeling of humanity!" Equiano exclaims; "this traffic . . . spreads like a pestilence, and taints what it touches!"[24] It was this material, with its allegedly first-hand account of the Middle Passage, that made his autobiography such a powerful contribution to abolitionist politics in 1789 and presumably helped to drive its high sales.

Knowing what goes on in the sugar islands, Equiano is desperate to return to Britain. He calls it his home, "where my heart had always been" – a remarkable act of rhetorical oblivion, blanking out his first decade of life. "I was now completely disgusted with the West Indies, and thought I never should be entirely free until I had left them," he declares, and breaks into verse:

With thoughts like these my anxious boding mind
Recall'd those pleasing scenes I left behind;
Scenes where fair Liberty, in bright array
Makes darkness bright, and e'en illumines day;
Where no complexion, wealth, or station can
Protect the wretch who makes a slave of man.

He concludes, "I determined to make every exertion to obtain my freedom, and to return to Old England."[25] In line with abolitionist geography, Equiano's rhetoric associates freedom with "Old England" and slavery with the colonies. Like Clarkson, and in contrast to Long and Edwards, he presents the slave-owning colonists as essentially different from their "countrymen at home."[26] His personified Liberty inhabits the "pleasing scenes" of "Old England" (the adjective invoking the nation's long history and ancient constitution), where slavery is not tolerated and any "wretch" who attempts it is punished. This personification is likely an allusion (although anachronistic, describing Equiano's state of mind in the 1760s) to the 1772 Mansfield Decision, the landmark verdict discussed in Chapter 3, which was often misconstrued to mean that slavery would not be tolerated on British soil. The lines' chiaroscuro imagery flatters "England" at the writer's expense: "fair Liberty" can brighten even the "darkness" of his African complexion.

Despite his joy at escaping from the West Indies, the peripatetic wanderer seems unable to stay away. After a supposedly "final farewell [to] the American quarter of the globe" in 1767, Equiano shipped out to Barbados and Grenada in April 1771 and then to Jamaica and Nevis in December of that year. His stint as an enslaved man in the West Indies provided Equiano with documentary material crucial to his book's political agenda; however, his later, post-manumission Caribbean sojourn puts a more personal spin on the region's corrupt and corrupting character. Chapter XI of *The Interesting Narrative* recounts an "adventure" – perhaps the strangest of Equiano's "chequered" life – the consequences of which seem to support abolitionist geography's description of the region as beyond the reach of morality and law.[27]

In 1775, after his Christian rebirth, Equiano's patron, "the celebrated Dr. Irving," decides to establish a plantation in Central America with Equiano as overseer. He and Irving stop in Jamaica to buy enslaved workers. "I chose them all of my own countrymen," Equiano writes.[28] As his biographer points out, in 1776, he did not yet oppose slavery. "Nearly a decade would pass before Equiano recognized that humane slavery was a contradiction in terms."[29] Although this is undoubtedly true, the outcome of this "adventure" suggests at least some ambivalence. Equiano quits his job, blaming Sabbath-breaking and "heathenish" behavior. What happens after he leaves is downright haunting. Irving hires a replacement overseer, who "beat and cut the poor slaves most unmercifully." They then try to escape in a large canoe "but, not knowing where to go, or how to manage the canoe, they were all drowned." Irving heads back to Jamaica to buy more enslaved workers for his plantation. Equiano does not comment on his employer's poor judgment. Although he reports Irving's death from food poisoning, he never speaks ill of this mentor and "amiable friend."[30]

Working his way back to Britain via Jamaica, Equiano must cross what he portrays as a type of "twilight zone," populated by human scum. He joins three different ships, all run by British captains who exploit and mistreat him – presumably "debauched by a West India climate." Reaching Plymouth in January 1777, Equiano writes, "I was happy once more to tread upon English ground."[31] The localized, Caribbean character of so much of the wickedness and madness reported in *The Interesting Narrative* supports abolitionist geography's assertion of a moral divide between colony and metropole. It also may have helped salve Equiano's guilt at his involvement, as a free man, in the institution of slavery. Although he certainly is not responsible for what happened after he left, the abused captives' escape and tragic drowning emblematize Caribbean slavery's massive waste of human life, the moral malaise that warps what Equiano calls the "American quarter of the globe."

The Interesting Narrative's imaginative geography of the Atlantic Rim – its moralized rendition of the Atlantic Triangle's nodes and the relationships among them – is indebted to abolitionist cultural politics and largely congruent with an abolitionist worldview. Yet, this congruence is not total. Under scrutiny, sly ironies and subtle inconsistencies emerge, putting space between Equiano and his white allies. His portrait of an idealized Africa does more than refute racist stereotypes – it subtly erodes his overt flattery of British civilization. His account of the colonial Caribbean as a geographical locus of evil is troubled by its disclosure of its author's participation, even if relatively benign, in the slave trade and the practice of plantation slavery.

Transformative voyages

Equiano represents the nodes of the Atlantic system in the process of narrating his numerous journeys between and among them. He criss-crosses the ocean on a succession of voyages that *The Interesting Narra-tive* presents as transformative. These voyages link stages in the narrator's personal growth – stages crucially associated with the places of the Atlantic: Africa, Britain, and the Caribbean islands. They are central to Equiano's personal transformation, or acculturation: becoming British while remaining black, the process Sonia Hofkosh describes as the "central problematic" of *The Interesting Narrative*.[32] Closer analysis of this chronicle of mobility, deracination, colonial mimicry, and eventual political maturity reveals a dialogically constituted narrative voice. I connect this narrative technique to the central presence of the ocean in the book and in Equiano's life.

Helen Thomas's landmark study, *Romanticism and Slave Narratives* (2000), puts black diaspora writers in dialogue with Romantic political and religious dissidents through their common participation in the Protestant religious idiom that she calls the "discourse of the spirit." She is especially interested in "the continuous processes of identity-transformation and negotiation within the diaspora, processes which disturb ideas of 'fixed' traditions, cultures or 'selves.'" Her chapter on Equiano notes *The Interesting Narrative*'s "emphasis on the sea . . . as a signifier of the author's cultural displacement and territorial dispossession." The ocean becomes "a trope of the diaspora itself, a 'no man's land' or middle passage in which 'identity' becomes amorphous and . . . epistemological boundaries and cultural ideologies are subjected to processes of instability, transition and miscegenation."[33] I propose to anchor the vital tropological presence of the "aquatic zone" in a pragmatic dimension of Equiano's life story: namely, his work as a deep-sea sailor.

To this end, I read the rather stylized meditation on the process of acculturation that opens Chapter IV alongside other sections of the book treating the narrator's ocean voyages – in particular, his (possibly fictional) description of the Middle Passage from Africa to the Americas. Chapter IV refers to Equiano's naval service with his owner, Lieutenant Pascal, in the Seven Years' War. The common thread linking that time on shipboard to the Middle Passage is the element of fear or terror, which Equiano cites as essential to his personal transformation. Henry Louis Gates's classic discussion of *The Interesting Narrative* is useful in thinking about Equiano's dramatized description of his acculturation as a black Briton. Gates identifies two voices in *The Interesting Narrative*: "the simple wonder with which the young Equiano approached the New World of his captors and a more eloquently articulated voice that he employs to describe the author's narrative present." Along with the temporal distinction between the voices of the naïve child and the sophisticated man, Gates notes their spatial or geographical affiliations: the child has an African worldview, whereas the man is largely assimilated to British culture. All of this serves Equiano's "apparent desire to represent a dynamic self that once was 'like that' but is now 'like this.'"[34]

A good example of the naïve early voice is the boy Equiano's initial response to Britain (discussed previously). The tension between the two voices – the unacculturated boy and the self-consciously worldly young man – gives *The Interesting Narrative* a dialogic dimension that is chronological, juxtaposing the protagonist's childhood with his youth, but also implicitly spatial or geographical: setting African and Anglicized perspectives in counterpoint, without definitively locating either speaker or reader. The geography of the Atlantic Triangle is narrated through a shifting or mobile consciousness that refracts heteroglossic "voices... world views [and] languages."[35] These are affiliated with places far apart yet linked by the routes of imperial travel and trade and the Atlantic representational network of which *The Interesting Narrative* forms a part.

This important passage, which I quote at length, connects Equiano's slavery and his acquired Britishness with his seamanship. The Britain to which the young slave is introduced, and for which he develops such a patriotic affection, is Britain not on land but instead at sea: the victorious international naval power that he and his owner, Lieutenant Pascal of the Royal Navy, served. Equiano's acculturation as a black Briton takes place, significantly, along with and as part of his initiation into life at sea. With Pascal, he takes part in major battles of the Seven Years' War in Europe and Canada. He grows up with the war, spending his teen years on a succession of battleships (i.e., HMS *Roebuck*, *Preston*, *Royal George*, and *Namur* and the fireship *Etna*) as Pascal is promoted.[36]

> It was now between three and four years since I first came to England, a great part of which I had spent at sea; so that I became inured to that service, and began to consider myself as happily situated; for my master treated me always extremely well; and my attachment and gratitude to him were very great. From the various scenes I had beheld on shipboard, I soon grew a stranger to terror of every kind, and was, in that respect at least, almost an Englishman. I have often reflected with surprise that I never felt half the alarm at any of the numerous dangers I have been in, that I was filled with at the first sight of the Europeans, and at every act of theirs, even the most trifling, when I first came among them, and for some time afterwards. That fear, however, which was the effect of my ignorance, wore away as I began to know them. I could now speak English tolerably well, and I perfectly understood every thing that was said. I not only felt myself quite easy with these new countrymen, but relished their society and manners. I no longer looked upon them as spirits, but as men superior to us; and therefore I had

the stronger desire to resemble them; to imbibe their spirit, and imitate their manners; I therefore embraced every occasion of improvement; and every new thing that I observed I treasured up in my memory.[37]

As the young Equiano becomes "inured to that service" (i.e., his work as a sailor), he also becomes inured – accustomed or habituated – to his "new countrymen," their "society and manners." He takes up a sophisticated tone that he attributes to his acquired "relish" for all things British. His extravagant deference, verging on self-caricature, highlights the insecurity of the boy torn from his original cultural milieu and thrown into a new one that is alien and powerful but also brutal. He cites the fear or terror he experienced on shipboard as essential to his transformation and its absence as defining his new British identity.

The terms of this meditation recall his first, vividly described ocean passage – the Middle Passage from Africa to the Caribbean – with its "horror almost inconceivable." The language in Chapter III that describes the Seven Years' War naval battles is not nearly as gripping as that in which the boy tells of his first encounter with Europeans and his voyage on the slave ship. His fear during that harrowing journey (whether fact or fiction) cannot be dismissed as the "effect of ignorance." Given the horrendous suffering and death that he reports, his terror would have been fully justified. The cannibalistic desires he attributes to the "white men with horrible looks" are a fitting metaphor for the slave-trade's consumption of African bodies.[38]

We also should recall the opening of The Interesting Narrative, in which Equiano puts the events of his life in cross-cultural perspective: "did I consider myself an European, I might say my sufferings were great; but, when I compare my lot with that of most of my countrymen, I regard myself as a particular favorite of Heaven." Critics have commented variously on the term "countrymen." It "suggests national identity," Boulukos notes, but "Equiano uses the term in very slippery ways."[39] In the opening, the phrase "most of my countrymen" situates him alongside his fellow Africans but with ambiguous implications. Does the phrase "most of my countrymen" refer to those Africans not fortunate enough to be enslaved or, rather, rescued – taken out of their backward country to live among Europeans? Or does it designate those Africans enslaved by Europeans but not fortunate enough to achieve manumission, as Equiano has done – still enduring the rigors of plantation labor and the cruel punishments described later in The Interesting Narrative?

Later in the book, when the young enslaved sailor of Chapter IV refers to his "new countrymen" – that is, the British sailors on the Navy ships where he has been serving – he marks aspiration rather than achieved fact. In this local context, as the narrator considers how far he has come in his process of acculturation, to be "almost an Englishman" is to be (almost) "a stranger to terror of every kind" – incidental patriotic flattery for British readers. However, read alongside *The Interesting Narrative's* earlier use of "countrymen," referring to Africans, this subsequent incidence yields a different perspective: a double exposure, juxtaposing two very different voyages – the Middle Passage and the imperial navy at war. Each is transformative in its own way for the young Equiano; both involve danger and fear, although of different kinds. Would the undoubted bravery of "these new countrymen" – the Royal Navy sailors – really have withstood the fetters, filth, stench, shrieks, groans, floggings, and continual death of the slave ship? Here, as elsewhere in *The Interesting Narrative*, Equiano's flattery of his adopted homeland carries – on closer scrutiny – a subtle challenge.

To grasp the narrator of this meditative passage as identified with neither the captive child's naiveté nor the young colonial mimic's self-proclaimed worldliness is to appreciate the unmoored artistry of Equiano's narrative method. Atlantic geography lends his narration its structure and texture: a structure that is restlessly mobile and ceaselessly on the move, and a texture correspondingly protean, arising from the dialogic or heteroglossic interplay of voices, languages, and worldviews associated with the various linked sites of the Atlantic system. Spatial dialogism as a structuring principle arises from Equiano's professional identity as a deep-sea sailor, the importance of which more critics have recently begun to notice. One language with a prominent role in *The Interesting Narrative* is the "polyglot, specialized lingo" of the ocean-going ship.[40] Marcus Rediker analyzed the sailor as cosmopolitan figure, member of an international laboring class that, along with the enslaved, provided muscle power for Britain's overseas expansion. The restless mobility that structures Equiano's *Narrative* both before and after he buys his freedom is the mobility of the sailor, shipping out for just one more voyage, seemingly unable to tarry long on shore. This unceasing circulation makes Equiano's life a fitting emblem for the geography of mercantile capitalism, the lifeblood of which circulated along the trade routes that Rediker calls the "arteries of the imperial body."[41]

The Interesting Narrative makes adroit use of its protagonist's putative roots on the dry land of Africa as well as his painstakingly acquired Britishness. However, as we follow his many journeys across and around the Atlantic, the Caribbean, the Mediterranean, and even the Arctic Ocean, "roots" give way to "routes." None of Equiano's geographically circumscribed characters – African native, enslaved West Indian, black British subject – defines the book as inclusively as the cosmopolitan roles of sailor and diasporan activist. Equiano's sailor identity provides *The Interesting Narrative* with a speaking voice and structural principle that breaks down national boundaries and ethnic stereotypes. Susan Marren describes his narrator as a "transgressive self": "not . . . a stable identity or essence in itself but rather . . . a fluid positioning, a mode of articulation of newly imagined, radically nonbinary subjectivities."[42] We can anchor such a fluid positioning in the concrete historical context of Equiano's working life at sea.

As Rediker points out, sailors and the enslaved had much in common: both the ship and the plantation – like the factory – concentrated large numbers of workers "under a watchful supervisory regime armed with violent disciplinary power . . . used to ensure their cooperation for the sake of profit." The "collectivism of necessity" that characterized both groups was a stateless, essentially deracinated group affinity, contrasting in this respect with the ethnic and national affiliations of Equiano's African and British selves. The ship, "a living, micro-cultural, micro-political system in motion" across the sea, makes an apt emblem for the "transcultural, international formation" that is the black Atlantic.[43] The mobile persona of the sailor, we also can say, corresponds to the rendering of geographical space in *The Interesting Narrative* as a fluid connective medium. Equiano the sailor is agent as well as product of the cultural crossing that characterizes the black Atlantic as a super-regional geographical entity.

Traveling black

The sailor's mobility also bears on the issue of genre. Critics have read *The Interesting Narrative* primarily as a slave narrative or a spiritual autobiography. Because Carretta cast doubt on Equiano's African birth, we also might classify at least its opening section as fiction. The other genre in which the book participates, of course, is that of abolitionist polemic; it was a crucial intervention in the slavery debate, providing the abolitionist movement with a first-person account of the Middle Passage. Similar to a number of the texts I consider in previous chapters, *The Interesting Narrative* is generically and discursively hybrid, overlapping with various types of prose works in circulation in its day. However, I believe Equiano's book is most fruitfully read as travel writing.

In this, I agree with Gretchen Gerzina but for different reasons. Equiano clearly did not fit the conventional image of the traveler: privileged, leisured, autonomous, moving voluntarily to destinations of his choice. Movement certainly marked the lives of many or most eighteenth-century black people, as Gerzina observes. She points to black sailors in particular as

benefiting from their mobility, entering an international black community that coalesced around the idea of Africa as home. Travel was thus an
important means of "forging a specific and positive black identity" in the
eighteenth-century Atlantic.[44] However, I understand the significance of
Equiano's sailor profession rather differently. His restless mobility – his life
at sea – enters his *Narrative* as both content and form. Its fluidly positioned,
elusive narrator, criss-crossing the Atlantic and circulating among its ports,
is best understood as a function or effect rather than a positive identity. In
Equiano's lifelong journey, as he tells it, geographical movement catalyzes
personal transformation under intense pressure. His narrative method, setting his earlier and later selves in dialogue, loosens or relativizes their spatial
affiliations to produce a narrating consciousness that passes through diverse
places, without becoming exclusively identified with one or another.

If this method is innovative, other aspects of his book's rhetorical strategy are less so – although perhaps surprising when practiced by a formerly enslaved writer. The sheer accumulation of "interesting" journeys
and adventures in *The Interesting Narrative* works to support its rhetorical
ethos.[45] To persuade British readers to abolish the slave trade, Equiano
marshals the authority of experience – specifically, the experience he has
gained through travel, both involuntary and voluntary. Travel traditionally
counted as a source of knowledge or wisdom – a valuable, indeed irreplace-
able, educational experience. The Grand Tour of Europe, for example, was
considered the capstone of a male British aristocrat's education.

Equiano's decision to include in his book so much of his life and travels
after his manumission (comprising approximately two fifths of its total
length) serves this rhetorical function in a way that his slave travels alone
could not have done. He certainly learned a great deal from his involuntary
travels while enslaved – knowledge that his book passes on to educate the
public about the evils of slavery. Yet, his later, voluntary journeys to Europe,
Turkey, and the Arctic, as well as back to the Caribbean, are important
to the book in a different way. The formerly enslaved traveler brings to
his travels the same intellectual curiosity about places and cultures that
characterizes "high" travel writing, but he turns his observations to a rather
different end. In Genoa, for example, he describes "rich and magnificent"
churches but adds that "all this grandeur was, in my eyes, disgraced by the
galley-slaves, whose condition . . . is truly piteous and wretched."[46] The
experience gained through travel enhances the traveler's authority to pass
moral as well as aesthetic judgment.

Aesthetic discourse, including the categories of beauty, elegance, and
taste among others, was a standard feature of travel writing by 1789. In its

use of such language, Equiano's account of his European travels occasionally resembles an unusual type of Grand Tour. "I was charmed with the richness and beauty of the countries, and struck with the elegant buildings with which they abound...I had frequent occasions of gratifying both my taste and curiosity." Even in the Arctic Circle, where he traveled with Phipps's expedition, aesthetic discourse elevates Equiano's descriptions (some cribbed from Phipps's own published account): "We had generally sunshine, and constant day-light; which gave cheerfulness and novelty to the whole of this striking, grand, and uncommon scene...the reflection of the sun from the ice gave the clouds a most beautiful appearance."[47] Chapter 1 explores the ways in which pro-slavery writers used the prestige of aesthetics to help legitimize colonial slavery while obscuring slavery's ugly realities. Equiano's anti-slavery autobiography also draws on the language of aesthetics to enhance his legitimacy as a participant in the slavery debate.

Aesthetic discourse figures in another of *The Interesting Narrative*'s dialogic moments: a transition that works paradoxically by abruptly shifting readers' perspective away from the horrors of slavery to bring them into better focus. This odd swerve occurs, not coincidentally, in Equiano's account of his Caribbean sojourn while enslaved. The colonial Caribbean took shape through a series of displacements that brought deracinated groups into often-violent contact: native Amerindians, African captives, and European settlers who came not always by choice (including transported convicts, indentured laborers, and political refugees). Equiano worked as a sailor and was able to observe the suffering of other enslaved people on a number of islands. The indignant reportage that resulted forms, along with the Middle Passage material, the core of *The Interesting Narrative*'s testimony against slavery.

At the beginning of Chapter VI, however, Equiano abruptly turns away from enumerating "those many instances of oppression, extortion and cruelty, to which I have been a witness in the West Indies." He treats his readers instead to a travelogue-like description of a visit to "a celebrated curiosity called Brimstone-Hill," a sulfur spring on the island of Montserrat. What could be his reason for juxtaposing this type of tourist discourse – which constructed the Caribbean for metropolitan readers as an exotic realm of beauty and "curiosity" – with Chapter V's gritty account of slavery's human toll? Geraldine Murphy comments: "Equiano seems determined to undermine the affective force of his own experience at a time when he felt the yoke of slavery most acutely." Why would he do this? He justifies his abrupt transition in the language of aesthetics. "The punishments of the slaves, on every trifling occasion, are so frequent, and so well known, together with the different instruments with which they are tortured, that it cannot any longer afford novelty to recite them; and they are too shocking to yield delight either to the writer or the reader."[48]

Novelty and delight were aesthetic categories familiar to British readers at least since Joseph Addison. Equiano's command of aesthetic discourse, conventional in travel writing, contributes to his ethos as a black gentleman, as discussed previously. His sulfur-springs tour also invokes another discourse that was conventional in travel writing, especially colonial travel, that is, natural history. Beginning in 1707 with Hans Sloane's book, a number of Caribbean natural histories – often illustrated with lavish plates of exotic flora and fauna –gave metropolitan readers access to the region's geography and culture as well as its plant and animal denizens. Several of these histories describe geothermal "curiosities": the Reverend William Smith's 1745 *Natural History of Nevis*, for example, describes a hot river, allegedly capable of curing leprosy, in which Smith bathes. "Some of my acquaintances," he reports, "would drink of it till they puked."[49] The discourses of aesthetics and natural history, sharing an emphasis on distance and control, collaborate in much writing about the Caribbean from this period. (Chapters 1 and 2 explore the presence of picturesque aesthetics in planter writing and the role of natural history in Stedman's narrative.)

At the beginning of Chapter VI, Equiano's narrative suddenly swerves from the perspective of the enslaved African majority to that of a privileged European – from a position under the boot heel, so to speak, of colonial slavery to one so far removed as to render the region's cruelties all but invisible. Equiano's incongruous shift from torture to tourism forcefully combines the disparate, place-identified perspectives of the enslaved African and the transient European, whose tense interaction forged the cruel, fragile culture of the plantation complex. Taking advantage of travel writing's conventional freedom to digress, *The Interesting Narrative* generates at this juncture a strange type of double vision. Readers experience the region from two incompatible discursive and social positions: that of the anonymous, vulnerable captive Africans whose oppression Equiano reports, and that of a white European such as the Reverend Smith. An ambiguous narrating voice reports both sadistically inflicted pain and touristic pleasure from a vantage point at least relatively privileged and safe.

This break in the momentum of Equiano's narrative helps us to focus on his uniqueness as a traveler and travel writer. An enslaved man can be a traveler, even a tourist. *The Interesting Narrative* encompasses widely divergent experiences in places around the Atlantic and far beyond by someone who has been both African and British, both enslaved and free. The book's broad scope, refracted through its protean persona, compels readers to rethink what we know of travel and travel writing. Through his travels, first involuntary and then voluntary, Equiano has been radically transformed. By narrating his personal transformation under the pressure of violent uprooting and forced immersion in an alien culture, he brings Atlantic geography to life for his readers. His autobiographical *The Interesting Narrative* crafts a unique life, spent traversing the captive spaces of the British Atlantic, into a powerful means of persuading readers that the slave trade must end: reading this eloquent account of transformation, his audience is meant to be transformed as well.

A key means of accomplishing this is the politics of place, which *The Interesting Narrative* pursues intertextually, as I have shown. Building on the work of other abolitionists, Equiano redraws the distorted map of the Atlantic purveyed by pro-slavery writers. His first-person testimony intervened decisively at a crucial point in the national debate over slavery, reaching thousands of readers; nine editions were published before the author's death in 1797. The book's inclusive account of enslavement features violent capture, inhumane transport, cruel punishment, and the indignities suffered by a nominally free black man in the slave societies of the Caribbean and the American South. Even if a key section, the Middle Passage, is actually fiction, we must recognize Equiano's literary achievement in bringing to life the experience of hundreds of thousands of his African brethren.[50]

His literary and business acumen led him to package his experience as travel writing. Travel writing – the literature of place – brings geography to life through first-person narrative. It draws readers in by embellishing that narrative with miscellaneous, "interesting" events and observations, such as Equiano's Caribbean sulfur-springs tour or the harrowing shipwreck of the *Nancy* in the Bahamas shortly after his manumission.[51] The decision to include in the book so much detail about his life after his manumission bespeaks the importance of travel – as a source of knowledge and wisdom – to Equiano's rhetorical ethos. The place-based identities of kidnapped African child, teenaged British sailor, and enslaved West Indian serve important purposes in the book. Yet, the mature voice that emerges from this complex record of a life spent en route from one corner of the Atlantic to another carries the weary, wise inflection of a black cosmopolitan – a citizen of the Atlantic world.

CHAPTER 5

At home with the "blackies"
Janet Schaw and Maria Nugent

The final two chapters are concerned with a type of place-making that contributed significantly to creating and maintaining the captive space of the slave colony. As Catherine Hall and Sonya Rose succinctly stated, "British women's roles in the colonies were envisioned as making new homes away from home."[1] What was involved in the gendered labor of colonial home-making? To answer this question, we first must ask a more basic one. What kind of place is home – home, in general, and home in the slave colony, in particular? What is the relationship between domesticity and the empire?

According to the OED, "home" is a "dwelling-place, house, or abode": the place where one lives, where one performs the basic functions of everyday life – eating, sleeping, washing, and dressing. Home provides shelter from the elements and from other people, so it must be secure and defensible. Hence, home is bounded: the inside is separated by boundaries or limits from the space outside. "Home is a way of establishing difference. Homes and home-countries are exclusive."[2] Home is a relational concept, which is important when we consider its status in the slave colony.[3] The OED further defines home as "the fixed residence of a family or household; the seat of domestic life and interests." It is "the place of one's dwelling or nurturing, with the conditions, circumstances, and feelings which naturally and properly attach to it." Feelings – the affective dimension of home – form the core of domesticity: "family, intimacy, and devotion to the home," with the house as the material embodiment of these sentiments.[4]

Feminist historians studying the rise of the middle-class British home in the eighteenth and nineteenth centuries view home in the context of economic history: the gradual but far-reaching economic and social reorganization leading up to the so-called Industrial Revolution. The removal of production from the home, or the separation between home and workplace, transpired unevenly throughout Britain's regions and localities.[5] The ideological consequences of establishing the home as a site of consumption rather than production have been analyzed under the rubric of "separate spheres." This familiar conceptual framework, qualified and critiqued over the years, remains useful for the purposes of my analysis. According to Catherine Hall, "Definitions of masculinity and femininity played an important part in marking out the middle class... The separation of spheres was one of the fundamental organizing characteristics of middle-class society in late eighteenth-century and early nineteenth-century England." The home as a feminized private sphere was a key ideological foundation of the middle classes, "the one place where moral order could be maintained."[6] Along with physical and emotional nurturance – the affective dimension of domesticity – middle-class women increasingly were entrusted with the moral and spiritual work of bourgeois life. Material cleanliness and physical nurturance, important in and of themselves, also could serve as tropes for the moral order and emotional sustenance for which these women were responsible. They made houses into homes.

However, the nation that this historiography describes, Great Britain, was the center of an empire. What, we now must ask, was the relationship of home to empire? An answer to this question can begin usefully with what Charlotte Sussman calls the "semantic slippage between 'the domestic,' meaning British national territory, and 'the domestic,' meaning the interior of the family. Defining these two domestic sites in terms of one another helps to reveal the crucial role played by constructions of female identity in articulating the relationship between Britain and its West Indian colonies." Sussman makes this slippage the basis of her analysis of a political tactic used by abolitionists: the sugar boycott of 1791–92. Abolitionist pamphlets invoked British women's compassion as part of their national identity – "a quality that distinguishes England from the rest of the world" – and used it to try to redefine England's relationship to its sugar-producing colonies by persuading women and – through their influence – men to abstain from slave-produced sugar.[7] The naturalized feminine quality of sympathy or compassion thus was brought to bear on colonial politics in the metropole, or the center of the empire. This example illustrates how the alternate meaning of "home" as "a place or region to which one naturally belongs or where one feels at ease" (OED) – that is, home as homeland – expands the affective associations of the home as domicile to the entire nation, thereby generating a political leverage for women that was exploited by the creative abolitionist tactic of the boycott.

In a modern empire, domesticity depends on and is permeated by the fruits of imperial rule. The associations of material comfort that surround the idea of "home" – food, cleanliness, and so forth – are embodied by imperial products, as Hall and Rose point out. For example, the comfort of a cup of tea, sweetened with sugar, was by 1790 already so well established in everyday British life that the sugar boycott demanded actual, painful sacrifice.[8] In a later instance, Anne McClintock's social history of soap finds the idea of cleanliness intertwined with Britain's imperial civilizing mission, as well as other middle-class values including monogamy, Christianity, and class control. "The cult of domesticity became indispensable to the consolidation of British national identity, and at the center of the domestic cult stood the simple bar of soap." To uncover the imperial networks, both material and ideological, that crosscut the metropolitan home is to realize how intimately "colony and metropole . . . were and are co-constituted."[9]

How did this co-constitution manifest on the colonial periphery? What forms did the gendered power of home take when no longer at home? In the colony, muses Ranajit Guha, the empire "*requires* no homes, if only because the authority, the imperium, from which it derives its form, function, and purpose, is easily sustained by forts and barracks and offices." Throughout history, however, these have not sufficed because the "empire too is seized by the urge to make a home of its territory." Something uncanny about imperial rule, Guha theorizes – a lack of boundaries, a discomforting unfamiliarity – provokes an anxiety in the rulers that makes them crave, in the words of British officer Francis Yeats-Brown, "a world whose limits were known." Boundary setting is a crucial founding act of the empire, invoking the logic of difference between rulers and ruled that underpins imperial governance. However, home-making, as a conceptual process, sets boundaries as well: a home must be bounded to be secure both physically and psychologically. The discourse of domesticity, in this sense, is well suited to its imperial use. It is "a mobile and often unstable discourse that can expand or contract the boundaries of home and nation."[10] Setting the boundaries of home, we might even say, helps to create an imperial subjectivity that is defined by its relationship to those outside of its boundaries: those from whom the inside of the home must be kept secure. The spatial and conceptual boundaries of the home thus can figure the boundaries of the imperial self.

Scholars in several disciplines have analyzed white women's ambiguous complicity in the imperial enterprise.[11] The majority of existing work treats the late-nineteenth and twentieth centuries – that is, high imperialism and its decline – rather than the earlier period that is of concern here. Anthropologists have studied white women in colonies such as India, Africa, Malaya, and Sumatra.[12] These "incorporated wives," as Shirley Ardener

and Hilary Callan call them, were viewed as bearers of a special civilizing mission to both the colonized and their countrymen. They made the
private domain available to colonial government, using its special power
as a platform to disseminate virtue for the nation. These wives were not
merely support staff. "In a colonial or settler society, a properly managed
home is more than a precondition of the 'civilizing mission': it is part of
it."[13] Colonial society profited from women's quotidian surveillance, their
monitoring of everyday life: managing servants, for example, or keeping a
journal. Women's contribution to colonization involved "the reconstruc-
tion of the ordinary"; amid colonial dirt and danger, white women strove
to enforce cleanliness as a "sociomoral condition."[14] Their work formed the
symbolic basis of a cultural hygiene intended to draw colonial men into
the home, away from "Mestizo customs [e.g., concubinage] and toward
metropolitan norms."[15] "The attribution of civilizing functions to domestic activities," Karen Hansen summarizes, "was a product of the colonial
encounter."[16]

    This chapter analyzes the journals of Janet Schaw and Maria Nugent,
white British women who traveled to the West Indies to accompany men
employed in serving the colonial government. These two women carry out
a number of "civilizing functions." Entering a society in which domesticity
was organized differently than in Britain, they exploit their special connection to home in both its senses. Schaw's journal strives to present colonial
life, particularly slavery, as morally acceptable and aesthetically appealing, whereas Nugent's journal records the ways in which she was able
to contribute to her husband's arduous work of colonial administration.
The discourse of domesticity at work in these journals encompasses affect –
feeling, sensibility, and sentiment – deployed in the service of the boundary
setting that was so essential to colonial life. Thus, Schaw – even before she
reaches her Caribbean destination – reworks her sentimental attachment to
her Scottish homeland into a portable set of affective ties among expatriate
Scots bound for the colonies. In the slave colony of Antigua, such bonds
could help to reinforce the solidarity among the relatively small population
of white colonizers over and against the enslaved majority, whom Schaw
depicts as lacking the capacity to feel in the same way as Europeans.

    Nugent's job as the wife of the lieutenant governor of Jamaica is more
complex and taxing. She runs the household in the governor's mansion,
managing the servants and working in various ways to achieve literal and
metaphorical cleanliness in this symbolically important enclave. Because
most of the servants are enslaved, the boundaries of home in this colonial
setting prove to be particularly complicated to maintain. Nugent's attempts

to impose metropolitan manners at the imperial periphery sometimes lead her into telling difficulties.

These two women bore the power of home in both senses across the Atlantic to what Schaw calls "the western world."[17] Although settled by the British for more than a century, the tropical Caribbean colonies remained persistently alien, resisting efforts to remake them in the image of the metropole. For the majority of their white population, "home" meant England or Scotland. James Stephen writes, "It would be difficult to find a white man in the island of Jamaica who does not regard England as his home and the colony as his place of exile."[18] Yet, those who sojourned in the colonies were no longer British. They became Creoles: that is, members of a colonial culture distinctly different from that of the British Isles, shaped by the islands' tropical environment and slave society. When they went back to the metropole, they carried their West Indian-ness with them and were "ridiculed and envied" for their un-British ways and their wealth, accrued – as was widely known – via slavery.[19]

White women sojourning in the colonial West Indies must have often felt out of place. Relatively few white women settled on the islands. Maria Nugent traveled through Jamaica for a week in 1802, staying in a different house each night, without meeting a single white woman. The West Indies were primarily exploitation colonies: men went there to make a fortune, which they planned to spend back home in Britain. Conditions on the islands were not such as to attract or to accommodate elite women. The living arrangements that first arose in the seventeenth century, when the Caribbean islands were the "Wild West" of the British Empire, included forms of domesticity that did not require a white woman's presence. Concubinage, as practiced by John Stedman in Suriname and many single colonial men (as well as by some with wives and families back in Britain or on the island), "characterized the gender order which developed as an integral part of the system of slavery."[20] The slave colony, in short, was no place for a lady, and the lady who ventured there faced significant challenges. The ways in which Janet Schaw and Maria Nugent negotiated these challenges have much to impart about gender, empire, and the portable virtues of home.

Yahoos

Janet Schaw sailed from her home in Edinburgh in October 1774 aboard the *Jamaica Packet*. She accompanied her brother Alexander, who had secured a job as searcher of customs on the island of Saint Christopher (Saint

Kitts). Her other brother, Robert, whom she would visit on another leg of her journey, was a planter in North Carolina. Janet and Alexander sailed with the three children of another North Carolina planter, John Rutherfurd, who had sent them home to Scotland for their education. Fanny Rutherfurd was 18 or 19, John Jr. was 11, and William (Billy) was 9 years old. Two servants accompanied the party: Schaw's maid, Mary Miller, and her brother's valet, whom she calls "Black Robert." Schaw's reasons for embarking on her journey are not entirely clear. By looking after the children, she did the typical family service of the unmarried woman. Based on ambiguous evidence in Schaw's text, Eve Tavor Bannet contends that she planned to live with her brother in Saint Kitts, having no remaining male relatives in Scotland to house her since her father's death in 1772.[21] If this were the plan, events disrupted it when the loyalist Schaws were forced to flee North Carolina at the outbreak of the American Revolution. Alexander was sent to London with secret dispatches from North Carolina's governor, and Janet traveled back to Scotland via Portugal.

Whatever her agenda, Janet Schaw saw more of the world than most genteel thirty-something Scottish spinsters. She recorded her experiences in a journal – unpublished in her lifetime – written in the form of letters to an unnamed Scottish friend. It was not published until the early twentieth century, although the survival of several manuscript copies suggests that it circulated among family and friends during the author's lifetime. Schaw's and Nugent's journals are the only unpublished writings I include in this study (Matthew Lewis's journal, although published posthumously, was intended for publication). Upper-class women, of course, were less inclined than men to publish for well-known reasons involving gender ideology.[22] Describing their West Indian experiences in journal form, these two women doubtless intended to share the exotic novelty of their travels with family and friends. Their journals strive to make sense of the radically unfamiliar.

Setting foot on Antigua for the first time, Schaw writes, "Every thing was as new to me, as if I had been but a day old."[23] The writer produces a version of herself in relation to unfamiliar places and people, exploiting the resources of the familiar to suture this new colonial reality into her existing view of the world. Implicitly justifying her presence in a place not so suitable for ladies, Schaw refashions the sugar colonies as a place where white women have important cultural work to accomplish. Bonding with the islands' Creole elite, particularly those of Scottish origin (there were many), she develops a strategic position between colonial Creoles and metropolitan readers as interpreter of and apologist for the institution of colonial slavery. Her ability to do so depends on her feminine expertise in sensibility, or feeling, and her special connection as a woman to home.

A talented writer, Schaw establishes an engaging persona – witty, resilient, and compassionate – starting with her narrative of the *Jamaica Packet*'s eventful Atlantic crossing. A surprising incident on shipboard helps to position Schaw to contribute to the colonial project after her arrival in Antigua. Harnessing the power of home, the resourceful traveler readjusts the boundaries among groups in the self-contained wooden world of the ship. When the Schaw party boards the *Jamaica Packet*, they think they have chartered the entire ship. Once out to sea, however, Janet hears strange noises like groans through her stateroom wall. She goes on deck to find it "covered with people of all ages, from three weeks old to three score, men, women, children and suckling infants. . . . Never did my eyes behold so wretched, so disgusting a sight. They looked like a cargo of Dean Swift's Yahoos newly caught." It turns out that the ship's owner has increased his profit by stashing in steerage a large party of emigrants from the Orkney Islands – "these wretched human beings," as Schaw calls them. Her revulsion seems visceral as she mentions the nasty smell "from the hole, where they had been confined" and the lice that she imagines they have brought onboard. "Faugh! let me not think of it; it affects my stomach more than . . . this shocking rough Sea."[24]

The emigrants packed in steerage bear distinct similarities to the enslaved people on the sugar islands to which the *Jamaica Packet* was bound, as the allusion to *Gulliver's Travels* suggests by invoking the Yahoos' links to eighteenth-century accounts of racial difference through such characteristics as body hair, uncleanliness, and stench. The Celtic peoples of the British Isles – specifically, the Irish and the Gaelic-speaking Scottish Highlanders – were viewed by many eighteenth-century English men and women as racially different and inferior.[25] As Bannet observes, "indentured servitude – or, in the language of the time, 'voluntary slavery' – preceded and accompanied African slavery, was its condition of possibility, and in many ways, gave it its characteristic forms." These emigrants form a human cargo, confined in conditions similar to those of a slave ship. Their indenture contracts will be sold on arrival in North America, where the hold will be repacked with colonial commodities for the return voyage.[26]

Schaw wrote during the largest-ever wave of Scottish emigration. Scots had been going to North America and the Caribbean since the seventeenth century. Emigrants included Civil War prisoners exiled by Cromwell and militant Covenanters banished by Charles II and his brother; transported criminals, indentured servants, and adventurers in search of fast cash; as well as respectable merchants, planters, and clerks. After the end of the Seven Years' War in 1763, the exodus of Scots to the American colonies "became a truly national phenomenon, drawing from all classes of society and most regions of the country." The scale of this diaspora was such as to alarm Britain's governing class because a large population was thought to be vital to the nation's economic and military might. Highlanders and Hebrideans like the *Jamaica Packet* emigrants were driven from their homes by agrarian modernization.[27] Although its social status appears well above that of the emigrants on the *Jamaica Packet*, the Schaw family was part of this movement as well. When Janet's father, Gideon Schaw, could not support his growing family by farming, he sent his eldest son, Robert, to be indentured to a Scottish-American merchant in Wilmington, North Carolina. "Conveniently related to titled people with sufficient patronage," Gideon Schaw later joined the customs service. There, his second son, Alexander, also found a post for which he was headed to the colonies, accompanied by his sister.[28]

Difference and similarity complexly configure Schaw's relationship to the emigrants below decks. It is nonetheless startling when she dramatically and self-consciously shifts her attitude toward them from disgust to sympathy. "You remember," she tells her friend, "how much I had been surprised, as well as disgusted, at the appearance of a company of Emigrants. . . . I . . . now find they are a company of hapless exiles, from the Islands we have just passed, forced by the hand of oppression from their native land." Getting more information about her fellow passengers helps her to reconfigure them as human. Lynn Festa's reading of this incident emphasizes the amount of work it takes to produce "suitable objects of feeling." A personified Pity is needed to help sweep away "dirty passion[s]" like pride and disdain and to substitute tenderness and kindness. In this interpretation, Schaw's own transformation, rather than that of the "Yahoos," takes center stage. Producing "the sentimentalized vision of a privileged observer," she allows her readers to identify with her as an "emotionally correct spectator." The pleasure of sentiment elevates both Schaw and her readers. It does not, however, make the emigrants her equals, as her condescending treatment of them during the rest of the voyage makes clear.[29]

Schaw's about-face is catalyzed by the power of home. As the *Jamaica Packet* sails past the Orkneys, the steerage passengers "all crowded to that side of the ship next to them, and stood in silent sorrow, gazing fondly on the dear spot they were never more to behold." Schaw continues for four and a half pages in language straight from a sentimental novel: "their hands clasped in silent and unutterable anguish, their streaming eyes raised to heaven in mute ejaculations," and so forth. She uses their emotional attachment to their Scottish home to humanize these lower-class families into "respectable sufferers."[30] This peculiar sequence works in several ways to help delineate Schaw's contribution, as a white woman, to West Indian colonialism. By highlighting her ties to her own Scottish home, she establishes a series of oppositions between home and colony that allow her to serve as a carrier of the feelings and values of home for the man she accompanies, as well as for those she will meet on arrival.

Before discovering the huddled masses in steerage, she has staged an elaborate farewell to her home alongside a defense of her decision to travel. "I had long taken root in my native Soil, yet it is not the spot of Earth that gave me being I call my country. No! it is the Social Circle of such friends, as few can boast . . . that constituted my happiness; the western world may shew me higher Scenes of riches . . . but never can they afford my soul such evening Conversations as I have feasted on in the friendly Circle of our chearfull Hearth."[31] The Scotland that Schaw invokes is warm and unpretentious, thriving on human connections and the exchange of ideas (which is ironic, given the mass emigration of eighteenth-century Scots in pursuit of colonial wealth). Contrasting external appearance with inner worth and material riches with emotional sustenance, she takes implicit responsibility for bearing Scotland's "Social Circle" with her wherever she goes. The two meanings of home converge as the British Isles, and Scotland in particular, take on the emotional valence that metropolitan gender ideology accords to woman-centered domesticity. Schaw will impart this emotion to her male companions as they go forth into the luxurious and showy yet difficult and dangerous world of colonial work.

However, the *Jamaica Packet*'s destination suggests an additional dimension to her abrupt shift in erasing the image of Yahoos to substitute respectable fellow Scots. This adjustment anticipates the shifted categories and alliances of the colonial setting. With the enslaved population outnumbering white colonists by as much as ten to one, white people needed to distinguish themselves from their human property. White Scottish men and women, no matter how grungy, cannot occupy the position of Yahoos – those abject others – which will be needed for the enslaved. On Schaw's first day on the island of Antigua, she reports, "a number of pigs run out at a door, and after them a parcel of monkeys. This not a little surprised me, but I found what I took for monkeys were negro children, naked as they were born."[32] This often-quoted gratuitous racism functions in Schaw's narrative to solidify racial boundaries at the threshold, so to speak, of her island stay.

Another feature she notices early in her stay on this small island is the cohesive social bond among the island whites. Antiguans dine, she reports, with their windows open, so that (white) passers-by can "come and chat in." This shocks Schaw's eighteenth-century sense of decorum, but she concludes that it is acceptable: "Every body in town is on a level as to station, and they are all intimately acquainted." This is due in part to the Scottishness of Antigua, a constant theme running throughout Schaw's journal: she meets "Duncans, Millikens, Blairs, Bairds, Hallidays, Tullidephs, Mackinnons and Malcolms" and sees more Scottish names on the graves in the island churchyard.[33] At least as compelling a motive, however, is the colony's racial composition: the white minority was far outnumbered by enslaved Africans. White solidarity overrides the distinctions of rank customary in the metropole. Home, in the slave colony, sets its limits mostly along racial lines.[34]

Sentiment has the power to turn Yahoos into respectable Scots and cement a Scottish "Social Circle" in the faraway tropics. Schaw later sees this power wielded by another colonial woman, her old friend Lady Isabella Hamilton, whom she visits on the neighboring island of Saint Kitts. Their Scottish contemporary Adam Smith proclaims in his *Theory of Moral Sentiments*, "Humanity is the virtue of a woman, generosity of a man." Humanity consists, he continues, "merely in the exquisite fellow-feeling which the spectator entertains with the sentiments of the persons principally concerned, so as to grieve for their sufferings, to resent their injuries, and to rejoice at their good fortune."[35] Generosity involves the sterner elements of self-command and self-sacrifice. When Lady Isabella takes her friend on a tour of her plantation, Schaw is "much entertained" by the boiling-house, the proto-industrial facility where cane juice is processed into raw sugar. The division of space on the plantation was emphatically gendered where white ladies were concerned: their place was in the great house, well removed from the working spaces of the cane field and processing plant. A rare visit by Lady Isabella to this area gives her the opportunity to exercise the virtue of humanity, specifically mercy. "There were several of the boilers condemned to the lash, and seeing her face is pardon," Schaw writes.[36] The gendered virtue of humanity mitigates the routine violence of the plantation, allowing Schaw to praise her friend while conveniently ignoring the norm of harsh punishment that has created the need for Lady Isabella's conspicuous display of mercy. Reporting in her journal on this colonial woman's adroit deployment of the feminine virtues of the domestic sphere, Schaw puts the anecdote in the service of her ongoing apology for slavery.

A complementary aspect of that apology is her depiction of slaves as lacking the capacity for finer feelings. The enslaved workers' "gratitude on this occasion [for Lady Isabella's pardon] was the only instance of sensibility that I have observed in them," Schaw comments dryly. She introduced the theme a few pages earlier in her description of a gang of field laborers, accompanied by drivers with whips:

> You will too easily guess the use of these weapons; a circumstance of all others the most horrid. They are naked, male and female, down to the girdle, and you constantly observe where the application has been made. But however dreadful this must appear to a humane European, I will do the creoles the justice to say, they would be as averse to it as we are, could it be avoided, which has often been tried to no purpose. When one comes to be better acquainted with the nature of the Negroes, the horror of it must wear off. It is the suffering of the human mind that constitutes the greatest misery of punishment, but with them it is merely corporeal. As with the brutes it inflicts no wound on their mind, whose Natures seem made to bear it, and whose sufferings are not attended with shame or pain beyond the present moment.[37]

Positioning herself along with her reader as "humane European[s]," Schaw elaborately rationalizes the corporal punishment of enslaved people.[38] This is the only moment when her journal renders the violence of slavery visible. In fact, she rarely mentions the enslaved majority, preferring to devote most of her space to the beauties of the islands and the manners and customs of the white Creole colonists. Her pious horror at seeing the whips and her euphemistic language – "the application" – place her strategically between colonial Creoles and readers back home as an interpreter of and apologist for slavery. Her ability to perform this task rests on her feminine expertise in sensibility. Because it is "the nature of the Negroes" to feel differently (and less) than whites, whipping is justified. Schaw's contemporary, Edward Long, offers a similar justification for slavery, although more harshly worded, denouncing Africans as a degenerate group without a single redeeming feature who lack everything that civilized Europeans value most about themselves (see Chapter 3). One thing they lack, according to Long, is "moral sensations."[39]

Traveling from her home in Scotland to colonial Antigua and Saint Kitts, Janet Schaw carried with her the gendered virtues of the domestic sphere. Such virtues had to be refunctioned in significant ways to become suited for the colonies. Although she did not stay very long, during her sojourn, Schaw contributed as she could to the cultural task of rendering the islands a fit home for those who would remain. Her journal, probably read by numerous members of her social circle of Edinburgh friends and family, marshals the discourse of domesticity in defense of the colonies' biggest difference from the "Mother Country": that is, the institution of colonial slavery.

The governor's lady and the "blackies"

The opening of Maria Nugent's Jamaica journal economically establishes the relationship between the colony and the metropole, or homeland, and the role of the colonial wife. When her husband, General George Nugent, received his posting to Jamaica, the couple had recently witnessed a bloody colonial revolt – the United Irishmen uprising of 1798:

> I must preface my intended Journal by saying, that it commences immedi-ately after we had terminated a residence of some years in Ireland, of which we were both heartily sick, tired, and disgusted; having witnessed during the Rebellion, which broke out in 1798, all the horrors of a civil war, during which my dear husband had the command in the north; so that he was not only obliged to meet the poor, infatuated, misguided people in the open field [battlefield], but, after defeating them there, had also the distressing task of holding courts martial, and signing the death warrants of very many, which was indeed heart-breaking to us both.
>
> After the suppression of the Rebellion, we wished to refresh ourselves and recruit our spirits, by returning to England. . . . A few days after our return, General Nugent was surprised by his appointment as Lt.-Governor and Commander-in-Chief of the Island of Jamaica. We were neither of us over well pleased; but, like good soldiers, we made up our minds to obey. . . . I should greatly have preferred remaining, instead of playing the Governor's lady to the *blackies*: but *we* are soldiers, and must have no will of our own.[40]

England is home, the place one goes to recruit one's spirits when one is "sick, tired, and disgusted" with colonial service. Home is where one would always prefer to be; however, when the imperial soldier's duty takes him (or her) far away, the thought of England is sustaining. It is noteworthy that Maria Nugent, born in colonial New Jersey of Scottish, Irish, and Dutch ancestry, insists that England is her home. Her husband also had roots in a colonized nation – Ireland, whose "misguided" rebels his forces had recently helped subdue. George Nugent was the illegitimate grandson of an Irish peer; before serving in Ireland, he took the field against another rebellious colony in the American war. After returning from Jamaica, General Nugent was posted to India from 1811 to 1813.[41]

These two colonials, serving the British Empire on the other side of the
Atlantic, identify England as their home. Nugent's journal records cozy
chats about home with her husband and other officers of the Jamaican
garrison. In 1801, for example, "General N. and I passed a comfortable
morning together... anticipating the delights of home, and talking over
our prospects of returning to dear England soon." She juxtaposes this
cheerful domestic scene with the evening's news: the "sad account of the
massacre of three hundred and seventy white persons in St. Domingo."
The neighboring island, of course, was the scene of an island-wide slave
revolt, a bloody process that began in 1791 and continued to unfold during
the four years of the Nugents' Jamaican sojourn and that culminated in
the founding of the Republic of Haiti in 1804.[42] The contrast between the
cozy metropole, "dear England," and the unstable and dangerous colony
forms the background for Maria Nugent's record of her colonial service.

The journal's opening communicates much about the nature of that service. Its insistent use of the first-person plural conveys a sense of corporate
identity. In Ireland, Nugent has put the affective dimension of the private
domain in the service of the empire, shouldering an extra share of the
emotional burden of colonial military service. When the General orders
the executions of the "poor, infatuated, misguided" Irish rebels, his wife
feels terrible about it and takes responsibility for proclaiming the couple's
mutual "heart-break" at this aspect of the General's duty. This division of
labor takes advantage of the wife's supposedly feminine virtue of humanity
or sensitivity, allotting to her husband the sterner responsibilities of martial
justice.

From her arrival in Jamaica, Maria Nugent was the active domestic
administrator of a large, high-profile household in the governor's mansion,
King's House – the symbolic center of the English presence in Jamaica.
She entertained the officers of the Jamaican garrison and other official
guests and oversaw a large staff, including a number of enslaved people.
The government provided the Nugents with 33 enslaved workers on their
arrival; they requested and received an additional 10 during their stay.[43]
The governor's lady starts out determined to view these captive workers
as contented. "August 4th [1801]. This day we have kept to ourselves, and
the house is put into as good order as we could prevail upon the poor
blackies to do it. They are all so good-humored, and seem so merry, that it
is quite comfortable to look at them. I wish, however, that they would be
a little more alert in clearing away the filth of this otherwise nice and fine
house." The boundaries of the colonial home are permeable to the extent
that enslaved people must work inside it. For the home's white inhabitants

to experience comfort, an essential element of domesticity, these black workers must be rendered "comfortable" from the whites' point of view. One way in which Maria Nugent seems to be trying to do this is with the diminutive "blackies." The word suggests a child or a pet – like the five-year-old mulatta girl whom Janet Schaw's friend, Lady Bell Hamilton, "retains as a pet," richly dressed for a flattering "contrast to the delicate complexion of her Lady."[44]

Nugent never completely succeeded in convincing herself of her captives' harmlessness. The atmosphere on the island had been tense for a decade by the time she arrived. The Saint Domingue rebellion had raised fears of a similar cataclysm happening on Jamaica, which had experienced its last island-wide insurrection 40 years earlier.[45] Haiti was ruled by Toussaint Louverture and subsequently by Dessalines (whom Governor Nugent privately called "that horrible brute"). The Nugent administration strove to address the massive security problem raised by the inevitable communication between revolutionary Haitians and enslaved Jamaicans. The latter were composing songs about the revolt within a month of its outbreak in 1791, as then-Governor Williamson reported. Of course, Jamaican slave owners also were well informed: the "garish images that filtered through from Cap Français in the autumn of 1791 must have seemed to the Jamaican planters like an enactment of their worst nightmares."[46] The Nugents well may have read *An Historical Survey of the French Colony in the Island of St. Domingo* (1797) by the Jamaican planter Bryan Edwards, with its hair-raising depiction of rebel atrocities (see Chapter 3).

In the domestic realm, Maria Nugent was uneasily aware that the enslaved people around her were watching and listening. She records the table talk at a King's House dinner party in 1804: "The splendor of the black chiefs of St. Domingo, their superior strength, their firmness of character . . . are the common topics at dinner; and the blackies in attendance seem so much interested, that they hardly change a plate, or do anything but listen. How very imprudent, and what *must* it all lead to!"[47] Because the Haitian revolutionaries had beaten the French – England's opponent in the ongoing Napoleonic war – *schadenfreude* forms an undercurrent to this "imprudent" conversation. Invisible to her guests, Nugent's house slaves are now unsettlingly visible to their owner. Were beings called "blackies" really capable of staging a bloody, island-wide revolt? She knew very well that they were.

Nugent gamely fulfilled her role throughout her four years on Jamaica: overseeing King's House, entertaining official guests, touring the island with her husband. Through it all she kept a stiff upper lip, confiding her sufferings to her diary while giving the General the emotional support he needed to carry out his duties. Hearing of a mutiny and upcoming court martial on board a navy frigate, she affirms, "I thank God that I am not a man, to run either the risk of such offences against society, or the being obliged to pass sentence upon them." Keeping a proper distance from masculine affairs, she also distances herself from the island economy. Like Schaw, she seldom enters the working areas of a plantation. On one occasion, she is taken on a tour of "the whole process of sugar making, which is indeed very curious and entertaining."[48] The adjective "curious" presents sugar agriculture as an interesting novelty, connecting it to the numerous curiosities of Jamaica's tropical nature.

However, it is not prudent for a woman in Nugent's position to be too curious. Her inquiries in the boiling house elicit too much information: "I asked the overseer how often his people were relieved. He said every twelve hours; but how dreadful to think of their standing twelve hours over a boiling cauldron, and doing the same thing; and he owned to me that sometimes they did fall asleep, and get their poor fingers into the mill; and he shewed me a hatchet, that was always ready to sever the whole limb, as the only means of saving the poor sufferer's life! I would not have a sugar estate for the world!"[49] Nugent's exclamations of pity for the overworked, mutilated laborers – "their poor fingers" – have a childlike air, reminiscent of her epithet, "blackies." As in Janet Schaw's boiling-house tour, mercy is linked to violence – here, the cutting off of a limb to save its owner's life. Distancing herself from the distasteful business of sugar planting – the economic mainstay of the island that her husband rules – Nugent withdraws to the feminized private domain of pity or sympathy. The role of the governor's lady requires her to maintain strict boundaries, staying out of the public realm so as to provide appropriate support for her husband's duties in it.

Cleaning up

From her arrival in Jamaica, Maria Nugent does her soldierly duty by trying her best to see the island's positive side. This is evident in her liberal use of the language of aesthetics, commonplace in discourse about the Caribbean, as described at length in Chapter 1. Nugent has the command of this idiom expected of educated Britons by 1801. Before she even sets foot on the island, sighting it from shipboard, she gushes, "It appears beautiful. – Such hills, such mountains, such verdure; every thing so bright and gay, it is delightful!" Throughout her journal, as she tours the island, she takes note of the "beautiful and romantic," the picturesque and the sublime, occasionally composing lengthy landscape descriptions. "Nothing, certainly," she declares, "can exceed the beauty and enchanting scenery of this country."[50] Yet we sense a heightening tension between the island's tropical beauty and its less appealing features.

Nugent's aestheticizing is offset by a heightened sensitivity to colonial dirt. Lord Balcarres, the outgoing lieutenant governor, has been living a bachelor's life in Jamaica, without a wife to keep him literally and figuratively clean. Nugent wishes he would wash his hands "and use a nail-brush, for the black edges of his nails really make me sick. He has, besides, an extraordinary propensity to dip his fingers into every dish. Yesterday he absolutely helped himself to some fricassé with his dirty finger and thumb." The new governor and his lady visit Lord Balcarres at the Government Penn (i.e., livestock farm). "Never was there such a scene of dirt and discomfort. Lord B. was in a sad fright, thinking that we should expect a breakfast. However, upon his Secretary's whispering me, that there was but one whole tea-cup and saucer and a half, we declared our intention of returning to the King's House." Gossip soon supplied another kind of dirt: "Major Gould . . . entertained me with an account of Lord B.'s *domestic* conduct, and his ménage here altogether. Never was there a more profligate and disgusting scene, and I really think he must have been more than half mad."[51] Her italics allude, with a typographical sneer, to Balcarres's participation in the colonial custom of concubinage, a parody (in a lady's eyes) of proper domesticity. The dirt of colonial life is metaphorical – in particular, moral – as well as literal.

Concubinage, in which women of color assumed white women's domestic as well as sexual roles, was the norm in the sugar colonies, as in Stedman's Suriname discussed in Chapter 2. Nugent was quickly made aware of this institution; on her second day in Jamaica, she reports, "The ladies told me strange stories of the influence of the black and yellow women, and Mrs. Bullock called them serpents." Visiting a rural plantation, she refers snidely to the "overseer's *chère amie*, and no man here is without one . . . the favorite Sultana of this vulgar, ugly, Scotch Sultan." On several occasions during her stay, Nugent feels called on to "remonstrate" with the young officers who surround her "upon the improper lives they lead, and the miseries that must result from the horrid connections they have formed." She even writes letters to "the young men of our staff . . . to guide them to what is for their future welfare." They make her "fair promises," which she receives skeptically: "[A]las! this is a sad country for the morals."[52] The colony, Nugent realizes, is a decidedly different place than her idealized England, from its attractive surface to its rotten core.

One woman, even the governor's lady, can do little to change an entire colony's alternative domestic arrangements. What she can do consists of token gestures: symbolic operations to transform Jamaica's alien space into something more closely resembling "dear England." On New Year's Day 1803, Nugent rejoices in the transformation of the Penn, with all traces of Lord B.'s dubious ménage swept away: "we got safe to the Penn, and found all so clean and nice there, that we felt the delight of being once more at home."[53] Seeing Jamaica's dirt makes Nugent want to clean up. The successful sanitizing of domestic space, presided over by the colonial wife, is an essential part of transporting something like home to the tropics. Her agents in this endeavor are those she calls "blackies," whom she also metaphorically cleans up in a couple of ways.

One way was to make them Christians, a project that took a fair amount of Nugent's time when she was not socializing or suffering from morning sickness (she bore the General two children, George and Louisa, during their stay on Jamaica). She writes of rehearsing her enslaved workers in their catechism and boning up on theology to explain it to them. Twenty-five were baptized in November 1801, receiving cake and wine after the ceremony. Slave conversion was controversial in the West Indies. Owners were less comfortable applying corporal punishment to fellow Christians, and respecting marriages between enslaved people could be an economic disadvantage to owners – a point with which Maria Nugent disagreed. In advocating both conversion and marriage for the enslaved, she was taking an unusually liberal position for 1801 – although she makes clear her support for the institution of slavery.[54]

The connection between cleanliness and conversion emerges from Nugent's language describing the celebration of her fourth wedding anniversary on Jamaica. Domestic imagery celebrates her properly circumscribed contribution, as a colonial wife, to domesticating the empire:

> I went to church with the staff. Delighted to see the black servants look so well, so orderly, and behave so properly during the Service. – Assembled them all afterwards, and gave them each a dollar for a wedding present. – Their wish was, that General N. and I might live happily together, till our hair was as white as their gowns. They don't know what snow is, or I suppose they would have said snow, rather than gowns; but their muslin was very clean and white.[55]

With their clean, white clothing; recently indoctrinated Christianity; and welcome deference, these sanitized captives make their owner proud. She has brought her little band of blackies closer to their British rulers' comfort zone or thinks she has (although the history of slave uprisings on Jamaica and elsewhere in the Caribbean might call that into question).[56] At the same time, the enslaved people's ignorance of snow keeps them at a safe symbolic distance from her real home, England, which they will never see. This entry brings together the two senses of "home" that make possible white women's contribution to the cultural work of the empire: (1) the domestic sphere over which Maria Nugent presides, comprising marriage and its attendant happiness, as well as proper behavior and clean gowns; and (2) the distant center of the empire, England, the homeland. The two meanings of "home" intersect yet diverge, preserving an imagined England pristinely free of blackies, as the governor's lady keeps them in order on the colonial periphery.

However, her ongoing effort to clean up Jamaica by imposing English manners and customs could cause trouble on occasion. In May 1803, the General, who was absent most of the month reviewing militia, announced his homecoming. His wife decided to celebrate by throwing a party for the enslaved staff of the governor's mansion. "Dined with the gentlemen of the family, before 3, and immediately after take our stations in the piazza, to see the blackies enjoy themselves." The refreshments include Creole favorites such as "barbecued hog, jerked hog, pepper-pot, yams, plantains, &c" along with "tubs of punch" and three glasses of Madeira apiece. With these, the grateful blackies drink three toasts: "Massa Gubernor, and Missis, and little Massa." Then came the dancing:

> I began the ball with an old negro man. The gentlemen each selected a partner, according to rank, by age or service, and we all danced. However, I was not aware how much I shocked the Misses Murphy by doing this; for I did exactly the same as I would have done at a servants' hall birthday in England. They told me, afterwards, that they were nearly fainting, and could hardly forbear shedding a flood of tears, at such an unusual and extraordinary sight; for in this country, and among slaves, it was necessary to keep up so much more distant respect! They may be right. I meant nothing wrong, and all the poor creatures seemed so delighted, and so much pleased, that I could scarcely repent it. I was, nevertheless, very sorry to have hurt their feelings, and particularly too as they seemed to think the example dangerous; as making the blacks of too much consequence, or putting them at all on a footing with the whites, they said, might make a serious change in their conduct, and even produce a rebellion in the island.[57]

The Misses Murphy were prominent Creoles, the daughters of Thomas Murphy, Member of the Jamaican Assembly for the Parish of Saint Mary and owner of the estates named The Decoy (formerly the property of Sir Charles Price) and The Ramble. Nugent's gaffe marks the limit of her work of domesticating the colony by imposing metropolitan manners and customs. Witnessing such close contact between black and white bodies – in particular, those of a white woman and a black man, the taboo combination in slave societies – triggers a visceral shock in women brought up on an island where enslaved people outnumber white colonists by as many as ten to one and rebellion is a constant fear. The Misses Murphy's reaction is immediate, physical, and intense: they are close to fainting, near "a flood of tears." Past a certain point, the difference or distance between colony and metropole is ineradicable. Transgressing this boundary, Creoles like the Murphy sisters believe, may lead to collapsing the difference between precariously orderly Jamaica and blood-soaked Saint Domingue.

Retreat

The longer she stayed in Jamaica, the more difficult it became for Maria Nugent to keep up her spirits. She is chronically homesick – "Feel low and unwell all dinner, thinking of England" – and less able to ignore the danger and discomfort of the tropics. People she knows die of tropical diseases such as yellow fever: Captain Bartlett in September 1802; two others in October; the husband of her wet nurse, Mrs. Hamilton; the mother of her favorite enslaved domestic worker, Cupid, in November; and Mrs. Ludford and Mr. Wolfrys in December. "Events like these fill the mind with horror and awe, and make us think indeed," Nugent writes. As 1803 wears on, the tropical creeping things she calls "reptiles" begin to crawl more frequently through the pages of her journal. Invading her domestic space – her bedroom, her baby's crib, her dinner table – these nasty creatures seem to demonstrate the futility of feeling safe anywhere in the Torrid Zone.[58] "At this season of the year we are really tormented with ants. My dressing table covered. My bason, jugs and goblets, full of them, and nothing can be more disgusting or distressing." Mosquitoes are "intolerable" to everyone, even baby George. After his mother has finished an hour-long purge of his netting, "just as we thought all was safe, close to his cot crept out a large centipede, and renewed all my distress and anxiety." Her disgust culminates at a dinner party in May 1804, when a scorpion crawls up a Miss Stewart's sleeve and attacks. "It was really frightful to see the reptile under the thin muslin sleeve, striking with all its force, and the poor girl in an agony; and it was some time before it could be got hold of . . . I sat opposite to her, between the two Admirals, and could not help crying from real fright."[59] The image of the creature invading the delicate sleeve to sting the white arm crystallizes Nugent's fear of the alien tropics and their monstrous denizens. The malignant side of tropical nature figures the erosion of her fragile colonial domesticity.

Her increasing sensitivity to vermin accompanies her growing sense that "this wretched country is devoted to the same destruction that has overtaken St. Domingo." During this tense time, the violence of slavery cannot be ignored, even on the way to church: "we were obliged to pass close by the pole, on which was stuck the head of the black man who was executed a few days ago." Hanged and beheaded for "rebellious conspiracy," the dead man (ironically named either Fidelle or Goodluck) is a grotesque public reminder that not all blackies are as contented as Nugent has fantasized. Little Georgie's first birthday occasions another fete; the governor's guests go "to see the blackies enjoying themselves... After which they drank young *Massa*, with a sort of shout, that was more like an Indian war-whoop than any thing else."[60] Even expressing their loyalty and joy, Nugent's own enslaved domestics sound to her like savages on the warpath.

She nonetheless persists in her determined efforts to civilize them – "Hear all the new blackies their prayers, &c. previously to their being made Christians" – and to view enslaved people as harmless, as in this ominous roadside encounter in early 1805:

> In returning home from our drive this morning, we met a gang of Eboe negroes, just landed, and marching up the country. – I ordered the postillions to stop, that I might see their countenances as they passed, and see if they looked unhappy; but they appeared perfectly the reverse. I bowed, kissed my hand, and laughed; they did the same. The women, in particular, seemed pleased, and all admired the carriage, &c. One man attempted to shew more pleasure than the rest, by opening his mouth as wide as possible to laugh, which was rather a horrible grin. He shewed such truly cannibal teeth, all filed as they have them, that I could not help shuddering. He was of Herculean size, and really a tremendous looking creature.[61]

Her curiosity to scrutinize the newly arrived Africans clearly has as a context the ongoing rumors of brewing revolt. Surveying the slaves, she clings to the belief that their emotions are transparent or legible. Short of declaring them "merry," she settles for an awkward double negative: they seem "perfectly the reverse" of unhappy, which would be happy. However, her description of the Africans' mimicry of her actions makes it seem less likely that their faces express their feelings. The unintentional oxymoron of the "horrible grin" captures the tension of the situation. Is the "Herculean" slave trying to show pleasure or intimidate? If the point of the exercise is self-reassurance, her involuntary shudder bespeaks the opposite. This experience approaches Burke's definition of the sublime as terror or awe experienced at a safe distance. As did Burke with the French Revolution, Nugent tries to "come to terms with [the possibility of slave revolt] by distancing it as a sublime experience, even while . . . realizing that it might not keep its 'distance.'"[62]

In a subsequent roadside encounter, distance and ambiguity are gone, along with any mention of pleasure. This time, little George and Louisa are with their mother. "We met a horrid looking black man, who passed us several times, without making any bow, although I recollected him as one of the boatmen of the canoe we used to go out in. . . . He was then very humble, but to-night he only grinned, and gave us a sort of fierce look, that struck me with a terror I could not shake off." The man's lack of deference profoundly unsettles Nugent. His grin is clearly meant to intimidate, and it succeeds. Mother and children are caught between two threats: a French invasion by sea and a slave revolt in the island interior. Nugent writes fearfully, "I have been told, by the few ladies who remain in Spanish Town, such horrid things of the savage ideas, &c. of the slaves, on the estates in the interior, that I am determined, if my dear N. is obliged to leave me to meet the enemy, that I will take my dear children on board a ship."[63] By early July 1805, they were on the merchant ship *Augustus Caesar*, en route with a navy convoy to "dear England."

Despite Maria Nugent's best efforts, by the end of her time in Jamaica, the island remained profoundly unhomely. Her assiduous work of home-making could not conjure comfort for herself and her fellow members of the colony's tiny white minority as rumors of bloody liberation continued to cross the water from Haiti. She could no longer view the enslaved people who surrounded her as comfortable blackies: these were clearly restless captives, catching the scent of freedom. Venturing far from their home in the British Isles, these two imperial women, Nugent and Schaw, were empowered by travel, achieving – at least in writing – "the kind of authoritative self associated with the modern female subject."[64] This female self had the capacity to serve the mother country by re-creating the domestic, in both its senses, on colonial soil. Such gendered cultural work of place-making depended on racial difference. The flexible boundary around Schaw's sentimental "social circle" of colonial Scots enclosed whiteness and excluded the unfeeling slaves. The semi-permeable domestic space of Nugent's Jamaican home away from home could enclose only a few select, domesticated blackies – evidence of the potential of England's civilizing mission at a time when it was poised to take off in Africa.[65]

My final chapter presents a decidedly different perspective on the slave colony and the idea of home: that of the enslaved woman, Mary Prince.

She did, however, have one element in common with these two white colonial women: all three were empowered, in different ways, by travel. Schaw and Nugent traveled as part of a family unit – carrying home, in that sense, with them to colonial soil. Mary Prince, in contrast, was torn from her family and thrust into white households where domestic labor signified the opposite of comfort or nurturance. Nonetheless – like that archetypical privileged traveler, the Grand Tourist – Mary Prince gained from her involuntary mobility a geographical knowledge that she eventually was able to translate into a limited form of power.

CHAPTER 6

A long way from home
Slavery, travel, and imperial geography in
The History of Mary Prince

Home for white Caribbean colonists, as discussed in Chapter 5, was both necessary and problematic. Part of the work of home-making for colonial women such as Janet Schaw and Maria Nugent consisted of remaking enslaved people into domestic creatures: "blackies" around whom white colonists could feel comfortable. What type of place was home for the enslaved? Could an enslaved person have a home? For geographers in the mid-twentieth century, home was an exemplary place. Home was where people could rest – where they could be sheltered, not just physically but also emotionally. For the phenomenologist Gaston Bachelard in his classic *The Poetics of Space*, "all really inhabited space bears the essence of the notion of home." Home signifies attachment, rootedness. It is the place where you can withdraw from the stress of the outside world, the space in which you control what happens. "Home is where you can be yourself. In this sense, home acts as a kind of metaphor for place in general."[1]

Feminist geographers retort that home is not necessarily comfortable for everyone. For women – some women, at least – home can be a place of oppression and abuse or at least of being taken for granted. For a gay teenager, for example, home can be a closet, a place where one cannot possibly be oneself. We can extend this line of thought from home as domicile to home as hometown or homeland. Not everyone, Doreen Massey points out, can "afford to locate their identities." The colonized or formerly colonized, for example, have a decidedly different sense of place from the inhabitants of the First World. Even within a single location or community, people in diverse positions have a widely varying sense of place determined in part by variables such as gender, class, and age.[2] Home is a privilege that not everyone shares.

A prominent scholar of slavery, Orlando Patterson, defines the state of being enslaved as a type of existential homelessness, what he terms "natal alienation." The constant threat of forced family separation, Patterson argues, transforms the way enslaved people think of themselves.

The enslaved person is a "genealogical isolate," denied any claims on living or dead family members. She or he is an outsider in a larger sense as well, suffering a "loss of native status," existing in a state of "deracination" involving "alienation . . . from any attachment to groups or localities other than those chosen . . . by the master." Because she has no legitimate power to form or maintain attachments to people or places, an enslaved person – in Patterson's view – cannot have a home in the way that a free person can.[3]

My study of the politics of place in British slavery concludes with a case that challenges the concept of home in both its senses: as cozy domicile and geographical locus of belonging. *The History of Mary Prince, a West Indian Slave, Related by Herself* (1831) is the only known published autobiography by an enslaved British woman. This unusual yet exemplary woman narrates her individual experience of displacement, which culminates in a transgressive movement toward freedom. Her narrative's strategic treatment of the term and concept of "home" contests the boundaries that white colonists set around their homes and the limits set by their racial ideology to what counts as human. The idea of travel as a privileged type of movement is similarly tested by Prince's *History*. She emerges, like Olaudah Equiano, as what James Clifford calls a "discrepant cosmopolitan": a subaltern who is able to exercise the privileged traveler's prerogative of turning geographical knowledge into power. I first consider the circumstances that brought Prince's *History* into print, particularly the importance of place for negotiations between the enslaved woman and her abolitionist sponsors. Next, I address the enslaved woman's relationship to home as domicile in the context of the ideology of gendered domesticity introduced in Chapter 5. Mary Prince's work as a domestic laborer in colonial households positioned her to challenge the idealized image of the home as nurturing haven. Finally, I turn to her involuntary travels – journeys that fostered a growing awareness of the imperial geography that slavery made.

Local color

Mary Prince dictated her life story to the abolitionist Susanna Strickland in the London home of Thomas Pringle, Secretary of the Anti-Slavery Society. Pringle hired Mary as a servant after she had walked away from her owners, Mr. and Mrs. John Wood of Antigua.[4] She was probably almost 40 years old at the time, worn down and scarred by a lifetime of hard labor and harsh physical abuse. She and her sponsors presumably shared the goal of emancipation, for which political momentum was building. (It was voted into law in 1833, two years after the *History* was published. However, it was delayed and qualified by the "apprenticeship" program, which was repealed in 1838.) Apart from that goal and Christianity, we can only guess that they did not have much in common. Producing the book, the sales of which were robust (i.e., three editions in 1831 alone), must have involved a complex cultural negotiation between the enslaved West Indian woman and the London abolitionists. Pringle notes in his preface that he "pruned" Mary's words, although he asserts that the text "is essentially her own, without any material alteration farther than was requisite to exclude redundances and gross grammatical errors, so as to render it clearly intelligible." We can begin here to chart the distance between the narrator and her sponsors.[5]

Extreme caution is warranted (as Gayatri Spivak famously warns) in any attempt to recover subaltern voices. *The History of Mary Prince* is the necessarily impure product of an awkward collaboration, involving unequal power relations and subject to social and political pressures. We may imagine Prince negotiating between West Indian culture and metropolitan abolitionist norms, a displaced person navigating treacherous shoals. Language posed the first difficulty. Her spoken language would have been patois, "the Creolized speech of slaves that combined English, Spanish, French, and West African languages."[6] Rendering Mary's patois narration into Standard English would necessarily have imprinted her editors' class, racial, and geographical (i.e., imperial) dominance on the enslaved woman's words. Pringle explains that her life story was first "written out fully, with all the narrator's repetitions and prolixities, and afterwards pruned into its present shape; retaining, as far as was practicable, Mary's exact expressions and peculiar phraseology." Sandra Pouchet Paquet finds traces of West Indian vernacular remaining in the published *History* even after Pringle's "pruning."[7] To white British readers, however, this would have been merely "peculiar phraseology," a quaint tinge of local color in an otherwise sanitized text.

To be intelligible and persuasive to its target audience of white, middle-class, metropolitan evangelicals, the slave's story would need to conform to that audience's norms in more than merely grammar. Critics have explored possible consequences of abolitionist mediation for the shape of Mary Prince's narrative.[8] Foremost among them is its silence about sex. The sexual morality of metropolitan, middle-class evangelical Protestants like Pringle and Strickland would not accept sexual activity of any type by a woman outside of marriage.[9] In addition, any representation of a black woman was forced to contend with racial stereotypes of black people in general and black women in particular as hypersexual or congenitally immoral. The *History* does not mention Prince's voluntary, possibly financially rewarding liaisons with free black and white men or her probable sexual exploitation by at least one of her owners.[10] The Anti-Slavery Committee's efforts on Mary's behalf prompted her former owner, Mr. Wood – in an attempt to discredit her – to raise allegations of immoral conduct.

To preserve Prince's credibility with her sponsors' target readership, these slurs had to be countered with the narrative projection of a virtuous Christian woman. Pringle added a supplement to the published *History* to preempt Wood's suggestions rather than allow readers to interpret Mary's silence to her detriment. Describing her efforts to get money for her manumission, Prince lets drop, "A gentleman also lent me some to help me buy my freedom – but when I could not get free he got it back again. His name was Captain Abbot." Sharpe speculates that Prince may have made an arrangement with Abbot to serve as his housekeeper (a euphemism for concubine) in return for her purchase price.[11]

In his effort to clear Mary's name, Pringle invokes an imaginary geography of the empire. He enlists as a character witness Joseph Phillips, an Antigua-based abolitionist, who comments:

> Of the immoral conduct ascribed to Molly [Prince's enslaved name] by Mr. Wood, I can say nothing farther than this – that I have heard she had at a former period (previous to her marriage) a connexion with a white person, a Capt. –, which I have no doubt was broken off when she became seriously impressed with religion. But, at any rate, such connexions are so common, I might almost say universal, in our slave colonies, that except by the missionaries and a few serious persons, they are considered, if faults at all, so very venial as scarcely to deserve the name of immorality.[12]

Pringle strategically chooses to introduce a discussion of colonial morality as different from and inferior to metropolitan morality to preserve Prince's assimilation to the "abolitionist construction of the slave woman as socioethical being."[13] Her story is told with constant reference to the only endpoint that abolitionists would accept: a person both free and morally enlightened. Sharpe discusses other subtle elisions that help to maintain this construction of Prince, but she does not focus on this use of geography. Prince is required, in effect, to shed one dimension of her West Indianness in favor of metropolitan morality if she is to serve as an abolitionist spokeswoman.

The cultural negotiation that led to the publication of *The History of Mary Prince* was thus a geographical negotiation as well: the editors "pruned" out colonial language and colonial morality and substituted metropolitan versions. The proportion of censorship to self-censorship involved in producing the *History* can never be fully known. Mary Prince knew her sponsors and presumably shared some of their goals, but this did not prevent them from subjecting her to cross-examination on "every fact and circumstance" of her story, with the help of the Antiguan Joseph Phillips. The perceived need for this interrogation by her supposed allies speaks eloquently of prevailing assumptions about the reliability of black people – almost as eloquently as the request by the Birmingham Ladies' Society for the Relief of Negro Slaves for verification of the whip scars on Prince's back before they would send any money. Their request was met with a physical examination performed by Pringle's wife, along with Strickland and two other white women.[14]

As to what was lost in the editing process beyond Pringle's censorship of sex, we only can speculate. Sharpe turns to hostile sources such as James MacQueen's refutation of the *History* in *Blackwood's Magazine* and the court records of the libel lawsuit and countersuit between Pringle and Wood. Based on her reading of these documents, Sharpe suggests that the need to represent Prince as "decent and docile" forced the elision of "less morally upright forms of self-defense, such as verbal abuse or acts of insubordination." From pro-slavery propaganda, Sharpe reconstructs a picture of Prince as "an outspoken and resourceful woman who considered herself to be something more than simply a slave."[15] I suggest further ways in which we may infer that Mary Prince's purposes occasionally differed from those of her sponsors, or at least ways in which forms of personal control could be represented in the interstices, as it were, of their moral agenda. My central concern, however, is with the *History*'s treatment of place and movement in rendering the identity of the enslaved woman.

Stones and timber

Chapter 5 surveys the idealized image of the home in nineteenth-century bourgeois ideology: a nurturing, spiritually uplifting haven, presided over by a pure and competent woman. We can assume that prescription and practice diverged to some extent as the ideology of gendered separate spheres unfurled in the daily lives of middle-class metropolitan men and women. In a slave colony, as previously discussed, even when a woman like Maria Nugent did her best to make a home away from home, doing so could be a discouraging task. Viewed from the perspective of enslaved people, however, home and family look decidedly different, indeed, from the prescriptions of metropolitan gender ideology.

The enslaved family has been subject to debate as part of the broader debate among historians over what Marietta Morrisey calls "the phenomenological status of slaves." The "social and cultural status of slaves has been debated [between] those who favor a structural explanation based on symbolic and legal orders and . . . those advocating a study of the culture of working peoples" or "history from below." Patterson's comparative study, *Slavery and Social Death*, with his concept of natal alienation (introduced previously), exemplifies the structural approach. More recently, however, historians' emphasis has shifted away from the oppressive structures imposed on the enslaved "from above." Although acknowledging the force of these structures – "slaves' culture and struggles were always impeded and framed by symbolic and legal orders"[16] – researchers emphasize enslaved people's active, creative responses to them – particularly the strength and endurance of the informal relationships that challenged the master's power of natal alienation.[17]

Mary Prince's skeptical treatment of "home" in her narrative makes rhetorical sense as an attempt to confront metropolitan readers with the profound incongruity between the institution of colonial slavery and their most cherished beliefs about gender, home, and family. "In contrast to the nineteenth-century ideal of family life in which the family was a discrete unit, enclosed within the private home, slave families were of necessity open and permeable, their members vulnerable to separation and unable to protect each other from violence."[18] The events of Prince's girlhood illustrate this well. She was born about 1788 in Bermuda and lived her first 12 years with her mother and siblings in the home of Captain Williams. Her father lived and worked nearby. Around 1800, Williams sold her and two of her sisters separately, breaking up the family.

Prince's narration of her parting from her mother and siblings responds to Captain Williams's cruel decision using language that brings out enslaved people's ability to feel emotional pain – contrary to stereotypes of blacks as insensitive – and makes clear the strength of this enslaved family's emotional ties[19]:

> Oh dear! I cannot bear to think of that day, – it is too much. – It recalls the great grief that filled my heart, and the woeful thoughts that passed to and fro through my mind, whilst listening to the pitiful words of my poor mother, weeping for the loss of her children. I wish I could find words to tell you all I then felt and suffered. The great God above alone knows the thoughts of the poor slave's heart, and the bitter pains which follow such separations as these. All that we love taken away from us – oh, it is sad, sad! and sore to be borne![20]

Her feelings extend to her white mistress, Mrs. Williams, whose death she mourned (not only because it occasioned her sale); to her white owner and playmate, Miss Betsey; and even to "the house in which I had been brought up," which she un-ironically calls "home." She makes clear, however, that her perceptions throughout this section are those of a child, based on ignorance: "I was too young to understand rightly my condition as a slave." She also notes that Captain Williams's reason for selling her and her sisters was to finance his remarriage: the white family, as Patterson puts it, is parasitical, built at the expense of the enslaved family.[21]

Prince describes her arrival at the house of her new owner, Captain I–, in pointed contrast to the relative happiness of her childhood. "It was night when I reached my new home. The house was large, and built at the bottom of a very high hill; but I could not see much of it that night. I saw too much of it afterwards. The stones and the timber were the best things in it; they were not so hard as the hearts of the owners."[22] Enslaved people, as Prince established, can feel pain. These owners, by contrast, display no emotion and, in that sense, are inhuman. The enslaved were widely spoken of as commodities, mere objects rather than human beings. Prince counters this conventional objectification by rendering her owners as a type of petrified object, like sticks or stones. In contrast to the affective richness of her early home with her own family and Mrs. Williams, Prince's description makes clear that this new house is just a building. It contains stones and timber but certainly no empathy or love.

By using the association-laden word "home" in a context that effectively strips it of all of the meaning familiar to white, middle-class, metropolitan readers, Prince highlights the disjunction between "home" as idealized in separate-spheres ideology – the foundation of civilization as such readers knew it – and as it was institutionalized in colonial slave society. Her approach was in line with a common and effective tactic of abolitionist propaganda, noted by the historian Diana Paton: "A crucial component of the critique of slavery was that it created a society in which gender relations diverged horribly from English bourgeois norms."[23] Those norms, we have seen, defined home as a site in which its private and feminine character was expressed through elevated morality and emotional nurturance, both markedly absent from the I– household.

The harsh life in that household eventually pushed Mary Prince to the breaking point. She was still in Bermuda, not far from her parents and their respective owners (i.e., Mr. Trimmingham and Mr. Richard Darrel). When she felt she could no longer stand life with Captain and Mrs. I–, she ran away to her mother: "She dared not receive me into the house, but she hid me up in a hole in the rocks near, and brought me food at night."²⁴ When her father heard of this subterfuge, he fetched Prince and escorted her back to her owners:

> When we got home, my poor father said to Capt. I–, 'Sir, I am sorry that my child should be forced to run away from her owner; but the treatment she has received is enough to break her heart. The sight of her wounds has nearly broke mine. – I entreat you, for the love of God, to forgive her for running away, and that you will be a kind master to her in future.' Capt. I– said I was used as well as I deserved, and that I ought to be punished for running away. I then took courage and said that I could stand the floggings no longer; that I was weary of my life, and therefore I had run away to my mother; but mothers could only weep and mourn over their children, they could not save them from cruel masters – from the whip, the rope, and the cow-skin.²⁵

This incident highlights the permeability and vulnerability of the slave family. Not only is this family dispersed among various owners but also the parents can do little to protect their child. The mother can offer only rocks as shelter; the father chooses to cooperate in enforcing slave ownership and family separation in an attempt to avoid worse. Neither parent has the power to avert their daughter's punishment by her sadistic owner. We may infer limited success for the joint rhetorical intervention of father and daughter from her remark that she was not flogged that day. However, she goes on to say that she remained five more years with Capt. I– "and almost daily received the same harsh treatment."²⁶ Again, narrating this complex compromise between resistance and accommodation, Prince begins by using the word "home" in a context that chafes against its cozy associations, as she had in describing her arrival at the I–house.

The institution of slavery thus endangered parent–child relationships. What about those between adult couples (whether or not formalized by marriage)? Historians disagree on the general prevalence of stable conjugal pairings among slaves. Some planters came to encourage Christian marriage in the belief that it served their interests by boosting fertility after the abolition of the slave trade.²⁷ In Mary Prince's case, however, her owners, Mr. and Mrs. Wood, clearly did not view her marriage as being in their interest. She married without asking their permission, presumably knowing she would not get it, and did not voluntarily tell them after the fact. Mr. Wood "flew into a great rage" when he found out, but his wife was beside herself:

Mrs. Wood was more vexed about my marriage than her husband. She could not forgive me for getting married, but stirred up Mr. Wood to flog me dreadfully with his horsewhip. I thought it very hard to be whipped at my time of life for getting a husband – I told her so. She said that she would not have nigger men about the yards and premises, or allow a nigger man's clothes to be washed in the same tub where hers were washed. She was fearful, I think, that I should lose her time, in order to wash and do things for my husband.[28]

Utilitarian concerns may have contributed to Mrs. Wood's rage, but its intensity suggests a less rational basis. Her fear of pollution by mixing clothes in a tub might be speculatively read as sexual rather than merely racial – hysterically denying the mistress's sexual jealousy of her female slave. Or, Mrs. Wood may have sensed in Mary Prince's marriage to a free man a sexual self-expression that was tantamount to a bid for freedom. The spiritual equality suggested by Prince's presumption to Christian marriage may have been another ground for the Woods' fury.[29] In any case, the owners clearly viewed their white family's needs as superseding the slave's desire for a family of her own. The labor power needed to support middle-class domesticity limits or precludes domesticity among the laboring class. Davidoff and Hall note a similar phenomenon among the Birmingham bourgeoisie, who had "difficulty in acknowledging claims of servants' own family and friends" and preferred to hire country girls, cut off from community ties.[30]

The crisis set off by Mary Prince's marriage underscores the difficult position of the domestic slave who lived and worked in her owners' home. Compared to the field labor that was the fate of the majority of Caribbean slaves (women as well as men), Prince's position as household slave would have been viewed as privileged, near the top of the occupational hierarchy. We should remember, however, how difficult and heavy nineteenth-century housework was compared to the present day: carrying water from pumps, fetching and carrying heavy tools and supplies, doing laundry by hand. Household work also involved frequent contact with masters and especially mistresses, like the sadistic Mrs. I–. House slaves were thus more vulnerable to physical punishment through "sadistic whims and personal caprice."[31]

Plantocratic writers often cite domestic servants as being especially difficult, complaining of their laziness, inefficiency, and disobedience. On larger plantations, "the most favored slaves, the house slaves and the skilled elite, were often in the vanguard of slave resistance at all levels."[32] Mary Prince's sharp tongue, presumably muted in her narrative by the demands of middle-class decorum, emerges occasionally, as it does in her forthright response to being flogged for getting married. The trajectory of her life, culminating in her transgressive seizure of a limited freedom, suggests a persistent tactical resistance against the indignities of slavery.[33]

Prince's position as a domestic slave highlights the incongruity between the state of slavery and the concept of "home." The house as home should be a place of relaxation, safety, comfort, nurturance, and family togetherness. For Prince, her owners' houses are places of near-incessant labor where she is at the mercy of her masters' and especially her mistresses' sadistic impulses. On her first night in the I– household, she lies awake listening to the screams of a fellow slave being beaten. She awakens to a harsh routine of work and punishment:

> The next morning my mistress set about instructing me in my tasks. She taught me to do all sorts of household work; to wash and bake, pick cotton and wool, and wash floors, and cook. And she taught me (how can I ever forget it!) more things than these; she caused me to know the exact difference between the smart of the rope, the cart-whip, and the cow-skin, when applied to my naked body by her own cruel hand. And there was scarcely any punishment more dreadful than the blows I received on my face and head from her hard heavy fist. She was a fearful woman, and a savage mistress to her slaves.[34]

This depiction of the colonial home squarely counters the idealized home of separate-spheres ideology on several fronts. By foregrounding household labor, Prince dispels the aura of relaxation and resuscitation that was supposed to pervade the home. Certainly, for Mary Prince, this home is in no sense a haven. By setting the list of household tasks in parallel with a list of punishments administered by the mistress of the house, Prince subverts the image of the middle-class lady – the crucial anchor of the middle-class home – as gentle, nurturing, pious, and morally pure. Mrs. I–'s domestic sadism and her "hard heavy fist" utterly belie her prescribed feminine role. Tassie Gwilliam comments that women "as bearers of domesticity best represent the destruction and perversion of home" in colonial slave society.[35]

My own country

To turn now to the significance of movement, displacement, or travel in Mary Prince's life is not to turn away from her troubled treatment of "home." Must a person have a home to experience displacement as hardship? Prince certainly experienced her owners' dwellings differently than they did, and she developed a critical perspective on "home" in the sense of domicile. We might expect her to turn a similarly jaundiced view on "home" in the larger sense of an attachment to a particular town, island, region, or even nation. Before turning to Prince's own references to home in this larger sense, I examine an exchange between her white contemporaries over an enslaved person's attachment to place.

In a "Supplement" to the published *History of Mary Prince*, the editor Pringle includes a letter written by her former master, Mr. Wood, to the secretary of the governor of Antigua, responding to the governor's request (instigated by abolitionists) for help in bringing Prince back to Antigua as a free woman. Among Wood's list of reasons why this should not happen, he claims that she "is not a native of this country, and I know of no relation she has here." (He also claims that her husband has taken another wife.) Pringle counters, "True: But was it not her home (so far as a slave can have a home) for thirteen or fourteen years? Were not the connexions, friendships, and associations of her mature life formed there? Was it not there she hoped to spend her latter years in domestic tranquillity with her husband, free from the lash of the taskmaster? These considerations may appear light to Mr. Wood, but they are every thing to this poor woman."[36] Abolitionist rhetoric emphasized the enslaved person's ability to form emotional bonds and enjoy "domestic tranquillity" – just like middle-class Britons (and more authentically than debased slave owners) – as part of the effort to establish enslaved people as human beings rather than livestock. In this, abolitionists had apparently been successful enough by 1830 to force a slave owner like Wood to argue on their terrain – denying specific facts – rather than dispute an enslaved person's ability to claim native status or her desire to be near family members.

In this context, Mary Prince's own claims to such a status take on a tactical air, in line with this aspect of abolitionist rhetoric. For example, narrating her departure from Turk's Island – where she has labored for 10 years in the salt works – for Bermuda, she explains that not only is she sick of the harsh work regime but also "my heart yearned to see my native place again, my mother, and my kindred." To articulate this yearning asserts human dignity by denying the slave's "natal alienation." We are never told whether she saw her family in Bermuda, only that life there "was not so very bad as Turk's Island."[37]

Prince later invokes attachment to place in a charged political context. Having walked away from her owners in London, she was left in a difficult bind. By British law, based on the 1772 Mansfield Decision, the Woods could not forcibly take her into custody or transport her to Antigua. If she were to go back of her own volition, she would again be enslaved, as Anti-Slavery Society lawyers advised her. Pringle, the secretary of the Society, had attempted to use her case to challenge this legal precedent, which had recently been upheld in the case of Grace Jones, an enslaved woman who was returned to Antigua against her will.[38] Although the Society's petition to Parliament on Prince's behalf had failed, she and her backers may have held out hope of influencing a future change in the precedent by which freedom entailed permanent exile – as it has for millions of refugees since then. Living with the Pringles, she says, "I . . . am as comfortable as I can be while separated from my dear husband, and away from my own country and all my friends and connections."[39] Linking family with country in this way again asserts the speaker's full humanity and her similarity to her white metropolitan readers. However, it seems to appeal to a sense of place more characteristic of comfortably rooted middle-class Britons than of someone whose life as a slave had uprooted her repeatedly from an early age.

To speculate on the significance of these displacements for Mary Prince's construction of her identity, we must begin by remembering that geographical movement is variously designated depending on who it is that moves. Chapter 4 discusses *The Interesting Narrative of . . . Olaudah Equiano* as travel writing, expanding the historically narrow definition of "travel" beyond "European, literary, male, bourgeois, scientific, heroic, recreational, meanings and practices" to encompass voluntary or involuntary mobility by those less secure and privileged, including enslaved or formerly enslaved travelers such as Equiano and Mary Prince. Their travel also generates knowledge and power, although rather differently than for more conventional travelers. The remainder of this chapter considers Mary Prince as what James Clifford calls a discrepant cosmopolitan: learning and growing through her involuntary and quasi-voluntary travels, each journey moving her closer to the sense of self that she will need to narrate her life story for publication.[40] The knowledge or wisdom she gains through travel – specifically, her geographic awareness of West Indian locations and later of the metropole – serves her in various situations and, ultimately, contributes to the sense of self-possession that allows her to walk away, free, from her owners in London.

Prince's journeys begin with the early sale that breaks up her family and takes her from her childhood home, teaching her among other things the irrelevance of emotional ties between owner and captive. "When I left my dear little brothers and the house in which I had been brought up, I thought my heart would burst," she laments. She uses the word "heart" throughout her narrative to invoke a network of affective connections and community values, attacked but never destroyed by slavery – connections and values that ground her identity amid maltreatment and repeated displacement. This usage is congruent with the language of her fellow enslaved people. After her sale, for example, her mother tells her to "keep up a good heart." On her arrival at the I– house, two enslaved women at work in the yard commiserate: "Poor child, poor child! . . . you must keep up a good heart, if you are to live here."[41] Her second sale, to Mr. D–, entails a journey to Turk's Island, hundreds of miles away from her already dispersed family members. Despite this, Prince reports "great joy" at leaving a bad situation for one she that hopes may be better; it turns out to be even worse. However, her horrific experience in the salt works brings her to identify herself as a spokeswoman for fellow captives, including old Daniel, beaten with briars and rubbed with salt, and Sarah, dead after being beaten and tossed in the prickly pears. "In telling my own sorrows, I cannot pass by those of my fellow-slaves – for when I think of my own griefs, I remember theirs." Thus, affective connections among members of enslaved communities – what they call "heart" – ground and give shape to Mary Prince's narration.[42]

Ten years later, Mr. D– leaves the salt business and retires to Bermuda, taking Mary with him to wait on his daughters. She is happy to be getting off Turk's Island, in addition to her hope of seeing her family again. The work in Bermuda proves to be "not so very bad as Turk's Island." However, Prince probably encountered an occupational hazard noted by historians of enslaved women to be especially prevalent for women domestic workers: sexual harassment or coercion by white men.[43] Immediately preceding her elliptical description of D–'s sexual advances, Prince narrates another violent encounter with him in which her cosmopolitanism – that is, the power-knowledge she has gained through her involuntary travels – plays a key role. This significant juxtaposition suggests how far she has come, in more than simply miles traveled, since her earlier stint in the I– household. I quote at length:

> My old master often got drunk, and then he would get in a fury with his daughter, and beat her till she was not fit to be seen. I remember on one occasion . . . I found my master beating Miss D– dreadfully. I strove with all my strength to get her away from him; for she was all black and blue with bruises. He had beat her with his fist, and almost killed her. The people gave me credit for getting her away. He turned round and began to lick me. Then I said, "Sir, this is not Turk's Island." I can't repeat his answer, the words were too wicked – too bad to say. He wanted to treat me the same in Bermuda as he had done in Turk's Island.

He had an ugly fashion of stripping himself quite naked and ordering me then to wash him in a tub of water. This was worse to me than all the licks. Sometimes when he called me to wash him I would not come, my eyes were so full of shame. He would then come to beat me. One time I had plates and knives in my hand, and I dropped both plates and knives, and some of the plates were broken. He struck me so severely for this, that at last I defended myself, for I thought it was high time to do so. I then told him I would not live longer with him, for he was a very indecent man – very spiteful, and too indecent; with no shame for his servants, no shame for his own flesh. So I went away to a neighboring house and sat down and cried till the next morning, when I went home again, not knowing what else to do.

After that I was hired to work at Cedar Hills. . . . [44]

In the beating incident, Prince's record of community recognition for her courageous act – "The people gave me credit" – prefaces D–'s grudging recognition of a type of capital, a knowledge or worldliness, that she has gained through her involuntary travel. Her retort when he starts to hit her – "Sir, this is not Turk's Island" – seems to succeed in checking his violence. This small triumph is grounded in the geographical awareness that her incredulous comment celebrates. "He wanted to treat me the same in Bermuda as he had done in Turk's Island." Here, an enslaved person shares to some extent in the privilege of the more traditionally defined traveler, whose mobility yields increased knowledge, prestige, and power.

This victory sets the stage for Prince's subsequent self-defense from D–'s "indecency," a term that again invokes community standards that support her and condemn him. Here, too, her verbal (and possibly physical) resistance is finally successful, resulting, as she tells it, in her no longer having to work in D–'s "indecent" household.[45] At Cedar Hills, Prince also hears news of the Woods' upcoming departure for Antigua: "I felt a great wish to go there, and I went to Mr. D–, and asked him to let me go in Mr. Wood's service."[46] Arranging her own sale, possibly through active persuasion ("Mr. Wood did not then want to purchase me") and thus her move to a new island, the enslaved woman actively intervenes in the geographical trajectory of her life. The whole sequence presents us with a tactically savvy woman whose limited power within the master–slave relationship is drawn in significant part from her cosmopolitanism. Another aspect of that cosmopolitanism – her awareness of her prospective readers' metropolitan morality – constrains her from revealing the full extent of D–'s "indecency." She nonetheless manages not to portray herself as the passive victim that abolitionist ideology ideally would demand in its drive to locate the agency for change firmly in England.[47]

Prince's move to Antigua, which she actively solicited, led to several steps toward greater independence. There, she began saving to buy her freedom, converted to Christianity, learned to read from Moravian missionaries, and married a free black man – initiatives to create safe affective and spiritual spaces. She left all of this behind, however, for a chance at freedom. "I was willing to come to England," she emphasizes. She says (rather implausibly) that she thought the climate would help her rheumatism, and that her husband had heard that the Woods intended to free her. Both proved to be false. Her owners worked her "without compassion," and when she spoke up, they threatened to turn her out of doors in a strange city: "I might go and try what freedom would do for me, and be d[amne]d," Wood snarls.[48] Eventually, the much-abused worker "took courage" and left.

Her final journey (the last one that we know of) was short but momentous.[49] Moving out of the Woods' house and in with her friend Mash, the shoe-black, and his wife, Prince openly transgressed the conceptual boundaries that had marked her owners' assumption of control over their human property. Their repeated threats to turn her out assume that her foreignness in London as a black West Indian woman would make it difficult, if not impossible, for her to survive there without their help. Indeed, without a character reference (or with the damning letter Wood had given her), it would have been difficult to find a job. There were from 10,000 to 20,000 black people in London at that time; many, if not most, were destitute.[50]

The Woods based their illusion of control over Mary Prince on the assumption that enslaved people were "locals," not cosmopolitans like themselves – that is, limited by knowing only their immediate colonial environment, threatened or immobilized by the strangeness of England. Prince proved them wrong. She knew more and found more resources than they had thought possible, garnering financial support, legal sponsorship, and eventually employment from missionaries and abolitionists – in addition to the initial solidarity of her white working-class friends, Mr. and Mrs. Mash. Her cosmopolitanism violated their expectations and transgressed the boundaries of their racialized map of the world. It is no wonder that Mrs. Wood was "very much hurt and frightened when she found [Prince] was determined to go out" and tried to convince her that "if she goes the people will rob her, and then turn her adrift."[51] It is a final, futile effort to paint London as the hostile foreign territory that she wants Prince to experience.

Dictating her story for publication – sending it on its own journey around the British Isles via the institutions of the print marketplace – constituted another scandalous transgression, as was evident in the reaction of the Scottish pro-slavery ideologue, James MacQueen.[52] His article in *Blackwood's Edinburgh Magazine*, entitled "The Colonial Empire of Great Britain," undertakes a detailed refutation of *The History of Mary Prince*, labeling her the "despicable tool" of a "set of mischievous moles" intent on "undermin[ing] our colonial empire" (744). In his cantankerous words (with original typography): "By tools like *Mary Prince*... PRINGLE, and the band of which Pringle is the tool and the organ, mislead and irritate this country, browbeat the Government, and trample upon, as they are permitted to trample upon, our most important transmarine possessions." The dire consequences that MacQueen predicts if the abolitionists win include "the LOSS OF ONE HUNDRED AND FORTY MILLIONS STERLING of British capital and property, vested in and secured over these colonies" as well as "deep national humiliation and degradation."[53] That MacQueen devotes a 20-page attack in an important journal to an enslaved woman's autobiography is a tribute to the power of the abolitionist movement as well as the power that one enslaved woman was able to achieve, based partly on the knowledge she had gained through travel.

Mary Prince's conclusion turns her cosmopolitan geographical awareness to the explicit support of the abolitionist cause. Addressing the "good people in England," she delivers a personalized version of the moral geography of the empire familiar in abolitionist rhetoric from the 1770s until emancipation in 1833 – a politics of place that also informs Equiano's *Interesting Narrative* (see Chapter 4). "[S]ome people in this country say, that the slaves do not need better usage, and do not want to be free. They believe the foreign people, who deceive them, and say slaves are happy. I say, Not so... I never heard a slave say so. I never heard a Buckra [white] man say so, till I heard tell of it in England." Prince had to cross the Atlantic – leaving behind a localized West Indian perspective for a broader cosmopolitan view – to learn the full extent of the deception that shields the colonists' bad behavior. "Since I have been here I have often wondered how English people can go out into the West Indies and act in such a beastly manner. But when they go to the West Indies, they forget God and all feeling of shame, I think, since they can see and do such things."[54] By backing this abolitionist geography with her hard-won authority as slave and traveler, Prince lends it the weight of authenticity. It is obvious that her credibility was feared by pro-slavery activists such as MacQueen.

As she punctures the mystifications of one side of the debate over slavery, however, Prince leaves those of her own side intact. By presenting the colonies as a wholly separate, degenerate world, abolitionist propaganda obscured the intimate links between worlds that were incommensurable but nonetheless inextricable – connected by the constant transatlantic circulation of goods, ideas, and people such as Mary Prince herself. Prince's ironic predicament as she dictated her story, dependent on the political will of the "good people in England" for imperial legislation that would allow her to cross the Atlantic once more, underscores the colonial and global interconnections the violent history of which produced a subaltern cosmopolitan such as herself.

Prince's story was published in 1831, close to the successful end of the decades-long fight for British emancipation. Her words, filtered through Pringle's editing and publicized in print through the Anti-Slavery Society's sponsorship, doubtless contributed to that event. I analyze her *History*'s canny politics of place: not only invoking (as Equiano did more extensively) the abolitionists' imaginary geography of the sites of slavery but also attacking slave owners' appropriation of English family values, their attempts to paint the slave colony as a cozy extension of the place called "home." Unpublished writings by pro-slavery women such as Janet Schaw and Maria Nugent reveal the contours of this political strategy of domestication: white women's powerful contribution to colonial ideology. Reading these decidedly different women authors with attention to their mutual focus on the gendered idea of home is one way that we can appreciate the importance of place in the debate over British slavery.

Essential to the long struggle for freedom was the struggle to represent – and, by representing, lay claim to – the places where enslaved people lived, worked, and suffered. When the engraver Duperly appropriated Hakewill's picturesque view of Montpelier Old Works Plantation in 1833 and drew a crowd of ragged revolutionaries onto its peaceful foreground (see Figures 1.1 and 1.4), he commemorated slavery's downfall by subverting the aesthetics of the picturesque. Pro-slavery writers routinely harnessed the power of aesthetic discourse (as I argue in Chapter 1) to defend slavery by obscuring the presence, labor, and oppression of enslaved people in places that white colonists claimed, along with those people, as their property. Yet, Duperly fights back. He removes the top-hatted white men on horseback whose surveillance lends Hakewill's peaceful scene an ominous edge. In their place, he populates the foreground with Afro-Jamaican freedom fighters – an unruly frieze of extravagantly individualized black humanity. In the background, staining Hakewill's serene, cloud-dotted sky, plumes of smoke ascend from the other plantations set on fire by these rebels' co-conspirators across western Jamaica. Duperly thus remakes one of the fraught places of British slavery. He transforms an idealized, timeless scene – where no one works and nothing is happening – into the site of one of the decisive events that helped to hasten slavery's end.[55]

I return to this pair of images at the conclusion of my study because they so powerfully epitomize what I mean by the politics of place. The dialogic relationship between the two scenes is a visual analogue of the relationship between the colonial historians' Atlantic geography and Equiano's polemical remapping of the Atlantic or between Schaw's and Nugent's domesticated colony and Mary Prince's bitter deconstruction of the notion of "home." From an individual plantation to an entire nation, even a continent, places mattered a great deal in the long, bitter political struggle over British slavery. Hakewill harnessed the familiar aesthetic conventions of the picturesque to produce the colonial plantation for metropolitan consumption. On the site of large-scale agribusiness and harsh, proto-industrial labor management, his art conjures an exotic tranquility. Duperly punctures this illusion by including something that those conventions proscribe: the vulgar, disorderly bodies of the enslaved, not even confined to appropriate areas (like the staffage figures that ornament picturesque scenes), but rather invading and discomposing the orderly space of the picturesque plantation. When we set side by side these dueling versions of the Jamaican plantation, what emerges is a greater understanding of both the power and the limitations of the resources available to artists seeking to represent the captive spaces of British slavery.

Intertextual dialogue thus sharpens our sense of what is at stake in slavery's politics of place. Yet, some of the most interesting interchanges emerge from individual books – those sprawling, hybrid prose works characteristic of the Romantic period. Ambiguously positioned authors such as John Gabriel Stedman and Matthew "Monk" Lewis record their interactions with enslaved people and Maroons, incorporating in their books a sense of place very different from the dominant colonial perspective.[56] Both writers avail themselves of the master discourses that pervaded published representations of the West Indies: Stedman of natural history and Lewis of aesthetics. My analysis reveals how these white authors' imaginative engagement with the black inhabitants of the colonies they visited interrupts these bifocal, imperial discourses, giving us mediated access to a local, Creolized, specifically Afro-Caribbean perspective. Of course, these tropicopolitans – the Maroons and their leader, Boni; enslaved people with names like Venus and Plato – lacked independent access to print. However, their discernible presence in white-authored texts supplements the contribution of the formerly enslaved authors, Olaudah Equiano and Mary Prince – the atypical subalterns whose words have actually survived.

The captive spaces of the colonial Caribbean were, in many ways, a laboratory for modernity. As a focal point for early modern European expansion, the region sustained dramatic demographic and ecological changes after 1492. It owes its peculiar character to multiple displacements, notably the massive movement of populations from Africa to the Americas caused by the Atlantic slave trade. Throughout three centuries, colonization and slavery forged societies from deracinated groups, uneasily coexisting under conditions of inequality and coercion. The large population of captive Africans joined a smaller, motley array of Europeans – not all of them there by choice – including convicts, political refugees, and indentured servants as well as settler-entrepreneurs.[57] Even the plants came from elsewhere: sugar cane, the region's predominant crop, was an introduced species taken from the Canary Islands to Hispaniola, from Sicily via Madeira to Brazil, and then to the Lesser Antilles.[58]

Formed by displacement, the Caribbean colonies could not have been sustained without the continuing circulation of money, goods, documents, and people across the Atlantic over the network of routes established by early modern globalization. All of the authors whose writings I analyze were mobile, impelled from place to place in the Atlantic system by the imperial logic of government and trade. Stedman, the soldier, collected hazard pay for a dangerous mission; Schaw and Nugent accompanied imperial civil servants to their posts; the planters commuted between the colonial lands (and enslaved workers) that produced their fortunes and the metropolitan retreats where they aspired to spend those fortunes. Of course, enslaved people, as human commodities, were shipped wherever their owners dictated, although both Olaudah Equiano and Mary Prince took control of their movement in the end. The textual work of place-making thus arose out of the modern phenomena of displacement and circulation, and it bears their mark.

Since the end of British slavery, the Caribbean has gradually dropped off the "cultural radar" of Western modernity. Ordinary Americans may glimpse it nowadays in tourist brochures or news reports of coups, drug gangs, and natural disasters (e.g., the April 2010 Haiti earthquake). In the words of C. L. R. James, the Caribbean is "in but not of the West."[59] However, during the period that concerns this study – the final decades of slavery, from its apogee in the 1770s to its end – this colonial region engaged the attention of metropolitan British investors, politicians, scientists, and the reading public. The potential of sugar as a high-value commodity, with slavery as its economic engine, built Britain's Caribbean colonies. The politics of slavery was never absent from those colonies' written representation, even when the ostensible topic was tropical scenery or natural history.

The imaginary geographies I analyze encompass not only the Caribbean sugar islands but also the entire Atlantic circuit that linked them with the source of the colonies' enslaved labor force – that is, Africa – and the imperial center that absorbed the resulting products and profits. Writers constructed the captive spaces of British slavery relationally, as this study argues. In this sense, *Slavery and the Politics of Place* contributes to postcolonial criticism, which is grounded in the analysis of place: places in asymmetrical relationships of power and dependency, exploitation and oppression. A colony is a captive space, a place defined by its relationship to a more powerful place. "The right to colonial rule," Catherine Hall explains, "was built on the gap between metropole and colony: civilization here, barbarism . . . there."[60] That gap – the conceptual distance between civilization and barbarism, temperate and tropical, free and enslaved – drove the cultural politics of place, the object of which was the fate of Britain's hundreds of thousands of actual captives. Crossing from slavery to freedom in a single step out of her owners' London door, Mary Prince symbolically remade a captive space into a place of liberation. A few years later, Duperly's audacious image of the enslaved rabble storming Lord Seaford's plantation commemorated the end of colonial slavery and the beginning of another chapter in the history of the places that slavery made.

Notes

INTRODUCTION: CAPTIVE SPACES

1 William Beckford, known as Beckford of Somerley (not to be confused with his cousin, the novelist of the same name) also published *Remarks on the Situation of the Negroes in Jamaica* (1788). For his biography, see Richard B. Sheridan, "Planter and Historian: The Career of William Beckford of Jamaica and England, 1744–1799," *Jamaican Historical Review*, Vol. 3, No. 1 (March 1957): 36–58.

2 David Brion Davis, *Slavery and Human Progress* (New York and Oxford: Oxford University Press, 1984), 81, quoted in David Lambert, *White Creole Culture, Politics and Identity During the Age of Abolition* (Cambridge: Cambridge University Press, 2005, 10).

3 Lambert, *White Creole Culture*, 11. Lambert's study explores the geographical "problem of slavery" from the perspective of white Creole society in Barbados. On humanitarian narratives, see Thomas Laqueur, "Bodies, Details, and the Humanitarian Narrative," in *The New Cultural History*, ed. Lynn Hunt (Berkeley, Los Angeles, and London: University of California Press, 1989). I use "Britain/British" to refer to the nation and its people after the 1707 Act of Union with Scotland and "England/English" for historical events or trajectories beginning before that (as well as for the geographical area of England, as distinct from Scotland and Wales). I refer to the legal proceedings in the Mansfield case as "English" because Scotland, of course, retained its own court system within Great Britain. The eighteenth-century writers I quote often use "English," where today's usage would dictate "British," especially to discuss the national inheritance of liberty. However, according to Linda Colley, "'English' and 'England'" were "giving way to 'British' and 'Great Britain' . . . in both official and everyday vocabulary by the 1750s." Colley, *Britons: Forging the Nation 1707–1837* (New Haven, CT: Yale University Press, 1992, 13). We may suspect this usage of sometimes having racial overtones; Kathleen Wilson's characterization of Englishness as "a trope of white civilization . . . that attempted to set off its performers" from various Others may apply. Wilson, *The Island Race: Englishness, Empire and Gender in the Eighteenth Century* (London and New York: Routledge, 2003, 17). The work of Wilson and other historians, in particular Colley, has helped to sensitize scholars to the distinctions among the three and, after 1801, four nations comprising Great Britain, and the necessity for precision in

nomenclature, while also reminding us that "Britishness and Englishness were not immutable and eternal formations, but sites of struggle whose tropes of representation are specific to particular periods." "No singular British system or idea of Englishness or indeed of empire emerged from the process of imperial expansion in the seventeenth and eighteenth centuries, but many systems and ideas, linked to each other through often disparate bonds of identity, experience and practice" (Wilson, *Island Race*, 4, 15). See also Catherine Hall, *White, Male, and Middle-Class: Explorations in Feminism and History* (New York: Routledge, 1992, 206).

4 Sidney Mintz suggests that "there might have been 'industry' on the colonial plantation before it existed in the homeland" – that the Industrial Revolution, for many years thought of as beginning in Europe and spreading to its peripheries, may instead have traveled from the periphery back to the center. *Sweetness and Power: The Place of Sugar in Modern History* (New York: Penguin, 1985, 48).

5 For an overview of the development of Atlantic Studies among historians, see Bernard Bailyn, "Introduction: Reflections on Some Major Themes," in *Soundings in Atlantic History: Latent Structures and Intellectual Currents, 1500–1830*, ed. Bernard Bailyn and Patricia L. Denault (Cambridge, MA, and London: Harvard University Press, 2009, 1–43). Examples of noteworthy work in literary and cultural studies include Paul Gilroy, *The Black Atlantic: Modernity and Double Consciousness* (Cambridge, MA: Harvard University Press, 1993); Joseph Roach, *Cities of the Dead: Circum-Atlantic Performance* (New York: Columbia University Press, 1996); Geoff Quilley and Kay Dian Kriz, ed., *An Economy of Color: Visual Culture and the Atlantic World, 1660–1830* (Manchester, UK: Manchester University Press, 2003); Philip Gould, *Barbaric Traffic: Commerce and Antislavery in the Eighteenth-Century Atlantic World* (Cambridge, MA, and London: Harvard University Press, 2003); Sean X. Goudie, *Creole America: The West Indies and the Formation of Literature and Culture in the New Republic* (Philadelphia: University of Pennsylvania Press, 2006); Kay Dian Kriz, *Slavery, Sugar, and the Culture of Refinement: Picturing the British West Indies, 1700–1840* (New Haven, CT, and London: Yale University Press, 2008); Christopher P. Iannini, *Fatal Revolutions: Natural History, West Indian Slavery, and the Routes of American Literature* (Chapel Hill: University of North Carolina Press, 2012); and Martha Schoolman and Jared Hickman, ed., *Abolitionist Places* (London and New York: Routledge, 2013).

6 Mary Pratt's *Imperial Eyes: Travel Writing and Transculturation* (New York and London: Routledge, 1993) broke important ground in the study of travel writing and colonialism. See also Paul Carter, *The Road to Botany Bay: An Essay in Spatial History* (London and Boston: Faber and Faber, 1987); P. J. Marshall and Glyndwr Williams, *The Great Map of Mankind: Perceptions of New Worlds in the Age of Enlightenment* (Cambridge, MA: Harvard University Press, 1982); Billie Melman, *Women's Orients: English Women and the Middle East, 1718–1918* (Ann Arbor: University of Michigan Press, 1992); Anthony Pagden, *European Encounters with the New World: From Renaissance to Romanticism* (New Haven, CT, and London: Yale University Press, 1993); Sara Mills, *Discourses of*

Difference: An Analysis of Women's Travel Writing and Colonialism (London and New York: Routledge, 1991); David Spurr, *The Rhetoric of Empire: Colonial Discourse in Journalism, Travel Writing, and Imperial Administration* (Durham, NC, and London: Duke University Press, 1993); and Sara Suleri, *The Rhetoric of English India* (Chicago: University of Chicago Press, 1992). More recent studies of note include Tim Fulford, *Romantic Indians: Native Americans, British Literature, and Transatlantic Culture, 1756–1830* (Oxford and New York: Oxford University Press, 2006); Jonathan Lamb, *Preserving the Self in the South Seas 1680–1840* (Chicago and London: University of Chicago Press, 2001); and Nigel Leask, *Curiosity and the Aesthetics of Travel Writing, 1770–1840* (Oxford: Oxford University Press, 2002); as well as the indispensable collection of primary texts edited by Tim Fulford and Peter J. Kitson, *Travels, Explorations and Empires: Writings from the Era of Imperial Expansion* (8 vols.) (London: Pickering and Chatto, 2001).

7 I use the word "enslaved" in preference to "slave" to emphasize that enslavement was a practice of subjection, not a state of being or essential category of people. See John F. Campbell, "Textualizing Slavery: From 'Slave' to 'Enslaved People' in Caribbean Historiography," in *Beyond the Blood, the Beach and the Banana*, ed. Sandra Courtman (Kingston, Jamaica, and Miami: Ian Randle, 2004, 34–45). (I have not altered the word "slave" in quotations, and I do use it as an adjective, as in "slave trade" and "slave society.")

8 James Clifford, *Routes: Travel and Translation in the Late Twentieth Century* (Cambridge, MA, and London: Harvard University Press, 1997, 33, 35–6, 257). Clifford points out that the Black Atlantic diaspora does not fit a paradigm "oriented by continuous cultural connections to a source and by a teleology of 'return,'" a model generated by the Jewish Diaspora, adding that we should be wary of "constructing our working definition of a term like 'diaspora' by recourse to an 'ideal type'" (249). Gilroy's *Black Atlantic* meditates on the ways in which displacement, loss, and violence were constitutive of black diaspora culture.

9 On the impact of postcolonial studies, see Felicity Nussbaum, "Introduction," *The Global Eighteenth Century*, ed. Felicity A. Nussbaum (Baltimore, MD, and London: Johns Hopkins University Press, 2003, 1–18); Suvir Kaul, *Eighteenth-Century Literature and Postcolonial Studies* (Edinburgh: Edinburgh University Press, 2009); and Elizabeth A. Bohls, *Romantic Literature and Postcolonial Studies* (Edinburgh: Edinburgh University Press, 2013). Important work on slavery and abolition includes that of Debbie Lee, *Slavery and the Romantic Imagination* (Philadelphia: University of Pennsylvania Press, 2002) and Helen Thomas, *Romanticism and Slave Narratives* (Cambridge: Cambridge University Press, 2000), who set Romanticism in dialogue with slavery. Ian Baucom, *Specters of the Atlantic: Finance Capital, Slavery, and the Philosophy of History* (Durham, NC: Duke University Press, 2005); George Boulukos, *The Grateful Slave: The Emergence of Race in Eighteenth-Century British and American Culture* (Cambridge: Cambridge University Press, 2008); and Lynn Festa, *Sentimental Figures of Empire in Eighteenth-Century Britain and France* (Baltimore, MD: Johns

Hopkins University Press, 2006) explore key tropes or figurations of slavery. Work on the abolitionist movement – in particular, the importance of sentiment or sensibility to abolitionist rhetoric – includes Moira Ferguson, *Subject to Others: British Women Writers and Colonial Slavery, 1670–1834* (New York and London: Routledge, 1992); Markman Ellis, *The Politics of Sensibility: Race, Gender and Commerce in the Sentimental Novel* (Cambridge: Cambridge University Press, 1996); Charlotte Sussman, *Consuming Anxieties: Consumer Protest, Gender and British Slavery, 1713–1833* (Stanford, CA: Stanford University Press, 2000, Chaps. 4 and 5); Marcus Wood, *Slavery, Empathy, and Pornography* (Oxford: Oxford University Press, 2002); Gould, *Barbaric Traffic*; Brycchan Carey, *British Abolitionism and the Rhetoric of Sensibility: Writing, Sentiment, and Slavery, 1760–1807* (Houndmills, Basingstoke, Hampshire: Palgrave Macmillan, 2005); and Schoolman and Hicks, ed., *Abolitionist Places*. Keith Sandiford, *The Cultural Politics of Sugar: Caribbean Slavery and Narratives of Colonialism* (Cambridge: Cambridge University Press, 2000) analyzes slavery's Creole apologists. Ian Haywood, *Bloody Romanticism: Spectacular Violence and the Politics of Representation, 1776–1832* (Houndmills, Basingstoke, Hampshire: Palgrave Macmillan, 2006, Chap. 1); and Sarah Salih, "Putting Down Rebellion: Witnessing the Body of the Condemned in Abolition-Era Narratives," in *Slavery and the Cultures of Abolition*, ed. Brycchan Carey and Peter J. Kitson (Cambridge: D. S. Brewer, 2007, 64–86) study slave resistance and insurrection. Jenny Sharpe's *Ghosts of Slavery: A Literary Archaeology of Black Women's Lives* (Minneapolis: University of Minnesota Press, 2003) is especially valuable for its painstaking and scrupulous attention to the elusive subjectivity of enslaved women. The essays in Philip Gould and Vincent Carretta, ed., *Genius in Bondage: Literature of the Early Black Atlantic* (Lexington: University Press of Kentucky, 2001) discuss enslaved authors, whereas those in Carey and Kitson, ed., *Slavery*, treat all aspects of slavery and abolition.

10 Paul Youngquist and Frances Botkin, "Introduction: Black Romanticism: Romantic Circulations," *Circulations: Romanticism and the Black Atlantic*, ed. Paul Youngquist and Frances Botkin, 2011, available at www.rc.umd.edu/praxis/circulations/index.html, 2. I use the term "West Indies" to refer to the Caribbean islands under British control; it also is used more broadly to refer to all of the islands of the Caribbean, including the Greater and Lesser Antilles. On its complex history, see Catherine Hall, "What Is a West Indian?" in *West Indian Intellectuals in Britain*, ed. Bill Schwarz (Manchester, UK: Manchester University Press, 2003, 33).

11 Miles Ogborn, "Historical Geographies of Globalization, c. 1500–1800," *Modern Historical Geographies*, ed. Brian Graham and Catherine Nash (Harlow, Essex, UK: Pearson Education Limited, 2000, 43). Felicity Nussbaum concurs ("Introduction," 3) but cautions us to rethink any "narrative that leads inexorably from the eighteenth century to modernity and its conjunctions with globalization." The literature on first globalization is substantial. J. M. Blaut, *The Colonizer's Model of the World: Geographical Diffusion and Eurocentric History* (New York and London: Guilford Press, 1993) influentially questions

European diffusionism, the idea that before 1492 Europe was already more advanced than the rest of the world: Europe's rise to dominance, Blaut writes, "resulted not from any European superiority of mind, culture, or environment" but rather from the profits of colonization and conquest (2, 51). Geoffrey C. Gunn, *First Globalization: The Eurasian Exchange, 1500–1800* (Lanham, MD: Rowman & Littlefield, 2003) reminds us that Western Hemisphere colonization and trade were only part of European expansion: they also went eastward, generating decidedly different interactions as Europeans in Asia "met their peers in civilization, military prowess, and science" (3). See also Brian Graham and Catherine Nash, ed., *Modern Historical Geographies* (Harlow, Essex, UK: Pearson Education Ltd., 2000) and Alan Lester, *Imperial Networks: Creating Identities in Nineteenth-Century South Africa and Britain* (London and New York: Routledge, 2001).

12 Tim Fulford, Peter J. Kitson, and Debbie Lee, *Literature, Science, and Exploration in the Romantic Era: Bodies of Knowledge* (Cambridge: Cambridge University Press, 2004, 117); also see pp. 9–13 and chap. 5 on Banks and breadfruit.

13 Richard B. Sheridan, *Sugar and Slavery: The Economic History of the British West Indies, 1623–1775* (Barbados, Jamaica, Trinidad, and Tobago: Canoe Press, 1994 [1974], 99).

14 Mintz, *Sweetness*, 185, 39, quoted in Catherine Hall, *Civilizing Subjects: Colony and Metropole in the English Imagination, 1830–1867* (Chicago: University of Chicago Press, 2002, 70, 455).

15 C. Hall, *Civilizing Subjects*, 72.

16 Trevor Burnard, *Mastery, Tyranny, and Desire: Thomas Thistlewood and his Slaves in the Anglo-Jamaican World* (Chapel Hill: University of North Carolina Press, 2004, 14). Although sugar dominated the economy of the colonial British Caribbean, other agricultural products (e.g., coffee and indigo) were cultivated as well. Mary Prince's *History* gives a harrowing account of an understudied aspect of the Caribbean economy, salt raking in the Turks and Caicos Islands off Bermuda; see Michelle Speitz, "Blood Sugar and Salt Licks: Corroding Bodies and Preserving Nations in *The History of Mary Prince, A West Indian Slave, Related by Herself*," *Circulations: Romanticism and the Black Atlantic*, ed. Paul Youngquist and Frances Botkin, 2011.

17 C. Hall, *Civilizing Subjects*, 72; Burnard, *Mastery*, 19.

18 Douglas Hall, *In Miserable Slavery: Thomas Thistlewood in Jamaica, 1750–1786* (London: Macmillan, 1989); Burnard, *Mastery*.

19 Burnard, *Mastery*, 15, 16; Stanley L. Engerman and B. W. Higman, "The Demographic Structure of the Caribbean Slave Societies in the Eighteenth and Nineteenth Centuries," *UNESCO General History of the Caribbean*, ed. Franklin W. Knight, Vol. 3, *The Slave Societies of the Caribbean* (Paris, London, and Oxford: UNESCO Publishing and Macmillan Publishers Ltd., 2003, 48).

20 Burnard, *Mastery*, 16. The historical literature on Caribbean slavery is vast. On slavery in Jamaica, see, e.g., Barbara Bush, *Slave Women in Caribbean Society 1650–1838* (Bloomington: Indiana University Press, 1990); Michael Craton, *Testing the Chains: Resistance to Slavery in the British West Indies*

(Ithaca, NY: Cornell University Press, 1982), and *Searching for the Invisible Man: Slaves and Plantation Life in Jamaica* (Cambridge, MA: Harvard University Press, 1979); B. W. Higman, *Slave Populations of the British Caribbean 1807–1834* (Baltimore, MD: Johns Hopkins University Press, 1984); Richard B. Sheridan, *Sugar and Slavery* and *Doctors and Slaves: A Medical and Demographic History of Slavery in the British West Indies, 1680–1834* (Cambridge: Cambridge University Press, 1985); Mary Turner, *Slaves and Missionaries: The Disintegration of Jamaican Slave Society, 1787–1834* (Urbana: University of Illinois Press, 1982); J. R. Ward, *British West Indian Slavery 1750–1834: The Process of Amelioration* (Oxford: Clarendon Press, 1988); and the essays in Knight, ed., *UNESCO General History.*

21 Franklin W. Knight, "Pluralism, Creolization, and Culture," in Knight, ed., *UNESCO General History*, Vol. 3, 275.

22 Quoted in Knight, "Pluralism," 275. Edward Long, the historian of Jamaica, observed this several decades earlier; it was one of his many criticisms of the planter class, to which his *History of Jamaica* reveals a deeply conflicted relationship.

23 Edward (Kamau) Brathwaite, *The Development of Creole Society in Jamaica, 1770–1820* (Oxford: Clarendon Press, 1971, 307). The term "Creole" applies to "anyone born in the Caribbean (and neighboring mainland) region of whatever descent, regardless of status or condition," enslaved or free (Knight, "Pluralism," 272). For the history of the term and varieties of regional usage, see Knight, "Pluralism," 272, and Lambert, *White Creole Culture,* 37. Also see the essays in Verene A. Shepherd and Glen L. Richards, ed., *Questioning Creole: Creolization Discourses in Caribbean Culture* (Kingston, Jamaica, and Oxford, UK: 2002), in particular, Caroline Allen, "Creole: The Problem of Definition" (47–63).

24 Eric Williams, *Capitalism and Slavery* (Chapel Hill and London: University of North Carolina Press, 1994 [1944], 7).

25 Peter J. Kitson, *Romantic Literature, Race, and Colonial Encounter* (Houndmills, Basingstoke, Hampshire: Palgrave Macmillan, 2007, 3–4). Discussions of race, racial theories, and racial discourse in the eighteenth and early nineteenth centuries are numerous. The best recent summary is Kitson, *Romantic Literature,* 11–37; see also Kitson's Introduction to Vol. 8, *Theories of Race,* in Kitson and Debbie Lee, ed., *Slavery, Abolition and Emancipation: Writings in the British Romantic Period* (8 vols.) (London: Pickering and Chatto, 1999, vii–xxvi). Other recent work on race and human variety in the long eighteenth century includes H. L. Malchow, *Gothic Images of Race in Nineteenth-Century Britain* (Stanford, CA: Stanford University Press, 1996); Felicity A. Nussbaum, *Torrid Zones: Maternity, Sexuality, and Empire in Eighteenth-Century English Narratives* (Baltimore, MD: Johns Hopkins University Press, 1995) and *The Limits of the Human: Fictions of Anomaly, Race, and Gender in the Long Eighteenth Century* (Cambridge: Cambridge University Press, 2003); Londa Schiebinger, *Nature's Body: Gender in the Making of Modern Science* (Boston: Beacon Press, 1993); Roxann Wheeler, *The Complexion of Race: Categories of Difference in*

Eighteenth-Century British Culture (Philadelphia: University of Pennsylvania Press, 2000); and Paul Youngquist, ed., *Race, Romanticism, and the Atlantic* (Surrey, UK, and Burlington, VT: Ashgate, 2013). Ania Loomba and Jonathan Burton's introduction to *Race in Early Modern England: A Documentary Companion* (Houndmills, Basingstoke, Hampshire: Palgrave Macmillan, 2007) questions the received historical timeline of racial theory, whereas Nancy Stepan's classic study, *The Idea of Race in Science: Great Britain 1800–1960* (Hamden, CT: Archon Books, 1982) addresses nineteenth-century developments. Robert J. C. Young, *Colonial Desire: Hybridity in Theory, Culture and Race* (London and New York: Routledge, 1995) discusses race in the context of postcolonial theory; Kathleen Wilson addresses the relationship between ideas of race and nation in the eighteenth century in *The Island Race*. David Theo Goldberg, *Racist Culture: Philosophy and the Politics of Meaning* (Oxford, UK, and Cambridge, MA: Blackwell, 1993) and Paul Gilroy, *Against Race: Imagining Political Culture Beyond the Color Line* (Cambridge, MA: Belknap Press of the Harvard University Press, 2000) both consider the implications of this history of racial ideology for the twentieth and twenty-first centuries.

26 Tim Cresswell, *Place: A Short Introduction* (Malden, MA: Blackwell, 2004), 12; Arif Dirlik, "Place-Based Imagination: Globalism and the Politics of Place," in *Places and Politics in an Age of Globalization*, ed. Arif Dirlik and Roxann Prazniak (Lanham, MD: Rowman & Littlefield, 2001, 15).

27 Doreen Massey, *Space, Place, and Gender* (Minneapolis: University of Minnesota Press, 1994, 154); Linda McDowell, *Gender, Identity and Place: Understanding Feminist Geographies* (Cambridge: Polity Press, 1999, 5). Arturo Escobar, "Culture Sits in Places: Reflections on Globalism and Subaltern Strategies of Localization," *Political Geography* 20 (2001): 139–74, helpfully surveys the field, as does Cresswell, *Place*. See the essays in Akhil Gupta and James Ferguson, ed., *Culture, Power, Place: Explorations in Critical Anthropology* (Durham, NC: Duke University Press, 1997) for an anthropological perspective. Cheryl McEwan, "Material Geographies and Postcolonialism," *Singapore Journal of Tropical Geography* 24 (2003): 340–55, incisively integrates geography and postcolonial theory. On the historical geography of modernization, see the introduction to David N. Livingstone and Charles W. J. Withers, ed., *Geography and Enlightenment* (Chicago: University of Chicago Press, 1999), as well as Withers, "Geography, Natural History and the Eighteenth-Century Enlightenment: Putting the World in Place," *History Workshop Journal* 39 (1995): 138–63; Lester, *Imperial Networks*; Ogborn, "Historical Geographies of Globalization"; and Catherine Nash, "Historical Geographies of Modernity," *Modern Historical Geographies*, ed. Brian Graham and Catherine Nash (Edinburgh Gate, Harlow, Essex: Pearson Education Limited, 2000, 13–40). Also note Neil Smith and Cindi Katz's cautionary stance on metaphor in "Grounding Metaphor: Towards a Spatialized Politics," in *Place and the Politics of Identity*, ed. Michael Keith and Steve Pile (London: Routledge, 1993, 67–83).

28 Gayatri Spivak's famous essay "Can the Subaltern Speak?" in *Marxism and the Interpretation of Culture*, ed. Cary Nelson and Lawrence Grossberg (Urbana:

University of Illinois Press, 1988) remains the starting point for thinking about this challenge, taken up by numerous scholars since she wrote. Among scholars of British slavery, Sharpe's *Ghosts of Slavery* perhaps best exemplifies the creative yet scrupulous strategies of interpretation needed for this important task.

29 John Durham Peters, "Seeing Bifocally: Media, Place, Culture," in Akhil Gupta and James Ferguson, ed., *Culture, Power, Place: Explorations in Critical Anthropology* (Durham, NC, and London: Duke University Press, 1997, 76). Important recent work connecting aesthetics with colonialism, slavery, and/or race includes Christine Battersby, *The Sublime, Terror, and Human Difference* (London: Routledge, 2007); David Bindman, *Ape to Apollo: Aesthetics and the Idea of Race in the Eighteenth Century* (Ithaca, NY: Cornell University Press, 2002); David Lloyd, "The Pathological Sublime: Pleasure and Pain in the Colonial Context," in *Postcolonial Enlightenment*, ed. Brycchan Carey and Lynn Festa (Oxford: Oxford University Press, 2009, 71–102); Ian Haywood, *Bloody Romanticism: Spectacular Violence and the Politics of Representation, 1776–1832* (Houndmills, Basingstoke, Hampshire: Palgrave Macmillan, 2006); Meg Armstrong, "'The Effects of Blackness': Gender, Race, and the Sublime in Aesthetic Theories of Burke and Kant," *Journal of Aesthetics and Art Criticism* 54 (1996): 213–36; and Paul Gilroy, "Cultural Studies and Ethnic Absolutism," in Lawrence Grossberg, Cary Nelson, and Paula Treichler, ed., *Cultural Studies* (New York: Routledge, 1992, 187–98).

30 For the purposes of this study, I use "discourse" to designate a body of language, encompassing a characteristic lexicon or vocabulary and a set of statements that deploy it in writing or speech. (I am primarily concerned with writing, although I touch on orality on a few occasions, such as Mary Prince's dictated narrative.) Different discourses encode different modes of representing experience, which arise within the framework of power relations, social institutions, and disciplines of knowledge. The resources of discourse determine what can be written or said or what counts as truth or fact within a given domain. Because it circulates through acts of writing and reading, discourse is not monolithic: I assume that all utterances and texts are "potentially splintered, formally open to contradictory uses." Dialogue is thus "the primary condition of discourse" and ideological struggle is at its heart; see Sara Mills, *Discourse* (London and New York: Routledge, 1997, 17, 9, 12). Key historical shifts give rise to new discourses, which enact new ways of knowing or organizing experience: the discourses with which I am concerned are central to the regime of truth known as the European Enlightenment. Linnaean classification, a key feature of the discourse of natural history, provides a useful example of the powerful effects that a discourse can have when implemented through colonial practice. Mary Pratt described the way that natural history could function to erase indigenous knowledge about plants, replacing it with colonial knowledge (*Imperial Eyes*, 32).

31 This is the thesis of Eric Williams's influential *Capitalism and Slavery*; others are less willing to draw this conclusion. For this ongoing debate, see Richard Pares,

Merchants and Planters, Economic History Review, Supplement No. 4, 1960; Stanley L. Engerman and Barbara Solow, *British Capitalism and Caribbean Slavery: The Legacy of Eric Williams* (Cambridge and New York: Cambridge University Press, 1987); Joseph E. Inikori, *Africans and the Industrial Revolution in England: A Study in International Trade and Development* (Cambridge: Cambridge University Press, 2002); and Selwyn H. H. Carrington, *The Sugar Industry and the Abolition of the Slave Trade 1775–1810* (Gainesville: University Press of Florida, 2003).

32 John Bender, "A New History of the Enlightenment?" *Eighteenth-Century Life,* 16 (1992), 9; Elizabeth A. Bohls, *Women Travel Writers and the Language of Aesthetics, 1716–1818* (Cambridge: Cambridge University Press, 1995, 69). Examples include William Smith, *Natural History of Nevis and the Rest of the English Leeward Charibee Islands in America* (London, 1745); Griffith Hughes, *Natural History of Barbados* (London, 1750); Janet Schaw, *Journal of a Lady of Quality: Being the Narrative of a Journey from Scotland to the West Indies, North Carolina, and Portugal, in the Years 1774 to 1776,* ed. Evangeline Walker Andrews and Charles Maclean Andrews, introduction by Stephen Carl Arch (Lincoln and London: University of Nebraska Press, 2005); Edward Long, *History of Jamaica* (London, 1774); Maria Nugent, *Lady Nugent's Journal of her Residence in Jamaica from 1801 to 1805,* ed. Philip Wright, revised edition (Kingston, Jamaica: Institute of Jamaica, 1968), and so forth.

33 Mimi Sheller, *Consuming the Caribbean: From Arawaks to Zombies* (London: Routledge, 2003, 38–44); Bohls, *Women Travel Writers,* chap. 2.

34 Simon Pugh, "Introduction," *Reading Landscape: Country – City – Capital,* ed. Simon Pugh (Manchester, UK: Manchester University Press, 1990, 5). John Stuart Mill saw Britain's trade with its Caribbean colonies as more like the trade between town and country than an external trade. "Our West Indian colonies," he wrote, "cannot be regarded as countries with a productive capital of their own . . . [but are rather] the place where England finds it convenient to carry on the production of sugar, coffee and a few other tropical commodities" (quoted in C. Hall, *Civilizing Subjects,* 70).

35 Michel Foucault, *The Order of Things [Les Mots et les choses]* (New York: Vintage, 1994, 124–65); Susan Scott Parrish, *American Curiosity: Cultures of Natural History in the Colonial British Atlantic World* (Chapel Hill: University of North Carolina Press, 2006). Here, I disagree with Pratt's influential analysis in *Imperial Eyes.* Other important recent work on natural history and scientific networks includes Alan Bewell, "Romanticism and Colonial Natural History," *Studies in Romanticism* 43 (2004): 5–34; Richard Drayton, *Nature's Government: Science, Imperial Britain, and the "Improvement" of the World* (New Haven, CT: Yale University Press, 2000); Fulford, Kitson, and Lee, *Literature, Science, and Exploration;* Joseph Gascoigne, *Joseph Banks and the English Enlightenment: Useful Knowledge and Polite Culture* (Cambridge: Cambridge University Press, 1994); and the collections of essays by N. Jardine, J. A. Secord, and E. C. Spary, ed. *Cultures of Natural History* (Cambridge: Cambridge University Press, 1996), and Londa Schiebinger and Claudia Swan, ed., *Colonial Botany: Science,*

Commerce, and Politics in the Early Modern World (Philadelphia: University of Pennsylvania Press, 2005).

36 Charles W. J Withers, "Geography, Natural History and the Eighteenth-Century Enlightenment: Putting the World in Place," *History Workshop Journal* 39 (1995), 138.

37 Withers, "Geography, Natural History and the Eighteenth-Century", 139.

38 Britain invaded Saint Domingue in 1794, a year after the start of its war with France, occupying parts of the island until the disproportionate financial and human cost of the venture forced a withdrawal in 1798. See David Geggus, *Slavery, War, and Revolution: The British Occupation of Saint Domingue, 1793–1798* (Oxford: Oxford University Press, 1982).

39 Equiano's editor and biographer, Vincent Carretta, found a baptismal register and a ship's roster on which Equiano (who went by his slave name, Gustavus Vassa) was listed as born in "Carolina." Carretta, *Equiano the African: Biography of a Self-Made Man* (Athens and London: University of Georgia Press, 2005, 2).

40 See Peter Linebaugh and Marcus Rediker, *The Many-Headed Hydra: Sailors, Slaves, Commoners, and the Hidden History of the Revolutionary Atlantic* (Boston: Beacon Press, 2000), on the role of sailors and ports in the transatlantic flow of revolutionary ideas.

41 Leonore Davidoff and Catherine Hall, *Family Fortunes: Men and Women of the English Middle Class, 1780–1850* (Chicago: University of Chicago Press, 1987), argue for separate-spheres ideology, critiqued in points by Amanda Vickery, *The Gentleman's Daughter: Women's Lives in Georgian England* (New Haven, CT, and London: Yale University Press, 1998); Margaret Hunt, *The Middling Sort: Commerce, Gender, and the Family in Eighteenth-Century England* (Berkeley: University of California Press, 1996); and Colley, *Britons*. See the discussion in Chapter 5.

42 Although the number of women publishing prose fiction rose dramatically in the course of the eighteenth century, by the end of the century, women were still far less likely than men to publish in some other genres, such as travel writing; hence, my inclusion of these unpublished works. (Matthew Lewis's journal, though intended for publication, also was not published until well after his death.)

43 Several seminal collections published in the mid-1990s address the issues of displacement and diaspora and helped to form my thinking on these issues. See Angelika Bammer, ed., *Displacements: Cultural Identities in Question* (Bloomington and Indianapolis: Indiana University Press, 1994); Caren Kaplan and Inderpal Grewal, ed., *Scattered Hegemonies: Postmodernity and Transnational Feminist Practices* (Minneapolis: University of Minnesota Press, 1994); Smadar Lavie and Ted Swedenburg, ed., *Displacement, Diaspora, and Geographies of Identity* (Durham, NC: Duke University Press, 1996); and Patricia Yaeger, ed., *The Geography of Identity* (Ann Arbor: University of Michigan Press, 1996).

1. THE PLANTER PICTURESQUE

1 Important work on the picturesque includes Christopher Hussey, *The Picturesque: Studies in a Point of View* (London: Frank Cass, 1927); Elizabeth Wheeler Manwaring, *Italian Landscape in Eighteenth-Century England* (New York: Oxford University Press, 1925); W. J. Hipple, *The Beautiful, the Sublime, and the Picturesque in Eighteenth-Century British Aesthetic Theory* (Carbondale: Southern Illinois University Press, 1957); Carl Paul Barbier, *William Gilpin* (Oxford: Clarendon Press, 1963); John Barrell, *The Idea of Landscape and the Sense of Place, 1730–1840: An Approach to the Poetry of John Clare* (Cambridge: Cambridge University Press, 1972); Ann Bermingham, *Landscape and Ideology* (Berkeley: University of California Press, 1986); Alan Liu, *Wordsworth: The Sense of History* (Stanford, CA: Stanford University Press, 1989, chap. 3); Kim Ian Michasiw, "Nine Revisionist Theses on the Picturesque," *Representations* 38 (1992): 76–100; Malcolm Andrews, *The Search for the Picturesque* (Stanford, CA: Stanford University Press, 1989); and the essays in Stephen Copley and Peter Garside, ed., *The Politics of the Picturesque* (Cambridge: Cambridge University Press, 1994). Of the relatively small body of work on colonial landscape, the most interesting has asked how metropolitan paradigms were adapted to specific colonial conditions: Leask, *Curiosity*; Suleri, *Rhetoric*, 75–110; J. M. Coetzee, *White Writing: On the Culture of Letters in South Africa* (New Haven, CT: Yale University Press, 1988, 36–62); Raymond Williams, *The Country and the City* (Oxford: Oxford University Press, 1973, 279–88). On explorers, see, e.g., Pratt, *Imperial Eyes,* chap. 3; John E. Crowley, "'Taken on the Spot': The Visual Appropriation of New France for the Global British Landscape," *Canadian Historical Review* 86 (2005): 1–28; and Simon Ryan, "Exploring Aesthetics: The Picturesque Appropriation of Land in Journals of Australian Exploration," *Australian Literary Studies* 15:4 (1992): 282–93. On settlers, see Coetzee, *White Writing*; and David Bunn, "'Our Wattled Cot': Mercantile and Domestic Space in Thomas Pringle's African Landscape" in *Landscape and Power,* ed. W. J. T. Mitchell (Chicago: University of Chicago Press, 1994, 127–73). Jill Casid, *Sowing Empire: Landscape and Colonization* (Minneapolis: University of Minnesota Press, 2005, chap. 2); and Geoff Quilley, "Pastoral Plantations: The Slave Trade and the Representations of British Colonial Landscape in the Late Eighteenth Century," in *An Economy of Color: Visual Culture and the Atlantic World, 1660–1830,* ed. Geoff Quilley and Kay Dian Kriz (Manchester, UK: Manchester University Press, 2003, 106–28), treat the West Indian picturesque; Casid's focus is transplantation, or material exchange between colony and metropole, whereas Quilley examines the work of the artist George Robertson in Jamaica and England. For important recent scholarship connecting aesthetics and race, see Introduction, Note 29 (this volume).

2 David Watts, *The West Indies: Patterns of Development, Culture and Environmental Change since 1492* (Cambridge: Cambridge University Press, 1987, 3).

3 I treat the picturesque as "a contested field of aesthetic theory and practice," its "indeterminate character" making it available to diverse appropriations by writers and illustrators in varied geographical locations and historical circumstances. Gary Harrison and Jill Heydt-Stevenson, "Variations on the Picturesque: Authority, Play, and Practice," *European Romantic Review* 13 (2002), 3.

4 David Harvey, *The Condition of Postmodernity* (Cambridge, MA, and Oxford, UK: Blackwell Publishing, 1990, 244).

5 Barrell, *Idea*, 2.

6 Andrews, *Search*, 3.

7 As Britain's biggest and most lucrative Caribbean slave colony, Jamaica generated a large proportion of the printed material in circulation about the British West Indies. Wilson, *Island Race*, chap. 4, discusses the "Janus-faced function" of the West Indies "in eighteenth-century English imagination and policy," reflecting "changing imperial strategies toward a cultural frontier at the heart of English prestige, wealth and authority.... As economic boon and cultural miasma, [the West Indies] hinted at the strangeness and hybridity of colonial power and the danger it posed to the honor of the English nation and the virtue and integrity of its imperial project" (Wilson, *Island Race*, 129–30).

8 In 1772, Lord Mansfield delivered his famous judicial decision on the case of the slave James Somerset, instigated by the abolitionist Granville Sharp. The decision forbade slave owners to force slaves to leave English soil, although it was often erroneously interpreted to abolish slavery in the British Isles. See Chapter 3, this volume.

9 The illustrations of the *Picturesque Tour of Italy* were prepared from Hakewill's sketches by a group of painters including J. M. W. Turner. See Cecilia Powell, *Turner in the South: Rome, Naples, Florence* (New Haven, CT: Yale University Press, 1987, 17–18), and "Topography, Imagination and Travel: Turner's Relationship with James Hakewill," *Art History* 5 (1982): 408–25, *passim*. The middle-class reading public of the 1820s "liked illustrated books with a text consisting solely of extended captions" (Powell, "Topography," 410). Hakewill's book is available from Google Books at http://books.google.com/books?hl=en&id=oL4NAAAAQAAJ&dq=hakewill&printsec=frontcover&source=web&ots=9Ifm5G-C41&sig=FdNgfMdoefHEFhMont6Hu91_kyA&sa=X&oi=book_result&resnum=6&ct=result#PPP6,M1.

10 Gad Heuman, "The British West Indies," *Oxford History of the British Empire*, ed. William Roger Louis (Oxford: Oxford University Press, 1999), Vol. III, *The Nineteenth Century*, ed. Andrew Porter, 470–72, 473; on Saint Domingue, see Chapter 3, this volume. Eric Williams's famous hypothesis in *Capitalism and Slavery* that the end of British slavery was due to economic decline and decreasing profitability has been largely refuted by the more recent work of Roger Anstey, *The Atlantic Slave Trade and British Abolition, 1760–1810* (Atlantic Highlands, NJ: Humanities Press, 1975); Seymour Drescher, *Econocide: British Slavery in the Era of Abolition* (Chapel Hill: University of North Carolina

Press, 2010); Hugh Thomas, *The Slave Trade: The Story of the Atlantic Slave Trade, 1440–1870* (New York: Simon and Schuster, 1997); and the contributors to Thomas Bender, ed., *The Antislavery Debate: Capitalism and Abolitionism as a Problem in Historical Interpretation* (Berkeley, Los Angeles, and Oxford: University of California Press, 1992), among others.

11 Robin Blackburn, *The Overthrow of Colonial Slavery 1776–1848* (London and New York: Verso, 1988, 421–22). He also notes that the slave population decline was more rapid in newer colonies, such as Demerara and Essequibo, and only slight in the more established colonies, which actually "represented an improvement on the appalling negative growth rate of the slave colonies in the previous century" (424). The decrease in the slave population also was linked to the growth of the free black or colored population.

12 Hakewill, *Picturesque Tour*, 3. See Bermingham, *Landscape and Ideology*, 83–5, on the standardization and popularization of picturesque composition through the guidebooks and tours of Gilpin and others.

13 Quilley, "Pastoral Plantations," 116.

14 Hakewill catalogs these as follows: "The first on the left is the barracks or residence of the book-keepers; the next the overseer's house and offices; on the knoll is the hospital; below is the cattle-mill [ox-powered mill to grind cane], and next the water-mill, between which a portion of the aqueduct is seen [perhaps a homage to Lorrain's famous bridge in the middle distance]. The next and largest building of the group is the boiling-house, and then the still-house. In the distance are the trash-houses [for storing canes with their juice removed]; and above, shaded and partly concealed by groves of cocoa-nut trees and plantations, are the cottages of the negroes."

15 William Gilpin, *Observations on the Mountains, and Lakes of Cumberland, and Westmoreland* (1786), in Malcolm Andrews, ed., *The Picturesque: Literary Sources and Documents* (Mountfield, East Sussex: Helm Information Ltd., 1994, 338); Liu, *Wordsworth*, 75.

16 Liu, *Wordsworth*, 93.

17 Liu, *Wordsworth*, 85.

18 Long, *History*, II: 185.

19 Richard Grove demonstrates "the extent to which tropical islands had by the mid-seventeenth century acquired a very specific role as the subject of a discourse based . . . on archetypal Utopian and Edenic precepts." *Green Imperialism: Colonial Expansion, Tropical Edens and the Origins of Environmentalism, 1600–1860* (Cambridge: Cambridge University Press, 1995, 72).

20 Long, *History*, II: 95. Sir Charles Price (1708–1772), one of the richest planters in Jamaica, served as Speaker of the Jamaican Assembly from 1745 to 1763 and was made a baronet in 1768. His eldest son, another Sir Charles (1732–1788), served as Speaker of the Assembly from 1763 to 1775, when he went back to England to try to recoup his declining fortunes. His widow sold The Decoy in 1789 for a paltry £2,500. See Michael Craton, "Reluctant Creoles: The Planters' World in the British West Indies," in *Strangers Within the Realm: Cultural Margins*

of the First British Empire, ed. Bernard Bailyn and Philip D. Morgan (Chapel Hill: University of North Carolina Press, 1991, 336, 333–5).

21 See Casid, *Sowing Empire*, 13–14 and 16–21, on Long's landscape descriptions.

22 Trevor Burnard, *Mastery, Tyranny, and Desire: Thomas Thistlewood and his Slaves in the Anglo-Jamaican World* (Chapel Hill: University of North Carolina Press, 2004), 117.

23 R. Williams, *Country*, 58–9, 115–16.

24 Long, *History*, II: 64, 65. Thomas Fearon of Clarendon Parish, Chief Justice in the 1760s, appears in the 1754 census with 8,941 acres. There were a number of Fearons, all rich, all local residents and heavily involved in planter politics. Thanks to Trevor Burnard for this information.

25 Long responded to the Mansfield Decision with an acidulous pamphlet entitled *Candid Reflections*, discussed in Chapter 3. On this "lanschape," see Casid, *Sowing Empire*, 13–14.

26 Bohls, *Women Travel Writers*, 95–6. Benjamin Colbert recently questioned the universality of this attitude, even in metropolitan landscape writing. "Aesthetics of Enclosure: Agricultural Tourism and the Place of the Picturesque," *European Romantic Review* 13 (2002): 25, 29. See also Quilley, "Pastoral Plantations," 116.

27 Long, *History*, I: 363; Thomson, *Summer* ll: 1452–3.

28 Born in Jamaica in 1744, this William Beckford is sometimes referred to as Beckford of Somerley, his Suffolk estate, to distinguish him from his more famous cousin, William Beckford of Fonthill, son of the Lord Mayor of London and author of the Orientalist Gothic novel *Vathek* (1786).

29 William Beckford, *A Descriptive Account of the Island of Jamaica* (London, 1790, I: xii, 243).

30 Sheridan, "Planter and Historian," 56–7; see Simon D. Smith, "*Merchants and Planters* Revisited," *Economic History Review* 55.3 (2002): 434–65, on the importance of mortgages to West Indian finance. The American war was a time of hardship for the West Indian colonies due to its interruption of trade with North America.

31 Boulukos, *Grateful Slave*, 201–2.

32 Harrison and Heydt-Stevenson, "Variations," 6.

33 Uvedale Price, "A Dialogue on the Picturesque and the Beautiful," in Malcolm Andrews, ed., *The Picturesque: Literary Sources and Documents*, 3 vols. (East Sussex: Helm Information Ltd., 1994, 232). On gypsies, see Katie Trumpener, "The Time of the Gypsies: A 'People Without History' in the Narratives of the West," *Critical Inquiry* 18 (1992): 843–84; and Anne Janowitz, "'Wild Outcasts of Society': The Transit of the Gypsies in Romantic Period Poetry," in Gerald MacLean, Donna Landry, and Joseph P. Ward. eds., *The Country and the City Revisited: England and the Politics of Culture, 1550–1850* (Cambridge: Cambridge University Press, 1999, 213–30). Malcolm Andrews points out a similar intercultural dimension in the picturesque tour of Scotland (*Search*, 201).

34 U. Price, "Dialogue," 233.

35 Suleri, *Rhetoric*, 103–106, 19, 76.

36 Beckford, *Descriptive Account*, I: 279.
37 Beckford, *Descriptive Account*, I: 9–10.
38 Sandiford, *Cultural Politics*, argues that the *Descriptive Account* "implicates the picturesque in a very complexly constructed legitimation of Creole culture" (145).
39 Beckford, *Descriptive Account*, 2: 279.
40 On the economics of sugar planting, see Pares, *Merchants and Planters*, and Smith, *"Merchants and Planters* Revisited."
41 Beckford made his Grand Tour of Europe in the 1760s accompanied by Patrick Brydone, who later wrote *A Tour Through Sicily and Malta in a Series of Letters to William Beckford, Esq., of Somerley in Suffolk*, published in 1791 while its addressee languished in gaol (Sheridan, "Planter and Historian," 42).
42 Beckford, *Descriptive Account*, I: 73, 214, 284, 286, 359; 2: 52.
43 W. J. T. Mitchell, "Imperial Landscape," *Landscape and Power*, ed. W. J. T. Mitchell (Chicago and London: University of Chicago Press, 1994, 10).
44 Tim Morton's chapter on sugar and slavery captures this well: "literature on sugar plantations... threatens to dissolve and decode all 'placedness' into the pure space of the sugar plantation: a supplementary island growing an imported, supplementary crop." *The Poetics of Spice* (Cambridge: Cambridge University Press, 2000, 182, 185).
45 Thomas D. Brumbaugh, quoted in Sheridan, "Planter and Historian," 44.
46 Beckford, *Descriptive Account*, I: 144. "Ratooning" is the practice of using the new shoots from old canes for a subsequent crop rather than clearing the field and planting it with new canes.
47 Beckford, *Descriptive Account*, I: vi, 80–81, 83.
48 See, respectively: Beckford, *Descriptive Account*, I: 193–4, 220–3, 251–3, 281–3, and 8–9, 26, 66, 70, 80, 286–305.
49 Michasiw, "Nine Revisionist Theses," 84, 82.
50 Beckford, *Descriptive Account*, I: 65–6.
51 Beckford, *Descriptive Account*, I: 103–106.
52 Beckford, *Descriptive Account*, II: 320, 397.
53 Sandiford, *Cultural Politics*, 145.
54 Beckford, *Descriptive Account*, II: 405. Caves enter the *Account* as a resting place for slaves on their way to their provision grounds (Beckford, *Descriptive Account*, I: 233, 237). The contrast between the cold, dark cave and the sun-drenched earth above suggests the contrast between Beckford's current confinement and his former life as planter-aesthete; for the chronically self-pitying author, the cave becomes a figure for the gaol. The "unhappy victims" to be found there include the bones of an extinct race, Jamaica's Amerindians (Beckford, *Descriptive Account*, I: 248). Are sugar planters also on the road to extinction? A fantasy sequence follows a slave tracker, chasing runaways, who meets a party of Maroons, who invite him to a cookout in a cave, "perhaps the refuge... of runaway negroes" (Beckford, *Descriptive Account*, I: 333). The runaway he finally catches is a "miserable outcast of human nature... his mind weighed down by terror and despair," locked up either on the plantation or in "a distant

gaol" (Beckford, *Descriptive Account*, I: 381–2). Runaway captive and bankrupt planter share the same plight. No longer the owner of land or enslaved people, the imprisoned Beckford co-opts an enslaved person's suffering.

55 Long, *History*, I: 5.

56 Louis F. Peck, *A Life of Matthew G. Lewis* (Cambridge, MA: Harvard University Press, 1961, 152); Judith Terry, "Introduction" to Matthew Lewis, *Journal of a West India Proprietor* (Oxford: Oxford University Press, 1999, xiv–xv). When Lewis inherited the plantations, he co-owned Hordley with a Mr. Scott, whose share he bought out before his death.

57 Heuman, "British West Indies," 475; Craton, *Testing*, 254–66.

58 Orlando Patterson, *The Sociology of Slavery* (Rutherford, NJ: Fairleigh Dickinson University Press, 1967, 174–81); Richard D. E. Burton, *Afro-Creole: Power, Opposition, and Play in the Caribbean* (Ithaca, NY: Cornell University Press, 1997), 49, 58; Lawrence Needham, "'Goody Two-Shoes'/'Goosee Shoo-Shoo': Translated Tales of Resistance in Matthew Lewis's *Journal of a West India Proprietor*" in Anuradha Dingwaney and Carol Maier, eds., *Between Languages and Cultures: Translation and Cross-Cultural Texts* (Pittsburgh, PA: University of Pittsburgh Press, 1995, 110–11).

59 Bermingham, *Landscape and Ideology*, 54.

60 Lewis, *Journal*, 56–7.

61 On the exclusion of work from the metropolitan picturesque, see Bohls, *Women Travel Writers*, 95–6.

62 Burton, *Afro-Creole*, 58, and see Needham, "Goody Two-Shoes."

63 I adopt Michel de Certeau's useful distinction between resistance and opposition, as summarized by Burton: "Resistance requires an 'elsewhere' from which the system may be perceived and grasped as a whole and from which a coherent *strategy* of resistance may be elaborated. *Opposition*, on the other hand, has no space it can properly call its own. It takes place of necessity *within* the system, on ground defined by the system ... moving from one *tactical* maneuver to another within and against the system" (*Afro-Creole*, 50).

64 Lewis, *Journal*, 104.

65 Judith Terry's glossary defines "hog's meat" as "a term applied to all species of *Boerhavia*, chiefly trailing or climbing plants, which were gathered to feed hogs" (Lewis, *Journal*, 291).

66 Lewis, *Journal*, 99.

67 Trap doors, or traps, were a standard feature of English theaters during the eighteenth and nineteenth centuries; see Michael R. Booth, Richard Southern, Frederick and Lise-Lone Marker, and Robertson Davies, *The Revels History of Drama in English, Vol. VI: 1750–1880* (London: Methuen, 1975, 71–6). The licenser's manuscript of Lewis's two-act melodrama *Rugantino; or, the Bravo of Venice* (1805) includes the stage direction, "Memmo, who has advanced into the middle of the Stage, almost falls thro' a trap-door, which opens suddenly. Pluto and Proserpine rise in a Car, drawn by black horses, breathing fire – They alight and the Car sinks" (Peck, *Life*, 93).

68 Lewis, *Journal*, 98.

69 Frank Felsenstein, ed., *English Trader, Indian Maid: Representing Gender, Race, and Slavery in the New World. An Inkle and Yarico Reader* (Baltimore, MD, and London: Johns Hopkins University Press, 1999, 88).

70 Felsenstein, *English Trader*, 173.

71 Felsenstein, *English Trader*, 213–14. Colman's line reads, "Yes, quite dark, but very elegant, like a Wedgwood tea-pot." Lewis's comment on emancipation is as follows: "Every man of humanity must wish that slavery, even in its best and most mitigated form, had never found a legal sanction, and must regret that its system is now so incorporated with the welfare of Great Britain as well as of Jamaica, as to make its extirpation an absolute impossibility, without the certainty of producing worse mischiefs than the one which we annihilate" (*Journal*, 249).

72 Sussman, *Consuming Anxieties*, 110–29.

73 Lewis, *Journal*, 98, 46–7.

74 Lewis, *Journal*, 46.

75 Historians disagree about its effect on the treatment of slaves. See, e.g., Ward, *British West Indian Slavery*, 209–10.

76 Lewis, *Journal*, 79–80, 237, 54.

77 Bush discusses the issue of slave fertility (*Slave Women*, 132–50), including "the possibility that the conditions of slavery reduced women's desire and ability to have children or may even have resulted in conscious forms of limitation such as abortion, contraception and infanticide." She concludes, "Deliberate management of their own fertility may have been a form of hidden, individual protest against the system over which slave masters had even less control than more overt forms of collective resistance" (*Slave Women*, 137, 150). Needham discusses Lewis's retelling of an Anansi story heard from a slave storyteller, noting, "Ultimately at issue in the story . . . is reproductive control and possession of the potentially wayward female body" ("'Goody Two-Shoes,'" 110, and see Lewis, *Journal*, 253–61).

78 Lewis, *Journal*, 46. Janet Schaw deploys the aesthetics of skin color in her earlier colonial picturesque, as I have noted (Bohls, *Women Travel Writers*, 57–8). See Chapter 5, this volume, on other aspects of Schaw's journal.

79 Lewis, *Journal*, 44–5, 105; Schaw 112–13. Also see Long's discussion of interracial sex, *History* II: 321–2. Bush provides a historical perspective on interracial sex in the colonial Caribbean: *Slave Women*, 110–18.

80 Jamaica Kincaid, *A Small Place* (New York: Penguin, 1988, 77, 14).

81 Patterson, *Slavery*, 57; Lewis, *Journal*, 83.

82 Lewis, *Journal*, 87, 88.

83 Lewis, *Journal*, 96.

84 Lewis, *Journal*, 231–2.

85 Lewis, *Journal*, 228, 229; Terry, "Introduction," xxxiii.

86 Lewis, *Journal*, 94, 114–15; Maureen Harkin, "Matthew Lewis's Journal of a West Indian Proprietor: Surveillance and Space on the Plantation," *Nineteenth-Century Contexts* 24 (2002), 147.

87 Patterson, *Sociology*, 174–81.

88 Burton, *Afro-Creole*, 49.
89 Lewis, *Journal*, 69, 36, 37–8. On Jonkonnu, see Michael Craton, "Decoding Pitchy-Patchy: The Roots, Branches, and Essence of Junkanoo," *Slavery and Abolition* 16 (1995): 14–44; and Judith Bettelheim, "Jonkonnu and Other Christmas Masquerades," in *Caribbean Festival Arts*, ed. John W. Nunley and Judith Bettelheim (Seattle: University of Washington Press, 1988, 39–83).
90 Burton, *Afro-Creole*, 66.
91 Bohls, *Women*, 87.
92 Bettelheim, "Jonkonnu," 35.
93 Lewis, *Journal*, 137.
94 Craton, *Testing*, 291.
95 Philip Sherlock and Hazel Bennett, *The Story of the Jamaican People* (Kingston, Jamaica: Ian Randle Publishers, 1998, 214).
96 Quoted in Burton, *Afro-Creole*, 73; Ward, *British West Indian Slavery*, 273; Craton, *Testing*, 294–5. Jamaica enjoyed local autonomy under a lieutenant governor and its legislative Assembly until London imposed Crown Colony government in 1865 in the aftermath of the Morant Bay rebellion and Governor Eyre's brutal suppression; see C. Hall, *Civilizing Subjects*, chaps. 4 and 7.
97 Craton, *Testing*, 300; Blackburn, *Overthrow*, 432. Blackburn puts the number of slaves involved at 20,000 to 30,000, considerably lower than Craton's estimate.
98 Turner, *Slaves and Missionaries*, 157.
99 Michel de Certeau, *The Practice of Everyday Life* (Berkeley: University of California Press, 1984, xi–xii, xix–xx); Burton, *Afro-Creole*, 81.
100 Sherlock and Bennett, *Story*, 214; the missionary Henry Bleby, quoted in Craton, *Testing*, 319.
101 This began with the provision of the emancipation legislation calling for a period of "apprenticeship," during which slaves would be paid for their labor but forbidden to leave their plantations. Apprenticeship was ended by legislation passed by the various Colonial Assemblies between March and July 1838, in response to a metropolitan campaign exposing widespread abuse of the system by former slave owners (Blackburn, *Overthrow*, 460).

2. STEDMAN'S TROPICS: THE MERCENARY AS NATURALIST

1 For details, see Sherlock and Bennett, *Jamaican People*, 75, 135–42. Historical work on marronage includes Mavis Campbell, *The Maroons of Jamaica, 1655–1796: A History of Resistance, Collaboration and Betrayal* (Granby, MA: Bergin & Garvey, 1988); Alvin O. Thompson, *Flight to Freedom: African Runaways and Maroons in the Americas* (Jamaica, Barbados, Trinidad, and Tobago: University of the West Indies Press, 2006); E. Kofi Agorsah, "Scars of Brutality: Archaeology of the Maroons in the Caribbean," in *Archaeology of Atlantic Africa and the African Diaspora*, ed. Akinwumi Ogundiran and

Toyin Falola (Bloomington and Indianapolis: Indiana University Press, 2007, 332–54); and Richard Price, ed., *Maroon Societies: Rebel Slave Communities in the Americas*, 3rd edn. (Baltimore, MD: Johns Hopkins University Press, 1996 [1979]). See also Wood, *Slavery*, 209–17, on the poet Southey's treatment of the Palmares maroon community, or *Quilombo*, in his *History of Brazil* (1817–19).

2 Wim Hoogbergen, *The Boni Maroon Wars in Suriname* (Leiden, New York, København, and Köln: E. J. Brill, 1990, 5); Richard Price and Sally Price, "Introduction," *Narrative of a Five Years Expedition against the Revolted Negroes of Suriname in Guiana on the Wild Coast of South-America from the Year 1772 to the Year 1777*, ed. Richard Price and Sally Price (Baltimore, MD, and London: Johns Hopkins University Press, 1988, xiv, xxi).

3 Alan Bewell calls this "military disease narrative." *Romanticism and Colonial Disease* (Baltimore, MD: Johns Hopkins University Press, 1999, 88–97). Others who analyze Stedman's representation of his relationship to his slave concubine, Joanna, include Pratt, *Imperial Eyes*, 90–102; Sharpe, *Ghosts*, 44–86; H. Thomas, *Romanticism*, 129–33; and Tassie Gwilliam, "'Scenes of Horror,' Scenes of Sensibility: Sentimentality and Slavery in John Gabriel Stedman's *Narrative of a Five Years Expedition against the Revolted Negroes of Suriname*," *ELH* 65 (1998): 653–73. Stedman's verbal and visual renderings of the sexualized violence of the Suriname slave society are discussed by Marcus Wood in *Blind Memory: Visual Representations of Slavery in England and America 1780–1865* (New York: Routledge, 2000, 230–9), and in *Slavery*, chap. 2; Haywood, *Bloody Romanticism*, 36–43; and Mario Klarer, "Humanitarian Pornography: John Gabriel Stedman's *Narrative of a Five Years Expedition Against the Revolted Negroes of Suriname* (1796)," *New Literary History* 36 (2005): 559–87. Linebaugh and Rediker, *Many-Headed Hydra* (344–50) and Debbie Lee, *Slavery*, chap. 4, discuss Stedman's *Narrative* in the context of Blake's role as his engraver. Emily Senior explores the significance of skin as "the motif through which Stedman imagines the corruptive influence of the colonial environment on the human body." "'Perfectly Whole': Skin and Text in John Gabriel Stedman's *Narrative of a Five Years' Expedition Against the Revolted Negroes of Suriname*," *Eighteenth-Century Studies* 44 (2010), 40.

4 To term Stedman a scientist is anachronistic because the word did not yet exist in his lifetime but rather was coined in 1833 (Fulford, Kitson, and Lee, *Literature, Science, and Exploration*, 5).

5 Drayton, *Nature's Government*, xiv. Also see Fulford, Kitson, and Lee, *Literature, Science, and Exploration*; Bewell, "Romanticism"; Gascoigne, *Joseph Banks*; and Schiebinger, *Nature's Body*, as well as the essays in Jardine et al., *Cultures of Natural History*; and Schiebinger and Swan, *Colonial Botany*. Deirdre Coleman's work on Henry Smeathman connects natural history, slavery, and the abolitionist movement. *Romantic Colonization and British Anti-Slavery* (New York and Cambridge: Cambridge University Press, 2005); "Henry Smeathman and the Natural Economy of Slavery," in *Slavery and the Cultures of Abolition: Essays Marking the Bicentennial of the British Abolition Act of 1807*, ed. Brycchan Carey and Peter J. Kitson (Cambridge: D. S. Brewer, 2007, 130–49). For a

classic, broad-based study of European science in an imperial context, see Michael Adas, *Machines as the Measure of Men: Science, Technology, and Ideologies of Western Dominance* (Ithaca, NY, and London: Cornell University Press, 1989).

6 Bruno Latour, *Science in Action: How to Follow Scientists and Engineers Through Society* (Cambridge, MA: Harvard University Press, 1987, chap. 6); Fulford, Kitson, and Lee, *Literature, Science, and Exploration*, 12 and *passim*.

7 Bewell, "Romanticism," 28.

8 Hans Sloane, *A Voyage to the Islands Madera, Barbados, Nieves, S. Christophers and JAMAICA, with the Natural History of the Herbs and Trees, Four-Footed Beasts, Fishes, Birds, Insects, Reptiles etc. of the last of those Islands* (London, 1707, 1725). This grew more common in the nineteenth century with the dramatic expansion of British colonial possessions. Bewell, "Romanticism," 22.

9 Stedman's *Narrative* relays the story of "the celebrated *Graman Qwacy*," born in Africa in the late seventeenth century, enslaved and brought to Suriname, where he worked as a healer and diviner for both enslaved people and white colonists, made a tidy profit, was later freed, and discovered a medicinal root that a colonist reported in a letter to Linnaeus himself in 1761. John Gabriel Stedman, *Narrative of a Five Years Expedition against the Revolted Negroes of Suriname in Guiana on the Wild Coast of South-America from the Year 1772 to the Year 1777*, ed. Richard Price and Sally Price (Baltimore, MD, and London: Johns Hopkins University Press, 1988, 581–4); Parrish, *American Curiosity*, 1–6.

10 Stedman, *Narrative*, 347; Stedman, *Journal of John Gabriel Stedman*, ed. Stanbury Thompson (London: The Mitre Press, 1962, 392); and see Richard Price and Sally Price, "John Gabriel Stedman's Collection of Eighteenth-Century Artifacts from Suriname," *Nieuwe West-Indische Gids* 53 (1979), 140. The Prices traced a number of Stedman's artifacts, in particular, the "musical instruments of the African Negroes" depicted in Plate 69 of his *Narrative*, including an early banjo, to the Rijksmuseum voor Volkenkunde in Leiden, Netherlands. Sir Joseph Banks in 1806 declined to purchase Sir Ashton Lever's vast collection of specimens and ethnological "curiosities" for the British Museum, probably on the grounds that it was too eclectic and insufficiently systematic (Gascoigne, *Joseph Banks*, 68).

11 On this practice, see, e.g., Wheeler, *Complexion*, 24–33.

12 Stedman, *Narrative*, 10. See Price and Price, "Introduction," for the textual history of Stedman's *Narrative*: the version published by Joseph Johnson in 1796 was bowdlerized by a ghostwriter whom Johnson hired to clean up Stedman's prose, William Thomson. Thomson's changes ranged from rephrasing to "substantial alterations of Stedman's views on race, slavery, and social justice" (Price and Price, "Introduction," lii). Stedman was furious at many of these alterations and fought Johnson to have them removed, with only partial success. For this reason, I cite his 1790 manuscript in Price and Price's modern edition. The diary that Stedman kept in Suriname also survives, held by the James Ford Bell Library at the University of Minnesota. Comparisons

make clear that Stedman's manuscript romanticizes parts of his experience, in particular, his relationship with the slave Joanna (Price and Price, "Introduction," xxxii–xxxiii).

13 Gascoigne, *Joseph Banks*, 108, 109. Beth Fowkes Tobin examines illustrated books on tropical plants from the late eighteenth to the early nineteenth century for what they can tell us about the "appeal, function, and significance of tropical plants in British life," another segment of the growing fascination with natural history. *Colonizing Nature: The Tropics in British Arts and Letters 1760–1820* (Philadelphia: University of Pennsylvania Press, 2005, 175).

14 Suriname also happened to be adjacent to some of the valuable colonies that Britain gained in the 1790s during the French wars: Demerara, Berbice, and Essequibo, united in 1831 as British Guiana. Ward, *British West Indian Slavery*, 415. Demerara would be the site of a large and bloody slave revolt in 1823; see Craton, *Testing*, 267–90.

15 Stedman, *Narrative*, 7, 8, 9.

16 Stedman, *Narrative*, 223, 144; 9, 429, 471.

17 Stedman, *Narrative*, 393, 394.

18 Pratt, *Imperial Eyes*, 31.

19 On cultural processes of decontextualization and recontextualization in the practice of botany, see Tobin, *Colonizing*, 170–1, 176.

20 Parrish, *American Curiosity*, 310. Kapil Raj explores "the construction of scientific knowledge in the contact zone" more broadly in a South Asian context, arguing that "important parts of what has been passed off as European or Western science were actually made elsewhere." Rather than the diffusion of metropolitan knowledge outward to the colonial periphery, he advocates "an alternative vision of the construction and spread of scientific knowledge through reciprocal, albeit asymmetric, processes of circulation and negotiation." *Relocating Modern Science: Circulation and the Construction of Knowledge in South Asia and Europe, 1650–1900* (Houndmills, Basingstoke, Hampshire: Palgrave Macmillan, 2007, 11, 13). On the role of local knowledge in the practice of natural history, see also Londa Schiebinger, "Nature's Unruly Body: The Limits of Scientific Description," in *Regimes of Description in the Archive of the Eighteenth Century*, ed. John Bender and Michael Marrinan (Stanford, CA: Stanford University Press, 2005, 30).

21 Linebaugh and Rediker, *Many-Headed Hydra*, 246; Stedman, *Narrative*, 82.

22 Price and Price, "Introduction," xxi.

23 Bewell, *Romanticism*, 69, 71; Johnson quoted in Bewell, *Romanticism*, 71.

24 Stedman, *Narrative*, 113, 607. Hoogbergen corrects Stedman by noting that a total of 1,650 soldiers, not 1,200, had actually come to Suriname. As of July 1776, nine months before Stedman left, Hoogbergen counts 366 soldiers still alive of 900 who had been sent to Suriname by that point; of those, 80 were seriously ill and 100 had been declared unfit for military service. Hoogbergen, *Boni Maroon Wars*, 104.

25 Stedman, *Narrative*, 119–20, 122.

26 Stedman, *Narrative*, 126, 199, 157.

27 Stedman, *Narrative*, 395–6.

28 Stedman, *Narrative*, 107, 190, 402. The Maroons preferred to attack when opponents were at their most vulnerable, as in this situation; see Hoogbergen, *Boni Maroon Wars*, 15, 83.

29 Parrish, *American Curiosity*, 267, and see M. Allewaert, "Swamp Sublime: Ecologies of Resistance in the American Plantation Zone," *PMLA* 123.2 (March 2008): 350–1, on this plate.

30 Stedman, *Narrative*, 408–9.

31 Srinivas Aravamudan, *Tropicopolitans: Colonialism and Agency, 1688–1804* (Chapel Hill, NC: Duke University Press, 1999, 4). See Parrish, *American Curiosity*, 270, on the particular association between runaway slaves and swamps in the American South.

32 Hoogbergen, *Boni Maroon Wars*, 22. In addition to having to defend themselves against the planters' forces, the Maroons faced anxiety over food supplies, a hostile natural environment full of swamps and insects, and other groups with obscure intentions roaming the bush (i.e., Amerindians were generally hostile to Maroons). They relied on plantation raids or trade with friendly slaves for essential goods such as knives and guns, and their leaders, like Boni, "had to cope with the problem of creating unity amongst a group of individuals with such a traumatic background as the slave trade and slave labor" (Hoogbergen, *Boni Maroon Wars*, 22).

33 Stedman, *Narrative*, 409, 410. Richard Price's ethnographic work with the twentieth-century descendants of Suriname's Saramaka Maroons suggests a sense of place that differs very much from that of Europeans'. Their oral history of their ancestors' flight from slavery and their struggle to establish themselves in the jungle involves negotiations with forest and river gods – rituals of propitiation and reciprocity with an animate nature. Price, *First-Time: The Historical Vision of an Afro-American People* (Baltimore, MD: Johns Hopkins University Press, 1983). See also Parrish, *American Curiosity*, 301–5.

34 Stedman, *Narrative*, 254–9, 172, 257. Colonial histories, such as those of Long and Edwards, discussed in Chapter 3 of this volume, similarly offer statistics on the cost and profit of sugar production and detailed accounts of how it was done.

35 On the concept of bifocality, see the Introduction to this volume.

36 Stedman, *Narrative*, 259. See Sussman, *Consuming Anxieties*, 110–29, on the politics of the sugar boycott. Chapter 3 in this volume discusses the planter-historian Edward Long's rhetorical sleight of hand as he purports to reconcile British liberty with his defense of slavery.

37 Stedman, *Narrative*, 188. On Stedman's use of the language of sensibility, see Gwilliam, "'Scenes of Horror.'"

38 Stedman, *Narrative*, 189, 190. See Thompson on the term "bush" and its symbolic associations for the planter class: "In the Caribbean the bush was contrasted with the plantation: the one primeval, the other cultivated; the one the work of nature in its uncultured state, the other the creation of civilized men." *Flight to Freedom*, 36.

39 Hoogbergen, *Boni Maroon Wars*, 23, 24, 64. Hoogbergen notes that Sted-man's information about the Maroons was sometimes less than reliable when compared with official records; he had not seen commanders' reports or the testimony of captured Maroons, and he did not have an accurate picture of the internal structure of the Boni Maroon group. He also may not have assessed Boni's own importance accurately. *Boni Maroon Wars*, 63.

40 Hoogbergen, *Boni Maroon Wars*, 52, 76, 80, 64. The Rangers were slaves recruited as soldiers to fight for the colonial government and offered free-dom and other compensation for successful service. The Maroons hated them passionately.

41 Stedman, *Narrative*, 225. Parrish discusses the concept of curiosity, central to her book, its use and importance in the eighteenth century: *American Curiosity*, 57–64.

42 The OED defines "Creole" as someone of European or African descent "born or naturalized in [the West Indies and other parts of America]." Creolization would then be the process of adapting to the New World natural and cultural environment. The Cuban historian Fernando Ortiz coined the term "transcul-turation" in 1947 as an alternative to "acculturation," designating "the process of transition from one culture to another, and its manifold social repercus-sions." He describes white immigrants and African slaves "torn loose" from their respective cultures of origin and "transplanted to a New World, where everything was new to them, nature and people, and where they had to readjust themselves to a new syncretism of cultures." *Cuban Counterpoint: Tobacco and Sugar* (Durham, NC, and London: Duke University Press, 1995 [1947], 98). Mary Pratt adapted the term to emphasize the way subordinate groups use and transform the materials of the dominant culture in the colonial contact zone, a coinage of hers that has come into wide usage to designate "the space of colonial encounters, the space in which peoples geographically and historically separated come into contact with each other," usually under "conditions of coercion, radical inequality, and intractable conflict" (*Imperial Eyes*, 6). My use of "transculturation" differs from hers in that Stedman is not a subaltern, although I am very interested in "the dynamic, mutual influence that a sub-ordinate and dominant culture effect upon each other in the 'contact zones' of colonial cultures." Frances R. Aparicio and Susana Chávez-Silverman, ed., *Tropicalizations: Transcultural Representations of Latinidad* (Hanover, NH, and London: Dartmouth College, 1997, 1). Stedman's transculturation, I argue, is given its shape through the agency of Creole interlocutors, including old Cramaca, Joanna, Boni, and the Maroons.

43 Stedman, *Narrative*, 127, 138; Parrish, *American Curiosity*, 216–17.

44 Sharpe, *Ghosts*, 44 ff., 57–9, 72.

45 Stedman, *Narrative*, 338, 220–1; Hoogbergen, *Boni Maroon Wars*, 101–102. Hoogbergen adds that Nepveu, the governor of Suriname, felt Boni's crossing over to the French side of the river "would do the colony no good . . . he could no longer search for and destroy Maroon villages whereas the Maroons could enter Suriname whenever they wanted to." Hoogbergen, *Boni Maroon Wars*,

102. See Parrish, *American Curiosity*, chap. 2, on earlier colonists' fears that living in the Americas would change their bodies in insidious and irreversible ways.

46 Stedman, *Narrative*, 326–7.

47 Stedman, *Narrative*, n.p.

48 Wood, *Slavery*, 405. Wood's discussion of Stedman's frontispiece centers on its "erotics of pain." Although he raises a number of interesting points, he oversimplifies the significance of the image by asserting that it merely "embodies a dominant violent white male colonizing sexuality." Wood, *Slavery*, 105.

49 Kay Dian Kriz, "Curiosities, Commodities and Transported Bodies in Hans Sloane's Voyage to . . . Jamaica," in *An Economy of Color: Visual Culture and the Atlantic World, 1660–1830*, ed. Geoff Quilley and Kay Dian Kriz (Manchester, UK: Manchester University Press, 2003, 86, 89–90).

50 Stedman, *Narrative*, 333, 145–6.

51 Stedman, *Narrative*, 145–6.

52 Stedman, *Narrative*, 147.

53 Price and Price, "Introduction," xiii; Stedman, *Narrative*, 105. Haywood discusses Stedman's depictions of slave punishment, including "Flagellation of a Female Samboe Slave," in *Bloody Romanticism*, 36–43.

54 Debbie Lee treats the image as Blake's, not Stedman's, labeling it "a sharp indictment of Stedman himself"; she interprets "the Stedman plates as being primarily a statement of Blake's artistic purpose." Lee, *Slavery*, 113, 96. I disagree: although we cannot discount Blake's contribution, the plates were based on Stedman's drawings. Unfortunately, few of these survive (none that I know of corresponding to Blake's engravings), so their relationship to the finished illustrations cannot be determined. In the absence of definitive evidence to the contrary, I chose to treat the illustrations as a component of the text, produced from Stedman's drawings under his supervision. See also Wood's discussion of this plate as "the Fetish of the Black Penis Serpent," *Slavery*, 114–21.

55 Stedman, *Narrative*, 148, 150.

56 Stedman, *Narrative*, 614. Stedman quotes Swift's "Satirical Elegy on the Death of a Late Famous General" at length in connection with the death of his commanding officer, Fourgeoud, with whom he often quarreled. *Narrative*, 621.

3. COLONIAL HISTORY AND ATLANTIC GEOGRAPHY

1 Charles W. J. Withers, "Geography, Natural History and the Eighteenth-Century Enlightenment: Putting the World in Place," *History Workshop Journal* 39 (1995): 139; Edward Said, *Culture and Imperialism* (New York: Alfred A. Knopf, 1993, 7, 78).

2 David Brion Davis, *The Problem of Slavery in the Age of Revolution 1770–1823* (Ithaca, NY, and London: Cornell University Press, 1975, 184–5, 188). Jefferson and Moreau each authored a planter history: *Notes on Virginia* (1785) and

Description topographique, physique, civile, politique et historique de la partie française de l'isle Saint-Domingue (1797–1798). Médéric Louis Élie Moreau de Saint-Méry (1750–1819) was a lawyer, slaveowner, and revolutionary leader who ended up in Philadelphia, where he finished and published his monumental history of a colony that, by that time, no longer existed in the form that his book described.

3 Philip Curtin, *The Image of Africa: British Ideas and Action, 1780–1850* (Madison: University of Wisconsin Press, 1964); Marshall and Williams, *Great Map*; George Boulukos, "Olaudah Equiano and the Eighteenth-Century Debate on Africa," *Eighteenth-Century Studies* 40, no. 2 (2007): 241–55.

4 David Brion Davis, *Inhuman Bondage: The Rise and Fall of Slavery in the New World* (Oxford: Oxford University Press, 2006, 158).

5 Bryan Edwards, *An Historical Survey of the French Colony in the Island of St. Domingo* (London, 1797, xx, 193).

6 Marcus Rainsford, *An Historical Account of the Black Empire of Hayti*, ed. Paul Youngquist and Grégory Pierrot (Durham, NC: Duke University Press, 2013 [1805], 133).

7 Blackburn, *Overthrow*, 35–6.

8 On my use of "British" and "English," see Introduction, Note 3, this volume.

9 Christopher Leslie Brown, *Moral Capital: Foundations of British Abolitionism* (Chapel Hill: University of North Carolina Press, 2006, 36, 48, 52).

10 C. L. Brown, *Moral Capital*, 49; Eliga Gould, "Zones of Law, Zones of Violence: The Legal Geography of the British Atlantic, circa 1772," *William and Mary Quarterly*, Third Series, 60 (2003), 474.

11 On the Somerset case and Mansfield's verdict, see F. O. Shyllon, *Black Slaves in Britain* (London: Oxford University Press, 1974, 76–140); Peter Fryer, *Staying Power: A History of Black People in Britain* (London: Pluto Press, 1984, 113–26); Simon Schama, *Rough Crossings: Britain, the Slaves, and the American Revolution* (London: BBC, 2005, 44–63); H. Thomas, *Romanticism*, 472–6; C. L. Brown, *Moral Capital*, 91–101; and Boulukos, *Grateful Slave*, 101–103. Brycchan Carey analyzes responses to the verdict in the press. *British Abolitionism and the Rhetoric of Sensibility: Writing, Sentiment, and Slavery, 1760–1807* (Houndmills, Basingstoke, Hampshire: Palgrave Macmillan, 2005, 175–9).

12 C. L. Brown, *Moral Capital*, 100, 78–87.

13 C. L. Brown, *Moral Capital*, 91, 92.

14 Shyllon, *Black Slaves*, 91, 93; Brown, *Moral Capital*, 97. The Scottish analogue to the Somerset case (Scotland retained its own courts after the Union) was that of Joseph Knight, whose owner, John Wedderburn, appealed to the Edinburgh Court of Session in 1777 to have Knight restored to him as a runaway slave but was denied by Lord Kames's verdict.

15 Quoted in Shyllon, *Black Slaves*, 92.

16 Bewell, *Romanticism and Colonial Disease*, 31–3, 37–9.

17 Quoted in Shyllon, *Black Slaves*, 106; Bewell, *Romanticism and Colonial Disease*, 286. The poet Cowper, an ardent abolitionist, writes in *The Task* (1785) that "Slaves cannot breathe in England; if their lungs / Receive our air, that moment

they are free." Quoted in Suvir Kaul, *Poems of Nation, Anthems of Empire: English Verse in the Long Eighteenth Century* (Charlottesville and London: University of Virginia Press, 2000, 238).

18 Quoted in C. L. Brown, *Moral Capital*, 94, 97.

19 Edward Long, *Candid Reflections upon the Judgment Lately Awarded by the Court of King's Bench, in Westminster-Hall, on What Is Commonly Called the Negroe-Cause* (London, 1772, 49); Samuel Estwick, *Considerations on the Negroe Cause Commonly So Called, Addressed to the Right Honorable Lord Mansfield, Lord Chief Justice of the Court of King's Bench &c., by a West Indian* (London, 1772, 44).

20 Long, *Candid*, 44, 43, 13–21, 21.

21 Wheeler, *Complexion*, 229, 214.

22 Wheeler, *Complexion*, 178, 210.

23 Wheeler, *Complexion*, 47. For scholarship on race and racial theory, see Introduction, Note 25, this volume.

24 Elsa V. Goveia, *A Study on the Historiography of the British West Indies to the End of the Nineteenth Century* (Washington, DC: Howard University Press, 1980, 54).

25 Edward Long, *The History of Jamaica*, 3 vols. (London, 1774, III: 964, I: 193).

26 Long, *History*, I: 5.

27 "Ethos" can be defined, following Aristotle and Quintilian, as the impression a speaker gives of himself by means of his words: the projected self whose credibility, authority, and prestige underwrite the argument. Chaim Perelman and L. Olbrechts-Tyteca, *The New Rhetoric: A Treatise on Argumentation*, trans. John Wilkinson and Purcell Weaver (Notre Dame, IN: University of Notre Dame Press, 1969, 319).

28 Robert Mowbray Howard, *Records and Letters of the Family of the Longs of Longville, Jamaica, and Hampton Lodge, Surrey* (London: Simpkin, Marshall, Hamilton, Kent & Co., 1925, 122, 359); Sheridan, "Planter and Historian." Long was thus related by marriage to both William Beckford Jr., author of *A Descriptive Account of the Island of Jamaica* (1790), and his cousin, another William Beckford, the author of the novel *Vathek* (1786).

29 Burnard, *Mastery*, 116. However, Burnard (and, of course, Long) cite evidence that "culture did exist in Jamaica": an active theater, a circulating library, literary and agricultural societies; members of the Royal Society, the Dilettante Society, and the Royal College of Physicians.

30 Long, *History*, I: 6–7.

31 John Barrell, *English Literature in History: An Equal, Wide Survey* (New York: St. Martin's Press, 1983, *passim*).

32 Long had a complicated relationship to the planter class, as his sarcasm in the passage quoted suggests. Wilberforce and others drew on his criticisms of fellow Creoles in *The History of Jamaica* as a source for abolitionist propaganda.

33 Long, *History*, I: 436; Francis Home, *The Principles of Agriculture and Vegetation* (Edinburgh, 1756). Burnard defines the British Enlightenment as "the creed of pragmatic worldly modernizers, devoted to progress and the increase of

both civility and civilization" (*Mastery*, 114). See his chapter, "In the Scientific Manner: Thistlewood and the Practical Enlightenment in a Slavery Regime": Burnard, *Mastery*, 101–36.

34 Fulford, Kitson, and Lee, *Literature, Science, and Exploration*, 34; on Banks's centrality to the imperialism of improvement, see Gascoigne, *Joseph Banks*, esp. 203–207, and Richard Holmes, *The Age of Wonder: How the Romantic Generation Discovered the Beauty and Terror of Science* (London: Harper Press, 2008, chap. 1).

35 Long, *History*, II: 353.

36 He labors for several pages to prove that the chimpanzee, or "oran-outang" as he calls it, has quasi-human characteristics and is especially obsessed with reports of "amorous intercourse" between apes and African women (Long, *History*, II: 360, 364, 370; and see Schiebinger, *Nature's Body*, chap. 3, on eighteenth-century perceptions of apes). Drawing extensively on travel writing as well as natural history, Long connects the phenotypical diversity of humankind, reported by explorers, to the possibility of plural human species. Boulukos emphasizes "the cultural centrality of recognition of African humanity," i.e., the marginal character of polygenist views like Long's (*Grateful Slave*, 100–116). Although Long's polygenist position was certainly a minority view in the eighteenth century, it was not completely isolated. Linnaean natural history, throughout the 13 editions of *Systema naturae* between 1735 and 1758, slid toward polygenism (i.e., the 1758 edition recognized at least two species of the genus *Homo*), and the great French natural historian Buffon, although maintaining a mono-genist stance, reports without explicit disbelief "intercourse . . . of Negresses with apes, the produce of which has penetrated into one or the other species." Quoted in Phillip Sloan, "The Gaze of Natural History," in Fox, Christopher, Roy Porter, and Robert Wokler, ed., *Inventing Human Science: Eighteenth-Century Domains* (Berkeley: University of California Press, 1995, 137, and see 123).

37 Long, *History*, II: 372, 373.

38 E.g., Robert Norris, *Memoirs of Bossa Ahadee, King of Dahomey* (London, 1789) and Archibald Dalzel, *The History of Dahomy, an Inland Kingdom of Africa . . .* (London, 1793).

39 Long, *History*, II: 387; Francis J. Barker, *The African Link: British Attitudes to the Negro in the Era of the Atlantic Slave Trade, 1550–1807* (London: Frank Cass, 1978, 130); and Andrew Battell, *The Strange Adventures of Andrew Battell, of Leigh, in Angola and the Adjoining Regions*, ed. E. G. Ravenstein, Hakluyt Society, 2nd Ser. No. 6 (Nendeln, Liechtenstein: Kraus Reprint, 1967). See Barker, *African Link*, 51, for a comprehensive, logical refutation of Long's attempt to apply the concept of gradation to racial difference.

40 Long, II: 353, 503, 354, 497.

41 Wheeler, *Complexion*, 217; Barker, *African Link*, 68, 70. Francis Williams (1702–1770) was a black Jamaican who was taken to England and educated at the expense of the Duke of Montagu as, in Long's words, "an experiment . . . to discover, whether, by proper cultivation, and a regular course of

tuition at school and the university, a Negroe might not be found as capable of literature as a white person" (II: 476). Returning to Jamaica, Williams became a schoolmaster and wrote Latin odes to each new governor of the island. Long tells Williams's story (*History* II: 475–85) to illustrate the limits to the improvability of "Negroes." He reprints one of his odes with a translation, asking sarcastically, "is it at all superior ... to any composition we might expect from a middling scholar at ... Eton or Westminster?" and he cites David Hume's notorious footnote to his essay "Of National Characters," saying of Williams, "'tis likely he is admired for very slender accomplishments, like a parrot who speaks a few words plainly" (quoted in Long, *History*, II: 477).

42 Edward (Kamau) Brathwaite, *The Development of Creole Society in Jamaica, 1770–1820* (Oxford: Clarendon Press, 1971, 307).

43 Long, *History*, II: 332, 265, 328.

44 Long, *History*, III: 326–7.

45 Wheeler, *Complexion*, 227.

46 The emerging middle-class idea that men could and should exercise at least some control over their sex drive is documented by Shawn Lisa Maurer, *Proposing Men: Dialectics of Gender and Class in the Eighteenth-Century English Periodical* (Stanford, CA: Stanford University Press, 1998, 31–2). It complemented an earlier paradigm of English masculinity, rooted in the Greek and Latin classics and praising the control of strong passions as manly. Carolyn D. Williams, *Pope, Homer, and Manliness: Some Aspects of Eighteenth-Century Classical Learning* (London: Routledge, 1993, 29, 37).

47 Wheeler, *Complexion*, 227; Long, *History*, II: 331. Doris Garraway traces in the colonial French Caribbean the displacement of responsibility for interracial sex onto black and mulatta women and their biracial progeny. *The Libertine Colony: Creolization in the Early French Caribbean* (Durham, NC: Duke University Press, 2005, chap. 4).

48 Long, *History*, II: 278.

49 Wheeler, *Complexion*, 227.

50 Long, *History*, III: 333, 503; Wheeler, *Complexion*, 222.

51 Beckford, *Descriptive Account*, I: 333; Parrish, *American Curiosity*, 266.

52 Long, *History*, II: 96–97, 100.

53 Blackburn, *Overthrow*, 133–7; see Baucom, *Specters, passim*, on the Zong scandal and its implications.

54 Blackburn, *Overthrow*, 138.

55 Signatures, which were limited to adult males, rose from 60,000–100,000 in 1788 to 380,000–400,000 in 1792 (Blackburn, *Overthrow*, 144). See Clare Midgley, *Women Against Slavery: The British Campaigns, 1780–1870* (London: Routledge, 1992, 23–5), and see 62–71 on women's role in the 1830–31 petition campaigns, when they were allowed to sign.

56 Sussman, *Consuming Anxieties*, chap. 4; Midgeley, *Women*, 35, 60–2.

57 Anthony Benezet, *Some Historical Account of Guinea* (London, 1788, 58, 8, 18, 26, 28, 30, 26).

58 Boulukos, "Olaudah Equiano," *passim.*
59 Carey, *British Abolitionism*, 133, and see his discussion of Clarkson, 130–7. See also Kitson, *Romantic Literature*, 106–109, and Haywood, *Bloody Romanticism*, 12–17, on Benezet and Clarkson; and Sarah Salih, "Putting Down Rebellion: Witnessing the Body of the Condemned in Abolition-Era Narratives," in *Slavery and the Cultures of Abolition*, ed. Carey and Kitson (Cambridge: D. S. Brewer, 2007, 71–2) on Clarkson.
60 Thomas Clarkson, *An Essay on the Slavery and Commerce of the Human Species, Particularly the African* (London, 1788, 118, 119); Benezet, *Some Historical Account*, 58, 69, 120. Other anti-slavery writings sharing this emphasis include the pseudonymous J. Philmore's early *Two Dialogues on the Man Trade* (1760) and James Ramsay's *Essay on the Treatment and Conversion of the African Slaves* (1784); Gould, *Barbaric Traffic*, 25.
61 Benezet, *Some Historical Account*, 77.
62 Clarkson, *Essay*, 82, 85, 86, italics in original.
63 Blackburn, *Overthrow*, 141–3.
64 Blackburn, *Overthrow*, 144; Turley, 27.
65 Ward, *British West Indian Slavery*, *passim*; see also Boulukos, *Grateful Slave*, 9–10 and 201–203, on the ameliorationist position as a point of convergence between the sides of the abolition debate and scholars' neglect of ameliorationism in writing the history of that debate.
66 Goveia, *Study*, 80, 81, 84, 87.
67 Goveia, *Study*, 81.
68 Olwyn M. Blouet, "Bryan Edwards, F.R.S., 1743–1800," *Notes and Records of the Royal Society of London* 54 (2000, 218).
69 Davis, *Problem*, 188, 195; Olwyn M. Blouet, "Bryan Edwards and the Haitian Revolution," in David P. Geggus, ed., *The Impact of the Haitian Revolution in the Atlantic World* (Columbia: University of South Carolina Press, 2001, 47). Blouet also notes that Jefferson heads the subscription list to the 1806 Philadelphia edition of Edwards's *History*.
70 Blouet, "Haitian Revolution," 45.
71 Blouet, "Haitian Revolution," 45.
72 Bryan Edwards, *A Speech Delivered at a Free Conference between the Honorable Council and Assembly of Jamaica . . . On the Subject of Mr. Wilberforce's Propositions in the House of Commons, Concerning the Slave Trade* (Kingston, Jamaica, 1789/London, 1790, 10, 57, 42).
73 Edwards, *A Speech*, 16, 43, 46.
74 Edwards, *History*, II: 137–8, 145, 151–2, 142, italics in original.
75 Edwards, *History*, II: 34.
76 Boulukos, *Grateful Slave*, 206, 204.
77 Edwards, *History*, II: 35.
78 Edwards, *History*, I: xv, xvi.
79 David Lambert, "'Taken captive by the mystery of the Great River': Towards an Historical Geography of British Geography and Atlantic Slavery," *Journal of Historical Geography* 35 (2009): 51.

80 Lambert, "Taken Captive," 54; Saidiya Hartman, *Scenes of Subjection: Terror, Slavery, and Self-Making in Nineteenth-Century America* (New York and Oxford: Oxford University Press, 1997, 5, 6), quoted in Lambert, "Taken Captive," 54. Of course, the scene MacQueen describes also may contain fictionalized elements, as Lambert concedes.

81 Edwards, *History*, II: 105, 106.

82 Edwards, *History*, II: 105.

83 Edwards, *History*, II: 105–106, 108, 69.

84 See, e.g., Lata Mani's research on Indian widow sacrifice in *Contentious Traditions: The Debate on Sati in Colonial India* (Berkeley: University of California Press, 1998), as well as A. M. Rauwerda, who suggests that critics can sometimes "make space for a subaltern or Other by inscribing and noting absence." "Naming, Agency, and 'A Tissue of Falsehoods' in *The History of Mary Prince*," *Victorian Literature and Culture* 29 (2001): 397–411, quoted In Lambert, 2009, 56.

85 Edwards, *History*, II: 107.

86 Edwards, *History*, II: 106, 105. Thomas Pringle's preface to *The History of Mary Prince* uses the word "pruned" to describe his editing of Prince's story; see Chapter 6, this volume.

87 Edwards, *History*, II: 107.

88 Edwards, *History*, II: 106.

89 Edwards, *History*, II: 75, 76. Characterizing the "Eboes," Edwards performs a deft rhetorical maneuver, as Boulukos points out: "He distances himself from the emergent discourse of race, though in doing so he also invokes it" (*Grateful Slave*, 206). "I believe indeed there is, in most of the nations of Africa, a greater elongation of the lower jaw, than among the people of Europe, but this distinction I think is more visible among the Eboes, than in any other Africans. I mean not however to draw any conclusion of natural inferiority in these people to the rest of the human race, from a circumstance which perhaps is purely incidental, and no more to be considered a proof of degradation, than the red hair and high cheek bones of the Natives of the North of Europe" (Edwards, *History*, II: 75).

90 Edwards, *History*, II: 68, 63, 68–9, italics in original; Sheridan, *Doctors*, chap. 3; Parrish, *American Curiosity*, 279–89.

91 Rainsford, *Historical Account*, 51.

92 Blackburn, *Overthrow*, 164; Laurent Dubois, *Avengers of the New World: The Story of the Haitian Revolution* (Cambridge, MA, and London: Belknap Press of Harvard University Press, 2004, 3).

93 Dubois, *Avengers*, 13.

94 Britain gained Dominica, Saint Vincent, Grenada, and Tobago as a result of the Seven Years' War (1756–63); the Revolutionary and Napoleonic Wars added Trinidad, Saint Lucia, and the three Dutch colonies of Demerara, Berbice, and Essequibo, united in 1831 as British Guiana. J. R. Ward, "The British West Indies in the Age of Abolition, 1748–1815," *Oxford History of the British Empire*, ed. William Roger Louis (Oxford: Oxford University Press, 1999), Volume II, *The Eighteenth Century*, ed. P. J. Marshall, 415.

95 Blackburn, *Overthrow*, 167. The history of the Haitian Revolution has generated a wealth of scholarship; see, e.g., Dubois, *Avengers*; Geggus, *Slavery, War, and Revolution*; Davis, *Inhuman*, chap. 8; Blackburn, *Overthrow*, chaps. V and VI; Blackburn, "Haiti"; Carolyn E. Fick, *The Making of Haiti: The Saint Domingue Revolution from Below* (Knoxville: University of Tennessee Press, 1990); and C. L. R. James, *The Black Jacobins: Toussaint L'Ouverture and the San Domingo Revolution*. 2nd edn. (New York: Vintage Books, 1989 [1963]).

96 Edwards, *Historical Survey*, i.

97 The Amis des Noirs, Blackburn points out, were never a campaigning group like the British abolition society, and like the French planter lobby, the Club Massiac; they were not actually very influential and were, in fact, nearly defunct by the time the Convention abolished slavery in 1794 (*Overthrow*, 172–3).

98 Edwards, *Historical Survey*, 62.

99 Edwards, *Historical Survey*, 62.

100 Edwards, *Historical Survey*, 193.

101 Edwards, *Historical Survey*, 192, 194.

102 Edwards, *Historical Survey*, 63–64, 69–70. See Haywood, *Bloody Romanticism*, 33–6, on the representation of violence in *An Historical Survey*. According to Robin Blackburn, "some tropes of counter-revolutionary propaganda, such as the famous dead white baby impaled on a pike supposedly used by the rebels as a standard, lack credible authentication." "Haiti, Slavery, and the Age of Democratic Revolution," *William and Mary Quarterly* 63, No. 4 (2006): 670.

103 Edwards, *History*, II: 59, 63.

104 Edwards, *History*, II: 66, 67–8.

105 Edwards, *History*, II: 70.

106 Edwards, *History Historical Survey*, 191, italics in original.

107 Geggus, *Slavery, War and Revolution*, 90.

108 Edwards, *Historical Survey*, 191–2, 193.

109 Rainsford's modern editors point out that the date he gives in his book for his adventures in Saint Domingue is incorrect, according to data from ship's musters and pay records; either he made a mistake or (more likely) misrepresented the facts to avoid addressing the issue of what a British officer was doing so far behind enemy lines. His assignment from 1795 on was to recruit soldiers for the Third West India Regiment, one of six units made up of white British officers and black rank-and-file (i.e., slaves secured by levy and perhaps also volunteers). See Youngquist and Pierrot, "Introduction," Marcus Rainsford, *An Historical Account of the Black Empire of Hayti*, ed. Youngquist and Pierrot (Durham, NC: Duke University Press, 2013 [1805], esp. xx–xxi and xxxiv). Thanks to Paul Youngquist for his response to my query.

110 Rainsford, *Historical Account*, 9; Youngquist and Pierrot, "Introduction," lv, lvi.

111 Rainsford, *Historical Account*, 133.

112 By the time the British withdrew in 1798, of 20,525 men sent to Saint Domingue, 12,695 were dead (Geggus, *Slavery, War and Revolution*, 362). Michael Duffy puts the total casualties of the British army in the Caribbean between 1793 and 1801 at 62,250 men, or roughly 70 percent of the 89,000 soldiers and sailors that the Empire sent there. *Soldiers, Sugar, and Seapower: The British Expeditions to the West Indies and the War Against Revolutionary France* (Oxford: Clarendon Press, 1987), 333. Exact figures are difficult to ascertain. The overwhelming majority died of disease, primarily yellow fever, rather than in combat (Geggus, *Slavery, War and Revolution*, 365).

113 Youngquist and Pierrot, "Introduction," xlvii, liii; Rainsford, *Historical Account*, 272.

114 Rainsford, *Historical Account*, 133.

115 Rainsford, *Historical Account*, 133–4.

116 Rainsford, *Historical Account*, 137.

117 Rainsford, *Historical Account*, 134, 139, 137, 138.

118 Rainsford, *Historical Account*, 138–9, 140.

119 Rainsford, *Historical Account*, 141.

120 Carolyn Fick, "The Haitian Revolution and Citizenship: Defining Citizenship in the Revolutionary Era," *Social History* 32, no. 4 (2007): 399. This illuminating discussion parses the meaning of citizenship when applied to former slaves, arguing that "The supreme, tragic paradox is that the implementation and preservation of the Rights of Man should have depended, *in the first instance*, upon coerced labor, militarization and the denial of individual rights to the agrarian masses" (414, italics in original).

121 Fick, *Making of Haiti*, 249, 250.

122 Rainsford, *Historical Account*, 5–6.

123 On historians' silence about the Haitian Revolution, see Blackburn, "Haiti"; Davis, *Inhuman*; Michel-Rolph Trouillot, *Silencing the Past: Power and the Production of History* (Boston: Beacon Press, 1995); and Sibylle Fischer, *Modernity Disavowed: Haiti and the Cultures of Slavery in the Age of Revolution* (Durham, NC, and London: Duke University Press, 2004). On later Haitian history, see David Nicholls, *From Dessalines to Duvalier: Race, Color, and National Independence* (Cambridge and New York: Cambridge University Press, 1979).

124 On eighteenth-century representations of Africa, see Marshall and Williams, *Great Map*, 227–57.

4. EQUIANO'S POLITICS OF PLACE: FROM ROOTS TO ROUTES

1 James Clifford, *Routes: Travel and Translation in the Late Twentieth Century* (Cambridge, MA, and London: Harvard University Press, 1997), 33.

2 Clifford, *Routes*, 34). Clifford notes, "I hang on to 'travel' as a term of cultural comparison precisely because of its historical taintedness, its associations with gendered, racial bodies, class privilege, specific means of conveyance, beaten paths, agents, frontiers, documents, and the like. I prefer it to more

apparently neutral, and 'theoretical,' terms, such as 'displacement,' which can make the drawing of equivalences across different historical experiences too easy" (39).
3 Clifford, *Routes*, 36.
4 Jonathan Elmer, "The Black Atlantic Archive," *American Literary History* 17:1 (2005), 161. Also see Carretta's introduction to *Unchained Voices: An Anthology of Black Authors in the English-Speaking World of the Eighteenth Century* (Lexington: University Press of Kentucky, 1996); Paul Youngquist, "The Afro Futurism of DJ Vassa," *European Romantic Review* 16 (2005): 181–92; William Boelhower, "'I'll Teach You How to Flow': On Figuring Out Atlantic Studies," *Atlantic Studies* 1:1 (2004): 28–48; and Srinivas Aravamudan, *Tropicopolitans: Colonialism and Agency, 1688–1804* (Chapel Hill, NC: Duke University Press, 1999, chap. 6). Other important recent discussions include Roxann Wheeler, *The Complexion of Race: Categories of Difference in Eighteenth-Century British Culture* (Philadelphia: University of Pennsylvania Press, 2000, chap. 5), reading Equiano in the context of theories of human variety; Felicity Nussbaum, *The Limits of the Human: Fictions of Anomaly, Race, and Gender in the Long Eighteenth Century* (Cambridge: Cambridge University Press, 2003, chap. 7), reading race and masculinity in the *Narrative* as mutually constitutive; and Lynn Festa, *Sentimental Figures of Empire in Eighteenth-Century Britain and France* (Baltimore, MD: Johns Hopkins University Press, 2006, 132–49), reading slave narratives in the context of talking things to interrogate the category of the person and the boundary (problematized by slavery) between person and thing.
5 See Paul Gilroy's meditation on these homonyms, *The Black Atlantic: Modernity and Double Consciousness* (Cambridge, MA: Harvard University Press, 1993, 19); and Youngquist, "Afro Futurism," 186.
6 Vincent Carretta finds the evidence that he uncovered – baptismal and naval records stating Equiano's, or Vassa's, place of birth as "Carolina" – to be inconclusive but adds, "The burden of proof... is now on those who believe that *The Interesting Narrative* is a historically accurate piece of nonfiction." *Equiano the African: Biography of a Self-Made Man* (Athens and London: University of Georgia Press, 2005, xv). Of course, it also could be a historically accurate piece of ethnography, put together not from Equiano's personal experience but rather from information collected over the years from slaves he knew who had come from Africa and endured the Middle Passage. I am indebted throughout this chapter to Carretta's years of labor as Equiano's editor and biographer.
7 Of Equiano's numerous critics, those who maintain that he was African include Catherine Obianju Acholonu, "The Home of Olaudah Equiano – A Linguistic and Anthropological Search," *Journal of Commonwealth Literature* 22.1 (1987): 5–16; A. E. Afigbo, *Ropes of Sand: Studies in Igbo History and Culture* (Ibadan, Nigeria: University Press, 1981); Paul Edwards, "Introduction," *The Life of Olaudah Equiano, or Gustavus Vassa, the African* (London: Dawsons of Pall Mall, 1969); Clement A. Okafor, "*The Interesting Narrative of the Life of Olaudah Equiano*: A Triple-Tiered Transatlantic Testimony," *The Literary Griot* 14 (2002): 160–83; and Robin Sabino and Jennifer Hall, "The Path Not Taken: Cultural

Identity in the Interesting Life of Olaudah Equiano," *MELUS* 24 (1999): 5–19.
Those who read him as a fully acculturated Briton include Tanya Caldwell,
"'Talking Too Much English': Languages of Economy and Politics in Equiano's
The Interesting Narrative," *Early American Literature* 34 (1999): 263–82; Katalin
Orban, "Dominant and Submerged Discourses in *The Life of Olaudah Equiano*
(or Gustavus Vassa?)," *African American Review* 27 (1993): 655–64; and Adam
Potkay, "Olaudah Equiano and the Art of Spiritual Autobiography," *Eighteenth-
Century Studies* 27 (1994): 677–92. Paul E. Lovejoy, the distinguished historian
of Africa and the African Diaspora, also contends that the Africa section of the
Narrative is true: "Autobiography and Memory: Gustavus Vassa, alias Olaudah
Equiano, the African," *Slavery and Abolition* 27 (2005): 317–47. Numerous oth-
ers read Equiano's identity as in some sense hybrid. These include Aravamudan,
Tropicopolitans; Boelhower, "I'll Teach You"; Terry S. Bozeman, "Interstices,
Hybridity, and Identity: Olaudah Equiano and the Discourse of the African
Slave Trade," *Studies in the Literary Imagination* 36 (Fall 2003): 61–70; Tess
Chakkalakal, "I, Hereby, Vow to Read The Interesting Narrative" in Jason
Haslam and Julia M. Wright, ed., *Captivating Subjects: Writing Confinement,
Citizenship and Nationhood in the Nineteenth Century* (Toronto: University of
Toronto Press, 2005, 86–109); Chinosole, *African Diaspora and Autobiographics*
(New York: Peter Lang, 2001); Eileen Razzari Elrod, "Moses and the Egyptian:
Literary Authority in Olaudah Equiano's *Interesting Narrative*," *African Ameri-
can Review* 35: 3 (2001): 409–25; Joseph Fichtelberg, *Critical Fictions: Sentiment
and the American Market, 1780–1870* (Athens: University of Georgia Press, 2003);
Susan M. Marren, "Between Slavery and Freedom: The Transgressive Self in
Olaudah Equiano's Autobiography," *PMLA* 108 (1993): 94–105; William Mot-
tolese, "'Almost an Englishman': Olaudah Equiano and the Colonial Gift of
Language," *Bucknell Review* 41 (1988): 160–71; Marion Rust, "The Subaltern
as Imperialist: Speaking of Olaudah Equiano," in *Passing and the Fictions of
Identity*, ed. Elaine K. Ginsberg (Durham, NC, and London: Duke University
Press, 1996), 21–36; Helen Thomas, *Romanticism and Slave Narratives* (Cam-
bridge: Cambridge University Press, 2000, chap. 8); and Youngquist, "Afro
Futurism."

8 S. E. Ogude, "Facts into Fiction: Equiano's Narrative Reconsidered," *Research
in African Literatures* 13 (1982): 31, 32. Equiano first appears in the historical
record when he was sold in Virginia in 1754 to Lieutenant Michael Henry
Pascal of the Royal Navy. The rest of his life as narrated in *The Interesting
Narrative* matches available data, as his biographer, Vincent Carretta, confirms.
He accompanied Pascal to England, briefly, and then on a series of navy vessels,
where Equiano worked through his adolescence. He fought in the Seven Years'
War in Canada and the Mediterranean before Pascal sold him, without warning,
to a slave dealer who took him to the West Indies. There, he became the slave of
a prosperous Quaker, Robert King, a humane owner who rewarded Equiano's
aptitude with considerable responsibility as a sailor on vessels plying among the
Caribbean islands. As a sailor, Equiano was able to engage in trade on his own
account, accumulating the requisite £40 to buy his freedom in 1766. Thereafter,
he returned to Britain, working variously as a sailor, hairdresser, and servant,

sailing to the Arctic in 1773 with Constantine Phipps's expedition and to Central America with the inventor-entrepreneur Dr. Charles Irving. Spiritually reborn on a voyage to Spain, Equiano eventually landed in London, working with a project to resettle destitute black people from London to Sierra Leone in the 1780s and joining the abolitionist movement by the time he wrote his life story.

9 Anthony Benezet, *Some Historical Account of Guinea* (London, 1788, 58).
10 George Boulukos contextualizes Equiano's defense of slavery within Africa and his assertion of an "English" political identity. "Olaudah Equiano and the Eighteenth-Century Debate on Africa," *Eighteenth-Century Studies* 40, no. 2 (2007): 241–55. Boulukos explores the ways in which Equiano resists the idea of essential race in *The Grateful Slave: The Emergence of Race in Eighteenth-Century British and American Culture* (Cambridge: Cambridge University Press, 2008).
11 Olaudah Equiano, *The Interesting Narrative and Other Writings*, ed. Vincent Carretta (New York: Penguin, 2003, 38, 37).
12 Equiano, *Interesting Narrative*, 34, 38. See Elizabeth A. Bohls, *Women Travel Writers and the Language of Aesthetics, 1716–1818* (Cambridge: Cambridge University Press, 1995, 71–3); Gilroy, *Black Atlantic*, 8–10; and Gilroy, "Cultural Studies and Ethnic Absolutism," in Lawrence Grossberg, Cary Nelson, and Paula Treichler, ed., *Cultural Studies* (New York: Routledge, 1992, 187–98). For recent work connecting aesthetics and race, see Introduction, Note 29, this volume. Equiano disagrees with the French natural historian Buffon, who redacts a prevalent European view as he proclaims, "The most temperate climate lies between the 40th and 50th degree of latitude, and it produces the most handsome and beautiful men. It is from this climate that the idea of the genuine color of mankind, and of the various degrees of beauty, ought to be derived." Quoted in P. J. Marshall and Glyndwr Williams, *The Great Map of Mankind: Perceptions of New Worlds in the Age of Enlightenment* (Cambridge, MA: Harvard University Press, 1982, 245–6).
13 Kerry Sinanan, "The Slave Narrative and the Literature of Abolition," in Audrey A. Fisch, ed., *The Cambridge Companion to the African-American Slave Narrative* (Cambridge: Cambridge University Press, 2007, 65).
14 Equiano, *Interesting Narrative*, 34, 36–7; Werner Sollors, "Introduction," *The Interesting Narrative of the Life of Olaudah Equiano, or Gustavus Vassa, the African, Written by Himself* (New York and London: W. W. Norton & Co., 2001, xvi–xix).
15 Equiano, *Interesting Narrative*, 35; John Sekora, *Luxury: The Concept in Western Thought, Eden to Smollett* (Baltimore, MD: Johns Hopkins University Press, 1977, 63–109); Suvir Kaul, *Poems of Nation, Anthems of Empire: English Verse in the Long Eighteenth Century* (Charlottesville and London: University of Virginia Press, 2000, 97–110).
16 Equiano, *Interesting Narrative*, 41.
17 Equiano, *Interesting Narrative*, 39; Benezet, *Some Historical Account*, 19; Thomas Clarkson, *An Essay on the Slavery and Commerce of the Human Species, Particularly the African* (London, 1786), 69.
18 Equiano, *Interesting Narrative*, 68.

19 John Matthews, *A Voyage to the River Sierra-Leone* (London: Frank Cass, 1966 [1788], 146–7, 148); Equiano, *Interesting Narrative*, 37, 40. Boulukos, "Olaudah Equiano," 248, contextualizes Equiano's positive portrayal of slavery within Africa.

20 Equiano, *Interesting Narrative*, 7.

21 One example of this approach is Phillis Wheatley's short poem, "On Being Brought from Africa to America," 1773; see Philip Gould, *Barbaric Traffic: Commerce and Antislavery in the Eighteenth-Century Atlantic World* (Cambridge, MA, and London: Harvard University Press, 2003, 65–6).

22 Equiano, *Interesting Narrative*, 55.

23 Lynn Orilla Scott defines slave narratives as "autobiographical accounts of the physical and spiritual journey from slavery to freedom." "Autobiography: Slave Narratives," *The Oxford Encyclopedia of American Literature,* ed. Jay Parini, Oxford African American Studies Center, available at www.oxfordaasc.com/article/opr/t197/e0019 (accessed July 9, 2010), 1. This definition, based primarily on nineteenth-century U.S. material, claims Equiano's book as a "prototype" (Scott, "Autobiography," 2) but has difficulty encompassing the amount of post-manumission material – in particular travels – that it includes. See also William L. Andrews, *To Tell a Free Story: The First Century of African-American Autobiography, 1760–1865* (Chicago: University of Illinois Press, 1986); Charles T. Davis and Henry Louis Gates Jr., ed., *The Slave's Narrative* (New York: Oxford University Press, 1985); Frances Smith Foster, *Witnessing Slavery: The Development of Antebellum Slave Narratives* (Madison: University of Wisconsin Press, 1994 [1979]). I argue that *The Interesting Narrative* is most fruitfully read as travel writing.

24 Equiano, *Interesting Narrative*, 98, 111; quoted in Equiano, *Interesting Narrative*, 97; and see Gould, *Barbaric Traffic*, 72–6, on the "motif of the African speaker's suicide" in anti-slavery poetry.

25 Equiano, *Interesting Narrative*, 147, 122.

26 Clarkson, *Essay*, 86. See Introduction, Note 3, this volume, on the usage of "English" and "British."

27 Equiano, *Interesting Narrative*, 159, 236.

28 Equiano, *Interesting Narrative*, 205. Irving employed Equiano as a servant beginning in 1768 and took him along on Phipps's Arctic expedition. The area known as the Mosquito Coast runs eastward from modern-day Honduras to the northern tip of what is now Nicaragua, and south to Costa Rica. It was what the historian Bernard Bailyn calls a marchland: a disordered border country in which violence was a way of life. Bailyn, *The Peopling of British North America* (New York: Knopf, 1986). Both Britain and Spain claimed the area until the very late 1700s, and it had been since the previous century a haven for pirates and runaway slaves. The indigenous Mosquito or Miskito Indians had hated the Spanish since the Conquest and were friendly with the English, who supplied them with arms to resist their mutual enemy, Spain (Carretta, *Equiano*, 180–1). Long's *History of Jamaica* encourages English settlement there, reporting that 30 families have already started sugar plantations on lands granted them

by the Indians, who help protect them from the Spanish, saving the cost of government troops. A Mr. Henry Corrin of Jamaica, Long writes, "settled here in 1752, and acquired a large fortune from the luxuriant productions of this district." Edward Long, *The History of Jamaica* (3 vols.) (London, 1774), 1: 317–24. Irving and his partner, Alexander Blair, wanted to cultivate plants used to produce oil for wool combing (Carretta, *Equiano*, 180). Equiano is referring to Irving's plantation in Chapter V when he contrasts slaves' cruel treatment by overseers who are "human butchers" with the "benevolence" of planters who live on their own estates and writes, "I myself, as shall appear in the sequel, managed an estate, where . . . the negroes were uncommonly cheerful and healthy, and did more work by half than by the common mode of treatment they usually do" (*Interesting Narrative*, 105–106). *The Interesting Narrative* does not take an emancipationist position; it explicitly advocates abolishing the slave trade, but not the institution of slavery, in line with the moderate political strategy of the national Society for Effecting the Abolition of the Slave Trade. Setting an example of amelioration, or reforming slavery from within through better treatment of slaves, is thus not inconsistent with the book's stated political aims.

29 Carretta, *Equiano*, 185.
30 Equiano, *Interesting Narrative*, 202, 205, 210, 217–18. The report of Irving's death was incorrect; see *Carretta*, Equiano, 192. For Boulukos, this episode illustrates that the good intentions "of individual owners or overseers are no match for the systemic violence of slavery." Boulukos, "Olaudah Equiano," 181.
31 Equiano, *Interesting Narrative*, 108, 219.
32 Sonia Hofkosh, "Tradition and the Interesting Narrative: Capitalism, Abolition, and the Romantic Individual," in Alan Richardson and Sonia Hofkosh, ed., *Romanticism, Race, and Imperial Culture, 1780–1834* (Bloomington: Indiana University Press, 1996, 338).
33 H. Thomas, *Romanticism*, 12, 229–30, 244. I cannot agree with Thomas's claim that *The Interesting Narrative* represents a "diasporic synchronization or fusion" of "the Ibo concept of 'chi,' the personal spirit of destiny" with the Protestant concept of the Holy Spirit (233). Publishing in 2000, she does not address Carretta's discovery of evidence casting doubt on Equiano's African birth. Given the inconclusive nature of the evidence, I neither deny nor affirm that he was African; rather, I am concerned with *The Narrative's* rhetoric and narrative technique. Rust, "Subaltern," also emphasizes the literal and metaphorical importance of water and travel by water in *The Narrative*, connecting it to Igbo spirituality.
34 Henry Louis Gates, Jr., *The Signifying Monkey: A Theory of African-American Autobiography* (New York: Oxford University Press, 1988, 153, 155).
35 M. M. Bakhtin, *The Dialogic Imagination: Four Essays*, ed. Michael Holquist, trans. Caryl Emerson and Michael Holquist (Austin: University of Texas Press, 1981, 325). I draw on the work of Bakhtin for the concept of dialogism in literary discourse; see especially his discussion of what he calls double-voiced discourse, 324–5; and Marren, "Between Slavery and Freedom," 99.

36 Boelhower, "'I'll Teach You How to Flow,'" lists all 26 ships named in the *Narrative* (31).
37 Equiano, *Interesting Narrative*, 77–8.
38 Equiano, *Interesting Narrative*, 58, 55. Cannibalism was, of course, stereotypically attributed to Africans – for example, in William Snelgrave's influential 1734 travel account, as Boulukos notes ("Olaudah Equiano," 244). On Equiano's use of the imagery of cannibalism, see C. L. Innes, *A History of Black and Asian Writing in Britain, 1700–2000* (Cambridge: Cambridge University Press, 2002, 39–41); and Mark Stein, "Who's Afraid of Cannibals? Some Uses of the Cannibalism Trope in Olaudah Equiano's *Interesting Narrative*," *Discourses of Slavery and Abolition: Britain and Its Colonies, 1760–1838*, ed. Brycchan Carey, Markman Ellis, and Sarah Salih (Houndmills, Basingstoke, Hampshire [UK]: Palgrave Macmillan, 2004, 96–107).
39 Equiano, *Interesting Narrative*, 31. Boulukos goes on to comment, "S.E. Ogude sees it as indicative of his 'pan-Africanism,' Felicity Nussbaum connects it to his Igbo identity, Srinivas Aravamudan links it to his flirtation with 'Ethnic separatist' nationalism, and C. L. Innes sees it as indicating Equiano's construction of an 'imaginary homeland' or an 'imagined community'" ("Olaudah Equiano," 243). One problematic occurrence of this term is when Equiano, working as Irving's overseer, buys his "countrymen" as slaves for the Central American plantation and later absconds, leaving them to their sad fate.
40 Youngquist, "Afro-Futurism," 187; see also Aravamudan, *Tropicopolitans*; Boelhower, "'I'll Teach You How to Flow'"; Chinosole, *African Diaspora*; Rust, "Subaltern"; W. Jeffrey Bolster, *Black Jacks: African American Seamen in the Age of Sail* (Cambridge, MA, and London: Harvard University Press, 1997); and Gretchen Holbrook Gerzina, "Mobility in Chains: Freedom of Movement in the Early Black Atlantic," *South Atlantic Quarterly* 100: 1 (Winter 2001): 41–59.
41 Marcus Rediker, *Between the Devil and the Deep Blue Sea: Merchant Seamen, Pirates, and the Anglo-American Maritime World, 1700–1750* (Cambridge: Cambridge University Press, 1987, 21).
42 Marren, "Between Slavery and Freedom," 95.
43 Rediker, *Between*, 293; Gilroy, *Black Atlantic*, 4. See also Rediker, *Between*, 160, 200–201, 211–12; and Sidney Mintz, *Sweetness and Power: The Place of Sugar in Modern History* (New York: Penguin, 1985, 47–8); as well as Peter Linebaugh and Marcus Rediker, *The Many-Headed Hydra: Sailors, Slaves, Commoners, and the Hidden History of the Revolutionary Atlantic* (Boston: Beacon Press, 2000, *passim*).
44 Gerzina, "Mobility in Chains," 42, 48; and see Bolster, *Black Jacks*, on black sailors, esp. 31–5 on the navy and 97–9 on Equiano and race at sea.
45 For the definition of "ethos," see Chapter 3, Note 24, this volume. The OED's definitions of "interest" include "7a. a feeling of concern for or curiosity about a person or thing; and 2b. good, benefit, profit, advantage." We might say that *The Interesting Narrative* aims to convert the curiosity typically awakened by adventure travel writing into concern for British slaves, to the interest (benefit or advantage) of the latter.
46 Equiano, *Interesting Narrative*, 169.

47 Equiano, *Interesting Narrative*, 167, 174.
48 Geraldine Murphy, "Olaudah Equiano, Accidental Tourist," *Eighteenth-Century Studies* 27 (1994), 567; Equiano, *Interesting Narrative*, 113.
49 William Smith, *Natural History of Nevis and the Rest of the English Leeward Charibee Islands in America* (London, 1745, 56).
50 Equiano doubtlessly knew numerous slaves who had experienced the Middle Passage, so this section of the *Narrative*, even if fictional, was probably informed by what we may call "ethnographic research." His biographer, Carretta, comments that "Equiano's literary achievements have been vastly underestimated" if "he invented his African childhood and his much quoted account of the Middle Passage" (*Equiano*, xiv).
51 This adventure gives the book its only illustration other than the frontispiece.

5. AT HOME WITH THE "BLACKIES": JANET SCHAW AND MARIA NUGENT

1 Catherine Hall and Sonya O. Rose, "Introduction: Being at Home with the Empire," in Catherine Hall and Sonya O. Rose, ed., *At Home with the Empire: Metropolitan Culture and the Imperial World* (Cambridge: Cambridge University Press, 2006, 27).
2 Rosemary Marangoly George, *The Politics of Home: Postcolonial Relocations and Twentieth-Century Fiction* (Cambridge: Cambridge University Press, 1996, 2). Scholars in several disciplines have studied the problem of home. George considers home in postcolonial literature, or "global English." Classic feminist meditations on home include bell hooks, *Yearnings: Race, Gender, and Cultural Politics* (Boston: South End Press, 1990); Caren Kaplan, "Deterritorializations: The Rewriting of Home and Exile in Western Feminist Discourse," *Cultural Critique* 6 (1987): 187–98; Biddy Martin and Chandra Talpade Mohanty, "Feminist Politics: What's Home Got to Do with It?," *Feminist Studies/Critical Studies*, ed. Teresa de Lauretis (Bloomington: Indiana University Press, 1986, 191–212); and Iris Marion Young, "House and Home: Feminist Variations on a Theme," *Intersecting Voices: Dilemmas of Gender, Political Philosophy, and Policy* (Princeton, NJ: Princeton University Press, 1997, 134–64). Alison Blunt and Robyn Dowling provide an invaluable introduction to recent research on home in geography and related fields: *Home* (London and New York: Routledge, 2006).
3 Witold Rybczinski, *Home: A Short History of an Idea* (New York: Viking, 1986, 75).
4 Rybczinski, *Home*, 75. The architectural historian Rybczinski analyzes modern bourgeois domesticity as a product of feminine control, correlating women's central position in the bourgeois home with the rise of domestic cleanliness and convenience and the evolution of bourgeois manners, all of which he traces to seventeenth-century Holland. This aspect of his analysis is helpful in its geographical and historical specificity, although his book elsewhere tends to romanticize home and family (see Blunt and Dowling, *Home*, 102).

5 This development depended on the needs of various forms of production (as well as, later, on individual choices, guided by a sense of propriety or gentility, for wives to stay home). The classic source for this shift is Alice Clark, *The Working Life of Women in the Seventeenth Century*, ed. Amy Louise Erickson (London and New York: Routledge, 1992). Amy Erickson's introduction to the 1992 reissue of this 1920 study notes that although "Clark's description of the development from 'domestic' to 'family' to 'capitalistic' industry is still largely accepted today," historians now assign a later chronology. "Many of the issues that Clark allocated to the late seventeenth century . . . are related today to the eighteenth and early nineteenth centuries." Amy Louise Erickson, "Introduction." Alice Clark, *The Working Life of Women in the Seventeenth Century*, ed. Amy Louise Erickson (London and New York: Routledge, 1992 [1919], ix–x). On voluntary separation between workshop and residential spaces, see Leonore Davidoff and Catherine Hall, *Family Fortunes: Men and Women of the English Middle Class, 1780–1850* (Chicago: University of Chicago Press, 1987), 364–9. The consequences of this reorganization for women have been debated. Middle-class women's role in productive labor probably did diminish, due also in part to economic diversification and the decline of the household economy, but revisionist accounts point out that there is no proof that this declining role in production necessarily caused a decline in women's status, which continued to be low within patriarchal households, as it had been since the Middle Ages; see Erickson, "Introduction," xv–xvii; and Amanda Vickery, "Golden Age to Separate Spheres? A Review of the Categories and Chronology of English Women's History," *Historical Journal* 36 (1993): 401–12. For speculations on the broader cross-cultural usefulness of the domestic–public division, see Michelle Zimbalist Rosaldo, "The Use and Abuse of Anthropology: Reflections on Feminism and Cross-Cultural Understanding," *Signs* 5 (1980): 389–417.

6 Catherine Hall, *White, Male, and Middle-Class: Explorations in Feminism and History* (New York: Routledge, 1992, 106); Davidoff and Hall, *Family Fortunes*, 89. Davidoff and Hall offer a complex rendering of the separate-spheres paradigm, critiqued by Vickery, "Golden Age to Separate Spheres?" John Smail, *The Origins of Middle-Class Culture: Halifax, Yorkshire, 1660–1780* (Ithaca, NY: Cornell University Press, 1994) agrees with Davidoff and Hall, whereas Margaret Hunt, *The Middling Sort: Commerce, Gender, and the Family in Eighteenth-Century England* (Berkeley: University of California Press, 1996) and Linda Colley, *Britons: Forging the Nation 1707–1837* (New Haven, CT: Yale University Press, 1992, 237–81), have major disagreements with them. Amy Kaplan, *The Anarchy of Empire in the Making of U.S. Culture* (Cambridge, MA: Harvard University Press, 2002, 23–50), represents an interesting recent application of the separate-spheres paradigm to the issue of American imperial expansion.

7 Charlotte Sussman, *Consuming Anxieties: Consumer Protest, Gender and British Slavery, 1713–1833* (Stanford, CA: Stanford University Press, 2000, 110, 126).

8 Hall and Rose, "Introduction," 25; Sidney Mintz, *Sweetness and Power: The Place of Sugar in Modern History* (New York: Penguin, 1985, 116).

9 Anne McClintock, *Imperial Leather: Race, Gender, and Sexuality in the Colonial Contest* (New York and London: Routledge, 1995, 208–209); Lester, quoted In Hall and Rose, "Introduction," 20.

10 Ranajit Guha, "Not at Home in Empire," *Critical Inquiry* 23 (1997): 482; Yeats-Brown, quoted in Guha, 483; A. Kaplan, *Anarchy of Empire*, 26. The South Asian context of Guha's theorizing may somewhat limit its applicability to the Caribbean context; also, women are notably absent from his essay.

11 E.g., McClintock, *Imperial Leather*; Nupur Chaudhuri and Margaret Strobel, ed., *White Women and Imperialism: Complicity and Resistance* (Bloomington: Indiana University Press, 1992); George, *Politics of Home*, chap. 2.

12 Hilary Callan and Shirley Ardener, ed., *The Incorporated Wife* (London: Croom Helm, 1984); Jean Comaroff and John Comaroff, "Home-Made Hegemony: Modernity, Domesticity, and Colonialism in South Africa," in Karen Tranberg Hansen, ed., *African Encounters with Domesticity* (New Brunswick, NJ: Rutgers University Press, 1992, 37–74); Ann Laura Stoler, "Making Empire Respectable: The Politics of Race and Sexual Morality in Twentieth-Century Colonial Cultures," in Anne McClintock, Aamir Mufti, and Ella Shohat, ed., *Dangerous Liaisons: Gender, Nation, and Postcolonial Perspectives* (Minneapolis: University of Minnesota Press, 1997, 344–73).

13 Callan and Ardener, *Incorporated Wife*, 9, 11.

14 Comaroff and Comaroff 67, 54.

15 Stoler, "Making Empire Respectable," 357.

16 Karen Tranberg Hansen, "Introduction," Karen Tranberg Hansen, ed., *African Encounters with Domesticity* (New Brunswick, NJ: Rutgers University Press, 1992, 3). Other work on this topic considers white women as symbols in the rhetoric of empire: e.g., Jenny Sharpe, *Allegories of Empire: The Figure of Woman in the Colonial Text* (Minneapolis: University of Minnesota Press, 1993); Laura Brown, *Ends of Empire: Women and Ideology in Early Eighteenth-Century English Literature* (Ithaca, NY: Cornell University Press, 1993). Felicity A. Nussbaum, *Torrid Zones: Maternity, Sexuality, and Empire in Eighteenth-Century English Narratives* (Baltimore, MD: Johns Hopkins University Press, 1995) argues influentially that representations of the "other" women of empire enabled the consolidation of the cult of domesticity of England.

17 [Janet Schaw], *Journal of a Lady of Quality: Being the Narrative of a Journey from Scotland to the West Indies, North Carolina, and Portugal, in the years 1774 to 1776*, ed. Evangeline Walker Andrews and Charles Maclean Andrews (Lincoln and London: University of Nebraska Press, 2005, 21).

18 Stephen, quoted in Catherine Hall, *Civilizing Subjects: Colony and Metropole in the English Imagination, 1830–1867* (Chicago: University of Chicago Press, 2002, 75).

19 Hall, *Civilizing*, 75. See Susan Scott Parrish, *American Curiosity: Cultures of Natural History in the Colonial British Atlantic World* (Chapel Hill: University of North Carolina Press, 2006, chap. 2), on colonists' fears that living in a different climate would change their bodies.

20 Hall, *Civilizing*, 69, 72.

21 Eve Tavor Bannet, "Trading Routes and Eighteenth-Century Migrations: Reframing Janet Schaw," in Dan Doll and Jessica Munns, ed., *Recording and Reordering: Essays on the Seventeenth- and Eighteenth-Century Journal* (Lewisburg, PA: Bucknell University Press, 2006, 153).

22 For text history, see Stephen Carl Arch, "Introduction," [Janet Schaw], *Journal of a Lady of Quality: Being the Narrative of a Journey from Scotland to the West Indies, North Carolina, and Portugal, in the years 1774 to 1776*, ed. Evangeline Walker Andrews and Charles Maclean Andrews (Lincoln and London: University of Nebraska Press, 2005, 1–18). Nugent's journal was printed for private circulation in 1839, five years after its author's death, perhaps as a tribute by her children. Philip Wright, "Introduction" to Maria Nugent, *Lady Nugent's Journal of her Residence in Jamaica from 1801 to 1805*, ed. Philip Wright, revised edn. (Kingston, Jamaica: Institute of Jamaica, 1968, ix, xvi).

23 Schaw, *Journal*, 78.

24 Schaw, *Journal*, 28, 30.

25 L. Brown, *Ends of Empire*, 194; and see Douglas Mack, *Scottish Fiction and the British Empire* (Edinburgh: Edinburgh University Press, 2006, 89–91).

26 Bannet, "Trading Routes," 138, 139; Keith Sandiford, *The Cultural Politics of Sugar: Caribbean Slavery and Narratives of Colonialism* (Cambridge: Cambridge University Press, 2000), 98.

27 T. M. Devine, *Scotland's Empire and the Shaping of the Americas 1600–1815* (Washington, DC: Smithsonian Books, 2003, 227, 108, 120–8); and see Michael Fry, *The Scottish Empire* (East Lothian and Edinburgh: Tuckwell Press and Birlinn, 2001, 57–82). Devine debunks the "persistent myth that early Highland emigration was mainly caused by the . . . failure of the Jacobite risings," attributing it to economic factors instead (130), although several hundred Scots Jacobites were transported to the Caribbean after 1746 as indentured servants (229).

28 Bannet, "Trading Routes," 140. Bannet argues that Janet Schaw understood very well the political implications of the mass emigration driving the *Jamaica Packet* emigrants and that this informs her sympathy for the Lawsons, whose fate the Schaws might well have shared had they lacked influential connections (141).

29 Schaw, *Journal*, 33, 36; Lynn Festa, *Sentimental Figures of Empire in Eighteenth-Century Britain and France* (Baltimore, MD: Johns Hopkins University Press, 2006, 172, 174).

30 Schaw, *Journal*, 33, 34, 36.

31 Schaw, *Journal*, 21.

32 Schaw, *Journal*, 78.

33 Schaw, *Journal*, 85; Devine, *Scotland's Empire*, 241. See Devine on the "complex networks of patronage, ethnic connection and family loyalty" underpinning "Scottish hegemony in the Caribbean." The island of Antigua in particular, where Schaw visited, experienced growing Scottish dominance through the eighteenth century (234, 238, 231). Sandiford, *Cultural Politics*, chap. 4, argues that Schaw's journal "theorizes a Scottish essentialism as the verifying criterion of culture in the colonies the author visits" (89).

34 Deirdre Coleman reads Schaw's journal in the context of the racialization of whiteness in the 1760s and 1770s. "Janet Schaw and the Complexions of Empire," *Eighteenth-Century Studies* 36 (2003): 169–93.

35 Adam Smith, *The Theory of Moral Sentiments*, ed. D. D. Raphael and A. L. Macfie (Indianapolis, IN: Liberty Classics, 1976 [1759], 190–91).

36 Schaw, *Journal*, 129.

37 Schaw, *Journal*, 129, 127.

38 Bohls, *Women Travel Writers*, 54–6.

39 Long, *History*, 2: 353.

40 Maria Nugent, *Lady Nugent's Journal of her Residence in Jamaica from 1801 to 1805*, ed. Philip Wright, revised edn. (Kingston, Jamaica: Institute of Jamaica, 1968, 1–2).

41 Wright, "Introduction," Maria Nugent, *Lady Nugent's Journal of her Residence in Jamaica from 1801 to 1805*, ed. Philip Wright, revised edn. (Kingston, Jamaica: Institute of Jamaica, 1968, xiii, xv). See Introduction, Note 3, this volume, on the usage of "English" as opposed to "British" in the eighteenth century and in this study.

42 Nugent, *Journal*, 40. Maria Nugent was in Jamaica from April 1801 until July 1805; her husband joined her in England the following year. British forces occupied parts of Hispaniola (i.e., the island containing the French colony of Saint Domingue and the Spanish colony of Santo Domingo) from 1793 until 1798, with massive casualties; see Chapter 3. During the Nugent administration, Napoleonic France was fighting the armies of Toussaint Louverture and, later, Dessalines, which defeated the French forces in 1803, followed by a series of massacres of white inhabitants. Laurent Dubois, *Avengers of the New World: The Story of the Haitian Revolution* (Cambridge, MA, and London: Belknap Press of Harvard University Press, 2004, 300).

43 Nugent, *Journal*, 38, footnote.

44 Nugent, *Journal*, 13; Schaw, *Journal*, 124. See Srinivas Aravamudan, *Tropicopolitans: Colonialism and Agency, 1688–1804* (Chapel Hill, NC: Duke University Press, 1999, 33–41) on the connection between pet-keeping and the use of black-child pages as props in paintings of aristocratic women.

45 This was known as Tacky's Revolt (1760): see Chapter 3 on Bryan Edwards's description of it in his *History of the West Indies*.

46 David Geggus, *Slavery, War, and Revolution: The British Occupation of Saint Domingue, 1793–1798* (Oxford: Oxford University Press, 1982, 90, 88).

47 Nugent, *Journal*, 198.

48 Nugent, *Journal*, 61, 62.

49 Nugent, *Journal*, 62–3.

50 Nugent, *Journal*, 10, 54, and see 25, 54, 61, 75, 115, 208, etc.

51 Nugent, *Journal*, 11, 15, 38.

52 Nugent, *Journal*, 12, 29, 172, 210.

53 Nugent, *Journal*, 140.

54 See Mary Turner, *Slaves and Missionaries: The Disintegration of Jamaican Slave Society, 1787–1834* (Urbana: University of Illinois Press, 1982, chap. 1), on the uneasy relations among planters, the Anglican Church, and non-Anglican

missionaries over the issue of slave conversion. Having read the 1791 publication of the "Evidence before the House of Commons, on the part of the Petitioners for the Abolition of the Slave Trade," Nugent comments, "As far as I at present see and can hear of the ill treatment of the slaves, I think what they say upon the subject is very greatly exaggerated. Individuals, I make no doubt, occasionally abuse the power they possess; but, generally speaking, I believe the slaves are extremely well used. Yet it appears to me, there would certainly be no necessity for the Slave Trade, if religion, decency, and good order, were established among the negroes; if they could be prevailed upon to marry; and if our white men would but set them a little better example" (Nugent, *Journal*, 86).

55 Nugent, *Journal*, 39.
56 See Michael Craton, *Testing the Chains: Resistance to Slavery in the British West Indies* (Ithaca, NY: Cornell University Press, 1982).
57 Nugent, *Journal*, 156.
58 Nugent, *Journal*, 108, 141. The BBC video "The Two Marys: Two Views of Slavery" (1997, from the series *Women: Word for Word*) makes effective visual use of this imagery. The production juxtaposes the stories of Maria Nugent and Mary Prince, contemporaries living in decidedly different relationships to the institution of slavery.
59 Nugent, *Journal*, 157, 162, 202.
60 Nugent, *Journal*, 164, 165, 178.
61 Nugent, *Journal*, 215, 220.
62 Ronald Paulson, *Representations of Revolution, 1789–1820* (New Haven, CT: Yale University Press, 1983, 67).
63 Nugent, *Journal*, 227, 240.
64 George, 36.
65 Cf. Mary Louise Pratt, *Imperial Eyes: Travel Writing and Transculturation* (New York and London: Routledge, 1993, 23): "By the last years of the eighteenth century, interior exploration had become the major object of expansionist . . . imaginings," in contrast with the paradigm of maritime exploration that had reigned for 300 years.

6. A LONG WAY FROM HOME: SLAVERY, TRAVEL, AND IMPERIAL GEOGRAPHY IN *THE HISTORY OF MARY PRINCE*

1 Gaston Bachelard, *The Poetics of Space* (Boston: Beacon Press, 1994, 5); Tim Cresswell, *Place: A Short Introduction* (Malden, MA: Blackwell, 2004, 24).
2 Doreen Massey, *Space, Place, and Gender* (Minneapolis: University of Minnesota Press, 1994, 165–6, 153–4); and see Bell Hooks, *Yearnings: Race, Gender, and Cultural Politics* (Boston: South End Press, 1990).
3 Orlando Patterson, *Slavery and Social Death: A Comparative Study* (Cambridge, MA: Harvard University Press, 1982, 5, 6, 7).
4 Prince could legally leave her owners under the Mansfield Decision precedent of 1772, which forbade forcible recapture of enslaved people on British soil or their transport back to the colonies against their will. This judgment is often

misinterpreted as making slavery unlawful on British soil, although its terms were actually more limited. See Chapter 3.

5 Mary Prince, *The History of Mary Prince, A West Indian Slave, Related by Herself*, ed. Moira Ferguson, revised edn. (Ann Arbor: University of Michigan Press, 1997 [1831], 55). Gillian Whitlock examines the relationship between Prince and her amanuensis, Susanna Strickland Moodie. "Volatile Subjects: *The History of Mary Prince*." *Genius in Bondage: Literature of the Early Black Atlantic*, ed. Vincent Carretta and Philip Gould (Lexington: University Press of Kentucky, 2001, 72–86).

6 Jenny Sharpe, "'Something Akin to Freedom': The Case of Mary Prince," *Differences: A Journal of Feminist Cultural Studies* 8 (1996): 38.

7 Prince, *History*, 55; Sandra Pouchet Paquet, "The Heartbeat of a West Indian Slave: The History of Mary Prince," *African American Review* 26 (1992): 131. Jessica L. Allen also discusses the importance of Prince's Caribbean Creole language to the impact of Pringle's editing. "Pringle's Pruning of Prince," *Callaloo* 35.2 (2012): 209–19.

8 Allen, "Pringle's Pruning"; Moira Ferguson, "Introduction," in Mary Prince, *The History of Mary Prince, A West Indian Slave, Related by Herself*, ed. Moira Ferguson, revised edn. (Ann Arbor: University of Michigan Press, 1997), and *Subject to Others: British Women Writers and Colonial Slavery, 1670–1834* (New York and London: Routledge, 1992, 281–98); Sharpe, "'Something Akin to Freedom'" and *Ghosts of Slavery: A Literary Archaeology of Black Women's Lives* (Minneapolis: University of Minnesota Press, 2003, 120–51); Whitlock, "Volatile Subjects."

9 Diana Paton, "Decency, Dependency, and the Lash: Gender and the British Debate over Slave Emancipation, 1830–34," *Slavery and Abolition* 17 (1996): 169.

10 Ferguson, *Subject to Others*, 281–98; Ferguson, "Introduction," 10–11; Sharpe, *Ghosts of Slavery*, 132.

11 Prince, *History*, 81; Sharpe, *Ghosts of Slavery*, 138.

12 Prince, *History*, 111.

13 Sharpe, "'Something Akin to Freedom,'" 42.

14 Prince, *History*, 55, 130–1; Clare Midgley, *Women Against Slavery: The British Campaigns, 1780–1870* (London: Routledge, 1992, 91).

15 Sharpe, "'Something Akin to Freedom,'" 42, 47.

16 Marietta Morrissey, *Slave Women in the New World: Gender Stratification in the Caribbean* (Lawrence: University Press of Kansas, 1989, 15, 13). Of course, historians of slavery have access to a rather different range of sources than do historians of the nineteenth-century middle classes because few slaves left behind testimony in their own words. Clare Robertson notes that the debate over the history of the slave family became politicized with attempts to blame present-day "black families, women members in particular, for African-American problems created by the dominant sector of society." "Africa into the Americas? Slavery and Women, the Family, and the Gender Division of Labor," in *More Than Chattel: Black Women and Slavery in the Americas*, ed. David

Barry Gaspar and Darlene Clark Hine (Bloomington: Indiana University Press, 1996, 12).

17 See, e.g., Michael Craton, "Changing Patterns of Slave Families in the British West Indies," *Journal of Interdisciplinary History* X (1979): 1–35; B. W. Higman, *Slave Populations of the British Caribbean 1807–1834* (Baltimore, MD: Johns Hopkins University Press, 1984, 364–78); Barbara Bush, *Slave Women in Caribbean Society 1650–1838* (Bloomington: Indiana University Press, 1990).

18 Paton, 169.

19 See, e.g., Janet Schaw's journal (discussed in Chapter 5, this volume): "When one comes to be better acquainted with the nature of the Negroes, the horror of [whipping] must wear off. It is the suffering of the human mind that constitutes the greatest misery of punishment, but with them it is merely corporeal. As to the brutes it inflicts no wound on their mind, whose Natures seem made to bear it, and whose sufferings are not attended with shame or pain beyond the present moment" (127).

20 Prince, *History*, 61.

21 Prince, *History*, 61, 60, 57; Patterson, 334–7.

22 Prince, *History*, 64.

23 Paton, "Decency," 163.

24 Prince, *History*, 70. Darrel was a prominent citizen, soon to become mayor of Hamilton, and Ferguson speculates that Prince "might have surmised that her escape to Darrel's house would in some way intimidate Captain Ingham" (Ferguson, *Subject*, 7).

25 Prince, *History*, 70.

26 Prince, *History*, 70.

27 Beckles, Hilary McD., *Natural Rebels: A Social History of Enslaved Black Women in Barbados* (New Brunswick, NJ: Rutgers University Press, 1989, 121–2). Craton, "Changing Patterns," Morrissey, *Slave Women*, and Beckles believe such stable pairing was in fact fairly prevalent; Bush, *Slave Women*, modifies their findings by cautioning, "The system of marriage and morality adhered to by slaves and the European proletariat differed considerably from that which prevailed amongst the middle and upper classes of eighteenth-century Europe" (90).

28 Prince, *History*, 84, 85.

29 Ferguson, "Introduction," 14; Sharpe, "'Something Akin to Freedom,'" 45–46; Beckles, *Natural Rebels*.

30 Davidoff and Hall, *Family Fortunes*, 389.

31 Bush, *Slave Women*, 34, 44; James Walvin, *Black Ivory: A History of British Slavery* (Washington, DC: Howard University Press, 1994), 124.

32 Bush, *Slave Women*, 61.

33 Ferguson, "Introduction," *passim*.

34 Prince, *History*, 66.

35 Tassie Gwilliam, "'Scenes of Horror,' Scenes of Sensibility: Sentimentality and Slavery in John Gabriel Stedman's *Narrative of a Five Years' Expedition against the Revolted Negroes of Surinam*," *ELH* 65 (1998, 666). Sussman, *Consuming Anxieties* (chap. 5), also analyzes the relationship among domestic ideology,

women's participation in the anti-slavery movement, and *The History of Mary Prince.*

36 Prince, *History*, 100, 104.

37 Prince, *History*, 75–6, 77.

38 Helen Cooper, "'Tracing the Route to England': Nineteenth-Century Caribbean Interventions into English Debates on Race and Slavery," *The Victorians and Race*, ed. Shearer West (Aldershot, Hants, UK: Scholar Press, 1996, 197).

39 Prince, *History*, 92.

40 James Clifford, *Routes: Travel and Translation in the Late Twentieth Century* (Cambridge, MA, and London: Harvard University Press, 1997, 33, 36).

41 Prince, *History*, 61, 63, 64. According to Paquet, "heart is an alternative to the material measure of the marketplace . . . a center of resistant subjectivity and interiority" ("Heartbeat," 142).

42 Prince, *History*, 70, 75. Michelle Speitz's recent essay focuses on the Bermuda salt industry, recovering a neglected part of the history of Caribbean slavery and examining the rhetorical function of salt in *The History of Mary Prince*. "Blood Sugar and Salt Licks: Corroding Bodies and Preserving Nations in *The History of Mary Prince, A West Indian Slave, Related by Herself.*" *Circulations: Romanticism and the Black Atlantic*, ed. Paul Youngquist and Frances Botkin. 2011. Accessed August 14, 2013. Available at www.rc.umd.edu/praxis/circulations/index.html. "Prince molds her many references to the salt industry of Turks Island into a compelling trope, grafting her figurations of a body and mind transformed by labor onto narratives of a British body politic and its ideological claims that purport to be working for freedom" (Speitz, "Blood Sugar," 11). Old Daniel's physical wounds that never heal figure the emotional and psychological as well as physical damage done to Mary Prince by slavery (Speitz, "Blood Sugar," 19).

43 C. Robertson, "Africa into the Americas?," 24; Ferguson, "Introduction," 10–11; Ferguson, *Subject*, 286; Walvin, *Black Ivory*, 126.

44 Prince, *History*, 77–8.

45 The BBC dramatization of this incident in *The Two Marys: Two Views of Slavery* imagines Prince menacingly putting the edge of a broken plate to her master's throat. Sharpe cautions in relation to this incident, "As much as Prince's scolding of Mr. D– shows a slave woman standing up to her master, one has to wonder whether morally upright speech could prevent a lashing from so ruthless a man. The episode has the narrative effect, however, of proving that a moral high ground can control the slaveholder's abuse of power. In doing so, it renders less morally upright forms of self-defense, such as verbal abuse or acts of insubordination, inappropriate as responses to slavery" ("'Something Akin to Freedom,'" 42).

46 Prince, *History*, 78. Ferguson contends, "Antigua was the most attractive island for any slave actively thinking of freedom. Free black men were permitted to vote there, and, although this law did not apply to Mary Prince, its relative liberality in the Caribbean islands was symbolically significant" ("Introduction," 12).

47 Sharpe, "'Something Akin to Freedom,'" 40.

48 Prince, *History*, 86, 87, 88.
49 The last evidence of Mary Prince that Moira Ferguson has found in more than a decade of searching is her testimony in the court case Pringle *v*. Cadell (i.e., Pringle is suing the publisher of Blackwood's for libel over MacQueen's article) in February 1833. We do not know how long she lived or whether she was able to return to Antigua after Parliament voted to emancipate the slaves later that year. Ferguson, "Introduction," 28.
50 Peter Fryer, *Staying Power: A History of Black People in Britain* (London: Pluto Press, 1984, 68). Wood's letter reads, "I have already told Molly, and now give it her in writing, in order that there may be no misunderstanding on her part, that as I brought her from Antigua at her own request and entreaty, and that she is consequently now free, she is of course at liberty to take her baggage and go where she pleases And, in consequence of her late conduct, she must do one of two things – either quit the house, or return to Antigua by the earliest opportunity, as she does not evince a disposition to make herself useful. As she is a stranger in London, I do not wish to turn her out, or would do so, as two female servants are sufficient for my establishment. If after this she does remain, it will be only during her good behavior; but on no consideration will I allow her wages or any other remuneration for her services" (Prince, *History*, 96).
51 Prince, *History*, 89.
52 David Lambert discusses MacQueen's career as an armchair geographer of Africa. "'Taken captive by the mystery of the Great River': Towards an Historical Geography of British Geography and Atlantic Slavery," *Journal of Historical Geography* 35 (2009): 44–65.
53 James MacQueen, "The Colonial Empire of Great Britain. Letter to Earl Grey," *Blackwood's Edinburgh Magazine* CLXXXVI (November 1831), 752, 754, 764.
54 Prince, *History*, 55, 93–4, 93. Prominent abolitionist writers such as Anthony Benezet, Thomas Clarkson, William Wilberforce, and James Stephen had developed the rhetoric of the division between good metropole and evil colony; see Chapter 3.
55 Philip Sherlock and Hazel Bennett argue persuasively for the importance of the Western Liberation Uprising in the series of events leading to Parliament's vote on August 28, 1833, to emancipate the slaves: "Through the uprising of 1831–32 Sam Sharpe and the other freedom fighters reset the timetable for freedom." *The Story of the Jamaican People* (Kingston, Jamaica: Ian Randle Publishers, 1998, 226).
56 Jenny Sharpe's *Ghosts of Slavery* is exemplary in its efforts to "piece together" the subjectivities of slave women from the textual fragments available (xiv).
57 The native Amerindians of the Caribbean islands were decimated during the century and a half following 1492 by colonial violence and European disease. A small but significant number, however, did survive in a few places. Documents about them are collected in Peter Hulme and Neil L. Whitehead, ed., *Wild Majesty: Encounters with Caribs from Columbus to the Present Day* (Oxford: Clarendon Press, 1992).

58 Richard B. Sheridan, *Sugar and Slavery: The Economic History of the British West Indies, 1623–1775* (Barbados, Jamaica, Trinidad, and Tobago: Canoe Press, 1994 [1974], 99); Sidney Mintz, *Sweetness and Power: The Place of Sugar in Modern History* (New York: Penguin, 1985, 30 ff.).

59 Quoted in Mimi Sheller, *Consuming the Caribbean: From Arawaks to Zombies* (London: Routledge, 2003, 1). Although British slaves were emancipated on August 1, 1834, a period of "apprenticeship" ensued, during which slaves had to be paid but could not leave their plantations. This ended in 1838.

60 C. Hall, *Civilizing Subjects*, 10.

Bibliography

Acholonu, Catherine Obianju. "The Home of Olaudah Equiano: A Linguistic and Anthropological Search." *Journal of Commonwealth Literature* 22.1 (1987): 5–16.

Adas, Michael. *Machines as the Measure of Men: Science, Technology, and Ideologies of Western Dominance.* Ithaca, NY, and London: Cornell University Press, 1989.

Afigbo, A. E. *Ropes of Sand: Studies in Igbo History and Culture.* Ibadan, Nigeria: University Press, 1981.

Agorsah, E. Kofi. "Scars of Brutality: Archaeology of the Maroons in the Caribbean." *Archaeology of Atlantic Africa and the African Diaspora*, ed. Akinwumi Ogundiran and Toyin Falola. Bloomington and Indianapolis: Indiana University Press, 2007. 332–54.

Allen, Carolyn. "Creole: The Problem of Definition." *Questioning Creole: Creolization Discourses in Caribbean Culture*, ed. Verene A. Shepherd and Glen L. Richards. Kingston, Jamaica: Ian Randle; Oxford, UK: James Currey, 2002. 47–63.

Allen, Jessica L. "Pringle's Pruning of Prince." *Callaloo* 35.2 (2012): 209–19.

Allewaert, M. "Swamp Sublime: Ecologies of Resistance in the American Plantation Zone." *PMLA* 123.2 (March 2008): 340–57.

Andrews, Malcolm, ed. *The Picturesque: Literary Sources and Documents* (3 vols.). East Sussex: Helm Information Ltd., 1994.

Andrews, Malcolm, ed. *The Search for the Picturesque.* Stanford, CA: Stanford University Press, 1989.

Andrews, William L. *To Tell a Free Story: The First Century of African-American Autobiography, 1760–1865.* Chicago: University of Illinois Press, 1986.

Anstey, Roger. *The Atlantic Slave Trade and British Abolition, 1760–1810.* Atlantic Highlands, NJ: Humanities Press, 1975.

Aparicio, Frances R., and Susana Chávez-Silverman, ed. *Tropicalizations: Transcultural Representations of Latinidad.* Hanover, NH, and London: Dartmouth College, 1997.

Aravamudan, Srinivas. *Tropicopolitans: Colonialism and Agency, 1688–1804.* Chapel Hill, NC: Duke University Press, 1999.

Arch, Stephen Carl. "Introduction." [Janet Schaw], *Journal of a Lady of Quality: Being the Narrative of a Journey from Scotland to the West Indies, North Carolina, and Portugal, in the Years 1774 to 1776*, ed. Evangeline Walker

Andrews and Charles Maclean Andrews. Lincoln and London: University of Nebraska Press, 2005. 1–18.

Armstrong, Meg. "'The Effects of Blackness': Gender, Race, and the Sublime in Aesthetic Theories of Burke and Kant." *Journal of Aesthetics and Art Criticism* 54 (1996): 213–36.

Augstein, Hannah Franziska, ed. *Race: The Origins of an Idea, 1760–1850*. Bristol: Thoemmes Press, 1996.

Bachelard, Gaston. *The Poetics of Space*. Boston: Beacon Press, 1994.

Back, Les, and John Solomos, ed. *Theories of Race and Racism: A Reader*. London and New York: Routledge, 2000.

Bailyn, Bernard. *The Peopling of British North America*. New York: Knopf, 1986.

Bailyn, Bernard. "Introduction: Reflections on Some Major Themes." *Soundings in Atlantic History: Latent Structures and Intellectual Currents, 1500–1830*, ed. Bernard Bailyn and Patricia L Denault. Cambridge, MA, and London: Harvard University Press, 2009. 1–43.

Baker, Houston. *Blues, Ideology, and Afro-American Literature: A Vernacular Theory*. Chicago: University of Chicago Press, 1984.

Bakhtin, M. M. *The Dialogic Imagination: Four Essays*. Ed. Michael Holquist, trans. Caryl Emerson and Michael Holquist. Austin: University of Texas Press, 1981.

Bammer, Angelika, ed. *Displacements: Cultural Identities in Question*. Bloomington and Indianapolis: Indiana University Press, 1994.

Bannet, Eve Tavor. "Trading Routes and Eighteenth-Century Migrations: Reframing Janet Schaw." *Recording and Reordering: Essays on the Seventeenth- and Eighteenth-Century Journal*, ed. Dan Doll and Jessica Munns. Lewisburg, PA: Bucknell University Press, 2006. 137–57.

Barker, Francis J. *The African Link: British Attitudes to the Negro in the Era of the Atlantic Slave Trade, 1550–1807*. London: Frank Cass, 1978.

Barbier, Carl Paul. *William Gilpin*. Oxford: Clarendon Press, 1963.

Barrell, John. *The Idea of Landscape and the Sense of Place, 1730–1840: An Approach to the Poetry of John Clare*. Cambridge: Cambridge University Press, 1972.

Barrell, John. *English Literature in History: An Equal, Wide Survey*. New York: St. Martin's Press, 1983.

Battersby, Christine. *The Sublime, Terror, and Human Difference*. London: Routledge, 2007.

Baucom, Ian. *Specters of the Atlantic: Finance Capital, Slavery, and the Philosophy of History*. Durham, NC: Duke University Press, 2005.

Beckford, William. *A Descriptive Account of the Island of Jamaica*. London, 1790.

Beckles, Hilary McD. *Natural Rebels: A Social History of Enslaved Black Women in Barbados*. New Brunswick, NJ: Rutgers University Press, 1989.

Bender, John. "A New History of the Enlightenment?" *Eighteenth-Century Life*, 16 (1992): 1–20.

Bender, Thomas, ed. *The Antislavery Debate: Capitalism and Abolitionism as a Problem in Historical Interpretation*. Berkeley, Los Angeles, and Oxford: University of California Press, 1992.

Benezet, Anthony. *A Short Account of that Part of Africa, Inhabited by the Negroes.* Philadelphia, 1762.

Benezet, Anthony. *Some Historical Account of Guinea.* London, 1788.

Bermingham, Ann. *Landscape and Ideology.* Berkeley: University of California Press, 1986.

Bettelheim, Judith. "Jonkonnu and Other Christmas Masquerades." *Caribbean Festival Arts,* ed. John W. Nunley and Judith Bettelheim. Seattle: University of Washington Press, 1988. 39–83.

Bewell, Alan. *Romanticism and Colonial Disease.* Baltimore, MD: Johns Hopkins University Press, 1999.

Bewell, Alan. "Romanticism and Colonial Natural History." *Studies in Romanticism* 43 (2004): 5–34.

Bindman, David. *Ape to Apollo: Aesthetics and the Idea of Race in the Eighteenth Century.* Ithaca, NY: Cornell University Press, 2002.

Blackburn, Robin. *The Overthrow of Colonial Slavery 1776–1848.* London and New York: Verso, 1988.

Blackburn, Robin. "Haiti, Slavery, and the Age of Democratic Revolution." *William and Mary Quarterly* 63:4 (2006): 643–74.

Blaut, J. M. *The Colonizer's Model of the World: Geographical Diffusion and Eurocentric History.* New York and London: Guilford Press, 1993.

Blouet, Olwyn M. "Bryan Edwards, F.R.S., 1743–1800." *Notes and Records of the Royal Society of London* 54 (2000): 215–22.

Blouet, Olwyn M. "Bryan Edwards and the Haitian Revolution." *The Impact of the Haitian Revolution in the Atlantic World,* ed. David P. Geggus. Columbia: University of South Carolina Press, 2001. 44–57.

Blunt, Alison, and Robyn Dowling. *Home.* London and New York: Routledge, 2006.

Boelhower, William. "'I'll Teach You How to Flow': On Figuring out Atlantic Studies." *Atlantic Studies* 1:1 (2004): 28–48.

Bohls, Elizabeth A. *Women Travel Writers and the Language of Aesthetics, 1716–1818.* Cambridge: Cambridge University Press, 1995.

Bohls, Elizabeth A. "The Gentleman Planter and the Metropole: Long's *History of Jamaica* (1774)." *The Country and the City Revisited: England and the Politics of Culture, 1550–1850,* ed. Gerald MacLean, Donna Landry, and Joseph P. Ward. Cambridge: Cambridge University Press, 1999. 180–96.

Bohls, Elizabeth A. *Romantic Literature and Postcolonial Studies.* Edinburgh: Edinburgh University Press, 2013.

Bolster, W. Jeffrey. *Black Jacks: African American Seamen in the Age of Sail.* Cambridge, MA, and London: Harvard University Press, 1997.

Booth, Michael R., Richard Southern, Frederick and Lise-Lone Marker, and Robertson Davies. *The Revels History of Drama in English, Volume VI: 1750–1880.* London: Methuen, 1975.

Bosman, William. *A New and Accurate Description of the Coast of Guinea.* London: Cass, 1967 (1705).

Boulukos, George. *The Grateful Slave: The Emergence of Race in Eighteenth-Century British and American Culture.* Cambridge: Cambridge University Press, 2008.

Boulukos, George. "Olaudah Equiano and the Eighteenth-Century Debate on Africa." *Eighteenth-Century Studies* 40:2 (2007): 241–55.

Bozeman, Terry S. "Interstices, Hybridity, and Identity: Olaudah Equiano and the Discourse of the African Slave Trade." *Studies in the Literary Imagination* 36 (Fall 2003): 61–70.

Brathwaite, Edward (Kamau). *The Development of Creole Society in Jamaica, 1770–1820*. Oxford: Clarendon Press, 1971.

Brown, Christopher Leslie. *Moral Capital: Foundations of British Abolitionism*. Chapel Hill: University of North Carolina Press, 2006.

Brown, Laura. *Ends of Empire: Women and Ideology in Early Eighteenth-Century English Literature*. Ithaca, NY: Cornell University Press, 1993.

Browne, Patrick. *The Civil and Natural History of Jamaica*. London, 1756.

Buck-Morss, Susan. *Hegel, Haiti and Universal History*. Pittsburgh, PA: University of Pittsburgh Press, 2009.

Bunn, David. "'Our Wattled Cot': Mercantile and Domestic Space in Thomas Pringle's African Landscape." *Landscape and Power*, ed. W. J. T. Mitchell. Chicago: University of Chicago Press, 1994. 127–73.

Burnard, Trevor. *Mastery, Tyranny, and Desire: Thomas Thistlewood and His Slaves in the Anglo-Jamaican World*. Chapel Hill: University of North Carolina Press, 2004.

Burton, Richard D. E. *Afro-Creole: Power, Opposition, and Play in the Caribbean*. Ithaca, NY: Cornell University Press, 1997.

Bush, Barbara. *Slave Women in Caribbean Society 1650–1838*. Bloomington: Indiana University Press, 1990.

Caldwell, Tanya. "'Talking Too Much English'": Languages of Economy and Politics in Equiano's *The Interesting Narrative.*" *Early American Literature* 34 (1999): 263–82.

Callan, Hillary, and Shirley Ardener, eds. *The Incorporated Wife*. London: Croom Helm, 1984.

Campbell, John F. "Textualizing Slavery: From 'Slave' to 'Enslaved People' in Caribbean Historiography." *Beyond the Blood, the Beach and the Banana*, ed. Sandra Courtman. Kingston, Jamaica, and Miami: Ian Randle, 2004. 34–45.

Campbell, Mavis. *The Maroons of Jamaica, 1655–1796: A History of Resistance, Collaboration and Betrayal*. Granby, MA: Bergin & Garvey, 1988.

Carey, Brycchan. *British Abolitionism and the Rhetoric of Sensibility: Writing, Sentiment, and Slavery, 1760–1807*. Houndmills, Basingstoke, Hampshire: Palgrave Macmillan, 2005.

Carey, Brycchan, and Peter Kitson, ed. *Slavery and the Cultures of Abolition*. Cambridge: D. S. Brewer, 2007.

Carretta, Vincent. *Equiano the African: Biography of a Self-Made Man*. Athens and London: University of Georgia Press, 2005.

Carretta, Vincent, ed. *Unchained Voices: An Anthology of Black Authors in the English-Speaking World of the Eighteenth Century*. Lexington: University Press of Kentucky, 1996.

Carrington, Selwyn H. H. *The Sugar Industry and the Abolition of the Slave Trade 1775–1810*. Gainesville: University Press of Florida, 2003.

Carter, Paul. *The Road to Botany Bay: An Essay in Spatial History*. London and Boston: Faber and Faber, 1987.

Casid, Jill. *Sowing Empire: Landscape and Colonization*. Minneapolis: University of Minnesota Press, 2005.

Chakkalakal, Tess. "I, Hereby, Vow to Read *The Interesting Narrative*." *Captivating Subjects: Writing Confinement, Citizenship and Nationhood in the Nineteenth Century*, ed. Jason Haslam and Julia M. Wright. Toronto: University of Toronto Press, 2005. 86–109.

Chaudhuri, Nupur, and Margaret Strobel, ed. *White Women and Imperialism: Complicity and Resistance*. Bloomington: Indiana University Press, 1992.

Chinosole. *African Diaspora and Autobiographics*. New York: Peter Lang, 2001.

Clark, Alice. *The Working Life of Women in the Seventeenth Century*, ed. Amy Louise Erickson. London and New York: Routledge, 1992 [1919].

Clarkson, Thomas. *An Essay on the Slavery and Commerce of the Human Species, Particularly the African*. London, 1786.

Clifford, James. *Routes: Travel and Translation in the Late Twentieth Century*. Cambridge, MA, and London: Harvard University Press, 1997.

Coetzee, J. M. *White Writing: On the Culture of Letters in South Africa*. New Haven, CT: Yale University Press, 1988.

Colbert, Benjamin. "Aesthetics of Enclosure: Agricultural Tourism and the Place of the Picturesque." *European Romantic Review* 13 (2002): 23–34.

Coleman, Deirdre. "Janet Schaw and the Complexions of Empire." *Eighteenth-Century Studies* 36 (2003): 169–93.

Coleman, Deirdre. *Romantic Colonization and British Anti-Slavery*. New York and Cambridge: Cambridge University Press, 2005.

Coleman, Deirdre. "Henry Smeathman and the Natural Economy of Slavery." *Slavery and the Cultures of Abolition: Essays Marking the Bicentennial of the British Abolition Act of 1807*, ed. Brycchan Carey and Peter J. Kitson. Cambridge: D. S. Brewer, 2007. 130–49.

Colley, Linda. *Britons: Forging the Nation 1707–1837*. New Haven, CT: Yale University Press, 1992.

Comaroff, Jean, and John Comaroff. "Home-Made Hegemony: Modernity, Domesticity, and Colonialism in South Africa." *African Encounters with Domesticity*, ed. Karen Tranberg Hansen. New Brunswick, NJ: Rutgers University Press, 1992. 37–74.

Cooper, Helen. "'Tracing the Route to England': Nineteenth-Century Caribbean Interventions into English Debates on Race and Slavery." *The Victorians and Race*, ed. Shearer West. Aldershot, Hants, UK: Scholar Press, 1996. 194–212.

Copley, Stephen, and Peter Garside, ed. *The Politics of the Picturesque*. Cambridge: Cambridge University Press, 1994.

Craton, Michael. "Changing Patterns of Slave Families in the British West Indies." *Journal of Interdisciplinary History* X (1979): 1–35.

Craton, Michael. *Searching for the Invisible Man: Slaves and Plantation Life in Jamaica.* Cambridge, MA: Harvard University Press, 1979.

Craton, Michael. *Testing the Chains: Resistance to Slavery in the British West Indies.* Ithaca, NY: Cornell University Press, 1982.

Craton, Michael. "Reluctant Creoles: The Planters' World in the British West Indies." *Strangers Within the Realm: Cultural Margins of the First British Empire*, ed. Bernard Bailyn and Philip D. Morgan. Chapel Hill: University of North Carolina Press, 1991. 314–62.

Craton, Michael. "Decoding Pitchy-Patchy: The Roots, Branches, and Essence of Junkanoo." *Slavery and Abolition* 16 (1995): 14–44.

Craton, Michael, James Walvin, and David Wright, ed. *Slavery, Abolition and Emancipation: Black Slaves and the British Empire.* London: Longman, 1976.

Cresswell, Tim. *Place: A Short Introduction.* Malden, MA: Blackwell, 2004.

Crowley, John E. "'Taken on the Spot': The Visual Appropriation of New France for the Global British Landscape." *Canadian Historical Review* 86 (2005): 1–28.

Curtin, Philip. *The Image of Africa: British Ideas and Action, 1780–1850.* Madison: University of Wisconsin Press, 1964.

Dalzel, Archibald. *The History of Dahomy, an Inland Kingdom of Africa.* London: T. Spilsbury and Son, 1793.

Davidoff, Leonore, and Catherine Hall. *Family Fortunes: Men and Women of the English Middle Class, 1780–1850.* Chicago: University of Chicago Press, 1987.

Davis, Charles T., and Henry Louis Gates Jr., ed. *The Slave's Narrative.* New York: Oxford University Press, 1985.

Davis, David Brion. *The Problem of Slavery in the Age of Revolution 1770–1823.* Ithaca, NY, and London: Cornell University Press, 1975.

Davis, David Brion. *Slavery and Human Progress.* New York and Oxford: Oxford University Press, 1984.

Davis, David Brion. *Inhuman Bondage: The Rise and Fall of Slavery in the New World.* Oxford: Oxford University Press, 2006.

Dayan, Joan. *Haiti, History, and the Gods.* Berkeley, Los Angeles, and London: University of California Press, 1998.

De Certeau, Michel, trans. Steven Rendall. *The Practice of Everyday Life.* Berkeley: University of California Press, 1984.

Devine, T. M. *Scotland's Empire and the Shaping of the Americas 1600–1815.* Washington, DC: Smithsonian Books, 2003.

Dirlik, Arif. "Place-Based Imagination: Globalism and the Politics of Place." *Places and Politics in an Age of Globalization*, ed. Arif Dirlik and Roxann Prazniak. Lanham, MD: Rowman & Littlefield, 2001. 15–51.

Douglas, Mary. *Purity and Danger.* London and New York: Routledge, 1991 [1966].

Drayton, Richard. *Nature's Government: Science, Imperial Britain, and the 'Improvement' of the World.* New Haven, CT: Yale University Press, 2000.

Drescher, Seymour. *Econocide: British Slavery in the Era of Abolition.* Chapel Hill: University of North Carolina Press, 2010.

Dubois, Laurent. *Avengers of the New World: The Story of the Haitian Revolution.* Cambridge, MA, and London: Belknap Press of Harvard University Press, 2004.

Duffy, Michael. *Soldiers, Sugar, and Seapower: The British Expeditions to the West Indies and the War Against Revolutionary France.* Oxford: Clarendon Press, 1987.

Edwards, Bryan. *A Speech Delivered at a Free Conference between the Honorable Council and Assembly of Jamaica . . . On the Subject of Mr. Wilberforce's Propositions in the House of Commons, Concerning the Slave Trade.* Kingston, Jamaica, 1789/London 1790.

Edwards, Bryan. *The History, Civil and Commercial, of the British Colonies in the West Indies: in Two Volumes.* 2nd edn. London, 1794.

Edwards, Bryan. *An Historical Survey of the French Colony in the Island of St. Domingo.* London, 1797.

Edwards, Paul. "Introduction." *The Life of Olaudah Equiano, or Gustavus Vassa, the African.* London: Dawsons of Pall Mall, 1969.

Ellis, Markman. *The Politics of Sensibility: Race, Gender and Commerce in the Sentimental Novel.* Cambridge: Cambridge University Press, 1996.

Elmer, Jonathan. "The Black Atlantic Archive." *American Literary History* 17:1 (2005): 160–70.

Elrod, Eileen Razzari. "Moses and the Egyptian: Literary Authority in Olaudah Equiano's *Interesting Narrative.*" *African American Review* 35:3 (2001): 409–25.

Engerman, Stanley L., and Barbara Solow, ed. *British Capitalism and Caribbean Slavery: The Legacy of Eric Williams.* Cambridge and New York: Cambridge University Press, 1987.

Engerman, Stanley L., and B. W. Higman. "The Demographic Structure of the Caribbean Slave Societies in the Eighteenth and Nineteenth Centuries." *UNESCO General History of the Caribbean,* ed. Franklin W. Knight, Vol. III, *The Slave Societies of the Caribbean.* 45–104. Paris, London, and Oxford: UNESCO Publishing and Macmillan Publishers Ltd., 2003, 45–104.

Equiano, Olaudah. *The Interesting Narrative and Other Writings,* ed. Vincent Carretta. New York: Penguin, 2003.

Erickson, Amy Louise. "Introduction." Alice Clark, *The Working Life of Women in the Seventeenth Century,* ed. Amy Louise Erickson. London and New York: Routledge, 1992 [1919]. vii–lv.

Escobar, Arturo. "Culture Sits in Places: Reflections on Globalism and Subaltern Strategies of Localization." *Political Geography* 20 (2001): 139–74.

Estwick, Samuel. *Considerations on the Negroe Cause Commonly So Called, Addressed to the Right Honorable Lord Mansfield, Lord Chief Justice of the Court of King's Bench &c., by a West Indian.* London, 1772.

Eze, Emmanuel Chukwudi, ed. *Race and the Enlightenment: A Reader.* Malden, MA, and Oxford, UK: Blackwell, 1997.

Felsenstein, Frank, ed. *English Trader, Indian Maid: Representing Gender, Race, and Slavery in the New World. An Inkle and Yarico Reader.* Baltimore, MD, and London: Johns Hopkins University Press, 1999.

Ferguson, Moira. *Subject to Others: British Women Writers and Colonial Slavery, 1670–1834*. New York and London: Routledge, 1992.

Ferguson, Moira. "Introduction." Mary Prince, *The History of Mary Prince, A West Indian Slave, Related by Herself*, ed. Moira Ferguson. Revised edn. Ann Arbor: University of Michigan Press, 1997.

Festa, Lynn. *Sentimental Figures of Empire in Eighteenth-Century Britain and France*. Baltimore, MD: Johns Hopkins University Press, 2006.

Fichtelberg, Joseph. *Critical Fictions: Sentiment and the American Market, 1780–1870*. Athens: University of Georgia Press, 2003.

Fick, Carolyn E. *The Making of Haiti: The Saint Domingue Revolution from Below*. Knoxville: University of Tennessee Press, 1990.

Fick, Carolyn E. "The Haitian Revolution and Citizenship: Defining Citizenship in the Revolutionary Era." *Social History* 32:4 (2007): 394–414.

Finseth, Ian Frederick. "In Essaka Once: Time and History in Olaudah Equiano's Autobiography." *Arizona Quarterly* 58 (2002): 1–35.

Fischer, Sibylle. *Modernity Disavowed: Haiti and the Cultures of Slavery in the Age of Revolution*. Durham, NC, and London: Duke University Press, 2004.

Foster, Frances Smith. *Witnessing Slavery: The Development of Antebellum Slave Narratives*. Madison: University of Wisconsin Press, 1994 (1979).

Foucault, Michel. *The Order of Things [Les Mots et les choses]*. New York: Vintage, 1994.

Fox, Christopher, Roy Porter, and Robert Wokler, ed. *Inventing Human Science: Eighteenth-Century Domains*. Berkeley: University of California Press, 1995.

Fry, Michael. *The Scottish Empire*. East Lothian and Edinburgh: Tuckwell Press and Birlinn, 2001.

Fryer, Peter. *Staying Power: A History of Black People in Britain*. London: Pluto Press, 1984.

Fulford, Tim. *Romantic Indians: Native Americans, British Literature, and Transatlantic Culture, 1756–1830*. Oxford and New York: Oxford University Press, 2006.

Fulford, Tim, and Peter J. Kitson. *Travels, Explorations and Empires: Writings from the Era of Imperial Expansion* (8 vols.). London: Pickering and Chatto, 2001.

Fulford, Tim, Peter J. Kitson, and Debbie Lee. *Literature, Science, and Exploration in the Romantic Era: Bodies of Knowledge*. Cambridge: Cambridge University Press, 2004.

Garfield, Peter. "Picturesque Figure and Landscape: Meg Merrilies and the Gypsies." *The Politics of the Picturesque*, ed. Stephen Copley and Peter Garside. Cambridge: Cambridge University Press, 1994. 145–74.

Garraway, Doris. *The Libertine Colony: Creolization in the Early French Caribbean*. Durham, NC: Duke University Press, 2005.

Gascoigne, John. *Joseph Banks and the English Enlightenment: Useful Knowledge and Polite Culture*. Cambridge: Cambridge University Press, 1994.

Gaspar, David Barry. *Bondmen and Rebels: A Study of Master–Slave Relations in Antigua with Implications for Colonial British America*. Baltimore, MD: Johns Hopkins University Press, 1985.

Gates, Henry Louis, Jr. *The Signifying Monkey: A Theory of African-American Autobiography.* New York: Oxford University Press, 1988.

Geggus, David. *Slavery, War, and Revolution: The British Occupation of Saint Domingue, 1793–1798.* Oxford: Oxford University Press, 1982.

George, Rosemary Marangoly. *The Politics of Home: Postcolonial Relocations and Twentieth-Century Fiction.* Cambridge: Cambridge University Press, 1996.

Gerzina, Gretchen Holbrook. "Mobility in Chains: Freedom of Movement in the Early Black Atlantic." *South Atlantic Quarterly* 100:1 (Winter 2001): 41–59.

Gilpin, William. *Observations on the Mountains, and Lakes of Cumberland, and Westmoreland (1786). The Picturesque: Literary Sources and Documents,* ed. Malcolm Andrews. East Sussex: Helm Information Ltd., 1994.

Gilroy, Paul. "Cultural Studies and Ethnic Absolutism." *Cultural Studies,* ed. Lawrence Grossberg, Cary Nelson, and Paula Treichler. New York: Routledge, 1992. 187–98.

Gilroy, Paul. *The Black Atlantic: Modernity and Double Consciousness.* Cambridge, MA: Harvard University Press, 1993.

Gilroy, Paul. *Against Race: Imagining Political Culture Beyond the Color Line.* Cambridge, MA: Belknap Press of the Harvard University Press, 2000.

Goldberg, David Theo. *Racist Culture: Philosophy and the Politics of Meaning.* Oxford, UK, and Cambridge, MA: Blackwell, 1993.

Goudie, Sean X. *Creole America: The West Indies and the Formation of Literature and Culture in the New Republic.* Philadelphia: University of Pennsylvania Press, 2006.

Gould, Eliga H. "Zones of Law, Zones of Violence: The Legal Geography of the British Atlantic, circa 1772." *William and Mary Quarterly, Third Series,* 60: 471–510.

Gould, Philip. *Barbaric Traffic: Commerce and Antislavery in the Eighteenth-Century Atlantic World.* Cambridge, MA, and London: Harvard University Press, 2003.

Gould, Philip, and Vincent Carretta, ed. *Genius in Bondage: Literature of the Early Black Atlantic.* Lexington: University Press of Kentucky, 2001.

Goveia, Elsa V. *A Study on the Historiography of the British West Indies to the End of the Nineteenth Century.* Washington, DC: Howard University Press, 1980.

Graham, Brian, and Catherine Nash. *Modern Historical Geographies.* Harlow, Essex, UK: Pearson Education Ltd. 2000.

Grove, Richard. *Green Imperialism: Colonial Expansion, Tropical Edens and the Origins of Environmentalism, 1600–1860.* Cambridge: Cambridge University Press, 1995.

Guha, Ranajit. "Not at Home in Empire." *Critical Inquiry* 23 (1997): 482–93.

Gunn, Geoffrey C. *First Globalization: The Eurasian Exchange, 1500–1800.* Lanham, MD: Rowman & Littlefield, 2003.

Gupta, Akhil, and James Ferguson, ed. *Culture, Power, Place: Explorations in Critical Anthropology.* Durham, NC: Duke University Press, 1997.

Gwilliam, Tassie. "'Scenes of Horror,' Scenes of Sensibility: Sentimentality and Slavery in John Gabriel Stedman's *Narrative of a Five Years' Expedition against the Revolted Negroes of Surinam.*" *ELH* 65 (1998): 653–73.

Hakewill, James. *A Picturesque Tour of the Island of Jamaica.* London, 1825. Google Books; available at http://books.google.com/books?id=oL4NAAAAQAAJ&printsec=frontcover&dq=Hakewill,+James&hl=en&ei=AMNITLroFojCsAPz-PBI&sa=X&oi=book_result&ct=result&resnum=1&ved=0CC8Q6AEwAA#v=onepage&q&f=false.

Hall, Catherine. *White, Male, and Middle-Class: Explorations in Feminism and History.* New York: Routledge, 1992.

Hall, Catherine. *Civilizing Subjects: Colony and Metropole in the English Imagination, 1830–1867.* Chicago: University of Chicago Press, 2002.

Hall, Catherine. "What Is a West Indian?" *West Indian Intellectuals in Britain*, ed. Bill Schwarz. Manchester, UK: Manchester University Press, 2003. 31–50.

Hall, Catherine, and Sonya O. Rose. "Introduction: Being at Home with the Empire." *At Home with the Empire: Metropolitan Culture and the Imperial World*, ed. Catherine Hall and Sonya O. Rose. Cambridge: Cambridge University Press, 2006. 1–31.

Hall, Douglas. *In Miserable Slavery: Thomas Thistlewood in Jamaica, 1750–1786.* London: Macmillan, 1989.

Hannaford, Ivan. *Race: The History of an Idea in the West.* Baltimore, MD, and London: Johns Hopkins University Press, 1996.

Hansen, Karen Tranberg, ed. *African Encounters with Domesticity.* New Brunswick, NJ: Rutgers University Press, 1992.

Hansen, Karen Tranberg. "Introduction: Domesticity in Africa." *African Encounters with Domesticity*, ed. Karen Tranberg Hansen. New Brunswick, NJ: Rutgers University Press, 1992. 1–33.

Harkin, Maureen. "Matthew Lewis's *Journal of a West Indian Proprietor:* Surveillance and Space on the Plantation." *Nineteenth-Century Contexts* 24 (2002): 139–50.

Harrison, Gary, and Jill Heydt-Stevenson. "Variations on the Picturesque: Authority, Play, and Practice." *European Romantic Review* 13 (2002): 3–10.

Hartman, Saidiya. *Scenes of Subjection: Terror, Slavery, and Self-Making in Nineteenth-Century America.* New York and Oxford: Oxford University Press, 1997.

Harvey, David. *The Condition of Postmodernity.* Cambridge, MA, and Oxford, UK: Blackwell Publishing, 1990.

Haywood, Ian. *Bloody Romanticism: Spectacular Violence and the Politics of Representation, 1776–1832.* Houndmills, Basingstoke, Hampshire: Palgrave Macmillan, 2006.

Heuman, Gad. "The British West Indies." Vol. III, *The Nineteenth Century*, ed. Andrew Porter. *Oxford History of the British Empire*, ed. William Roger Louis. Oxford: Oxford University Press, 1999. 470–93.

Higman, B. W. *Slave Populations of the British Caribbean 1807–1834.* Baltimore, MD: Johns Hopkins University Press, 1984.

Higman, B. W. *Plantation Jamaica 1750–1850: Capital and Control in a Colonial Economy.* Jamaica, Barbados, Trinidad, and Tobago: University of the West Indies Press, 2005.

Hinds, Elizabeth Jane Wall. "The Spirit of Trade: Equiano's Conversion, Legalism, and the Merchant's Life." *African American Review* 32 (1998): 635–47.

Hipple, W. J. *The Beautiful, the Sublime, and the Picturesque in Eighteenth-Century British Aesthetic Theory.* Carbondale: Southern Illinois University Press, 1957.

Hochschild, Adam. *Bury the Chains: Prophets and Rebels in the Fight to Free an Empire's Slaves.* Boston and New York: Houghton Mifflin Company, 2005.

Hofkosh, Sonia. "Tradition and *The Interesting Narrative*: Capitalism, Abolition, and the Romantic Individual." *Romanticism, Race, and Imperial Culture, 1780–1834,* ed. Alan Richardson and Sonia Hofkosh. Bloomington: Indiana University Press, 1996.

Holmes, Richard. *The Age of Wonder: How the Romantic Generation Discovered the Beauty and Terror of Science.* London: Harper Press, 2008.

Hoogbergen, Wim. *The Boni Maroon Wars in Suriname.* Leiden, New York, København, Köln: E. J. Brill, 1990.

hooks, bell. *Yearnings: Race, Gender, and Cultural Politics.* Boston: South End Press, 1990.

Howard, Robert Mowbray. *Records and Letters of the Family of the Longs of Longville, Jamaica, and Hampton Lodge, Surrey.* London: Simpkin, Marshall, Hamilton, Kent & Co., 1925.

Hudson, Nicholas. "From 'Nation' to 'Race': The Origin of Racial Classification in Eighteenth-Century Thought." *Eighteenth-Century Studies* 29 (1996): 247–64.

Hughes, Griffith. *Natural History of Barbados.* New York: Arno Press, 1972 [1750].

Hulme, Peter. *Colonial Encounters: Europe and the Native Caribbean 1492–1797.* London and New York: Routledge, 1986.

Hulme, Peter, and Ludmilla Jordanova, ed. *The Enlightenment and Its Shadows.* London: Routledge, 1990.

Hulme, Peter, and Neil L. Whitehead, ed. *Wild Majesty: Encounters with Caribs from Columbus to the Present Day.* Oxford: Clarendon Press, 1992.

Hunt, Margaret. *The Middling Sort: Commerce, Gender, and the Family in Eighteenth-Century England.* Berkeley: University of California Press, 1996.

Hussey, Christopher. *The Picturesque: Studies in a Point of View.* London: Frank Cass, 1927.

Iannini, Christopher P. *Fatal Revolutions: Natural History, West Indian Slavery, and the Routes of American Literature.* Chapel Hill: University of North Carolina Press, 2012.

Inikori, Joseph E. *Africans and the Industrial Revolution in England: A Study in International Trade and Development.* Cambridge: Cambridge University Press, 2002.

Innes, C. L. *A History of Black and Asian Writing in Britain, 1700–2000.* Cambridge: Cambridge University Press, 2002.

James, C. L. R. *The Black Jacobins: Toussaint L'Ouverture and the San Domingo Revolution.* 2nd edn. New York: Vintage Books, 1989 [1963].

Janowitz, Anne. "'Wild Outcasts of Society': The Transit of the Gypsies in Romantic Period Poetry." *The Country and the City Revisited: England and the Politics of Culture, 1550–1850*, ed. Gerald MacLean, Donna Landry, and Joseph P. Ward. Cambridge: Cambridge University Press, 1999. 213–30.

Jardine, N., J. A. Secord, and E. C. Spary, ed. *Cultures of Natural History.* Cambridge: Cambridge University Press, 1996.

Jordan, Winthrop. *White Over Black: American Attitudes Toward the Negro, 1550–1812.* Chapel Hill: University of North Carolina Press, 1968.

Kaplan, Amy. *The Anarchy of Empire in the Making of U.S. Culture.* Cambridge, MA: Harvard University Press, 2002.

Kaplan, Caren. "Deterritorializations: The Rewriting of Home and Exile in Western Feminist Discourse." *Cultural Critique* 6 (1987): 187–98.

Kaplan, Caren, and Inderpal Grewal, ed. *Scattered Hegemonies: Postmodernity and Transnational Feminist Practices.* Minneapolis: University of Minnesota Press, 1994.

Kaul, Suvir. *Poems of Nation, Anthems of Empire: English Verse in the Long Eighteenth Century.* Charlottesville and London: University of Virginia Press, 2000.

Kaul, Suvir. *Eighteenth-Century Literature and Postcolonial Studies.* Edinburgh: Edinburgh University Press, 2009.

Kelleter, Frank. "Ethnic Self-Dramatization and Technologies of Travel in *The Interesting Narrative* of Olaudah Equiano (1789)." *Early American Literature* 39 (2004): 67–84.

Kincaid, Jamaica. *A Small Place.* New York: Penguin, 1988.

Kitson, Peter J. *Romantic Literature, Race, and Colonial Encounter.* Houndmills, Basingstoke, Hampshire: Palgrave Macmillan, 2007.

Kitson, Peter J. "Introduction," Vol. 8, *Theories of Race. Slavery, Abolition and Emancipation: Writings in the British Romantic Period*, ed. Peter J. Kitson and Debbie Lee. London: Pickering and Chatto, 1999. vii–xxvi.

Kitson, Peter J., and Debbie Lee, ed. *Slavery, Abolition and Emancipation: Writings in the British Romantic Period* (8 vols.). London: Pickering & Chatto, 1999.

Klarer, Mario. "Humanitarian Pornography: John Gabriel Stedman's *Narrative of a Five Years' Expedition Against the Revolted Negroes of Surinam* (1796)." *New Literary History* 36 (2005): 559–87.

Knight, Franklin, ed. *UNESCO General History of the Caribbean.* Vol. III: *The Slave Societies of the Caribbean.* London and Basingstoke: UNESCO Publishing, 1997.

Knight, Franklin, "Pluralism, Creolization and Culture." *UNESCO General History of the Caribbean.* Vol. III: *The Slave Societies of the Caribbean.* London and Basingstoke: UNESCO Publishing, 1997. 271–86.

Kriz, Kay Dian. "Curiosities, Commodities and Transported Bodies in Hans Sloane's Voyage to . . . Jamaica." *An Economy of Color: Visual Culture and the*

Atlantic World, 1660–1830, ed. Geoff Quilley and Kay Dian Kriz. Manchester: Manchester University Press, 2003. 85–106.

Kriz, Kay Dian. *Slavery, Sugar, and the Culture of Refinement: Picturing the British West Indies, 1700–1840*. New Haven, CT, and London: Yale University Press, 2008.

Lamb, Jonathan. *Preserving the Self in the South Seas 1680–1840*. Chicago and London: University of Chicago Press, 2001.

Lambert, David. *White Creole Culture, Politics and Identity During the Age of Abolition*. Cambridge: Cambridge University Press, 2005.

Lambert, David. "'Taken Captive by the Mystery of the Great River': Towards an Historical Geography of British Geography and Atlantic Slavery." *Journal of Historical Geography* 35 (2009): 44–65.

Laqueur, Thomas. "Bodies, Details, and the Humanitarian Narrative." *The New Cultural History*, ed. Lynn Hunt. Berkeley, Los Angeles, and London: University of California Press, 1989. 176–204.

Laqueur, Thomas. *Making Sex: Body and Gender from the Greeks to Freud*. Cambridge, MA, and London: Harvard University Press, 1990.

Latour, Bruno. *Science in Action: How to Follow Scientists and Engineers Through Society*. Cambridge, MA: Harvard University Press, 1987.

Lavie, Smadar, and Ted Swedenburg, ed. *Displacement, Diaspora, and Geographies of Identity*. Durham, NC: Duke University Press, 1996.

Leask, Nigel. *Curiosity and the Aesthetics of Travel Writing, 1770–1840*. Oxford: Oxford University Press, 2002.

Lee, Debbie. *Slavery and the Romantic Imagination*. Philadelphia: University of Pennsylvania Press, 2002.

Lester, Alan. *Imperial Networks: Creating Identities in Nineteenth-Century South Africa and Britain*. London and New York: Routledge, 2001.

Lewis, Mathew Gregory. *Journal of a West India Proprietor*, ed. Judith Terry. Oxford: Oxford World's Classics, 1999.

Ligon, Richard. *A True & Exact History of the Island of Barbadoes*. London: Frank Cass & Co., Ltd., 1970 (1657).

Linebaugh, Peter, and Marcus Rediker. *The Many-Headed Hydra: Sailors, Slaves, Commoners, and the Hidden History of the Revolutionary Atlantic*. Boston: Beacon Press, 2000.

Liu, Alan. *Wordsworth: The Sense of History*. Stanford, CA: Stanford University Press, 1989.

Livingstone, David N., and Charles W. J. Withers, ed. *Geography and Enlightenment*. Chicago: University of Chicago Press, 1999.

Lloyd, David. "The Pathological Sublime: Pleasure and Pain in the Colonial Context." *Postcolonial Enlightenment*, ed. Brycchan Carey and Lynn Festa. Oxford: Oxford University Press, 2009. 71–102.

Long, Edward. *Candid Reflections upon the Judgment Lately Awarded by the Court of King's Bench, in Westminster-Hall, on What Is Commonly Called the Negroe-Cause*. London, 1772.

Long, Edward. *The History of Jamaica*. 3 Vols. London, 1774.

Loomba, Ania, and Jonathan Burton, ed. *Race in Early Modern England: A Documentary Companion*. Houndmills, Basingstoke, Hampshire: Palgrave Macmillan, 2007.

Lovejoy, Paul E. "Autobiography and Memory: Gustavus Vassa, alias Olaudah Equiano, the African." *Slavery and Abolition* 27 (2005): 317–47.

Mack, Douglas. *Scottish Fiction and the British Empire*. Edinburgh: Edinburgh University Press, 2006.

MacQueen, James. "The Colonial Empire of Great Britain. Letter to Earl Grey." *Blackwood's Edinburgh Magazine* CLXXXVI (November 1831): 744–64.

Malchow, H. L. *Gothic Images of Race in Nineteenth-Century Britain*. Stanford, CA: Stanford University Press, 1996.

Mani, Lata. *Contentious Traditions: The Debate on Sati in Colonial India*. Berkeley: University of California Press, 1998.

Manwaring, Elizabeth Wheeler. *Italian Landscape in Eighteenth-Century England*. New York: Oxford University Press, 1925.

Marren, Susan M. "Between Slavery and Freedom: The Transgressive Self in Olaudah Equiano's Autobiography." *PMLA* 108 (1993): 94–105.

Marshall, P. J., and Glyndwr Williams. *The Great Map of Mankind: Perceptions of New Worlds in the Age of Enlightenment*. Cambridge, MA: Harvard University Press, 1982.

Martin, Biddy, and Chandra Talpade Mohanty. "Feminist Politics: What's Home Got to Do with It?" *Feminist Studies/Critical Studies*, ed. Teresa de Lauretis. Bloomington: Indiana University Press, 1986. 191–212.

Massey, Doreen. *Space, Place, and Gender*. Minneapolis: University of Minnesota Press, 1994.

Matthews, Gelien. *Caribbean Slave Revolts and the British Abolitionist Movement*. Baton Rouge: Louisiana State University Press, 2006.

Matthews, John. *A Voyage to the River Sierra-Leone*. London: Frank Cass, 1966 (1788).

Maurer, Shawn Lisa. *Proposing Men: Dialectics of Gender and Class in the Eighteenth-Century English Periodical*. Stanford, CA: Stanford University Press, 1998.

McBride, Dwight A. *Impossible Witnesses: Truth, Abolition, and Slave Testimony*. New York: New York University Press, 2001.

McClintock, Anne. "'No Longer in a Future Heaven': Gender, Race, and Nationalism." *Dangerous Liaisons: Gender, Nation, & Postcolonial Perspectives*, ed. Anne McClintock, Aamir Mufti, and Ella Shohat. Minneapolis and London: University of Minnesota Press, 1997. 89–112.

McClintock, Anne. *Imperial Leather: Race, Gender, and Sexuality in the Colonial Contest*. New York and London: Routledge, 1995.

McDowell, Linda. *Gender, Identity, and Place: Understanding Feminist Geographies*. Cambridge: Polity Press, 1999.

McEwan, Cheryl. "Material Geographies and Postcolonialism." *Singapore Journal of Tropical Geography* 24 (2003): 340–55.

Melman, Billie. *Women's Orients: English Women and the Middle East, 1718–1918*. Ann Arbor: University of Michigan Press, 1992.

Mendyk, Stan A. E. *"Speculum Britanniae": Regional Study, Antiquarianism, and Science in Britain to 1700.* Toronto: University of Toronto Press, 1989.

Michasiw, Kim Ian. "Nine Revisionist Theses on the Picturesque." *Representations* 38 (1992): 76–100.

Midgley, Clare. *Women Against Slavery: The British Campaigns, 1780–1870.* London: Routledge, 1992.

Mills, Sara. *Discourses of Difference: An Analysis of Women's Travel Writing and Colonialism.* London and New York: Routledge, 1991.

Mills, Sara. *Discourse.* London and New York: Routledge, 1997.

Mintz, Sidney. *Sweetness and Power: The Place of Sugar in Modern History.* New York: Penguin, 1985.

Mintz, Sidney, and Richard Price. *The Birth of African-American Culture: An Anthropological Perspective.* Boston: Beacon Press, 1992.

Mitchell, W. J. T. "Imperial Landscape." *Landscape and Power,* ed. W. J. T. Mitchell. Chicago and London: University of Chicago Press, 1994. 5–34.

Morrissey, Marietta. *Slave Women in the New World: Gender Stratification in the Caribbean.* Lawrence: University Press of Kansas, 1989.

Morton, Tim. *The Poetics of Spice.* Cambridge: Cambridge University Press, 2000.

Mottolese, William. "'Almost an Englishman': Olaudah Equiano and the Colonial Gift of Language." *Bucknell Review* 41 (1988): 160–71.

Murphy, Geraldine. "Olaudah Equiano, Accidental Tourist." *Eighteenth-Century Studies* 27(1994): 551–68.

Nash, Catherine. "Historical Geographies of Modernity." *Modern Historical Geographies,* ed. Brian Graham and Catherine Nash. Edinburgh Gate, Harlow, Essex: Pearson Education Limited, 2000. 13–40.

Needham, Lawrence. "'Goody Two-Shoes'/'Goosee Shoo-Shoo': Translated Tales of Resistance in Matthew Lewis's Journal of a West India Proprietor." *Between Languages and Cultures: Translation and Cross-Cultural Texts,* ed. Anuradha Dingwaney and Carol Maier. Pittsburgh, PA: University of Pittsburgh Press, 1995. 103–18.

Nelson, E. Charles. "Patrick Browne (ca. 1720–1790), Irish Physician, Historian, and Caribbean Botanist: A Brief Biography with an Account of his Lost Medical Dissertations." *Huntia* 11 (2000): 5–16.

Nicholls, David. *From Dessalines to Duvalier: Race, Color, and National Independence.* Cambridge and New York: Cambridge University Press, 1979.

Norris, Robert. *Memoirs of Bossa Ahadee, King of Dahomey.* London, 1789.

Nugent, Maria. *Lady Nugent's Journal of her Residence in Jamaica from 1801 to 1805,* ed. Philip Wright. Revised edn. Kingston, Jamaica: Institute of Jamaica, 1968.

Nussbaum, Felicity A. *Torrid Zones: Maternity, Sexuality, and Empire in Eighteenth-Century English Narratives.* Baltimore, MD: Johns Hopkins University Press, 1995.

Nussbaum, Felicity A. "Introduction." *The Global Eighteenth Century,* ed. Felicity A. Nussbaum. Baltimore, MD, and London: Johns Hopkins University Press, 2003. 1–18.

Nussbaum, Felicity A. *The Limits of the Human: Fictions of Anomaly, Race, and Gender in the Long Eighteenth Century*. Cambridge: Cambridge University Press, 2003.

O'Brien, Karen. "Imperial Georgic, 1660–1789." *The Country and the City Revisited: England and the Politics of Culture, 1550–1850*, ed. Gerald MacLean, Donna Landry, and Joseph P. Ward. Cambridge: Cambridge University Press, 1999. 160–79.

Ogborn, Miles. "Historical Geographies of Globalization, c. 1500–1800." *Modern Historical Geographies*, ed. Brian Graham and Catherine Nash. Harlow, Essex, UK: Pearson Education Limited, 2000. 43–69.

Ogborn, Miles. *Spaces of Modernity: London's Geographies 1680–1780*. New York and London: The Guilford Press, 1998.

Ogude, S. E. "Facts into Fiction: Equiano's Narrative Reconsidered." *Research in African Literatures* 13 (1982): 31–43.

Okafor, Clement A. *"The Interesting Narrative of the Life of Olaudah Equiano*: A Triple-Tiered Transatlantic Testimony." *The Literary Griot* 14 (2002): 160–83.

Orban, Katalin. "Dominant and Submerged Discourses in *The Life of Olaudah Equiano* (or Gustavus Vassa?)." *African American Review* 27 (1993): 655–64.

Ortiz, Fernando. *Cuban Counterpoint: Tobacco and Sugar*. Durham, NC, and London: Duke University Press, 1995 (1947).

Outram, Dorinda. *The Enlightenment*. Cambridge: Cambridge University Press, 1995.

Pagden, Anthony. *European Encounters with the New World: From Renaissance to Romanticism*. New Haven, CT, and London: Yale University Press, 1993.

Paquet, Sandra Pouchet. "The Heartbeat of a West Indian Slave: The History of Mary Prince." *African American Review* 26 (1992): 131–46.

Pares, Richard. "Merchants and Planters." *Economic History Review Supplement No. 4*, 1960.

Pares, Richard. *A West-India Fortune*. London: Longmans, Green & Co., 1950.

Parrish, Susan Scott. *American Curiosity: Cultures of Natural History in the Colonial British Atlantic World*. Chapel Hill: University of North Carolina Press, 2006.

Paton, Diana. "Decency, Dependency, and the Lash: Gender and the British Debate Over Slave Emancipation, 1830–1834." *Slavery and Abolition* 17 (1996): 163–84.

Patterson, Orlando. *The Sociology of Slavery*. Rutherford, NJ: Fairleigh Dickinson University Press, 1967.

Patterson, Orlando. *Slavery and Social Death: A Comparative Study*. Cambridge, MA: Harvard University Press, 1982.

Paulson, Ronald. *Representations of Revolution, 1789–1820*. New Haven, CT: Yale University Press, 1983.

Peck, Louis F. *A Life of Matthew G. Lewis*. Cambridge, MA: Harvard University Press, 1961.

Perelman, Chaim, and L. Olbrechts-Tyteca. *The New Rhetoric: A Treatise on Argumentation*. Trans. John Wilkinson and Purcell Weaver. Notre Dame, IN: University of Notre Dame Press, 1969.

Peters, John Durham. "Seeing Bifocally: Media, Place, Culture." *Culture, Power, Place: Explorations in Critical Anthropology*, ed. Akhil Gupta and James Ferguson. Durham, NC, and London: Duke University Press, 1997. 75–92.

Potkay, Adam. "Olaudah Equiano and the Art of Spiritual Autobiography." *Eighteenth-Century Studies* 27 (1994): 677–92.

Powell, Cecilia. *Turner in the South: Rome, Naples, Florence*. New Haven, CT: Yale University Press, 1987.

Powell, Cecilia. "Topography, Imagination, and Travel: Turner's Relationship with James Hakewill." *Art History* 5 (1982): 408–25.

Pratt, Mary Louise. *Imperial Eyes: Travel Writing and Transculturation*. New York and London: Routledge, 1993.

Price, Richard. *First-Time: The Historical Vision of an Afro-American People*. Baltimore, MD: Johns Hopkins University Press, 1983.

Price, Richard, ed. *Maroon Societies: Rebel Slave Communities in the Americas*, 3rd edn. Baltimore, MD: Johns Hopkins University Press, 1996 (1979).

Price, Richard, and Sally Price. "Introduction." *Narrative of a Five Years' Expedition against the Revolted Negroes of Suriname in Guiana on the Wild Coast of South-America from the Year 1772 to the Year 1777*, ed. Richard Price and Sally Price. Baltimore, MD, and London: Johns Hopkins University Press, 1988.

Price, Richard, and Sally Price. "John Gabriel Stedman's Collection of Eighteenth-Century Artifacts from Suriname." *Nieuwe West-Indische Gids* 53 (1979): 121–40.

Price, Uvedale. "A Dialogue on the Picturesque and the Beautiful." *The Picturesque: Literary Sources and Documents* (3 vols.), ed. Malcolm Andrews. East Sussex: Helm Information Ltd., 1994. 231–64.

Prince, Mary. *The History of Mary Prince, A West Indian Slave, Related by Herself.* Ed. Moira Ferguson. Revised edn. Ann Arbor: University of Michigan Press, 1997 [1831].

Pudaloff, Ross J. "No Change Without Purchase: Olaudah Equiano and the Economies of Self and Market." *Early American Literature* 40 (2005): 499–527.

Pugh, Simon. "Introduction." *Reading Landscape: Country – City – Capital*, ed. Simon Pugh. Manchester: Manchester University Press, 1990.

Quilley, Geoff. "Pastoral Plantations: The Slave Trade and the Representations of British Colonial Landscape in the Late Eighteenth Century." *An Economy of Color: Visual Culture and the Atlantic World, 1660–1830*, ed. Geoff Quilley and Kay Dian Kriz. Manchester: Manchester University Press, 2003. 106–28.

Quilley, Geoff, and Kay Dian Kriz, ed. *An Economy of Color: Visual Culture and the Atlantic World, 1660–1830*. Manchester: Manchester University Press, 2003.

Rainsford, Marcus. *An Historical Account of the Black Empire of Hayti*, ed. Paul Youngquist and Grégory Pierrot. Durham, NC: Duke University Press, 2013 [1805].

Raj, Kapil. *Relocating Modern Science: Circulation and the Construction of Knowledge in South Asia and Europe, 1650–1900*. Houndmills, Basingstoke, Hampshire: Palgrave Macmillan, 2007.

Rauwerda, A. M. "Naming, Agency, and 'A Tissue of Falsehoods' in *The History of Mary Prince.*" *Victorian Literature and Culture* 29 (2001): 397–411.

Rediker, Marcus. *Between the Devil and the Deep Blue Sea: Merchant Seamen, Pirates, and the Anglo-American Maritime World, 1700–1750.* Cambridge: Cambridge University Press, 1987.

Rice, Alan. *Radical Narratives of the Black Atlantic.* London and New York: Continuum, 2003.

Roach, Joseph. *Cities of the Dead: Circum-Atlantic Performance.* New York: Columbia University Press, 1996.

Robertson, Clare. "Africa into the Americas? Slavery and Women, the Family, and the Gender Division of Labor." *More Than Chattel: Black Women and Slavery in the Americas*, ed. David Barry Gaspar and Darlene Clark Hine. Bloomington: Indiana University Press, 1996.

Robertson, William. *History of America.* London, 1778.

Rosaldo, Michelle Zimbalist. "The Use and Abuse of Anthropology: Reflections on Feminism and Cross-Cultural Understanding." *Signs* 5 (1980): 389–417.

Rust, Marion. "The Subaltern as Imperialist: Speaking of Olaudah Equiano." *Passing and the Fictions of Identity*, ed. Elaine K. Ginsberg. Durham, NC, and London: Duke University Press, 1996. 21–36.

Ryan, Simon. "Exploring Aesthetics: The Picturesque Appropriation of Land in Journals of Australian Exploration." *Australian Literary Studies* 15: 4 (1992), 282–93.

Rybczinski, Witold. *Home: A Short History of an Idea.* New York: Viking, 1986.

Sabino, Robin, and Jennifer Hall. "The Path Not Taken: Cultural Identity in the Interesting Life of Olaudah Equiano." *Multi-Ethnic Literature of the United States* 24 (1999): 5–19.

Said, Edward. *Culture and Imperialism.* New York: Alfred A. Knopf, 1993.

Salih, Sarah. "Introduction." *The History of Mary Prince, a West Indian Slave, Related by Herself,* ed. Sarah Salih. New York: Penguin, 2000 [1831].

Salih, Sarah. "Putting Down Rebellion: Witnessing the Body of the Condemned in Abolition-Era Narratives." *Slavery and the Cultures of Abolition*, ed. Brycchan Carey and Peter Kitson. Cambridge: D. S. Brewer, 2007. 64–86.

Sandiford, Keith. *The Cultural Politics of Sugar: Caribbean Slavery and Narratives of Colonialism.* Cambridge: Cambridge University Press, 2000.

Schama, Simon. *Rough Crossings: Britain, the Slaves, and the American Revolution.* London: BBC, 2005.

[Schaw, Janet.] *Journal of a Lady of Quality: Being the Narrative of a Journey from Scotland to the West Indies, North Carolina, and Portugal, in the Years 1774 to 1776,* ed. Evangeline Walker Andrews and Charles Maclean Andrews. Introduction by Stephen Carl Arch. Lincoln and London: University of Nebraska Press, 2005.

Schiebinger, Londa. *Nature's Body: Gender in the Making of Modern Science.* Boston: Beacon Press, 1993.

Schiebinger, Londa. "Nature's Unruly Body: The Limits of Scientific Description." *Regimes of Description in the Archive of the Eighteenth Century*, ed. John Bender and Michael Marrinan. Stanford, CA: Stanford University Press, 2005. 25–43.

Schiebinger, Londa, and Claudia Swan, ed. *Colonial Botany: Science, Commerce, and Politics in the Early Modern World*. Philadelphia: University of Pennsylvania Press, 2005.

Schoolman, Martha, and Jared Hickman, ed. *Abolitionist Places*. London and New York: Routledge, 2013.

Scott, Lynn Orilla. "Autobiography: Slave Narratives." *The Oxford Encyclopedia of American Literature*, ed. Jay Parini. Oxford African American Studies Center, available at www.oxfordaasc.com/article/opr/t197/e0019 (accessed July 9, 2010).

Sekora, John. *Luxury: The Concept in Western Thought, Eden to Smollett*. Baltimore, MD: Johns Hopkins University Press, 1977.

Senior, Emily. "'Perfectly Whole': Skin and Text in John Gabriel Stedman's *Narrative of a Five Years' Expedition Against the Revolted Negroes of Suriname*." *Eighteenth-Century Studies* 44 (2010): 39–56.

Seymour, Susanne, Stephen Daniels, and Charles Watkins. "Estate and Empire: Sir George Cornewall's Management of Moccas, Herefordshire and La Taste, Grenada, 1771–1819." *Journal of Historical Geography* 24: 3 (1998), 313–51.

Sharpe, Jenny. *Allegories of Empire: The Figure of Woman in the Colonial Text*. Minneapolis: University of Minnesota Press, 1993.

Sharpe, Jenny. "'Something Akin to Freedom': The Case of Mary Prince." *Differences: A Journal of Feminist Cultural Studies* 8 (1996): 31–56.

Sharpe, Jenny. *Ghosts of Slavery: A Literary Archaeology of Black Women's Lives*. Minneapolis: University of Minnesota Press, 2003.

Sheller, Mimi. *Consuming the Caribbean: From Arawaks to Zombies*. London: Routledge, 2003.

Shepherd, Verene A., and Glen L. Richards, ed. *Questioning Creole: Creolization Discourses in Caribbean Culture*. Kingston, Jamaica: Ian Randle; Oxford, UK: James Currey, 2002.

Sheridan, Richard B. "Planter and Historian: The Career of William Beckford of Jamaica and England, 1744–1799." *Jamaican Historical Review* Vol. III, No. 1 (March 1957): 36–58.

Sheridan, Richard B. *Sugar and Slavery: The Economic History of the British West Indies, 1623–1775*. Barbados, Jamaica, Trinidad, and Tobago: Canoe Press, 1994 [1974].

Sheridan, Richard B. *Doctors and Slaves: A Medical and Demographic History of Slavery in the British West Indies, 1680–1834*. Cambridge: Cambridge University Press, 1985.

Sherlock, Philip, and Hazel Bennett. *The Story of the Jamaican People*. Kingston, Jamaica: Ian Randle Publishers, 1998.

Shyllon, F. O. *Black Slaves in Britain*. London: Oxford University Press, 1974.

Sinanan, Kerry. "The Slave Narrative and the Literature of Abolition." *The Cambridge Companion to the African-American Slave Narrative*, ed. Audrey A. Fisch. Cambridge: Cambridge University Press, 2007. 61–80.

Sloan, Phillip. "The Gaze of Natural History." *Inventing Human Science: Eighteenth-Century Domains*, ed. Christopher Fox, Roy Porter, and Robert Wokler. Berkeley: University of California Press, 1995. 112–51.

Sloane, Hans. *A Voyage to the Islands Madera, Barbados, Nieves, S. Christophers, and JAMAICA, with the Natural History of the Herbs and Trees, Four-Footed Beasts, Fishes, Birds, Insects, Reptiles etc. of the Last of those Islands*. London, 1707, 1725.

Smail, John. *The Origins of Middle-Class Culture: Halifax, Yorkshire, 1660–1780*. Ithaca, NY: Cornell University Press, 1994.

Smith, Adam. *The Theory of Moral Sentiments*. Ed. D. D. Raphael and A. L. Macfie. Indianapolis, IN: Liberty Classics, 1976 [1759].

Smith, Bernard. *European Vision and the South Pacific*. 2nd edn. New Haven, CT: Yale University Press, 1985 (1960).

Smith, Neil, and Cindi Katz. "Grounding Metaphor: Towards a Spatialized Politics." *Place and the Politics of Identity*. Ed. Michael Keith and Steve Pile. London: Routledge, 1993. 67–83.

Smith, Simon D. "*Merchants and Planters* Revisited." *Economic History Review* LV.3 (2002): 434–65.

Smith, William. *Natural History of Nevis and the Rest of the English Leeward Charibee Islands in America*. London, 1745.

Snelgrave, William. *A New Account of Some Parts of Guinea and the Slave Trade*. London, 1734; 2nd edn., 1754.

Sollors, Werner. "Introduction." *The Interesting Narrative of the Life of Olaudah Equiano, or Gustavus Vassa, the African, Written by Himself*. New York and London: W. W. Norton & Co., 2001. ix–xxxi.

Spary, Emma. "Political, Natural, and Bodily Economies." *Cultures of Natural History*, ed. Jardine et al. Cambridge: Cambridge University Press, 1996. 178–96.

Speitz, Michelle. "Blood Sugar and Salt Licks: Corroding Bodies and Preserving Nations" in *The History of Mary Prince, A West Indian Slave, Related by Herself." Circulations: Romanticism and the Black Atlantic*, ed. Paul Youngquist and Frances Botkin. 2011. Accessed August 14, 2013. Available at www.rc.umd.edu/praxis/circulations/index.html.

Spivak, Gayatri Chakravorty. "Can the Subaltern Speak?" *Marxism and the Interpretation of Culture*, ed. Cary Nelson and Lawrence Grossberg. Urbana: University of Illinois Press, 1988.

Spurr, David. *The Rhetoric of Empire: Colonial Discourse in Journalism, Travel Writing, and Imperial Administration*. Durham, NC, and London: Duke University Press, 1993.

Stanfield, James Field. *Observations on a Voyage to the Coast of Africa, in a Series of Letters to Thomas Clarkson, by James Field Stanfield, Formerly a Mariner in the African Trade*. London, 1788.

Stedman, John Gabriel. *Narrative of a Five Years' Expedition against the Revolted Negroes of Suriname in Guiana on the Wild Coast of South-America from the Year 1772 to the Year 1777*, ed. Richard Price and Sally Price. Baltimore, MD, and London: Johns Hopkins University Press, 1988.

Stedman, John Gabriel. *Journal of John Gabriel Stedman*, ed. Stanbury Thompson. London: The Mitre Press, 1962.

Stein, Mark. "Who's Afraid of Cannibals? Some Uses of the Cannibalism Trope in Olaudah Equiano's *Interesting Narrative.*" *Discourses of Slavery and Abolition: Britain and Its Colonies, 1760–1838*, ed. Brycchan Carey, Markman Elllis, and Sarah Salih. Houndmills, Basingstoke, Hampshire (UK): Palgrave Macmillan, 2004. 96–107.

Stepan, Nancy. *The Idea of Race in Science: Great Britain 1800–1960*. Hamden, CT: Archon Books, 1982.

Stephen, James. *The Slavery of the British West India Colonies Delineated*, Vol. 1. London, 1824.

Stewart, John. *An Account of Jamaica*. Freeport, NY: Books for Libraries Press, 1971.

Stoddart, David. *On Geography and its History*. Oxford: Basil Blackwell, 1985.

Stoler, Ann Laura. "Making Empire Respectable: The Politics of Race and Sexual Morality in Twentieth-Century Colonial Cultures." *Dangerous Liaisons: Gender, Nation, and Postcolonial Perspectives*, ed. Anne McClintock, Aamir Mufti, and Ella Shohat. Minneapolis: University of Minnesota Press, 1997. 344–73.

Suleri, Sara. *The Rhetoric of English India*. Chicago: University of Chicago Press, 1992.

Sussman, Charlotte. *Consuming Anxieties: Consumer Protest, Gender and British Slavery, 1713–1833*. Stanford, CA: Stanford University Press, 2000.

Terry, Judith. "Introduction" to Matthew Lewis, *Journal of a West India Proprietor*. Oxford: Oxford University Press, 1999. ix–xxxiv.

Thomas, Helen. *Romanticism and Slave Narratives*. Cambridge: Cambridge University Press, 2000.

Thomas, Hugh. *The Slave Trade: The Story of the Atlantic Slave Trade, 1440–1870*. New York: Simon & Schuster, 1997.

Thomas, Nicholas. *Colonialism's Culture: Anthropology, Travel and Government*. Princeton, NJ: Princeton University Press, 1994.

Thompson, Alvin O. *Flight to Freedom: African Runaways and Maroons in the Americas*. Jamaica, Barbados, Trinidad, and Tobago: University of the West Indies Press, 2006.

Thomson, James. *The Seasons*, ed. James Sambrook. Oxford: Clarendon Press, 1987.

Thornton, John. *Africa and Africans in the Making of the Atlantic World, 1400–1800*, 2nd edn. Cambridge: Cambridge University Press, 1998 (1992).

Tobin, Beth Fowkes. *Colonizing Nature: The Tropics in British Arts and Letters 1760–1820*. Philadelphia: University of Pennsylvania Press, 2005.

Tobin, Beth Fowkes. *Picturing Imperial Power: Colonial Subjects in Eighteenth-Century British Painting*. Durham, NC: Duke University Press, 1999.

Trouillot, Michel-Rolph. *Silencing the Past: Power and the Production of History*. Boston: Beacon Press, 1995.

Trumpener, Katie. "The Time of the Gypsies: A 'People Without History' in the Narratives of the West." *Critical Inquiry* 18 (1992): 843–84.

Turner, Mary. *Slaves and Missionaries: The Disintegration of Jamaican Slave Society, 1787–1834*. Urbana: University of Illinois Press, 1982.

Vickery, Amanda. "Golden Age to Separate Spheres? A Review of the Categories and Chronology of English Women's History." *Historical Journal* 36 (1993): 383–414.

Vickery, Amanda. *The Gentleman's Daughter: Women's Lives in Georgian England*. New Haven, CT, and London: Yale University Press, 1998.

Wahrman, Dror. *The Making of the Modern Self: Identity and Culture in Eighteenth-Century England*. New Haven, CT: Yale University Press, 2004.

Walvin, James. *Black Ivory: A History of British Slavery*. Washington, DC: Howard University Press, 1994.

Ward, J. R. *British West Indian Slavery 1750–1834: The Process of Amelioration*. Oxford: Clarendon Press, 1988.

Ward, J. R. "The British West Indies in the Age of Abolition, 1748–1815." Volume II, *The Eighteenth Century*, ed. P. J. Marshall. 415–39. *Oxford History of the British Empire*, ed. William Roger Louis. Oxford: Oxford University Press, 1999.

Watts, David. *The West Indies: Patterns of Development, Culture and Environmental Change since 1492*. Cambridge: Cambridge University Press, 1987.

Wheeler, Roxann. *The Complexion of Race: Categories of Difference in Eighteenth-Century British Culture*. Philadelphia: University of Pennsylvania Press, 2000.

Whitaker, Katie. "The Culture of Curiosity." *Cultures of Natural History*, ed. Jardine et al. Cambridge: Cambridge University Press, 1996. 75–90.

Whitlock, Gillian. "Volatile Subjects: *The History of Mary Prince.*" *Genius in Bondage: Literature of the Early Black Atlantic*, ed. Vincent Carretta and Philip Gould. Lexington: University Press of Kentucky, 2001. 72–86.

Wilberforce, William. *An Appeal to the Religion, Justice, and Humanity of the Inhabitants of the British Empire, in Behalf of the Negro Slaves of the West Indies*. London, 1823.

Wiley, Michael. "Consuming Africa: Geography and Identity in Olaudah Equiano's *Interesting Narrative.*" *Studies in Romanticism* 44 (2005): 165–79.

Williams, Carolyn D. *Pope, Homer, and Manliness: Some Aspects of Eighteenth-Century Classical Learning*. London: Routledge, 1993.

Williams, Eric. *Capitalism and Slavery*. Chapel Hill and London: University of North Carolina Press, 1994 [1944].

Williams, Raymond. *The Country and the City*. Oxford: Oxford University Press, 1973.

Wilson, Kathleen. *The Island Race: Englishness, Empire and Gender in the Eighteenth Century*. London and New York: Routledge, 2003.

Withers, Charles W. J. "Geography, Natural History and the Eighteenth-Century Enlightenment: Putting the World in Place." *History Workshop Journal* 39 (1995): 138–63.

Wood, Marcus. *Slavery, Empathy, and Pornography*. Oxford: Oxford University Press, 2002.

Wood, Marcus. *Blind Memory: Visual Representations of Slavery in England and America 1780–1865*. New York: Routledge, 2000.

Wright, Philip. "Introduction." *Lady Nugent's Journal of her Residence in Jamaica from 1801 to 1805*, ed. Philip Wright. Kingston: Institute of Jamaica, 1966. xi–xxxii.

Yaeger, Patricia, ed. *The Geography of Identity*. Ann Arbor: University of Michigan Press, 1996.

Young, Iris Marion. "House and Home: Feminist Variations on a Theme." *Intersecting Voices: Dilemmas of Gender, Political Philosophy, and Policy*. Princeton, NJ: Princeton University Press, 1997. 134–64.

Young, Robert J. C. *Colonial Desire: Hybridity in Theory, Culture and Race*. London and New York: Routledge, 1995.

Youngquist, Paul. "The Afro Futurism of DJ Vassa." *European Romantic Review* 16 (2005): 181–92.

Youngquist, Paul, and Grégory Pierrot. "Introduction." Marcus Rainsford, *An Historical Account of the Black Empire of Hayti*, ed. Youngquist and Pierrot. Durham, NC: Duke University Press, 2013 [1805]. xvii–lviii.

Youngquist, Paul, and Frances Botkin. "Introduction: Black Romanticism: Romantic Circulations." *Circulations: Romanticism and the Black Atlantic*, ed. Paul Youngquist and Frances Botkin. 2011. Accessed August 14, 2013. Available at www.rc.umd.edu/praxis/circulations/index.html.

Youngquist, Paul, ed. *Race, Romanticism, and the Atlantic*. Surrey, UK, and Burlington, VT: Ashgate, 2013.

Index

CAMBRIDGE STUDIES IN ROMANTICISM

General Editor
James Chandler, *University of Chicago*

Made in the USA
Columbia, SC
21 October 2020

23234724R00154